Beyond Sovereignty

STUDIES IN INTERNATIONAL RELATIONS

Charles W. Kegley, Jr., and Donald J. Puchala,
Series Editors

BEYOND SOVEREIGNTY

THE

CHALLENGE OF

GLOBAL POLICY

by MARVIN S. SOROOS

UNIVERSITY OF SOUTH CAROLINA PRESS

Copyright © University of South Carolina 1986

Published in Columbia, South Carolina, by the
University of South Carolina Press

Manufactured in the United States of America

Second printing, 1987

Library of Congress Cataloging-in-Publication Data

Soroos, Marvin S., 1945–
    Beyond sovereignty.

    (Studies in international relations)
    Includes bibliographies.
    1. International relations.   I. Title.
II. Series: Studies in international relations
(Columbia, S.C.)
JX1391.S64   1986   327.1′1′09048   85-31495
ISBN 0-87249-474-8
ISBN 0-87249-478-0 (pbk.)

CONTENTS

v

EDITORS' PREFACE

The pace of global change has accelerated greatly in the last decades of the twentieth century, and new problems occurring under novel conditions are challenging the academic study of International Relations. There is today a renaissance in scholarship directed toward enhancing our understanding of world politics, global economics, and foreign policy. To examine the transformed structure of the international system and the expanded agenda of global affairs, researchers are introducing new concepts, theories, and analytic modes. Knowledge is expanding rapidly.

Our goal in this series of books is to record the findings of recent innovative research in International Relations, and make these readily available to a broader readership of professionals and students. Contributors to the series are leading scholars who are respectively expert in particular subfields of the discipline of International Relations. Their contributions represent the most recent work located at the discipline's research frontiers. Topics, subjects, approaches, methods and analytical techniques vary from volume to volume in the series, as each book is intended as an original contribution in the broadest sense. Common to all volumes however are careful research and the excitement of new discovery.

The present volume by Professor Marvin S. Soroos is in many ways a model beginning for Studies in International Relations. In a well-organized progression of chapters, the author reconcep-

tualizes the fundamental nature of international politics, redefines
the objectives of inquiry in the discipline of International Relations, and systematically proceeds to empirically establish the
importance of his theoretical reformulations. Soroos introduces
the concept of international public policy and astutely shows how
the need for such policy and its implementation affect the agendas
of governments and the lives of people in all parts of the world.
The book is about collaboration across national borders which is
increasingly critical because of the deteriorating global social,
economic, demographic, and physical environment. There is, of
course, no world government. However, Professor Soroos shows
that there is today a modicum of world governance which varies in
scope and impact in different problem areas. He explains exactly
where and why the global capacity for collective action is increasing. But, he quite deliberately leaves us wondering whether this
capacity will be adequate to manage the strains of inhospitable
environmental developments predicted for the early decades of
the next century.

—Charles W. Kegley, Jr., and Donald J. Puchala

ABBREVIATIONS

ACP	African, Caribbean, and Pacific countries
CIEO	Conference on International Economic Cooperation
CMEA	Committee for Mutual Economic Assistance
COMSAT	Communications Satellite Corporation
COPUOS	Committee on the Peaceful Uses of Outer Space
DBS	direct broadcast satellite
OECD	Organization for Economic Cooperation and Development
ECE	Economic Commission for Europe
ECOSOC	Economic and Social Council
EEC	European Economic Community
EEZ	exclusive economic zone
ENDC	Eighteen Nation Disarmament Committee
EURATOM	European Atomic Energy Commission
FAO	Food and Agricultural Organization
GATT	General Agreement on Tariffs and Trade
GEMS	Global Environmental Monitoring System
GNP	gross national product
HF	high frequency band
IAEA	International Atomic Energy Agency
IBRD	International Bank for Reconstruction and Development
ICAO	International Civil Aviation Organization
ICJ	International Court of Justice
ICRC	International Committee of the Red Cross
ICSU	International Council of Scientific Unions
IDA	International Development Association
IEA	International Energy Agency
IFC	International Finance Corporation
IFRB	International Frequency Regulation Board
IGO	international governmental organization
ILO	International Labor Organization
IMF	International Monetary Fund
IMO	International Maritime Organization
INFCE	International Nuclear Fuel Cycle Evaluation
INGO	international nongovernmental organization
INTELSAT	International Communications Satellite Organization
ISPA	international scientific and professional association
ITU	International Telecommunications Union
MARPOL	International Convention for the Prevention of Pollution from Ships
MSY	maximum sustainable yield

NAM	Non-Aligned Movement
NATO	North Atlantic Treaty Organization
NGO	nongovernmental organization
NIC	newly industrialized country
NIEO	new international economic order
NPT	Non-Proliferation Treaty
NWIO	new world information order
OPEC	Organization of Petroleum Exporting Countries
PAC	Program Activity Center
PQLI	physical quality of life index
SBT	segregated ballist tank
SDR	special drawing rights
SOLAS	International Convention for the Safety of Life at Sea
SWAPO	South-West Africa Peoples Organization
TDF	transborder data flow
TNC	transnational corporation
UNCLOS I	First United Nations Conference on the Law of the Sea (1958)
UNCLOS II	Second United Nations Conference on the Law of the Sea (1960)
UNCLOS III	Third United Nations Conference on the Law of the Sea (1973–1982)
UNCTAD	United Nations Conference on Trade and Development
UNDP	United Nations Development Programme
UNEP	United Nations Environmental Programme
UNESCO	United Nations Educational, Scientific, and Cultural Organization
UNFPA	United Nations Fund for Population Activities
UNICEF	United Nations Children's Fund
UNIDO	United Nations Industrial Development Organization
UNISPACE	United Nations Conference on the Exploration and Peaceful Uses of Outer Space (1982)
UPU	Universal Postal Union
WARC	World Administrative Radio Conference
WHO	World Health Organization
WMO	World Meteorological Organization

Beyond Sovereignty

1 INTRODUCTION

Global Policy in an Interdependent World

As the 1970s gave way to the current decade, the world seemed to be in an advanced state of disorder. On November 4, 1979, international attention was drawn to Teheran where militants had stormed the American embassy, taking more than sixty hostages from among its staff, 52 of whom remained in captivity for more than a year. They demanded that United States extradite the hated former Shah of their country, Mohammed Rezi Pahlavi, who in exile had been permitted to undergo emergency medical treatment in New York City. Later, the revolutionary government of the Ayatolla Khomeini endorsed the seizure of the embassy and threatened to put some of the hostages on trial in flagrant disregard for international law on the treatment and security of diplomats. President Carter responded by declaring an embargo on most United States trade with Iran, including imports of petroleum, and by freezing the accounts of the Iranian government in American banks, accounts estimated to be worth as much as $12 billion. When diplomatic efforts failed to win the release of the hostages, a daring military rescue was attempted, but was aborted because of equipment failures in the Iranian desert.

In mid-December of the same year, the decision was made at a ministerial meeting of the NATO countries in Brussels to base 572 highly accurate missiles bearing nuclear warheads at locations in Western Europe. They would be the first missiles deployed in this region with sufficient range to strike major Soviet cities, including Moscow, and they could reach their targets within eight to ten minutes. This action was ostensibly taken in response to the Soviet deployment of medium-range SS-20 missiles targeted at Western Europe. Initiatives taken by the Soviet Union to encourage a postponement of the deployment until further negotiations could take place were rebuffed by the West, presumably in the interests of establishing a stronger bargaining position for future arms talks.

Earlier in the year, President Carter made a commitment to increase American defense spending in an effort to win Senate support for ratification of the beleaguered SALT II treaty, which presumably had been negotiated to reduce burdensome expenditures on arms. Included in the President's program were funds for the deployment of a new generation of land-based missiles, the mobile MX system estimated to cost a minimum of $35 billion (or, more probably, two or three times that figure). In addition, a severe environmental impact on several western states, where it was to be deployed in a mobile-basing mode, was foreseen by critics.

Then, in the first weeks of the 1980s, what remained of a decade of detente between the superpowers unraveled quickly following the occupation of Afghanistan by Soviet ground forces. This move was apparently designed to quash growing Moslem resistance to a succession of socialist, pro-Soviet regimes in Afghanistan that, it was feared, might encourage similar restiveness in the Moslem population in the Soviet Union. Reacting to what he denounced as a Soviet "invasion," President Carter cut back sharply on sales of grain and high technology to the Soviet Union and restricted the fishing privileges of its fleet in American coastal waters. The SALT II treaty was withdrawn from further consideration in the Senate and 36 nations participated in an American-led boycott of the 1980 summer Olympic Games in Moscow. Concern was expressed in the West that the Soviet Union would proceed to invade Iran and take control of the rich oil fields of the Persian Gulf area. United States and Chinese defense planners talked of closer military cooperation and an arms package was offered to Pakistan despite its refusal to comply with the terms of the Non-Proliferation Treaty.

And in far-off, war-ravaged Kampuchea, millions were on the brink of starvation as hostilities continued between the remnants of the once potent forces of the Khmer Rouge and the invading Vietnamese army, which had overrun the country and was resisting all efforts of international relief agencies to provide emergency food and medical supplies to refugees caught in the cross-fire. The continuing conflict between these two communist states of Southeast Asia heightened tension between the Soviet Union and China, which then took the sides of the Vietnamese and Kampuchean governments, respectively. In the West there was anxiety that the Vietnamese forces, buoyed up by their recent military successes, posed a serious threat to the neighboring state of Thailand.

Not all of the events occurring toward the close of the 1970s took the form of political conflicts, military confrontations, and arms races. After five years of talks the Tokyo Round of trade negotiations taking place under the auspices of the General Agreement on Tariffs and Trade (GATT) came to a conclusion in the spring of 1979 with the signing of an agreement in Geneva that would slash remaining tariffs by an average of 35 to 38 percent and significantly reduce nontariff barriers to trade. One participant from an industrial country described the treaty as the "biggest trade negotiation package ever," despite its failure to address several issues of special concern to representatives from the Third World.

Several other developments took place on the economic front. During the last half of August, a major United Nations conference was held in Vienna to discuss how science and technology could be adapted more effectively to the fulfillment of the economic needs of the developing world. In October, the World Bank and the International Monetary Fund (IMF) held their annual joint meetings in Belgrade, Yugoslavia, in an effort to stabilize the international monetary system. There was widespread agreement that fighting inflation should be given top priority. Steps were also taken to ease some of the pressure on the weakened American dollar by allowing holders to convert them to a new asset denominated in special drawing rights (SDRs).

Also during the fall, a 10-week World Radio Administrative Conference (WARC) was held in Geneva under the auspices of the International Telecommunications Union (ITU). Major WARCs of this type are held at 20-year intervals to update international rules pertaining to a wide variety of forms of international communication. Advertised as the largest international conference ever held, the WARC made decisions that would shape global communications networks for the remainder of the century.

Simultaneously, at a brief meeting of the Economic Commission for Europe (ECE), an agreement was signed by the United States, Canada, and 32 other countries of eastern and western Europe on a treaty to curb transboundary air pollution. The ECE treaty was aimed primarily at limiting the amount of sulfur dioxide emitted into the atmosphere from burning fossil fuels and was viewed as a check on a potential stampede to coal as an alternative to oil and nuclear power. Douglas Costle, then the Director of the United States Environmental Protection Agency, remarked that "a decade ago the idea that a group of nations with clear differences would unite to protect the environment would have seemed doubtful at best. Indeed many would have said it was impossible."

Finally, after a decade of negotiation, first in a special committee of the General Assembly and then at the most recent United Nations Conference on the Law of the Sea, which commenced in 1973, agreement was within reach on a comprehensive new ocean law that sought to resolve many of the conflicts that have arisen over a variety uses of the seas and seabed by more and more states. Among the interests at stake were the rights to exploit the vast natural wealth of the oceans, including fisheries, off-shore oil and natural gas, and mineral-rich nodules on the seabed; to navigate scores of straits critical to international shipping; and to conduct scientific research.

World politics is a rich and perplexing mixture of trends and countertrends. In this regard, what was observed during 1979–80 was not unusual. Numerous examples can be cited of conflict and military confrontation occurring concurrently with international cooperation and accommodation for any other year-long period in recent history. Moreover, it is not unusual for the same states to be involved in both conflictive and collaborative interactions with one another simultaneously. Thus, it might be said that world politics has a dual nature or, to borrow a concept from psychology, appears to be "schizophrenic," as it displays its two personalities.

In the aftermath of World War II, it was widely assumed that world politics, when stripped to its essential nature, was almost exclusively a struggle for power in which national governments attempt to impose their wills on weaker states. Many recent events, such as the seizure of the Falkland Islands by Argentina and the subsequent war with the United Kingdom, the escalation of hostilities between Iran and Iraq that included attacks on shipping in the Persian Gulf, and the United States invasion of Grenada and "covert" support for anti-Sandinista "contras" in Central America, are evidence that conflict-ridden, power politics continues to be a salient feature of world politics.

Such a perspective on world politics does not, however, adequately take into account the evolution in the commitment of most national governments, international institutions, and numerous nongovernmental actors to address global problems. This commitment is reflected in the upwards of 1,000 international conferences that are convened annually in addition to the regular sessions of hundreds of international institutions. Significant among these developments were the arrangements worked out by the IMF in 1983 to rescue countries from the verge of economic bankruptcy, an event that could have had reverberations through the international banking community. In 1984 Mexico City was the site for a major international conference on population, which was convened to assess the progress that had been made in the ten years since the landmark World Population Conference was held in Bucharest. In 1985 Nairobi hosted a major world conference that assessed the achievement of the United Nations Decade for Women and adopted a plan of action for the remainder of the century. The myriad of activities of this type occurring on a day-by-day basis illustrate what has become a substantial undercurrent of world politics directed toward cooperative efforts at international problem solving.

What attracts attention in the study of world politics is greatly influenced by the observer's theoretical perspective, or paradigm. This book focuses on the cooperative aspects of world politics, in particular the efforts of the international community to address problems of global scope. In doing so, it adopts the approach, as well as some of the concepts and theories, of the field of policy studies, which during its relatively brief history has been oriented almost exclusively to the policies of national governments and their subunits. Often overlooked, however, is a substantial body of international public policy and varied policy processes by which it is made and developed that are a significant feature of world political scene. In adopting a policy perspective, the intention is not to deny the reality of international conflict and power politics. Rather, it is to call attention to a dimension of world politics that is too often ignored or downplayed, partly because it is less dramatic and thus not considered to be as newsworthy. Before elaborating further on global public policy and how it is made, let us view it in the larger context of the many perspectives from which international affairs have been studied.

POLITICAL REALISM

In the aftermath of World War II, a paradigm emphasizing the role of power in the relations among states gained widespread acceptance among students of world affairs (see Vasquez, 1983). Since then, this general theory, which became known as "political realism," has been the leading shaper of perceptions of the nature of politics in international arenas. The basic precepts of political realism, which can be traced back to the classical theories of Machiavelli and Hobbes, have been expounded by numerous scholars of the contemporary era—Edward H. Carr (1939, 1964), George Kennan (1952), Kenneth W. Thompson (1960), Arnold Wolfers (1962), Henry A. Kissinger (1964), Robert W. Tucker (1977), and Robert Gilpin (1981), to mention a few. The realist perspective has, however, been most frequently associated with Hans Morganthau's *Politics Among Nations* (1948). The influence of political realism has diminished gradually as circumstances have changed and its assumptions have come under attack on numerous grounds. Nevertheless, its basic tenets are still subscribed to by many, both in academic circles and among political leaders and foreign policy makers, as well as in Western publics at large.

The rise of realist theory was a response to the aggressive self-serving machinations of several national leaders during the 1930s, which triggered the second global war of the twentieth century. The failure of the League of Nations, the Permanent Court of International Justice, and international law to prevent this conflagration fueled a general disillusionment with the prevailing "idealist" tradition of scholarship, which had put faith in the capacity of rational human beings to create institutions that would preserve peace and order in the relations between states. Not surprisingly, scholars reacted strongly to these catastrophic experiences by developing theories which assumed that the essence of international politics was to be found in conflict between nation-states locked in a Darwinian struggle for dominance and ultimately self-preservation. States were seen as predominant actors in an international system that was not only separate from domestic political systems, but also very different in its lack of a governing authority strong enough to restrain its members. Each nation existing in this anarchic world was seen as having no viable alternative but to adopt a strategy of self-help in pursuit of its basic needs and interests.

In its purist form, realist theory presumes that the primary objective of national governments is to increase their power relative to other states as a means of enhancing their security, wealth, and influence in international affairs. While it was recognized that numerous factors, such as population, education, industry, technology, natural resources, and geography, contribute to the power of nations, the capacity to use military force was looked upon as the critical instrument for pursuing national interests. Accordingly, states can be expected to make great sacrifices to build and maintain as potent a military force as the resources of a country permit. To ambitious leaders of the stronger states, military power becomes the means for preying upon weaker states, possibly even to seize part or all of their territory, thereby taking control of the population and resources that are located within it. Weaker states attempt to secure their territory and independence against the onslaughts of predatory nations, usually by building up their own military strength or aligning with other states that will come to their defense in the event of an armed attack from a common enemy. So close is the relationship between military power and other national interests often perceived to be, there is a tendency for power to be looked upon an end unto itself, perhaps even the ultimate objective of national policy.

Thus, from the perspective of political realism, international politics is an inherently competitive game that states play with one another. The extent to which a state wins out over others depends upon the relative power of the two. What a country accomplishes in raising its stature in the international system is achieved by diminishing the ability of others to resist its influence. Therefore, it is impossible for all states to increase simultaneously their power relative to one another. Such situations in which the gains of any participant are automatically offset by the loses of its competitors have been described as being "zero-sum" games. Leaders who believe they are locked into such a zero-sum situation are quite often guided in making foreign policy by the anticipated impact that their decisions will have on the relative strength of their enemies, rather than by an independent assessment of what is in the best interests of the population of their own country.

The realist school of thought places little stock in the possibility of reforming the international system through international cooperation. The quest for power is believed to be too deeply rooted in human nature for other states to be trusted to observe international law or to be reliable partners in significant collaborative undertakings that address major world problems. Furthermore, there is deep skepticism about the possibility that international institutions could be established that are strong enough to constrain states determined to use force to elevate their standing in international politics. Lulls in the amount of warfare, referred to as peace, are usually attributed either to the military hegemony of a dominant state that is strong enough to enforce order or to a balance of military strength that prevails among pairs or larger groups of states. Such a balance can be observed in the flexible alliances of nineteenth-century Europe and in the nuclear stalemate between the United States and Soviet Union.

ALTERNATIVES TO POLITICAL REALISM

Not all students of world affairs are as persuaded as the realists of the inevitability of an international political order that is so thoroughly shaped by a struggle for power among nation-states. Nor are they all willing to concede that power politics is the only, or even the predominant, contemporary reality in international affairs. It is argued by many that much of what occurs in world politics is not adequately explained by the theories of the political realists, including the numerous and varied cooperative activities among states and the cross-national activities of nongovernmental actors that are so much a part of the international scene. Generally speaking, the critics of political realism are more optimistic about the potential for constructive international efforts to address the many problems that transcend the boundaries of states. Paradoxically, they also tend to express greater anxiety about these problems, which they fear are becoming ever more numerous and severe, even to the point of jeopardizing human survival. Thus, cooperation on a global scale is viewed by many as not only being possible, but also essential for the future welfare of humanity.

Scholars who assign greater significance to the cooperative or integrative aspects of world politics have not coalesced around a single theory. Rather, they have approached the subject from a variety of perspectives, some of which are difficult to distinguish because of extensive overlap in the phenomena being observed and the way that concepts, theories, and insights are shared. There are, however, differences in their primary foci, which are reflected in the questions that each is designed to answer. The brief survey of these perspectives that follows groups them on the basis of whether the primary focus is on (a) the structure and process of international organization, (b) emerging problems that dictate international responses, or (c) strategies for addressing international problems that either have already been tried or are being proposed for the future.

The Structure and Process of International Organization

The subject of international organization has itself been approached in two basically different ways. Some scholars have concentrated on international governmental organizations (IGOs) that either exist currently, did so in the past, or could be created in the future. Others have analyzed the broader phenomenon of international organization as an integrative political process, either on global or regional scope.

Much has been written about IGOs. Some students of IGOs have delved into the *historical evolution* of international institutions, which can be traced to the Delian League of the ancient Greek city-states, the Hanseatic League of German towns that was formed in the eleventh century to facilitate trade, and the Concert of Europe which contributed to the measure of international order during much of the nineteenth century. The history of the two major experiments with international organization on a global basis during the twentieth century, the League of Nations and the United Nations, has been scrutinized by numerous scholars (e.g., Claude, 1956). The growth over the past century and a half in the numbers of various types of IGOs—universal and regional in membership, general and specific in function—has also been plotted (Skjelsbaek, 1971). The politics of *decision making* in international bodies has been another subject of interest, as can be seen in studies of roll-call votes that reveal blocs that typically appear on certain types of issues (Hovet, 1969). Questions have also been raised about the roles played by the delegates in representing their countries, in particular the extent to which their actions are guided by instructions from their home governments (Cox and Jacobson, 1973). Finally, the operations of the *bureaucracies* of international organizations have been a subject of inquiry. The secretariats of IGOs face many administrative problems on matters such as personnel and budgeting that in some ways are more complicated than those that must be dealt with by national bureaucracies (see Jordan, 1971, 1972).

Some scholars have been intrigued by the more general phenomenon of international organization and the long-term direction that it might be taking. The *functionalist* school of thought espoused by David Mitrany (1966) envisioned a world in which more and more public functions on such matters as health, agriculture, transportation, telecommunication, and scientific development would be transferred to international agencies, each of which would be designed to perform a limited range of tasks. It was anticipated that the success of the first "functionally-specific" organizations, in which politics would be downplayed in favor of technical considerations, would spawn more of these narrowly focused IGOs. Gradually, political divisions between states would be overlain by a "web of international activities and agencies" (Mitrany, 1966, pp. 10–11). As a growing number of the tasks formerly performed by states were shifted to international agencies, loyalties of people would be divided between national and international institutions. In such a world, states would be both less inclined and less able to wage war with each other.

Fascination with Western Europe's dramatic plunge toward economic union with the establishment of the European Coal and Steel Community in 1952 and the European Economic Community in 1957 led to a preoccupation with *integration* theory that lasted for little more than a decade. The concept was a confusing one because of very different conceptions of what was to be the end product of an integrative process. To one influential theorist, integration was the achievement of "sense of community" and "institutions and practices strong and widespread enough to assure, for a 'long' time, dependable expectations of 'peaceful change'" (Deutsch, 1957, p. 5). To another, integration was a shifting of "loyalties, expectations, and political activities toward a new and larger center, whose institutions possess or demand jurisdiction over the preexisting national states" (Haas, 1958, p. 16). Others found it useful to distinguish political integration, which involved institutions and loyalties, from economic and social integration, which could be observed in the growth of international transactions and interactions, such as trade, mail, and air travel (Nye, 1971, p. 24). Much of the research on the subject was directed toward developing ways of measuring the degree of integration that had taken place and to identifying the conditions that are favorable or necessary to the formation of integrated communities, such as the homogeneity of the societies involved in the process. In the background was the question of whether the experiences with regional integration could be transferred to the world as a whole.

As the integration process in Europe and other regions showed signs of stagnating during the late 1960s, interest shifted back to global arenas, in particular to the phenomena that became known as *transnational* relations. In contrast to "interstate relations" taking place between the governments of two or more states, transnational interactions involve at least one party that is not governmental in character. In the process, the government of at least one of the interacting countries is bypassed (Nye and Keohane, 1971, p. 332–33; see also Rosenau, 1980). Among the participants in transnational relations are international nongovernmental organizations (INGOs), which were increasingly becoming involved in global policy making through their consultative relationships with IGOs. Notable also are the transnational corporations which because of their sheer size and far-flung operations have become substantial factors in national economies. A related phenomenon is the numerous and varied direct links that municipal groups have to foreign countries that also often bypass national governments (see Alger, 1977). The transnationalist perspective is especially significant for challenging what was seen as the "state-centric" bias of political realists, who have been reluctant to acknowledge the significance of the role played by nongovernmental actors in the contemporary global system.

A Focus on Global Problems

During the 1970s there was a greater tendency to look beyond the organizational aspects of world politics to the problems that confronted the international system and humanity generally, or what have become known as "global issues." To most observers of the international scene, the preeminent international problem of modern times is to prevent war, especially those conflicts that could lead to the use of the nuclear arsenals of the superpowers. Other global challenges of an economic, social, or ecological nature also have become the subject of increasing concern (Falk, 1972; Sterling, 1974). Interest in a broader range of global issues was partly a response to several dramatic developments. One was the floating of the American dollar in 1972, which added uncertainties to the international monetary order. Another was the "energy crisis" touched off by the oil embargo and price rises dictated by OPEC in 1973–74, which caused serious economic disruptions in both developed and less developed countries. There was also a growing uneasiness about the long-term consequences of more gradual changes, such as the very rapid growth in the world's population and the buildup of pollutants in the environment.

One reason why it appears that these problems have assumed international and global proportions is the way in which the destinies of nations are becoming intertwined in ever more complex ways. The concept used most frequently to describe these underlying changes in the international system is *interdependence*. At the international level, interdependence implies that nations are sensitive or vulnerable in significant ways to developments taking place beyond their borders, some of which are, or at least potentially could be, under the control of foreign actors (see Keohane and Nye, 1977, pp. 12–14). Thus, governments of increasingly interdependent states become less the masters of what occurs within their countries, even though they continue to claim legal sovereignty. The trend toward interdependence in economic matters has been especially pronounced due to spectacular rises in international trade and investment that have taken place in recent decades. During the same era, multinational corporations, including some that dwarf many of the economies of entire nations, have been rationalizing production with little regard being given to political boundaries (see Vernon, 1971; Barnet and Müller, 1974).

Some forms of interdependence can prove to be advantageous for states, but also pose stern challenges for them. In the economic sphere, international trade and investments have contributed greatly to the prosperity of many states, but there can be significant drawbacks. Most states, particularly the smaller and less developed ones, are buffeted by strong economic forces over which their governments have little control. Economic problems that arise in one country or region, such as a downturn in growth or large trade imbalances, can quickly reverberate throughout the world. Interdependent relationships are often ripe for a rise in international tensions, especially when governments appear to be insensitive to the impacts that their policies have on others, as when they act to protect their domestic markets from imports. Thus, whatever peace and prosperity is enjoyed in an interdependent world can be a very fragile condition, particularly when international institutions are inadequate to manage the relations between states (see Scott, 1982).

To those sensitive to the frustrations of less developed countries, the compelling feature of the modern world has not been interdependence, but unidirectional *dependency*. A web of relationships created and controlled by the developed countries of the West, both of an economic and political nature, is seen as an obstacle to the efforts of Third World countries to develop and achieve a greater share of the world's wealth. Thus, rather than there being mutual and balanced dependence among all countries, as the concept of interdependence implies, it is argued that dependence has been much more of an oppressive reality for the poorer countries of the Third World on the "peripheries" of the world economy than it is for the advanced developed states which are at the "center" (see Chirot, 1977). The dependency of the Third World is not, of course, as recent a phenomenon as modern forms of interdependence referred to in the preceding paragraph. These scholars of the "world systems" school have traced contemporary patterns of dependence to the social upheavals taking place in sixteenth- and seventeenth-century Europe that led to several centuries of rampant colonialism (Wallerstein, 1974). Whatever the causes of dependence and the badly skewed distribution of the world's wealth, reform of the prevailing economic and political order is the first order of business for those who would like to see a more balanced partnership between developed and less developed countries.

The 1970s were also notable for the emergence of a new *ecological* consciousness that questioned whether the natural environment could sustain a rapidly growing and industrializing world population (Ward and Dubois, 1972). These concerns were fanned by a controversial yet very influential book bearing the ominous title *The Limits to Growth,* which was one of several reports commissioned by an INGO named the Club of Rome (Meadows et al., 1972; see also Mesarovic and Pestel, 1974). The report warned of a global ecocatastrophe within a century, which would be marked by a precipitous drop in population, a collapse of the world economy, and severe damage to the global environment, unless steps were taken promptly to sharply reduce the rapid rates of growth in population and industrialization that had prevailed in the postwar era. The world "food crisis" and "energy crisis" of the mid-1970s appeared to bear out these gloomy forecasts and to usher in an era of resource scarcity. While these conditions ameliorated somewhat in the ensuing years, evidence mounted of other environmental problems, such as depletion of ocean fisheries, climate change due to the "greenhouse effect," desertification, and tropical deforestation. A number of scholars were alert to the implications that ecological factors could have for world politics (e.g., Sprout and Sprout, 1971; Caldwell, 1972). Some contended that impending ecological crises could be averted only by replacing the decentralized international political order composed of sovereign states with a more centralized system of authority that could coerce states into acting in an ecologically responsible manner (Heilbroner 1974; Ophuls, 1977).

The crescendo of concern over a spate of interrelated global problems that appeared to be growing ever more severe left the impression that the challenges confronting humanity were of a historically unprecedented magnitude. In some circles, the studies warning of nuclear armageddon, economic collapse, and ecological calamity were referred to pejoratively as "doomsday" literature. It should be recognized, however, that the global issues approach conveys more optimism than political realism in at least one important sense—the conviction that humanity can muster the will and discipline to deal with the serious problems it faces. Whether this task can be accomplished using the existing institutions, or will require a major transformation of the global political order, continues to be a subject of considerable dispute.

An Emphasis on Global Problem Solving

Several schools of inquiry have not shared the skepticism of the political realists about the inherent futility of constructive, international efforts designed to tackle global problems. Of these approaches, the study of *international law* perhaps has the longest history. There are, however, very different philosophies on the basic nature of international law and what it can contribute to the solution of global problems. The more traditional view, which is still held by some legal scholars, is that international law is simply a set of norms that evolves gradually in the community of states and is generally acknowledged to be binding on all of its members. These norms define the limits of acceptable behavior and, thus, are appropriate criteria for resolving disputes that arise between states (see Nardin, 1983, pp. 198–220). In recent decades, a competing perspective that looks upon international law as a instrument of international cooperation has gained acceptance. As elaborated by one of its early proponents, Myres S. McDougal (1960), this approach contends that international law can also be a form of public policy that is consciously created by states to serve their common interests on a wide variety of problems that concern them, such as the conduct of war, arms control, pollution, and the use of outer space.

Recently, it has been fashionable to analyze efforts at international cooperation in terms of the role that *international regimes* play in addressing a wide range of problems. Differing connotations of the term "regime" as applied to governing arrangements at the national and international levels have led to considerable confusion about what the concept implies. Furthermore, the vagueness of the concept has made it susceptible to varied interpretations, especially in the international context. As defined in one of the seminal works on the subject, a regime comprises a set of "governing arrangements" that include "networks of rules, norms, and procedures that regularize behavior and control its effects" (Keohane and Nye, 1977, p. 19). Individual regimes are identified in terms of the problem areas that they address, such as international trade, monetary order, shipping, disaster relief, weather, health, or a region such as Antarctica. One or more IGOs are an integral part of most regimes, and numerous IGOs are involved in several regimes. Thus, rather than selecting a certain IGO as the subject of inquiry, the regime approach singles out an international problem area of interest and then seeks to identify the network of IGOs that is active in addressing it. Thus, if international trade is the problem area under study, the applicable regime would include the rules, norms, and procedures of several IGOs, the most centrally involved being GATT, IMF, and the United Nations Conference on Trade and Development (UNCTAD) (see Krasner, 1982).

Finally, there are two notable streams of scholarship on international problem solving that are explicitly normative in orientation. *Peace research,* which dates back to the 1950s, was originally directed almost exclusively to developing knowledge of how war could be avoided—with particular emphasis on resolving conflicts peacefully. Later, the concept "peace" was broadened to include justice in social relationships, which entailed addressing the "structural violence" inherent in the existing economic order (Galtung, 1971). Contemporary *world order studies* got its start in the 1960s with the publication of Clark and Sohn's (1966) design for a future in which the means of war would be drastically reduced, with the preponderance of the remaining arms being transferred to a world government. Most of the recent work of world orderists has been guided by an expanded set of core values—peace, economic and social welfare, human rights, and environmental balance (see Falk, 1975; Kim, 1984). Their writings reveal a deep disillusionment with the state-centric character of the existing global order and the accompanying weakness of both global institutions and the international legal system (e.g., Johansen, 1980). In most instances, the product of world order inquiry is a vision of a "preferred future" that is radically different from the existing global political system, especially in regard to the autonomy of the states. Designing a preferred future is, however, only part of the task of the world orderist. The other is the formidable challenge of devising a plausible strategy for transforming the existing world into the preferred one (see Beres and Targ, 1974; Mendlovitz, 1975).

GLOBAL POLICY STUDIES

The perspective of *policy studies,* which is being adopted in this book, can be grouped along with the international law and regime approaches, and with peace research and world order studies as well, as ways of analyzing actual or potential responses to global problems. While the roots of policy studies run deep in intellectual history, the stimulus for contemporary policy studies is frequently acknowledged to be a book edited by Daniel Lerner and Harold D. Lasswell, *The Policy Sciences: Recent Developments in Scope and Method,* published in 1951. It was not until the mid-1960s, however, that policy studies blossomed into an identifiable sub-field of the social sciences devoted to enhancing the effectiveness of public policies. To this date, the approach has been applied almost exclusively to policies adopted by national and local governments and only infrequently to comparable international efforts. The primary reasons for the neglect of international policy would appear to be the widely held but questionable notion that policies are exclusively the products of governments of a type that does not exist at the international level.

A *policy* is a purposeful course of action designed and implemented with the objective of shaping future outcomes in ways that will be more desirable than would otherwise be expected (Anderson, 1979, p. 24). Discrete actions, in and of themselves, are normally not considered policies. On the contrary, a policy establishes criteria for deciding on an entire series of actions. Thus, the arrest of a single motorist for excessive speed does not constitute a policy. But a directive to the state patrol to strictly enforce a posted speed limit on all drivers is an example of a policy. How human beings will react to a policy is often difficult to predict, nor is it usually possible to anticipate all of the ramifications the policy will have in complex social or natural environments. Thus, it is by no means inevitable that a policy will have the desired effect, even when it is laid out with considerable care. As a policy is carried out, there may be unforeseen results, which more often than not are unfavorable. It is not inconceivable for a policy to go badly awry with catastrophic consequences.

A *public policy* is a course of action adopted by a government. While it is customary to refer to governments as single actors, in actuality their policies are typically the product of either a bureaucratic or legislative process that involves numerous groups and individuals from both within and outside of government. At the level of world politics, it is important to distinguish foreign and international public policies. *Foreign policies* are adopted by individual national governments to guide their actions toward actors who are beyond their jurisdiction, in particular the governments of other states. In contrast, *international policies* are joint responses to common problems that two or more national governments work out with one another, often with the active participation of IGOs and INGOs. Foreign and international policies are integrally related, for it would be impossible to adopt and implement international policies without supportive foreign policy decisions by key states.

The *global policies* examined in this book are a subset of the larger group of international public policies. They are the products of the international community as a whole in contrast to policies that are adopted by a smaller group of actors defined by geographical region, level of economic development, or status as a producer of a certain commodity. For a policy to be considered global, it is not necessary that all potential national actors be direct participants in the policy making, but that representatives of each of the principal types of states and geographical regions be involved. Most global policies are set forth in treaties or resolutions, which are adopted either in the regular meetings of the central organs of United Nations, in the affiliated specialized agencies, or in ad hoc conferences convened to focus world attention on a particular problem of widespread concern.

Students of global policy can make use of much of the information and many of the insights generated by the other analytical perspectives on world politics that were briefly surveyed in this chapter. Studies that probe into the patterns of interdependence and the nature of global problems illuminate the challenges that confront international policy makers. Knowledge of the rapidly growing number of international organizations is perhaps of even more direct relevance. Not only do IGOs provide the arenas in which global policies are made, but their directors and staffs also play an important role at several points in the policy process, including the implementation of policies. Awareness of voting procedures in IGOs and the politics of voting blocs is crucial to understanding how decisions are made on policies. Studies of transnationalism have illuminated the variety of roles played by INGOs in the international policy process, which parallel those of pressure groups in national political arenas. Finally, familiarity with international law is essential to global policy studies because so many policies have the status of either customary or treaty law, and are therefore subject to various legal canons. However, not all international laws are expressions of international policies nor do all global policies have the status of law.

The relationship of global policy analysis to international regime perspective and world order studies is more ambiguous. The regime and policy approaches have much in common, but whereas regimes are oriented toward a more encompassing problem area, policies are responses to a more narrowly defined problem. Thus, it could be said that there is an international regime that deals with the broad range of matters related to Antarctica, while there are international policies that address specific questions pertaining to the region, such as territorial claims of states, pollution, the conduct of scientific research, the establishment of military installations, the exploitation of mineral and oil resources, and the conservation of wildlife. Furthermore, whereas the regime approach focuses on the international arrangements that have evolved for devising a cooperative response to matters pertaining to a certain problem area, policies are the actual course of action adopted to deal with a specific problem. Thus, the two approaches have a complementary relationship in the sense that regimes are the institutional environment within which international policies are made.

The policy approach has more in common with peace research than with world order studies. Much of peace research is directed toward identifying policies, both national and international, that will reduce the incidence of war and contribute to social justice on a global basis. Global policy studies differ in several fundamental ways from world order inquiry, even though both are designed to have an impact on future developments. One divergence is in the treatment of values. Policy studies are normally guided by the priorities of policy makers, while in world order studies—and peace research as well—the guiding values are those of the theorist. Second, a large proportion of the effort in policy studies is devoted to empirical analyses of policies that have already been adopted. In world order studies, more of a premium is placed on creatively envisioning preferred futures. Third, policy studies and peace research generally assume a greater willingness to accept existing mechanisms for bringing about change, although there is openness to relatively minor, pragmatic reforms that would enhance the effectiveness of the policy-making process. In contrast, world orderists display little faith in the capacity of contemporary institutions to cope with global problems and achieve the values they espouse. They seek instead a deeper transformation of the institutions that operate at the global level. Finally, policy analysts and peace researchers usually focus on problems and responses on a one-by-one basis, whereas world order studies encourages a holistic perspective on world affairs that illuminates the way that the many challenges confronting humanity are interrelated.

In what remains of this chapter, we will return to the dual "personality" of world politics that was noted earlier and consider the adaptability of both power and policy oriented politics to a highly interdependent world in which the means are at hand to destroy all of civilization. Naturally, there is little doubt about which of these strategies is better suited to the contemporary realities.

POWER POLITICS VERSUS GLOBAL POLICY IN AN INTERDEPENDENT WORLD

An interdependent community of states can be likened to the heavily used network of streets in a densely populated urban area. Imagine what the flow of traffic will be like if there are no traffic rules and each operator of a vehicle and each pedestrian is left to his own means to reach his destination. The more daring drivers would perhaps resort to a game of "chicken" in which they lay on their horns and accelerate wildly in hopes of intimidating less aggressive drivers and pedestrians into clearing the way for fear of being hit. Inevitably, collisions would take place, causing deaths, injuries, and paralyzing traffic jams; and nobody would reach his destination without major delays. Playing chicken in traffic has some parallels with engaging in games of power politics in an interdependent world.

Can it still be that the practice of power politics is a rational strategy for states, assuming of course that it once was? Because of their relative military weakness, most states have no realistic option but to cope with their dependencies in a cooperative rather than a forceful manner. At best, only a small proportion of the stronger nations are in position to contemplate using either force or coercion for coping with an interdependent world. But can even they take advantage of their superior military capability to successfully extend their domination over the outside forces that affect them? For example, can a dependence on foreign sources of vital natural resources be overcome by seizing poorly defended geographical areas that are richly endowed with them? Historically, overcoming dependence on unreliable foreign suppliers was one of the motivations for the expansionary drives of Germany, Japan, and Italy that triggered World War II, which by the war's end proved to be disastrous for these aggressors.

Power politics makes sense as a strategy for coping with dependence only if force can be effectively applied without absorbing costs as great as the value of what is gained. It would, of course, be extremely difficult to conceive of a justification for any action that would significantly heighten the danger of a nuclear catastrophe. Modern conventional warfare is also likely to be a very costly undertaking. Moreover, a clear-cut, military victory can be an elusive objective even when dealing with a much weaker opponent, a lesson learned by the United States in Indochina and, more recently, by the Soviet Union in Afghanistan. With the acceleration of exports of sophisticated conventional armaments to the Third World, it is becoming less possible for any state to reduce its dependencies through foreign military domination without paying a price that is disproportionately high relative to whatever benefits are derived.

Not only has warfare become very costly in human life and devastation, but it also disrupts the many mutually beneficial international relationships that exist in an interdependent world. Part of the price the Soviet Union paid for indulging in power politics in Afghanistan was the temporary loss of imports of low-cost grain and of advanced technologies from the United States.

Concurrently, American farmers lost a lucrative market they had come to depend upon to keep grain prices high enough to be profitable. Also among the costs of competitive, military strife are countless opportunities for future collaboration, which are often not as readily apparent. Directors of multinational corporations emphasize the importance of a stable, peaceful world as a prerequisite to the profitability of their decentralized operations and decry what some view as the failure of the art of international diplomacy to have progressed much beyond the sixteenth-century theories of Machiavelli.

The exercise of power politics would be a much less costly proposition for the stronger states if the threat of using military force would suffice to influence the actions of those upon whom they depend. Threats are normally not credible, however, unless the states making them have demonstrated a willingness to use force in similar circumstances in the past. Nor will threats be taken seriously if it is obvious that the costs of following through on them would be greater than what would be gained if they were successful. Even in the most favorable circumstances, coercion is a clumsy if not completely inappropriate tactic for exerting influence. It is difficult, for example, to imagine how military threats could be used to induce other countries to cooperate in banning the use of aerosol sprays containing chemicals that are believed to be depleting the ozone layer, to take steps to prevent an epidemic from spreading beyond a country's borders, to help coordinate airline scheduling, or to exercise restraint in devaluing currencies. Less threatening tactics of influence, such as negotiation, would appear to hold much more promise for dealing with a myriad of forms of interdependence.

Even if it is true that power politics has become counterproductive in the modern, interdependent world, it does not necessarily follow that nations will discontinue its practice, even when it is inappropriate or irrational. Beliefs about the nature of international politics can be expected to lag significantly behind the changes in the basic nature of the world political system, especially those that evolve gradually. Ways of coping with the outside world that have become deeply entrenched habits are discarded by governments only with great reluctance and a sense of uneasiness, particularly if they are reinforced by a strong sense of nationalism. Nor is it prudent for states completely to disengage from power politics unless all other players simultaneously do likewise. Otherwise, those who let down their guard first may be vulnerable to coercion from those who continue to play the game by building up their military forces.

Let us now imagine a few changes in the analogy of urban traffic. Rather than leaving it to each driver to fend for himself in a situation of anarchy, traffic lights and stop signs are installed. Speed limits are established, as are rules banning left turns at major intersections. Lanes are clearly marked indicating the direction in which traffic is permitted and where pedestrians may cross streets. Policemen are hired and instructed to strictly enforce the rules. The result is an orderly flow of traffic that makes it possible for a large volume of vehicles to pass safely through the city with a minimum of delay and a reduced likelihood of accidents and injuries. Adopting such a strategy for managing traffic has parallels to a policy response to interdependence in the contemporary world.

As with dense traffic, a highly interdependent world must be managed to avoid disruptions and chaos that can be detrimental to the interests of all the nations whose destinies are intertwined. International public policies embodying rules, responsibilities, and programs can be the instruments for bringing about the measure of order, stability, and equity that makes it possible for interdependence to work to the benefit of all states. Such policies are more likely to be effective in coping with the many forms of interdependence than a strategy of leaving it up to each nation to decide on its own what it should do to be a responsible member of the interdependent community. If there is widespread compliance, international policies can contribute a measure of predictability to the actions of states upon which others have come to depend. Thus, common sense would seem to dictate that statesmen gradually set aside the tactics of power politics and hone their skills at negotiating cooperative arrangements with their counterparts in other states.

Nevertheless, national governments frequently display a reluctance to work together to manage interdependence. They persist in pursuing self-help strategies, failing to consider that the welfare of their societies in an interdependent world may be better served by sacrificing some of the prerogatives of state sovereignty in order to play a more constructive role in tackling the problems of the larger community. Important international public policies are all too often derailed by disagreements over specific provisions of minor importance when compared to the much greater rewards that can be derived from implementing the policy. Likewise, it is not uncommon for governments to refuse to commit themselves to international policies, not because of the immediate costs or sacrifices that would be incurred, but out of concern for how they may be interpreted in the future and the precedents that could be set for other policy issues. If constructive ways of coping with interdependence are to be developed, it behooves states to display a willingness to compromise by occasionally going along with policies that do not serve their immediate interests. This is the price that must be paid in exchange for the promise of significantly greater benefits that accrue to them as a result of concessions made by other states in the interest of addressing common problems. It may, of course, be necessary to exert pressure on actors that refuse to comply with international policies, just as traffic rules must be enforced to be effective. Unfortunately, enforcement of international policies is a task that the international community is not well equipped to do.

This book offers an analysis of contemporary world politics from a policy perspective. As has been just observed, cooperative problem solving is not the only game being played out in international circles, nor does it appear to be the dominant one of this era or any previous one. While more has been accomplished in tackling global problems than many observers are willing to acknowledge, the degree of progress that has been made in resolving them has been mixed. As we shall see, there have been some successes and numerous failures in the efforts of global policy makers to come to grips with the challenges before them.

Part I looks at global policy in general way and, in doing so, presents a theoretical framework for examining responses to individual policy problems. Most of Chapter 2 is devoted to an overview of policy problems that have been appearing on the agendas of the decision-making bodies of the United Nations system. Two questions about the global agenda are also raised: (1) What is implied when a problem is said to have policy implications? (2) What attributes of a problem merit its inclusion on the global agenda? Chapter 3 explores the policy process through which global problems are addressed, beginning with a rundown of the actors that are involved and the conflicts that typically arise among them. The policy process is then broken down into a series of steps that serves as a theoretical framework for analyzing how global policies are made and carried out. The arenas in which global policy processes take place are noted, as well as the types of conflicts that arise among those involved in the process. The products of these policy-making efforts are reviewed in Chapter 4. Attention is given to the forms that policies take, usually either treaties or resolutions; the goals and principles that guide the making of policies; the actual content of policies, which normally comprise regulations and programs; and, lastly, the provisions that are set forth for carrying out policies, which involves inducing compliance with rules and generating funding for programs.

Part II applies the elements of this theoretical framework in a series of six case studies, each of which examines the response of the international community to a selected policy problem. The policy problems chosen for the case studies include one from each of six major problem areas identified in the second chapter. Chapter 5 examines a political problem of a military nature—the potential for further proliferation of nuclear weapons. Extensive international efforts grounded on the Non-Proliferation Treaty of 1968 have been directed at a two-fold objective: preventing the acquisition of nuclear weapons by additional state or nonstate actors while facilitating the development of nuclear power for peaceful purposes throughout the world. Chapter 6 discusses one of the most prominent problems on the global economic agenda— the slow and faltering rate of development of many of the Third World countries. The demands of their leaders for a "new international economic order," which is the central topic in North-South politics, are treated as an integrated set of policy alternatives to the prevailing economic order. Turning next to the social agenda, Chapter 7 focuses on efforts to promote the observance of fundamental human rights. The establishment and enforcement of global standards on human rights is a notable encroachment on the sovereignty of states in dealing with their populations.

The three remaining case studies examine the international response to policy problems that are less publicized but are nevertheless of considerable importance. The issue of who can make use of the living and nonliving resources of ocean areas was selected from among the resource-related items on the global agenda. Accordingly, Chapter 8 delves into the work of three United Nations Law of the Sea Conferences at which extensive attempts were made to codify and update the traditional ocean law, the principal tenets of which date back several centuries. Chapter 9 takes up the subject of pollution, the policy problem chosen from the environmental agenda. Thus far, much more has been done to establish international public policy on contamination of the marine environment than on that of atmospheric pollution, which because of the "green house" and "acid rain" phenomena, has been a matter of heightened concern during the past decade. The final case study, the subject of Chapter 10, explores several problems in the field of telecommunications, which have arisen with spectacular technological advancements in the field. Attention is given to the task of managing the frequencies of the radio spectrum, which has been the province of the ITU for many years. The advent of satellite communications has added several new issues to the international telecommunications agenda, including managing use of the geosynchronous orbit and regulating remote-sensing activities, applications of direct broadcast satellites, and transborder data flows.

The concluding chapter summarizes and compares the experiences of the global community in addressing these six policy problems, referring back to the theoretical framework presented in Part I. It also includes a brief assessment of the future prospects for global problem solving and of the usefulness of the policy perspective for analyzing world politics.

REFERENCES

Alger, Chadwick F. (1977). " 'Foreign' Policies of U.S. Publics," *International Studies Quarterly,* Vol. 21, No. 2., pp. 277–318.

Anderson, James E. (1979). *Public Policy-Making* (2d ed.). New York: Holt, Rinehart and Winston.

Barnet, Richard J. and Ronald E. Müller (1974). *Global Reach: The Power of the Multinational Corporations.* New York: Simon and Schuster.

Beres. Louis R. and Harry R. Targ, eds. (1975). *Planning Alternative World Futures: Values, Methods, and Models.* New York: Praeger.

Caldwell, Lynton K. (1972). *In Defense of Earth: International Protection of the Biosphere.* Bloomington: Indiana University Press.

Carr, Edward Hallett (1939, 1964). The Twenty Years' Crisis, 1919–1939:

An Introduction to the Study of International Relations. London: Macmillan.

Chirot, Daniel (1977). *Social Change in the Twentieth Century*. New York: Harcourt Brace Jovanovich Inc.

Clark, Grenville and Louis Sohn (1966). *World Peace Through World Law*. Cambridge: Harvard University Press.

Claude, Inis L., Jr. (1956, 1984). *Swords into Plowshares*. New York: Random House.

Cox, Robert W. and Harold K. Jacobson (1973).*Anatomy of Influence: Decision-making in International Organization*. New Haven: Yale University Press.

Deutsch, Karl et al. (1957). *Political Community and the North Atlantic Area*. Princeton: Princeton University Press.

Falk, Richard A. (1972). *This Endangered Planet: Prospects and Proposals for Survival*. New York: Random House.

Falk, Richard A. (1975). *A Study of Future Worlds*. New York: Free Press.

Galtung, Johan (1969). "Violence, Peace, and Peace Research," *Journal of Peace Research*, pp. 167–91.

Gilpin, Robert (1981). *War and Change in World Politics*. Cambridge: Cambridge University Press.

Haas, Ernst B. (1958). *The Uniting of Europe: Political, Social, and Economic Forces, 1950–1957*. Stanford: Stanford University Press.

Heilbroner, Robert (1974). *An Inquiry into the Human Prospect*. New York: Norton.

Hovet, Thomas Jr. (1969). *Bloc Politics in the United Nations*. Cambridge: Harvard University Press.

Keohane, Robert O. and Joseph S. Nye (1977). *Power and Interdependence: World Politics in Transition*. Boston: Little, Brown and Company.

Kim, Samuel (1984). *The Quest for a Just World Order*. Boulder, Co.: Westview Press.

Kissinger, Henry A. (1961). *The Necessity of Choice*. New York: Harper and Row.

Krasner, Stephen D., ed. (1983). *International Regimes*. Ithaca, N.Y.: Cornell University Press.

Johansen, Robert C. (1980). *The National Interest and the Human Interest: An Analysis of U.S. Foreign Policy*. Princeton: Princeton University Press.

Jordan, Robert S., ed. (1971). *International Administration: Its Evolution and Contemporary Applications*. New York: Oxford University Press.

Jordan, Robert S. (1972). *Multinational Cooperation: Economic, Social, and Scientific Development*. New York: Oxford Press.

Lerner, Daniel and Harold D. Lasswell (1951). *The Policy Studies*. Stanford: Stanford University Press.

McDougal, Myres S. et al. (1960). *Studies in World Public Order.* New Haven: Yale University Press.

Meadows, Donella H., Dennis L. Meadows, Jørgen Randers, and William H. Behrens (1972). *The Limits to Growth.* New York: Signet.

Mendlovitz, Saul H., ed. (1975). *On the Creation of a Just World Order: Preferred Worlds for the 1990s.* New York: Free Press.

Mesarovic, Mihajlo and Eduard Pestel (1974). *Mankind at the Turning Point.* New York: Free Press.

Mitrany, David (1966). *A Working Peace System.* Chicago: Quadrangle.

Morganthau, Hans J. (1948, 1985). *Politics Among Nations: the Struggle for Power and Peace.* New York: Alfred A. Knopf.

Nardin, Terry (1983). *Law, Morality, and the Relations of States.* Princeton: Princeton University Press.

Nye, Joseph S. (1971). *Peace in Parts.* Boston: Little, Brown and Company.

Nye, Joseph S. and Robert O. Keohane (1971). "Transnational Relations and World Politics: An Introduction," *International Organization,* Vol. 25, No. 3 (Summer), pp. 329–49.

Ophuls, William (1977). *Ecology and the Politics of Scarcity.* San Francisco: Freeman.

Rosenau, James N. (1980). *The Study of Global Interdependence: Essays on the Transnationalization of World Affairs.* London: Francis Pinter.

Scott, Andrew M. (1982). *The Dynamics of Interdependence.* Chapel Hill: University of North Carolina Press.

Skjelsbaek, Kjell (1971). "The Growth of International Non-governmental Organization in the Twentieth Century," *International Organization,* Vol. 25, No. 3, pp. 420–42.

Sprout, Harold and Margaret Sprout (1971). *The Ecological Perspective on Human Affairs.* Princeton: Princeton University Press.

Sterling, Richard W. (1974). *Macropolitics: International Relations in a Global Society.* New York: Alfred A. Knopf.

Thompson, Kenneth W. (1960). *Political Realism and the Crisis of World Politics.* Princeton: Princeton University Press.

Tucker, Robert W. (1977). *The Inequality of Nations.* New York: Basic Books.

Vernon, Raymond (1971). *Sovereignty at Bay: The Multinational Spread of U.S. Enterprises.* New York: Basic Books.

Wallerstein, Immanuel (1974). *The Modern World System: Capitalist Agriculture and the Origins of European World Economy in the Sixteenth Century.* New York: Academic Press.

Ward, Barbara and René Dubois (1972). *Only One Earth: The Care and Maintenance of a Small Planet.* New York: Norton.

Wolfers, Arnold (1962). *Discord and Collaboration.* Baltimore: The Johns Hopkins University Press.

PART I

ELEMENTS OF GLOBAL POLICY

2 | THE AGENDA

The Problems That Confront Humanity

Perhaps it is inevitable that each generation believes that it lives in both the best and the worst of times, to borrow a phrase from Charles Dicken's *A Tale of Two Cities*. There are ample reasons why current generations might come to such a conclusion. On the positive side, modern science and technology has made it possible for a significant part of world's population to enjoy a standard of living that is substantially higher than that of previous generations, while being relieved of much of the suffering and drudgery endured by their ancestors as they struggled to survive. Advances in agriculture, such as in fertilization, pest control, and genetic engineering, have dramatically increased the amount of food that can be grown per acre. Debilitating and fatal diseases have been greatly reduced and health care has been vastly improved, leading to reduced rates of infant mortality and increasing life expectancies. Almost limitless opportunities for an enriched life style have been opened by dramatic advances in technologies used for communication, transportation, and information processing. Space exploration is satisfying more and more of man's curiosity about the universe.

Nevertheless, it is also evident that these are very troubled times. The problems that now confront humanity may be more challenging than those faced by any previous generation. There is concern, for example, that despite the spectacular advances in agriculture, the world's farmers will be unable to provide sufficient food for the rapidly expanding population. Expanding industrial production in many countries is depleting scarce fossil fuels and other natural resources and polluting the environment in ways that will have serious future consequences, such as threats to human health and major climate changes. There are also anxieties that an inability to manage the large volume of transnational financial transactions could lead to a collapse of the global economy; that the sharp disparities in the distribution of wealth will heighten tension between the rich and poor of the world; that regional conflicts could escalate into wars in which increasingly destructive weapons will be used; and that the very survival of the human species is jeopardized by the huge arsenals of nuclear weapons possessed by the superpowers and by the prospect that more countries will have nuclear weapons in the near future. In view of the many relationships between these contemporary problems, some observers suggest that we are in the throes of a "crisis of crises," or world "problematique," which will require an unprecedented level of international cooperation in order to avoid what could evolve into a global cataclysm (see Ruggie, 1979–80). Ironically, some of these problems, such as the spectacular growth of the world's population, are the consequence of the same scientific and technological breakthroughs that contribute to the improvement of the human condition.

This chapter offers an overview of the global policy problems that have appeared on the agendas of international institutions, including the numerous assemblies, councils, and agencies of the United Nations system, most notably the General Assembly. But before commencing with the overview, let us briefly reflect upon the meaning of the terms "problem" and "agenda." After the survey of the problems appearing on global agendas, we shall consider what attributes of them dictate an international response as opposed to purely national policy efforts.

THE NATURE OF PROBLEMS AND AGENDAS

Being preoccupied with our frustrations and anxieties, we rarely reflect on what it means to say that there is a problem. There is a tendency to think of a problem as any adverse circumstance, such as poverty, hunger, pollution, disruptive conflict, or nuclear devastation, which is either a current reality or a realistic possibility in the future. It should be kept in mind, however, that problems are in the eyes of the beholder, for to refer to any actual or potential condition as being problematical presumes a certain interpretation of it. A *problem* is a situation that diverges significantly from what is considered to be a desirable state of affairs. How serious a problem is perceived to be depends in part on the degree to which the actual or potential conditions differ from what is preferred. Furthermore, problems are judged to be more critical when they affect fundamental values, such as survival or the satisfaction of basic human needs. It follows that individuals and societies with contrasting values or priorities may not come to the same conclusions about what, if any, problems are present in any given situation.

Our concern is with *policy problems.* Problems are regarded as policy problems only when there is the prospect of diminishing, if not eliminating, the gap between the actual and desired circumstances, assuming a suitable course of action is adopted. Looked at in another way, a policy problem is the challenge to devise and implement a strategy that will bring about a more favorable result. If there is no possibility of altering the state of affairs in a desired direction, it would be inappropriate to describe the situation as a policy problem. Thus, even though earthquakes often have disastrous consequences, they are not policy problems because nothing can be done to prevent them. On the other hand, limiting the amount of damage that will result from earthquakes or rebuilding from past ones can be policy problems, for it is possible to act in ways that will achieve these outcomes. Likewise, nuclear arms races are under human control and, therefore, can be looked upon as being a policy problem.

It would be a mistake to think exclusively of policy problems in the negative sense, as the task of alleviating or preventing what is undesirable or harmful. Opportunities for enhancing what is already a reasonably desirable and acceptable state of affairs may also be looked upon as a policy problem (Mansbach and Vasquez, 1981, p. 88). Examples of such policy problems might include the challenge of bringing about cultural enrichment by stimulating achievements in the arts, improving crops by genetic engineering, establishing global communications networks using satellites, realizing greater efficiency in industry through freer trade and by developing and applying computer technologies and robotics, enhancing man's capacity to forecast and even control the weather, or exploiting the resources of the deep seas and outer space. Whether a policy problem is looked upon as reacting to a difficulty or taking advantage of an opportunity may be a matter of perspective and expectations. For example, developing medical techniques for organ transplants can be looked upon either in a positive way as an opportunity to extend what is already an ample life span, or in a negative sense, as addressing health problems that cause premature deaths.

There are many other ways in which policy problems vary and pose diverse challenges for policy makers. Some are long-standing conditions which have not yet been adequately addressed, such as the widespread use of torture by governments along with many other abuses of human rights. Others are relatively new, such as the perceived need to regulate transnational data flows. Some problems are very broad, such as speeding up the rate of economic development in the poorer countries of the Third World. Others are narrow by comparison, such as preserving endangered species of whales. Some problems are highly complicated, such as reducing the degree of monetary instability in the international economic system; others are relatively simple, such as the protection of diplomats stationed in foreign countries. Some problems are dramatic and attract immediate attention in the world's press, such as terrorism. Sometimes these problems require an immediate response, as in the case of international political crises or suffering of earthquake victims. Other problems such as the erosion of top soil of prime farmland are hardly noticed and, because they develop very gradually, can be addressed in a more measured manner. Finally, there are problems that are heartrending, such as the plight of political refugees as they drift at sea on rafts or are crowded into squalid border camps, in contrast to others that are primarily technical in nature and thus evoke little emotion, such as standardizing weights and measures.

Once recognized, policy problems may become a part of two types of agendas, both of which comprise a number of problems on which action might be taken. A *formal* agenda is an official listing of specific items before a decision-making body in the order in which they will be taken up for discussion, as in the case of the agenda drawn up by the Secretary-General for the annual session of the General Assembly. By contrast, the problems on a *public* agenda are not written down and ordered, but are on the minds of many members of a community, who believe that they should be addressed by an appropriate governmental institution. (Cobb et al., 1976, pp. 126–27). Not all problems appear on an agenda of either type, for it is quite possible that those who formulate them are not alert to the existence of undesirable circumstances or threatening possibilities or, alternatively, of attractive opportunities that could be exploited. The problems that have not been recognized yet may have greater consequences than the agenda items that preoccupy policy makers or a community as a whole. For example, until recently there was little awareness of the serious dangers to human health posed by the improper disposal of toxic substances. It is also possible to believe mistakenly that a problem exists, as later analysis proved to be the case with President Kennedy's concern over a "missile gap" and President Reagan's warnings of a "window of vulnerability" in strategic nuclear weapons.

The limited time available to most policy-making bodies allows them to consider and act on only a small part of the public agenda. Furthermore, they lack the resources needed to tackle the full range of problems that confront them. Thus, decisions must be made on priorities. Ideally, problems having a significant bearing on the core values of a society will receive the greatest amount of attention and resources. Moreover, it is normally advisable to focus on problems on which the prospects for making concrete progress are favorable and to play down those that are less susceptible to solution. In actual practice, however, formal agendas rarely reflect the relative importance of the matters on public agendas. Problems with localized consequences that are immediate and dramatic usually receive more attention than do more serious conditions that evolve slowly and are widely dispersed. Thus, there is more commitment to ameliorating the suffering due to temporary famines and wars than addressing the problem of chronic malnutrition affecting many more people (Hopkins and Puchala, 1978, pp. 601–2). There is also a tendency for new policy problems, such as those related to the environment, to be short-shrifted in favor of issues like arms control or colonialism that have traditionally occupied a prominent position on formal agendas. Finally, the composition of agendas is the product of a political struggle among those inclined to cooperate with one another (Lindblom, 1980, p. 5). Thus, disproportionate attention is normally given to the priorities of the more numerous, powerful, or politically astute members of an organization or community. Political influence may also be used to keep certain items high on the public agenda from being placed on a formal agenda.

As time passes, the agenda of any community can be expected to undergo change. Modifications may be a response to new threats or to previously existing problems that have only recently been widely recognized, as has been the case with a number ecological concerns such as the spread of deserts and deforestation of tropical areas. Opportunities brought about by new technologies also expand agendas; thus, developments in genetic engineering have raised new policy issues. Agendas may also be transformed by raising expectations with the result that what was once not considered a problem is later perceived to be one. There has, for example, been a general tendency to expect more of governments in matters such as eradicating poverty, reducing unemployment, guaranteeing human rights, and protecting the environment. Finally, agendas are modified as new actors, or ones that have recently acquired greater influence, press for action on their priorities, as has been especially noticeable in the United Nations with the influx of recently independent states of the Third World.

A SURVEY OF THE GLOBAL AGENDA

What then are the policy problems that appear on the global agenda? The survey that follows calls attention to many of the diverse problems that have had a place on global agendas in recent decades, each of which poses distinctive challenges for international policy makers. It is not, however, an exhaustive catalog of all of the policy problems that engage them, which is well beyond the scope of this book. The survey is drawn heavily from, but not restricted to, matters written into the formal agendas of bodies such as the General Assembly and the specialized agencies of the United Nations. Most issues on the public agendas of global problems are taken up in one or more of these institutions. There are occasionally, however, some concerns that arise in other circles, such as the scientific community, that do not appear immediately on any of the formal agendas.

For purposes of the overview, the policy problems have been grouped into six more narrowly focused agendas: political, economic, social, resource, environmental, and transportation and communication. While the problems on each of these specialized agendas have some characteristics in common, many could have been placed on one or more of the other agendas.

The Political Agenda

No international policy problem can be entirely divorced from politics. Political considerations are a significant factor in which problems appear international on agendas and the ways in which they are addressed and implemented. This section discusses two interrelated types of problems that are political in substance, which have traditionally been preoccupations of international policy makers. The first is the often mundane, but sometimes highly controversial, question of who can legitimately exercise political authority over a given geographical area or population and, in addition, take part in international forums that discuss and make international policies. A second and perhaps more conspicuous part of the global political agenda involves problems related to war and peace, in particular the tasks of deterring military aggression, defusing crises and resolving international conflicts that could lead to war, bringing an end to ongoing wars and other types of armed hostilities, and containing the buildup of armaments. Security from aggression and the ravages of war was the primary motivation for the establishment of both the League of Nations and the United Nations. These two parts of the political agenda are often intertwined. Not only are disputes over political authority a leading cause of war, but it is not uncommon for wars to result in changes of government and a redrawing of political boundaries. Moreover, not only are arms build-ups by nations an effort to protect the political authority of their own governments against foreign or domestic challenges, but they can also pose a threat to the security of the authority of other states.

Several types of political authority are widely regarded as being improper, and, therefore, a legitimate subject of international concern. Perhaps the most harshly denounced type of authority has been colonialism, which came into being as less developed societies succumbed to the rule of foreign states endowed with more advanced military technologies and forms of social organization. Such a fate befell the traditional societies of large areas of Latin

America, Africa, and Asia beginning in the fifteenth century as they were forcibly brought under the control of European states that sought to exploit their labor and natural resources. Colonialism emerged as a major issue in the United Nations during the 1950s and 1960s as the swelling ranks of newly independent, Third World members clamored for the "self-determination" of all societies. Most of these areas had become self-governing by the mid-1970s, after the last sizable colonial holdings, Angola and Mozambique, were relinquished by Portugal. Since then, several other colonial enclaves have become self-governing or were incorporated into neighboring states. The issue of colonialism has not faded away completely, however. Indonesia, a former Dutch colony, is accused of a "second-generation" type of colonialism for having annexed East Timor, a former Portuguese colony whose natives have fought fiercely for self-rule. A similar charge has been made against Morocco for its efforts to take over the Western Sahara, a former Spanish colony, despite the armed resistance of an indigenous political movement named the Prolisario. Cuba has attempted unsuccessfully to have the control of the United States over Puerto Rico condemned as colonialism. Spain has objected to Britain's continuing occupation of the Rock of Gibralter.

There are other circumstances in which the legitimacy of political authority has been challenged on the grounds that it violates the principle of self-determination. Such is the case with puppet regimes that foreign states impose on countries against the will of their people. Thus, the Soviet Union was roundly condemned in the United Nations for intervening in Afghanistan with a military force of 100,000 to establish a client government led by Babrak Kamal. A similar case is Kampuchea, which was overrun by Vietnamese forces who deposed the Khmer Rouge regime of Pol Pot and installed a new government under their control led by Heng Samrin. The General Assembly continues to seat the Pol Pot government as the legitimate representative of Kampuchea in the United Nations, despite its failure to control the country and its previous documented practice of genocide. South Africa's control over Southwest Africa, or Namibia, which was declared illegal by the General Assembly in 1966, had a very different origin. A former colony of Germany, the territory was temporarily mandated by the League of Nations to South Africa, which had occupied the area during World War I and made known its desire to permanently annex the territory. In 1973 the General Assembly recognized an indigenous group, the South West Africa People's Organization, as the authentic representative of the Namibian people. Another distinctive case was the white, minority government headed by Ian Smith in Southern Rhodesia. Shortly after unilaterally announcing the independence of the colony from the United Kingdom in 1965, the Smith government was declared to be illegitimate by the United Nations, which subsequently imposed an embargo on trade with the country.

Disputes over who is entitled to control certain territories also appear on the global political agenda. This has been the case with areas taken by military force, such as the lands seized by Israel during the Six Day War of 1967, most notably the West Bank of the Jordan River, which is now dotted with newly established Israeli settlements. Argentina and the United Kingdom went to war in 1982 over conflicting claims to the Falkland (Malvinas) Islands. A few years earlier, Somalia attacked Ethiopia in an attempt to take control of the Ogaden region, which is populated by ethnic Somalis. Both Iran and Iraq claim the Shatt al Arab waterway between the two countries, which has been one of the primary issues in their ongoing war. Controversies have also arisen over how much of the ocean area falls within the jurisdiction of coastal states (one of the principal issues addressed at the Law of the Sea Conferences) and over overlapping claims to territory in Antarctica.

War has been a scourge of humanity throughout recorded history, but especially during the twentieth century. Despite the establishment of the United Nations, wars continue to be a widespread phenomenon. By one count, 120 wars were waged during the period 1945 to 1976. They were fought on the territories of 71 countries, involved the armies of 82 nations, and resulted in the deaths of 25 million people (Kende, 1977, p. 60). Another study lists 40 armed conflicts taking place during 1983 involving 45 countries (Center for Defense Information, 1983, p. 1). In contrast to earlier eras, few of the recent wars and armed conflicts were fought between states in the traditional manner across international boundaries; the Arab-Israeli, Iran-Iraq, and Argentina-United Kingdom wars being notable exceptions. Most are internal conflicts that take the form of revolutions fought by guerrilla forces or of civil wars between regions of states. While these wars are described as being "internal," they often take on an international dimension as the belligerents receive support from the outside in the form of financial assistance, arms shipments, or troop deployments. And even though most wars of the contemporary era have been fought on the territories of less developed countries, industrialized countries, including the superpowers, have frequently been involved, sometimes deeply, as in the case of the lengthy interventions of the United States and the Soviet Union in the hostilities in Vietnam and Afghanistan, respectively. There is the danger, moreover, what starts out as an internal war could evolve into a confrontation between outside powers who believe that vital interests are at stake.

Most governments build up their armed strength for security both from revolutions originating within their countries and from attack by other states. Unfortunately, what each state does to protect itself can pose a threat to other countries. As a result, the competitive quest for protection through armed strength by states throughout the world has diminished the security of all nations, including the superpowers, while contributing to the potential destructiveness of the wars that do take place. Arms build-ups are also regarded as being one of the most serious global problems because of their financial cost, an estimated $660 billion worldwide in 1983, which substantially reduces the resources available for pursuing other priorities such as domestic social programs or foreign economic assistance (Sivard, 1983, p. 6). For these reasons, arms control has been a prominent item on global agendas during the post-World War II era as a strategy for enhancing the security of states. The 58 resolutions passed in 1982 by the General Assembly are indicative of the amount of attention the issue continues to receive (Puchala et al., 1983, p. 61).

Most international efforts to constrain the development and deployment of weapons have been directed toward nuclear weapons. The accumulation of huge nuclear arsenals by the two superpowers, what is sometimes referred to as "vertical proliferation" of arms, has been of particular concern because the detonation of large numbers of them would inevitably have catastrophic social, economic, and environmental consequences for most of the world. Between them, the United States and Soviet Union now have approximately 50,000 nuclear bombs, a large proportion of which are far more powerful than the atomic bombs dropped on Japan in World War II. Even more worrisome is the erosion of the tenuous measure of "crisis stability" that has prevailed during most of the nuclear age as a consequence of the deployment of "first-strike" weapons accurate and powerful enough to destroy many of the retaliatory weapons of the enemy within minutes. Rationality dictates launching vulnerable missiles with great haste if it is believed, correctly or incorrectly, that an attack on them is either imminent or is already in progress. The potential acquisitions of nuclear weapons by additional countries, or what is known as "horizontal proliferation," has also been in a subject of considerable international anxiety since the advent of nuclear age. Thus far, the roster of countries acknowledged to have nuclear weapons has grown much more slowly than was initially feared. Nevertheless, there are continuing fears that in the coming decades more countries will acquire nuclear weapons and that these countries might be tempted to use them if regional and global tensions persist.

The Economic Agenda

Two distinct, but integrally related, economic agendas continue to occupy prominent positions on global agendas. The first is the vitality and stability of the international economic system. This concern became part of the original mission of the United Nations largely as a reaction to the miseries of the Great Depression which had had such a disastrous impact on nations throughout the world and added to the popular support for the aggressive policies of the fascist governments of Germany and Italy. Although it is difficult to isolate the causes of the economic chaos of the period, the pronounced trend toward economic protectionism by a number of the leading states is widely credited with deepening and prolonging the depression. Even before the end of World War II, Western leaders meeting at Bretton Woods in 1944 agreed upon the need and design for a liberalized international economic order. They hoped that a freer flow of goods and capital between states would facilitate a rebuilding of the war-ravaged societies and would stabilize the global economy in a way that would prevent depressions in the future.

The second overriding global economic concern of the contemporary era is the economic development of the Third World. The development issue can, in turn, be looked upon as a two-fold policy problem. Not only are there the persistent conditions of economic stagnation and severe poverty in the poorer nations, but there are also the serious injustices inherent in the sharply skewed distribution of the world's wealth. The development issue rose to a high position on the global agenda as large numbers of newly independent, less developed countries forged a relatively cohesive voting majority in the General Assembly in the late 1950s and early 1960s. The issue came to a head in the General Assembly in 1974 when Third World proposals for a "new international economic order" were presented, intensively debated, and finally approved by large majorities composed mostly of the less developed countries. Third World representatives challenged the legitimacy of the then existing economic order, known as the Bretton Woods System, pointing out that because it was in place before most of their countries became independent, obviously they could play no role in designing it. These demands for a major reform of the existing international economic order have been the subject of the continuing "North-South" dialogue, which has taken place in a variety of international forums over the past decade.

Trade has been a central issue on both of these international economic agendas. Achieving the liberalized order envisioned at Bretton Woods required disassembling many of the impediments to commerce between countries that had been erected in the protectionist era of the 1930s. Then it was customary for states to use trade barriers and exchange controls to limit imports that were believed to be contributing to the extraordinarily high rates of unemployment. When trading partners reciprocated by sealing off their markets to imports, the rising protectionism was economically damaging to all, and the economic miseries of the period were prolonged. Since World War II, efforts to reduce trade restrictions have been concentrated in several rounds of intensive multinational trade negotiations, each lasting several years, the most recent being the six-year Tokyo Round that ended in 1979. These negotiations have taken place under the auspices of the GATT, which was established in 1947 to facilitate orderly international trade. Trade has increased dramatically as tariffs and other restrictions have been reduced or eliminated, but clearly more to the benefit the industrialized countries than to the less developed ones.

A different agenda of trade-related issues has been raised by the Third World countries, primarily in the forum provided by UNCTAD. Concerned that the less developed countries cannot compete on equal terms with the highly developed states, Third World leaders have worked for global policies that would increase and stabilize the import revenues of their nations. Among their primary objectives is an end to trade restrictions that make it difficult for products from the Third World, especially processed or manufactured goods, to penetrate the much more lucrative markets of the developed world. It is argued further that the exports of less developed countries should receive preferential access to these markets over those of other states. At the same time, less developed countries would not be required to fully reciprocate, but would be permitted to maintain higher trade restrictions of their own in order to at least temporarily preserve domestic markets for infant industries that would be overwhelmed by much larger and more efficient foreign firms.

Mutually beneficial trading relationships can be disrupted when monetary problems arise. States that persistently run sizable trade deficits or are confronted by temporary cash-flow shortages may be unable to pay for their imports. In such circumstances, governments are tempted to correct the imbalance by devaluing their national currencies, a step that makes the exports of their country more competitive in world markets, simultaneously reducing the financial capacity of their citizens to purchase imports. Unfortunately, currency devaluations work hardships on trading partners, prompting them to adopt similar tactics in order to cope with trade imbalances of their own. Under the Bretton Woods system, the problem of maintaining monetary stability became the responsibility of the IMF. As the primary public source of short-term loans to tide countries over temporary shortages of the hard currencies needed to pay their accounts, the IMF plays a critical role in ensuring sufficient liquidity in the international system to keep trade moving. In performing this role, the IMF has been criticized for the strict conditions attached to its loans, which are designed to enhance the borrower's capacity to repay the loan.

The financial austerity that these conditions dictate has on several occasions touched off political unrest in the recipient countries, which have sometimes been referred to as "IMF riots."

Over the past two decades the rapid growth in foreign investments in most countries, even in the bastions of socialism—the Soviet Union and China—has been an important factor increasing the degree of international economic interdependence. Particularly notable is the spectacular growth in direct foreign investments, which include tens of thousands of subsidiaries that have been made by several thousand multinational corporations, representing the full gamut of industries and businesses. The impact of these direct investments on the economies of host states can be considerable, especially in the case of the largest of the multinational corporations whose annual sales exceed the GNP of most states (see Ray, 1983, pp. 348–49). The impact of the decisions of corporate directors on the economies of foreign countries may be seen in overall rates of economic growth, the products that are manufactured, the goods that are marketed and consumed, the ways agricultural land is used, the pace at which natural resources are developed, the balance of trade, the value of national currencies, employment opportunities and wage rates, tax revenues, and access to modern technologies..

What, if anything, should be done internationally to regulate the activities of these multinational corporations that have so seriously undermined the sovereignty of foreign governments? In some industries, it is increasingly possible for the largest corporations to act in a monopolistic or oligopolistic manner to dominate production and marketing on a global basis to the disadvantage of consumers everywhere. Third World leaders contend that their countries have been exploited by the machinations of corporations upon which they have become dependent for capital investment and advanced technology. The profit-oriented directors are criticized for being insensitive to the impact that their decisions have on the economy, society, and environment of the countries that host their operations. Moreover, several instances have come to light in which large multinational corporations have meddled in the internal politics of countries where they have investments, a celebrated case being ITT's efforts to undermine the Allende government in Chile during the early 1970s. Alternatively, having committed large amounts of financial resources abroad, corporate officials fear being victimized by arbitrary changes in national policies that could jeopardize the profitability of their subsidiaries or even lead to the nationalization of their holdings without fair compensation. Negotiations have been taking place for nearly a decade on fashioning an international "code of conduct" for multinational corporations that will not only improve the bargaining position of host states, but also offer greater security to investors.

Over the past fifteen years, several shocks to the global economic order occurred that brought an end to an era of relative stability under the Bretton Woods System, during which rapid economic growth and prosperity had taken place in much of the world. The first of these shocks was the decision of the United States in 1971 to discontinue its practice of allowing foreign countries to convert dollars into gold at the fixed rate of $35 to the ounce. This action was taken in the face of a run on American gold stocks when confidence in the dollar began to wane as a result of large balance of payments deficits during the Vietnam War. Thus, the value of the dollar, rather than being constant and hence a stable anchor of the international monetary order, fluctuated daily on currency markets. The floating of the dollar has had a major destabilizing effect on international trade both because it had become the world's primary reserve currency and because many traded goods, including petroleum, were priced in dollars. Another consequence is that the domestic economic policies of the United States, such as the tight monetary policies that were adopted to cool the economy and thereby reduce inflation, affect the value of the dollar and subsequently trade balances and patterns of investment.

Sharp increases in the price of oil that were engineered by OPEC in 1973–74 and 1979 were also major shocks to the stability of the international economic order. They are credited with being a major factor contributing to the economic malaise that descended on the industrialized world during the latter 1970s and early 1980s, which was characterized by slow economic growth and high inflation rates, or what became known as "stagflation". The accompanying unemployment rates, the highest in some countries since the 1930s, combined with large balance of payments deficits due to the larger payments for imported oil, increased political pressures in developed nations for a return to trade protectionism. The impact of the oil price rises has also been serious on the countries of the Third World that do not produce oil. Their foreign indebtedness increased dramatically as they borrowed heavily to pay the much higher prices for imported oil. Many of these loans came from the commercial banks that were "recycling" surplus "petrodollars" that some of the OPEC countries deposited in them. Ironically, some of the oil-producing countries, most notably Mexico and Venezuela, have also accumulated large debts because of the plummeting demand for their high-priced oil. What to do about this "debt crisis" of the Third World countries, who by 1983 owed more than $750 billion to foreign lenders, has been a major challenge for international economic policy makers. Not only is there the danger of defaults that would have widespread reverberations, but also there exists the dire prospect of shrinking markets in the less developed countries for exports from the developed countries.

The Social Agenda

The global social agenda can be distinguished from the economic one by its emphasis on the actual conditions of life that hundreds of millions of people experience on a day-by-day basis, such as poverty, hunger, overcrowding, disease, illiteracy, drug addiction, unemployment, inhumane working conditions, discrimination, government repression, and general hopelessness. Obviously, the state of national economies and the global economic environment can have a significant bearing on the prevalence of many social problems in both developed and less developed countries. Robust economic growth and industrialization do not, however, inevitably translate into an improvement in the social conditions of all sectors of a population. All too often the poorer classes are bypassed as the fruits of economic growth go disproportionately to those who are relatively well off. Significant improvement in the social conditions of the world's hard-core poor requires much more than a purely economic approach.

One of leading issues on the global social agenda is health, which on a societal basis is often measured in terms of infant mortality rates and average life expectancy. Disease continues to be a major cause of death and suffering, even though much has been learned from medical research on how to prevent or cure disease. Thus, while smallpox and several other diseases have been virtually irradicated or are significantly less prevalent—largely because of the programs of the World Health Organization (WHO)—many others still affect the populations of large areas. The problem of disease remains the most serious for Third World peoples, many of whom live in tropic areas where organisms thrive that cause illness such as malaria, sleeping sickness, yellow fever and dengue, cholera, diarrhoea, schistosomiasis, bilharzia, filariasis, onchocerciasis, Rift Valley fever, hookworm, and leprosy (see Eckholm, 1977). These people are often more susceptible to diseases because their natural resistances have often been weakened by malnutrition and because of the inadequacies of health care services. Disease is also more prevalent in the Third World because much of the population docs not have access to potable water and, thus, may have no alternative to using water contaminated with raw human wastes. This problem that is being highlighted by the Drinking Water and Sanitation Decade declared for the 1980s by the United Nations. Disease and malnutrition attributable to the improper use of aggressively marketed infant formulas in these regions has been a concern of WHO as has the growth in lung cancer as a result of increased cigarette consumption. The residents of developed countries are spared many of these health related miseries of Third World peoples, but yet must contend with illnesses such as influenza, cancer, and heart disease.

Hunger, either of a continuing or temporary nature, continues to be one of the basic realities experienced by much of the world's population. According to Food Agriculture Organization (FAO) estimates, approximately 500 million people suffer from severe, chronic malnourishment, while an additional billion are undernourished to a lesser degree. If inadequate amounts of food were being produced on a global basis, the problem of hunger would be appropriately regarded as a resource problem. However, this does not appear to be the case in view of FAO estimates that world food production is sufficient to satisfy the nutritional requirements of the world's population. Furthermore, it is ironic that the proportion of the world's population that is severely malnourished has apparently increased in recent decades despite increases in per capita food production (FAO, 1983, p. 261). Thus, the prevalence of chronic hunger can in large part be explained by gross inequalities in the consumption of food which result from many of the poorest people and countries simply being priced out of the market for food. The inability of the rural poor in many Third World countries to secure adequate food can be attributed to the concentration of land ownership in the hands of a small wealthy minority, a problem that was addressed at the World Conference on Agrarian Reform and Rural Development that was held in Rome in 1979. Famines resulting from adverse weather conditions or political instabilities take a heavy toll on the population of some regions, in recent years most notably the drought-plagued sub-Saharan region of Africa. Food security was a major issue on the agenda of the World Food Conference held in Rome in 1974 and the World Food Council which it spawned.

Another serious concern is population growth, which on a worldwide basis reached the historically unprecedented rate of nearly 2 percent annually in the 1960s and 1970s. Most of this growth has been in the Third World where substantial improvements in health care in the postwar era have sharply lowered mortality rates. The most rapid growth has been in Africa and Latin America, where the annual increase is nearly 3 percent a year. If these rates were to continue, the populations of these two continents would double within twenty-five years and mushroom to sixteen times the original figure within a century. In Africa 45 percent of the people are fifteen years of age or less compared to only 24 percent in the developed countries (Population Reference Bureau, 1981). Disproportionately large numbers of young people burden society not only because they are largely nonproductive economically, but also because of the heavy demands they put on the limited educational resources of less developed countries. As the young grow older, they will severely tax the capacity of the economies of their countries to generate employment and, in the absence of strong antinatalist policies of their governments, perpetuate the already high population growth rates. The problem of how to dampen these trends has been taken up at major United Nations conferences convened in Bucharest in 1974 and Mexico City in 1984. The United Nations Fund for Population Activities has assisted Third World countries in implementing family planning programs.

Large migrations of people both within and between countries pose another type of demographic problem. Within many of the less developed countries there has been a vast movement of people from rural to urban areas, causing cities to grow at a much faster rate than has been the case when the industrial countries were at a similar stage of development. Currently, there are 22 urban areas in the Third World that have a population in excess of 4 million, a figure that is projected to grow to 60 by the year 2000, 18 of which could have more than 10 million people (Holdgate et al., 1982, p. 328). Faced with overpopulation and a lack of opportunity in rural areas, these migrants have sought a better life in cities that are poorly prepared to provide either opportunities for employment or essential services, such as a safe water supply, sanitary disposal of wastes, education, medical care, electricity, and transportation. Large numbers take up residence in overcrowded, disease-ridden slums or squatter settlements, which together are home to more than half of the population of cities such as Addis Ababa, Abidjan, Ibadan, Lomé, Dar es Salaam, Lusaka, Kinshasa, Dakar, Mombasa, Ankara, and Bogota and more than a quarter of the residents of many cities of Asia and Latin America (Linn, 1983, pp. 12–13). Many of the squatter settlements are illegal, but nevertheless spring up at a faster rate than the overall growth of many Third World cities (Holdgate et al., 1982, p. 343). The quality of life in these urban areas is looked upon as an environmental problem as well as a social one by the United Nations Environment Programme (UNEP), which in 1976 convened the Conference on Human Settlements in Vancouver, British Columbia (see Ward, 1976).

Migrations of people across national boundaries have more obvious international implications. Many migrants are refugees fleeing war, political persecution, and famine. Over the decade of the 1970s the worldwide flow of refugees tripled to an annual figure of 7.4 million, with the greatest numbers being in Africa and Asia (Office of the UN High Commissioner for Refugees quoted in Holdgate et al., p. 319). In recent years the plight of the "boat people," who fled Vietnam on the seas, and the "foot people," who walked across the border from Cambodia into Thailand, has been the subject of considerable international discussion. Pakistan has received more than 2 million refugees from Afghanistan; Somalia and the Sudan have experienced large influxes from neighboring states. Political turmoil in Central America is generating a smaller, but growing flow of refugees. Migrations of refugees in sizable numbers can be a serious strain on the limited resources and the shakey political stability of the less developed countries that receive them. Moreover, their activities, including support of rebels in their homeland, can be a persistent source of international conflict. Changing conditions may permit these uprooted people to return before long to their homelands. For others like the Palestinians who fled their homes during the 1948 war, there is no foreseeable prospect of such a return. The special needs and vulnerabilities of refugees, who typically live in wretched, disease-ridden camps, have been a concern of the Office of the United Nations High Commissioner for Refugees and the United Nations Relief and Works Agency for Palestine Refugees.

Opportunities for employment have been the stimulus for another type of international migration. During the economic boom of the 1960s and early 1970s, several of the Western European states recruited "guest" workers from northern Africa and Asia to overcome their labor shortages. More recently, Saudi Arabia and several oil-rich states of the Middle East imported millions of workers from as far away as Pakistan, India, and South Korea. What to do about a large flow of undocumented immigrants from Mexico and Haiti, who desire to escape the unemployment and economic miseries of their home countries, has been a controversial political issue in the United States. But even for the foreign workers who are invited, many issues arise in regard to the economic rights that they should enjoy in the host country to prevent their labor from being unfairly exploited. Moreover, should guest workers be permitted to bring their families and to make full use of the social services of the countries that invited them? May a host state deport foreign workers during periods of economic downturn and high unemployment, as was recently done by the Nigerian government to foreign workers from Ghana and other west African states?

Questions of human rights have been raised in regard to other types of people that have been mistreated or have special needs. Recognition of the second-class treatment women receive in many countries prompted the declaration of the United Nations Decade for Women, which was launched in 1976 with a major international conference held in Mexico City. Women have been the victims of practices such as enslavement, sexual coercion, forced marriages, sexual mutilation by excision, and even murder over dowry disputes. In many societies, women are given fewer opportunities for education than their male counterparts. And even though women are often expected to assume a dual work load, full-time wage earning employment in addition to household responsibilities, their fraction of the wealth of the society remains very meager compared to that of men. Children are another vulnerable group whose needs and rights are often neglected or ignored, a problem the United Nations publicized when it proclaimed 1979 as the International Year of the Child, in an effort to generate more support for the United Nations Children's Fund (UNICEF). In addition, 1985 has been designated as the International Youth Year. The 1982 World Assembly on the Aging examined the special problems of people at the other end of the life cycle, which are becoming more serious in the industrialized countries as the proportion of the elderly in the population swells and in less developed countries with the demise of extended families which offered security in old age. The United Nations Decade for Disabled Persons, which began in 1985, will focus international attention on the difficulties faced by the handicapped throughout the world.

The Resource Agenda

The global resource and environmental agendas can be difficult to separate because both are concerned with the natural endowments of the planet that are essential to human life. Whereas the resource agenda, which we will consider in this section, pertains to the *use* of nature to satisfy human needs and ambitions, the environmental agenda, which will be discussed in the next section, is oriented toward the *preservation* of nature.

What in nature qualifies as a resource depends on an appraisal by human beings of what is useful to them (Larkin et al., 1981). Down through the ages, humanity has adapted much from the natural world to its uses—fertile land, forests, fossil fuels, minerals, fish, water, and solar energy are but a few examples. The catalog of resources changes over time depending upon human values and the technologies employed. Previously ignored materials, such as rubber and uranium, become resources only after human ingenuity makes it possible to use them advantageously. Conversely, when substances become obsolete for certain uses, as happened with whale oil, they are no longer a resource unless they are employed in some other way. It should also be kept in mind that a substance may be a critical resource in some societies, while in other societies, it may be discarded as a waste. Such is the case with cattle dung, an important source of fertilizer and cooking fuel in much of the Third World, but largely disdained in the developed world.

Rather than being distributed evenly over the surface of the planet, many natural substances that are in high demand are concentrated in a few geographical areas. Conversely, the majority of countries are poorly endowed with natural resources. Thus, the quest for secure access to adequate supplies of critical resources by those who lack them has been a major factor shaping world history through the ages. The famous explorers of the fifteenth and sixteenth centuries who discovered the American continents and new trade routes to the Far East set out in a search for resources such as gold, silver, and spices. Later, the resource poverty of the European countries spurred the establishment of colonial empires as a stable and inexpensive source of the natural resources essential to their industrial development and to the maintenance of their preferred style of life. In more modern times, the aggression of Japan, Germany, and Italy that sparked World War II was motivated at least in part by the desire to guarantee a secure supply of vital natural resources (Eckes, 1978, pp. 57–59). Reliable access to natural resources at affordable prices is a continuing concern, especially in the aftermath of the oil embargo of 1973–74, the dramatic rises in the price of oil during the decade, and the international tensions in the Persian Gulf area upon which much of the world relies heavily for imports of petroleum. No state in the contemporary world is endowed with adequate reserves of all of the natural resources that are necessary to sustain an industrialized economy. Thus, one of the challenges for the makers of global resource policy is to ensure that all countries will have access to an adequate supply of the planet's natural endowment without resort to armed conflict.

Recently, insecurity about resources has been compounded by projections that the resource base of the planet may be insufficient to satisfy the demands of a mushrooming world population. These concerns were fanned by the first of the reports to the Club of Rome, which projected an uncontrollable decline in population and industrial production within a century, if not sooner, if strong, corrective action were not taken to bring growth trends under control promptly (Meadows et al., 1972). The Malthusian specter foreseen in that study appeared to be unfolding much sooner than predicted when a combination of circumstances—adverse climatic conditions, interruptions in the oil trade, and the collapse of the anchovy fishery off the coast of Peru—tightened world food supplies during a period in the mid-1970s, which became known internationally as the "world food crisis." During the same period, OPEC's success in raising oil prices as rapidly growing oil consumption cut deeply into proven global reserves led to a widespread perception that the world was also in the throes of an "energy crisis" which would progressively become more severe. These developments were reasons for pessimism about whether the resource base of the planet would be sufficient to permit the Third World countries to achieve a very high level of industrialization. The worst fears of a decade ago have been dispelled by a series of better crop years and by sharp declines in the demand for fossil fuels and minerals caused by the price rises and the resultant economic recession through much of the world. Higher prices were an incentive for exploration that led to the discovery of additional reserves of many natural resources and eventual price reductions. Nevertheless, there is continuing concern in some circles that the time is not too distant when human demand for resources will run up against planetary limits if consumption remains high in the developed countries and increases substantially elsewhere (Trainer, 1982).

Conflicts over the ownership of natural resources and the right to exploit them also pose important international policy problems. Among the reforms that Third World leaders have been seeking in a new economic order is an internationally recognized right to exercise "sovereignty," or control, over the development of the natural resources within the boundaries of their countries. This demand challenges the legitimacy of past concessions made to foreign corporations to extract their resources, which they contend were negotiated when they were politically weak and international resource markets were glutted. The question of resource rights also arises in reference to areas beyond the territorial jurisdiction of states, in particular the oceans and the seabed beneath them, Antarctica, and outer space. Disputes have arisen as the

demand for the resources of these regions has grown and technologies have been developed for exploiting them. Thus, the fundamental question for global policy is: who has the right to
develop the natural wealth of these nonnational areas and under
what conditions? Should those possessing the advanced technologies needed to exploit the resources of the deep seabed or
outer space be expected to share the wealth they generate with the
societies that lack them? This type of question has been addressed
extensively in the most recent United Nations Law of the Sea
Conference and the UNISPACE conference held in Vienna in
1982.

The terms of trade in primary commodities, such as coffee, tea,
jute, copper, bauxite, or petroleum, is another resource-related
problem on global agendas, one which could as appropriately be
classified as an economic item. Exports of a small number of
these primary commodities are relied upon by many of the Third
World countries for the revenues needed to finance their plans for
development. Unfortunately, commodity prices are notorious for
sharp fluctuations from one year to the next. This roller coaster
tendency in prices is caused by variations both in the demand,
which reflects economic conditions in importing countries, and in
the supply, as new producers try to take advantage of high prices.
The supply of agricultural commodities is of course affected by
erratic weather conditions. Spokesmen for the less developed
countries complain that the average prices of the primary commodities they sell have not, over the long run, kept pace with the
prices of the industrial products they must import from the West.
In forums such as UNCTAD, international policy makers have
been grappling with the question of whether to simply allow
market forces to determine the world prices of primary commodities, or whether prices should be subject to international
control designed to stabilize them and thus ensure that they will
keep pace with increases in the cost of manufactured goods.

Less developed countries that have had to satisfy their resource
needs through imports have also experienced hard times. The oil
price rises of the 1970s wreaked havoc with the trade balances of
Third World states and would have been much worse were it not
for their meager consumption of oil in comparison to the industrialized West (see Sivard, 1981). The economic miseries of many
of these states were compounded by sharp increases in the price

of food during the years of the "world food crisis" of the mid-1970s, causing the United Nations to list them in a specially designated category of countries called the "most seriously affected" that would qualify them for special forms of multilateral assistance. The larger problem faced by most Third World states is the prospect that the natural resources they need to develop, in particular fossil fuels, will not be nearly as plentiful and will be much more expensive than was the case when the Western countries underwent rapid industrialization. Thus, economic growth and an improvement in living conditions in Third World countries can be accomplished only if they discover and exploit more of their own resources, possibly with outside help, or adopt development strategies that require fewer resources, using what are commonly referred to as "alternative technologies." Possibilities for helping less developed countries make use of domestic sources of energy, ranging from fossil fuels to solar power, were explored and debated at the Conference on New and Renewable Sources of Energy held in Nairobi in 1981.

The Environmental Agenda

Over the past century, human beings have perhaps done more irreparable harm to the natural environment essential to their survival than the combined impact of earlier generations over tens of thousands of years. This is not to say, however, that earlier civilizations did not also damage the environment (see Hughes, 1975). What is unique about modern times is the scope and degree of the environmental degradation brought about by a mushrooming world population and the rapid industrialization that has taken place in some regions.

In view of the relatively recent acceleration in the pace of environmental deterioration and a lag in awareness of the consequences of this trend, it is not surprising that the global environment is a relatively new addition to international agendas. In fact, it was not until 1968 that the deteriorating condition of the natural environment attracted the attention of the General Assembly. That year, a Swedish resolution was adopted that provided for the United Nations Conference on the Human Environment, convened in Stockholm in 1972 following an extensive series of preparatory meetings. In taking up the recommendations of the

Conference, the General Assembly established UNEP, which has become the catalyst for international efforts aimed at preserving the natural environment. Likewise, it was not until the late 1960s and early 1970s that the major industrialized countries set up national environmental ministries and adopted comprehensive legislation to limit further damage to the environment (Holdgate et al., 1982, p. 8). Even then, the environmental agenda did not receive nearly as much attention as other international policy problems, such as regional conflicts, arms control, and economic development, even though the deteriorating condition of the environment may have very serious consequences for humanity as a whole (Soroos, 1981).

Human activities have contaminated land, sea, and air with a myriad of substances. Initially it was believed that the primary consequences of pollution were aesthetic, but gradually scientific evidence has been mounted on the ill effects on plant and animal life, including human beings. Among the most troublesome pollutants are emissions from industries, smelters, power plants, and automobiles that contribute to the "acid rain" phenomenon, which has killed aquatic life in freshwater lakes and damaged forests in large regions of North America and Europe. Pesticides containing highly toxic substances that have been used intensively in agriculture have entered the food chain through which they have had a devastating impact on birds and other wildlife and have been a cause of cancer and a variety of other human health problems, including sterility, birth defects, and nervous disorders. Moreover, there is evidence that the buildup of other pollutants has the potential for either warming or cooling the atmosphere and for destroying the stratospheric ozone layer that shields the earth from the sun's ultraviolet rays. Extensive additional research is needed to sort out all of the consequences of these and a multitude of other substances that are being introduced into the environment. Some pollutants may prove to be "time bombs" in the sense that their harmful effects will become apparent only with the passage of time. Little progress can be expected on international public policies on pollution until such a knowledge base has been generated.

Much of the environmental agenda involves the deterioration or outright destruction of the renewable resources of the planet, a tendency that is being addressed by the World Conservation Strategy that was announced in 1980 by UNEP. Especially alarming has been the loss or degrading of agricultural land in an era of very rapid population growth. Large amounts of fertile land have been converted to nonagricultural uses, in particular for human "living space" in sprawling urban areas as well as for factories, highways, reservoirs, and mining operations. In many areas, intensive use of croplands and inadequate rotation of crops has depleted the soil of its natural fertility. Improper farming practices have resulted in the loss of great amounts of top soil due to wind and water erosion. Where irrigation is excessive and drainage poor, the soil has become waterlogged and eventually salinized as salt and minerals percolate to the surface forming a hard crust. Since reclamation designed to reverse this process is very costly, these new deserts are usually abandoned for agricultural purposes. Desertification has also been a serious and widespread problem in areas such as the Sahel region of Africa, the Middle East, Pakistan, and China where dry lands have been heavily grazed and severe droughts recur (Holdgate et al., 1982, pp. 255–73). These problems received worldwide attention in 1977 with the convening of the United Nations Conference on Desertification in Nairobi and have been the subject of continuing programs of UNEP and FAO.

The forest cover of the planet has been disappearing at an alarming rate, especially in tropical regions of the Third World. In some areas large forested tracts are being burned or cut down so that the land can be used for cultivation or grazing. Elsewhere, forests are being harvested rapidly often in a very wasteful manner and with little or no investment in replanting, to satisfy the booming market international market for lumber and wood products. In many of the poorer countries, wooded areas have been stripped for fuel by swelling rural populations that cannot afford other fuels for cooking and heating. Deforestation can have very serious environmental consequences both locally and globally. Water gushing off steep, denuded hillsides, such as those of Himalayas of Nepal, erode away large amounts of soil causing extensive flooding and siltation downstream. The shrinking size of the tropical rain forests of Latin America, Sub-Sahara Africa, and Southeast Asia could have an even more extensive impact on the ecology of the planet, in particular on its climate. Not only do rain forests moderate surface temperatures as they take in great quantities of energy from the sun while retarding heat reflection, but they also release moisture that causes rain in other areas. Forests play an important role in maintaining the chemical balance of the atmosphere by absorbing carbon dioxide from the atmosphere while in turn being a major producer of oxygen (Guppy, 1984). Tropical forests are also home to millions of species of plants and animals, approximately 40 percent of all that live on the earth, many of which are in danger of becoming extinct as deforestation proceeds (see Myers 1984).

The loss of numerous species that once lived in rain forests is part of the larger problem of declining genetic diversity. Human beings have had a profound effect on many of the estimated 10 million species of fauna and flora with which they share the planet's ecosystem. Ecologists warn that we may be in the midst of an "extinction spasm" which could claim as many as one million species during the last quarter of the twentieth century, or an average of 100 extinctions a day (Myers, 1979, p. 31). Some of the more noticeable, exotic species, such as elephants, rhinoceroses, tigers, cranes, eagles, and whales, have been hunted to near extinction either for sport or for their economic value. Some species of birds are unintended victims of toxic chemicals used as pesticides and herbicides in agriculture. The survival of a far greater number of species, many of which are inconspicuous species of insects and plants, is threatened by the encroachment of rapidly growing human populations on their habitats as cities expand, forests are cleared, swamps are drained, and rivers are dammed. The accelerated rate of extinctions may cost humanity dearly, ironically at a time when dramatic scientific breakthroughs in genetic engineering are greatly increasing the potential usefulness of the planet's great diversity of species. Some of the unrecorded species that are lost may have proved to be invaluable in breeding new strains of high-yield, disease-resistant crops. The qualities of others could have been an essential ingredient in new drugs that combat the diseases that afflict humanity or in a wide range of industrial products such as lubricants, glues, waxes, rubber, insecticides, fibers, and cosmetics (Myers, 1979, p. 31; see also Ehrlich and Ehrlich, 1981).

The Communication and Transportation Agenda

It has been said that contemporary man lives in a "global village" following a series of remarkable technological advancements that make it possible to communicate and travel over much greater distances in much less time and at reduced cost. The first significant breakthroughs in the telecommunications revolution were the inventions of the telegraph and telephone in the nineteenth century, which were followed by the introduction of the broadcast media of radio and television in the twentieth century. Virtually instantaneous communication to even the most distant parts of the planet later became possible using satellites orbiting the Earth in outer space. Even more recently, the linking of new computer technologies to telecommunications networks has opened up many more possibilities, including teleconferencing, electronic mail, and the electronic transmission of data. Turning to transportation, the powering of train locomotives and ships with steam engines, beginning in the nineteenth century, speeded up greatly the movement of people and goods by both land and sea and made arrival times more predictable. The advent of air travel early in the twentieth century followed by the introduction of jet engines increased many-fold the speed of long-distance transportation. These modern technologies greatly enhanced the potential for human contacts and the exchange of goods across international boundaries, but did not make them inevitable. The remarkable increase in international interactions and transactions which followed could not have taken place in the absence of international cooperation on many related matters.

The need for international cooperation of a functional nature in the field of communications and transportation has been recognized for more than a century. The international flow of mail requires arrangements for the routine transfer of letters and parcels from the postal services of the nations in which they originate to those of the states in which they are to be delivered. In addition, some mail must be handled by one or more intermediary states. This task has been ably performed by the Universal Postal Union (UPU) since its founding in 1874. It has also been necessary to reach understandings on revenue matters to spare the senders the cumbersome task of acquiring and affixing stamps for every country that will handle their letters. The telegraph and telephone could be used for international communication only after states cooperated in laying cables between fixed locations in different countries, in some cases across oceans. Furthermore, these and the other types electronic media can be used for international communication only if the equipment that transmits the signals in one country is compatible with receivers in other states. International cooperation has also been needed to avoid interference between users of the airwaves. These and many other problems related to international communication via the electronic media have been on the agenda of the ITU since it was created in 1865.

Global coordination has also been critical to travel and the shipment of goods between countries, both by sea and by air. Uniform specifications for equipment and standardized procedures make it possible for ships and planes of all nations to land or dock at harbors and airports throughout the world. Internationally established ways of communicating information to pilots have been needed to assist them in navigation and to warn them of adverse weather conditions and other hazards. Concerns for safety dictate minimal international standards for equipment, inspections, and training of crews as well as rules on the use of certain shipping lanes or airs corridors to avoid collisions. Recognition of the right to use the air space or the territorial waters of third countries are needed if carriers are to take the most direct route to their destinations. Commercial development of shipping and air travel has required the establishment of networks of routes so that travelers or cargo can be transferred to connecting carriers. In the case of the heavily traveled routes, agreements may be needed that limit the number and capacity of carriers and set minimum fares to avoid excessive competition. Many of these policy problems, in particular those that pertain to safety, have been on the agendas of the International Maritime Organization (IMO), which oversees international shipping, and the International Civil Aviation Organization (ICAO), which regulates international air travel. Not to be overlooked is a long tradition of efforts by nongovernmental organizations formed by shipping and airline companies, most notably the Comité Maritime International and International Air Transport Association, to establish private regulations that supplement or reduce the need for global public policies.

Most of communications and transportation agenda evokes relatively little political controversy. However, several somewhat more contentious issues have arisen in recent years. There is, for example, concern that an expanded flow of information across national frontiers made possible by modern technologies poses a serious threat to the sovereignty of national governments. For example, representatives from closed societies express fear that communications satellites may be used to beam foreign propaganda directly to the home receivers of their citizens as part of a strategy to stir up political unrest. Satellites equipped with remote-sensing equipment can be used to collect many types of information on countries such as on reserves of natural resources, the condition of crops, and the location of military installations. It is clearly possible that information of this type could be used to the disadvantage of the country being photographed. The privacy of the citizens of a country could be compromised when data about them is transmitted to foreign countries that have less stringent regulations on how it may be used. Transboundary data flows can also affect the operations of multinational corporations, such as by making it possible for more of the corporate decision making to be even more centralized at the headquarters (Sauvant, 1983, p. 366). Furthermore, large financial transactions made instantaneously using electronic forms of telecommunication can undermine the ability of governments to regulate the economies of their nations.

Third World delegates to international bodies posed other policy questions within the larger framework of their demands for a "new international economic order." One such matter is international shipping, a subject that has received considerable attention in UNCTAD's permanent Committee on Shipping. It is argued that international shipping practices, especially those agreed upon by associations of shipping companies, known as "liner conferences," treat Third World countries unfairly on matters such as fares. The liner conferences have also been accused of monopolizing the shipping industry in ways that prevent firms based in Third World countries from carrying a share of the world's cargo that reflects the proportion which originates in them (Juda, 1981, pp. 497–98). In a quite different context, at the 1982 UNISPACE conference in Vienna, concern was expressed that advanced countries would use their exclusive access to the technologies of satellite communication and space exploration to increase their economic and social dominance of the less developed nations unless opportunities were made available to Third World countries to participate in these activities.

Imbalances in the flow of news have become one of the most contentious and highly publicized policy problems in the field of international communication. Third World representatives in bodies such as UNESCO and the more recently formed United Nations Committee on Information call attention to the fact that four Western-based news agencies—United Press International, the Associated Press, Reuters, and Agence France-Press—account for approximately 85 percent of the news copy that crosses international boundaries (Puchala, 1982, p. 130). They contend that this dominance introduces a strong Western bias, especially when insensitive reporters have only a superficial knowledge of the societies they are describing to the outside world. Moreover, it is alleged that the profit motive leads the wire services to devote a disportionate amount of their coverage of the Third World to "hard" news, such as coups, communal violence, and disasters, while underreporting of less newsworthy accomplishments, such as an increases in agricultural production, reductions of illiteracy rates, or the successes of family planning programs. As a step toward correcting the situation, a New World Information and Communication Order has been proposed that would establish standards for reporting and make it possible for governments to exercise more influence over how their countries are being portrayed to the outside world. These proposals have drawn heavy criticism in the West for being a major assault on the principle of press freedom. Another approach to balancing the flow of news is a strengthening of the news reporting capabilities of Third World countries on an individual or collective basis (see Righter, 1978).

WHAT TYPES OF PROBLEMS APPEAR ON GLOBAL AGENDAS?

The overview of the global agendas presented in the previous section identified a diverse assortment of policy problems. The only characteristic these problems appear to have in common is the breadth of concern that has been expressed. What other characteristics of these problems account then for the widespread attention they receive, as evidenced by inclusion on the agendas of global institutions? A variety of explanations are offered in this section, any one of which may be sufficient to warrant a place on a global agendas for any given policy problem. These explanations will be presented in two stages. The first discusses several reasons why problems are treated as being *international* in character as opposed to being solely national. The second looks at what distinguishes a problem of *global* proportions from problems that are simply international.

Problems involving a relationship between two or more countries are appropriate subjects of international policy because normally they cannot be addressed effectively by nations acting on their own. This is true of many types of *interactions and transactions* taking place between the governmental officials or private parties of different states. These include the flow of people across borders—diplomats, businessmen, tourists, students, workers, athletes, performers, and refugees, not to mention spies, criminals, smugglers, mercenaries, terrorists, and other less welcome individuals. Not to be overlooked are cross-national contacts that take place when military forces engage one another in armed combat. Mail and the many forms of electronic telecommunication are also major forms of international interactions, as are transnational shipping and air transport. Among the principal types of international transactions are foreign trade in goods and services along with investments of financial capital. The challenge for policy makers is to facilitate the international activities that are beneficial to the larger community, as in the case of most types of telecommunication, transportation, and trade. As dependence on these interactions and transactions increases, the task becomes one of routinizing them so that they will be more reliable and predictable. In the case of undesirable international contacts or exchanges, such as war or the flow of illicit drugs across national boundaries, the task is to prevent or stop them.

Problems transcend national boundaries in several other ways. For one, certain harmful conditions can *spill over the boundaries* of the state in which they originate, thus becoming a problem for other states. Transboundary air pollution, such as acid precipitation, is one of the most conspicuous examples of an international spillover problem. Likewise, what begins as a localized outbreak of a contagious disease afflicting human beings or livestock can spread rapidly across national boundaries and eventually take on the proportions of a pandemic, as was the case with the "black plague" in fourteenth-century Europe, influenza during World

War I, and strains of Asian flu in more recent times. Nor do political boundaries impede swarms of desert locusts and other insects that can devastate crops and forests. The economic difficulties occurring in one state, especially if it has a large economy or a sizable foreign debt, can reverberate throughout the highly interdependent international economic order. Obviously, the larger international community has an interest in preventing potential spillover problems from getting started. But once an occurrence is detected, the challenge is to keep it from spreading. When containment is beyond the means of the countries in which the problems originate, the interests of other states may be best served by extending timely assistance.

States acting on their own often cannot effectively address problems that are caused or complicated by the *actions or policies of foreign actors.* Foreign governments understandably seek to satisfy the domestic groups that keep them in power, even at the expense of other countries whose people are not part of their political constituency. Such is the case when foreign governments adopt a "beggar-thy-neighbor" approach of higher tariffs and currency devaluations to ease large trade deficits and high unemployment, thereby shifting the burdens of economic adjustment to their trading partners. The external origins of some problems can be traced to the policies of international organizations, a good example being the economic woes that many countries experienced as a result of the oil price increases engineered by OPEC in the 1970s. The relevant foreign actors may also be nongovernmental ones, such as the large multinational corporations. Decisions made in the boardrooms of corporations headquartered in New York, Tokyo, or London can have a major economic and social impact on the countries in which they invest—especially the smaller, less developed ones. The challenge for international policy makers is to make both governmental and nongovernmental actors more sensitive to the impacts that their decisions can have on other countries. Beyond that, there is a need to identify and prohibit actions that will have predictably harmful consequences for foreign societies, while encouraging those that will have a beneficial impact.

An international response is also needed to moderate *competition that is mutually disadvantageous* to all states that are engaged in it. The dynamics of such a situation commonly parallel those of the game known as the "prisoner's dilemma," which is played between a pair of prisoners accused of having committed a joint crime. However, neither of the prisoners can be convicted of the crime without the testimony of the other. Eschewing the opportunity to go free if they both remain silent, each prisoner decides that it is in his interests to confess and to testify against the other in return for a promise of a lesser sentence. By remaining silent, each would risk a much stiffer sentence if his partner testifies against him, unless they have a credible prior agreement that neither will testify against the other. In the international realm, the dynamic of an arms race parallels the "prisoner's dilemma." Each state elects to absorb the expense of a continuing military buildup for fear that to do otherwise would make it vulnerable to conquest or coercion by states that keep adding to their military power. All would save on military expenditures if they could agree to an international policy that sets verifiable limits on the acquisition of new weapons that threaten the other states. A similar rationale underlies the negotiations on a "code of conduct" that would impose international standards on the terms under which multinational corporations invest in foreign countries. Without such an understanding, pressures mount on states to undercut one another in offering ever greater concessions, such as on tax rates, to the corporations they hope to attract. Such inducements can significantly diminish the contribution the corporate investments make to the economic development of Third World countries.

A second group of problems are international in character, not because they cut across national jurisdictions, but because they involve areas that are beyond the boundaries of any state. This is the case with *nonself-governing territories,* such as Namibia and the other inhabited areas treated as trust territories by the League of Nations and the United Nations. The *international commons* mentioned earlier in this chapter—the oceans, the seabed, outer space, and the moon and other extraterrestrial bodies—are vaster. Antarctica is also usually looked upon as a nonnational area despite the territorial claims of some states. Traditionally, parties from any state were legally entitled to help themselves to the resources of these areas for their own gain. This arrangement for taking advantage of what common property has to offer can lead to the depletion or destruction of limited resources through a social dynamic Garrett Hardin (1968) calls the "tragedy of commons." Such a tendency has been noted in the decline of a several ocean fisheries due to overharvesting by the vessels from many nations. It is also not unusual for one use of a commons to interfere with others. For example, the huge off-shore platforms used for drilling off-shore oil can be a hindrance to fishing or shipping operations. Such circumstances dictate international policies that referee the competing or conflicting uses of these nonnational areas. Otherwise, the potential of these areas may be wasted or destroyed, and armed conflict becomes a distinct possibility.

The types of policy problems discussed thus far are inherently international in that they are not confined to the territory of individual states. They either cut across national boundaries or involve areas that are beyond the borders of any state. Curiously, a substantial proportion of the global agendas are taken up with problems that are not international in either of these senses. Rather these agenda items refer to conditions that are internal to countries, which potentially could be dealt with at the national level, assuming the commitment is there and sufficient resources are available within the state. However, under certain circumstances, which we shall now briefly explore, these essentially domestic problems are regarded as a proper subject of international policy.

This is true of domestic problems that are *common to many, if not all, countries*. Thus, the problems raised by vast internal migrations of people from rural areas to mushrooming cities unprepared to accommodate them that is taking place in many Third World countries appears on global agendas. Social conditions, such as high rates of infant mortality and illiteracy, and environmental degradation in the form of deforestation or soil erosion are among many other essentially internal problems that are addressed by global institutions. Why do these problems become a subject of international policy? One reason is the potential benefits of exchanging information on the successes and failures of the various approaches that nations have used to address common problems, such as the family planning programs used to restrain population growth. Furthermore, the limited resources that are available worldwide for researching a problem, such as developing a cure for cancer, can be used more efficiently if they are pooled or coordinated internationally rather than being wasted in the duplicated efforts of individual countries. International cooperation in addressing common internal problems is especially beneficial to the smaller countries that cannot begin to assemble the range of expertise and resources needed to investigate the entire range of problems faced by a complex, modern society. The poorer, less developed countries have a special need for international programs to address domestic problems, which may be the only source of the funding and expertise required to satisfy the basic needs of their populations, to accelerate their rate of economic development, and to share in the opportunities opened up by new technologies. International programs are also dictated in the case of large-scale disasters, such as floods, earthquakes, and droughts, that can overwhelm the relief services of smaller countries.

Conditions that are indigenous to individual states may also become the subject of global policy when the *outside community takes a special interest* in them. Gross violations of human rights have been considered a legitimate concern of outside groups even though they involve the way that governments treat the inhabitants of their own country. A problem of this type does not have to be common to a large number of states to become a subject of global policy making, but could be a situation that is unique to a particular state. Thus, South Africa's apartheid system of racial discrimination and segregation has been a prominent item on the agenda of the General Assembly. On a different front, international action may be needed to preserve what is extraordinary about the natural endowments of a particular country, such as a spectacular river gorge or waterfall or endangered species of plants or animals that inhabit its rain forests. Preservation of the irreplaceable artifacts of earlier civilizations—temples, tombs, paintings, and sculptures—is a similar type of international challenge. Because of their historical significance and the way they enrich the lives of people throughout the world, such structures and works of art have been described as being part of the "cultural heritage" of humanity as a whole, even though each is located within the boundaries of a single country. If often behooves the international community to offer expertise and to share the financial burdens of preservation, rather than to expect the states in which they are located to bear all of the costs, which they may be reluctant or unable to do.

Are the problems that appear on the agendas of global organizations truly global in scope? While the term global can be readily defined as the quality of being worldwide or planetary in scope, it is not always clear what this means in the context of policy problems. The type of problem that first comes to mind as being global is one that transcends national boundaries on such a scale that it affects much if not all of humanity as an undivided unit. Thus, the prospect of a gradual warming of the atmosphere attributable to the "greenhouse effect" causing a more rapid melting of the polar icecaps and a general rise in sea levels throughout the world, is a prototype of the problems that affect the entire world in a unitary way. Likewise, economic slowdowns and instabilities that reverberate through the entire international economic order, such as those following the oil price shocks of the 1970s, have consequences for the world as a unit.

Most of the problems mentioned in this chapter are not global in this holistic sense. International commons cover either only part of the Earth's surface, albeit a major part in the case the oceans and seabed, or realms in outer space well beyond the surface of the planet. They are global in the sense that all countries claim the right to make use of them. A greater number of the problems discussed in the survey of global agendas are actually composed of many localized problems of the same type, which are global in the sense that cases of them can be observed throughout much of world. Some of these problems, such as urbanization, are confined within the boundaries of individual states; others, such as the security of diplomats or the pollution of a shared river systems, involve the relationship among limited groupings of states. Issues pertaining to oceans are also often of a reoccurring, localized nature, such as depletion of choice fishing grounds or passage of shipping through straits. Problem situations that are unique to a particular state or region and have little or no direct impact beyond its borders, such as South Africa's practice of apartheid, are global only by virtue of the geographical breadth of the interest in them.

CONCLUSION: A GLOBAL PROBLEMATIQUE?

The global agenda poses a variety of formidable challenges for the community of international public policy makers. Among them are the tasks of alleviating what is unpleasant or intolerable in the existing world, preventing the undesirable or catastrophic from happening in the future, and realizing opportunities for enhancing the human condition. While some items on international agendas truly transcend political boundaries, and in a few instances in ways that affect the entire world, many are localized conditions that appear on international agendas either because they afflict many states or because they have attracted worldwide interest.

Is the international community in the throes of an unprecedented "global problematique?" To answer this question we might ask whether the contemporary assortment of problems is more numerous, more serious, and more interrelated than those of the past. These are difficult questions to answer. The number of items on both the global public agendas and the formal agenda of the General Assembly appears to have grown considerably over the past several decades. This trend reflects in part the increased complexity of the relationships between states in the contemporary world. It may also, however, be at least partly an artifact of a growing tendency to seek international solutions to problems that were once addressed exclusively at the national or local level. Are contemporary problems more serious than those of earlier eras? Again the answer appears to be yes. Clearly, nuclear weapons have introduced the possibility of a catastrophe of an entirely new magnitude, one that is all the more frightening in view of recent warnings of a "nuclear winter" following a war in which large numbers of them would be detonated. Industrialization has cut deeply into the resource base of the planet in a matter of a few generations and severely contaminated the ecosphere with many pollutants. Population growth has added substantially to the gravity of social problems in the Third World, especially in south Asia and Africa.

Are the problems which the global agenda comprises interrelated? In many respects they are. Insecurities over access to natural resources can lead to international tensions and war. The contamination of the environment with pollutants is a major factor contributing to human health problems. Political upheavals and unemployment contribute to the flow of refugees. Inequalities and social problems within countries trigger political revolutions that can be a threat to world peace. Poverty is a factor in many ecological problems as is industrialization. The status of women in a society affects population growth. Arms races reduce the amount of monetary resources that are available for development programs. Efficient communication and transportation networks are essential to worldwide economic progress. These are but a few of the ways in which global problems are interrelated and that must be taken into account by those who attempt to address them.

The global agenda appears to have the elements of a problematique. In coming to such a conclusion, there is the danger of becoming awed or overwhelmed by the constellation of problems to the point of becoming immobilized by the belief that nothing can be done to cope with them and prevent a cataclysmic future. While there are certainly ample reason for pessimism, it should also be recognized that substantial progress has been previously made on addressing many policy problems. Numerous other problems described in this chapter can be significantly ameliorated by appropriate international public policies. Some, however, will be very difficult to address.

REFERENCES

Center for Defense Information (1983). "A World at War—1983," *The Defense Monitor,* Vol. 12, No. 1.

Cobb, Roger W., Jennie Keith-Ross, and Marc Howard Ross (1976). "Agenda Building as a Comparative Political Process," *American Political Science Review,* Vol. 70, No. 1 (March), pp. 126–38.

Eckes, Alfred D. (1979). *The United States and the Global Struggle for Minerals.* Austin: University of Texas Press.

Eckholm, Erik P. (1977). *The Picture of Health: Environmental Sources of Disease.* New York: Norton.

Ehrlich, Paul and Ann Ehrlich (1981). *Extinction: the Causes and Consequences of the Disappearance of Species.* New York: Random House.

Food Agriculture Organization (1983). *1982 FAO Production Yearbook.* Rome: FAO.

Gold, Edgar (1981). *Maritime Transport: The Evolution of Marine Policy and Shipping Law*. Lexington, Mass.: Lexington Books.

Guppy, Nicholas (1984). "Tropical Deforestation," *Foreign Affairs*, Vol. 62, No. 4 (Spring), pp. 928–64.

Hardin, Garrett (1968). "The Tragedy of the Commons," *Science*, Vol. 162, pp. 1243–48.

Holdgate, Martin W., Mohammed Kassas, and Gilbert White (1982). *The World Environment: 1972–1982*. Dublin: Tycooly International Publishing Limited.

Hopkins, Raymond F. and Donald J. Puchala (1978). "Perspectives on the International Relations of Food," *International Organization*, Vol. 32, No. 3 (Summer), pp. 581–616.

Hughes, Donald J. (1975). *Ecology in Ancient Civilizations*. Albuquerque: University of New Mexico.

Juda, Lawrence (1981). "World Shipping, UNCTAD and the New International Economic Order," *International Organization*, Vol. 35, No. 3 (Summer), pp. 493–516.

Kende, Istvan (1977). "Dynamics of Wars, of Arms Trade and of Military Expenditure in the 'Third World', 1945–1976," *Instant Research on Peace and Violence*, No. 2, pp. 59–67.

Larkin, Robert P., Gary L. Peters, and Christopher H. Exline (1981). *People, Environment, and Place: an Introduction to Human Geography*. Columbus, Ohio: Charles E. Merrill.

Lindblom, Charles E. (1980). *The Policy Making Process*. New Haven: Yale University Press.

Linn, Johannes F. (1983). *Cities in the Developing World: Policies for Their Equitable and Efficient Growth*. New York: Oxford University Press.

Mansbach, Richard W. and John A. Vasquez (1981). *In Search of Theory: A New Paradigm for Global Politics*. New York: Columbia University Press.

Meadows, Donella H., Dennis L. Meadows, Jørgen Randers, and William W. Behrens (1972). *The Limits to Growth*. Universe Books.

Myers, Norman (1979). *The Sinking Ark: the Shocking Story of the World's Endangered Species*. New York: Macmillan, 1975.

Myers, Norman (1984). *The Primary Source: Tropical Forests in Our Future*. New York: W. W. Norton.

Population Reference Bureau (1981), "1981 World Population Data Sheet."

Ray, James L. (1983). *Global Politics* (2d ed.). Boston: Houghton Mifflin Company.

Righter, Rosemary (1978). *Whose News? Politics, the Press and the Third World*. New York: New York Times Books.

Ruggie, John Gerard (1979–80). "On the Problem of 'The Global Problematique': What Roles for International Organizations?" *Alternatives,* Vol. 5, No. 4, pp. 517–50.

Sauvant, Karl P. (1983). "Transborder Data Flows," *International Organization,* Vol. 32, No. 2 (Spring), pp. 359–71.

Sivard, Ruth Leger (1983). *World Military and Social Expenditures—1983.* Washington, D.C.: World Priorities.

Soroos, Marvin S. (1981). "Trends in the Perception of Ecological Problems in the United Nations General Debates," *Human Ecology,* Vol. 9, No. 1, pp. 665–77.

Spero, Joan Edelman (1981). *The Politics of International Economic Relations* (2d ed.). New York: St. Martin's.

Trainer, F.E. (1982). "Potentially Recoverable Resources: How Recoverable?" *Resources Policy,* Vol. 8, No. 1.

Ward, Barbara (1976). *The Home of Man.* New York: Norton.

3 | THE POLICY PROCESS

Actors, Procedures, Arenas

A frustrated United Nations delegate once remarked that the task of making global policies resembled the mating of elephants in several key respects. Not only are both undertakings slow and awkward, but they also require the willing participation of all relevant parties (Gardner, 1972, p. 238). Global policy making is typically a long, drawn-out process. Several decades may elapse between the time a problem is identified to the date at which a policy goes into effect upon having been formally accepted by the requisite number of states. A noteworthy example is the "international bill of rights" that is discussed in Chapter 7, which did not become official international policy until 1976, thirty years after work began on formulating it. Global policy making is almost always an awkward process, but especially when delegates from 150 or more independent states are involved in negotiations on a long list of complex, interrelated issues. Such was the case with the United Nations Conference on the Law of the Sea, which came to an end in 1982 after nearly a decade of intermittent meetings. Finally, under most circumstances, global policies cannot be imposed against the will of the actors responsible for carrying them out, namely the governments of states. Thus, the often elusive objective of global policy makers is to reach a consensus among states on how to address the problems that concern them.

This chapter is devoted to an analysis of the ungainly and typically protracted processes by which attempts are made to address the global problems mentioned in the preceding chapter. The first step is to consider the cast of actors that form what is sometimes referred to as the "international community," who through their structured interactions make and implement global public policies. The ultimate decision-making authority resides, of course, with the governments of territorial states, but other types of actors can play a significant role in the policy enterprise. Policy-related activities will then be looked upon as a process consisting of a sequence of nine basic steps, beginning with the recognition of a policy problem and concluding with a decision on the future of the policy that was adopted and implemented. In doing so, the roles played by the various actors in carrying out each of these steps will be noted. Next, the different types of arenas in which the policy process takes place are examined, including not only the permanent organs of international institutions, but also the ad hoc, single-issue conferences that have been in vogue since the early 1970s. International activity directed at some major policy problems shifts from one arena to another as the policy process proceeds through the steps that are identified earlier in the chapter. Finally, brief attention will be given to the types of conflict that commonly arise which can delay or thwart efforts to address global problems.

POLICY ACTORS

Public policies are made and implemented within larger social contexts. They are adopted as responses to the problems or needs of a certain social grouping, such as the population of a city, nation, international region, or, in the case of global policy, humanity as a whole. The willingness of people to seriously consider cooperative strategies for addressing their common problems is indicative of some sense of community among them. Despite all the conflicts and tensions that are obvious in the world, there is also evidence of what can be called a global community. Whether the social bonds are strong enough at this level to support effective efforts at collective problem solving is a debatable proposition to which we shall return later in this chapter. Clearly, much stronger ties bind many of the smaller social groupings, such as nations and regions.

Within each community, there is a relatively small circle of *policy actors* that play an active role in developing or implementing its public policies. By virtue of their positions, some policy actors are accorded the right to participate directly in policy decisions, others seek to take advantage of opportunities to have an indirect influence on those who actually make the decisions. These active participants in the policy process usually form a much more closely knit community among themselves as they come into regular and frequent contact with one another. Members of the larger community who are affected by the policies, but do not play either a direct or indirect role in making them, are not normally considered policy actors.

In this section, we shall identify some of the actors that commonly play roles in global policy processes. Naturally, each type of policy problem attracts a unique cast of policy participants. There are, however, certain categories of actors—governments of states, international governmental organizations (IGOs), and a broad assemblage of international nongovernmental organizations (INGOs)—which play roles that are to some extent predictable regardless of the type of policy problems being addressed. There are other assorted actors that do not readily fall into any of these categories, a prominent example being the Palestinian Liberation Organization, which has been granted observer status in the United Nations.

In matter of fact, aren't the policy actors human beings rather than organizations? Governments and international organizations, it could be argued, are simply abstractions that refer to networks of people who make the actual policy decisions and carry them out. In a technical sense, this is clearly the case. Only rarely, however, do people acting in their own capacity become important participants in international policy processes. In most cases they are performing a role defined by the organizations that will be referred to as actors; for example, a permanent delegate appointed by a government to represent it in an international body. There are, however, exceptions that should be noted, including numerous international commissions and working groups whose members are selected as individuals for their expertise, a noteworthy example being the Executive Board of the World Health Organization. Then, of course, there are some dynamic or highly skilled individuals whose impact on global policy transcends the role their official role; among these would be Dag Hammarskjold, who expanded the role of Secretary General of the United Nations, as well as Arvid Pardo and Maurice Strong, who left their marks on the law of the sea and environmental policy, respectively. Nevertheless, in this volume only infrequent reference will be made to specific individuals.

States as Policy Actors

States have been the principal political and legal units in the world community since the Treaty of Westphalia of 1648, which brought an end to the Thirty Years War, a long period of political strife in Europe between local princes, national kings and queens, and the papal authorities of the Roman Catholic Church. The state was born at that time as a new type of political entity that was recognized to be an impersonal and sovereign authority over a defined territory and population. Sovereignty implies that the governments of these political units have the supreme decision-making and rule-enforcing authority within their territorial boundaries and, thus, are not subject to any higher political authorities (Held, 1983, p. 1).

For reasons of style, the common practice of using the terms "nation," "nation-state," and "country" interchangeably with "state" has been adopted in this work. In doing so, however, we should not overlook distinctions which have been drawn between these terms that may be meaningful in some contexts. Jews, Scots, Basques, Tamils, and Armenians are examples of the many groupings of people who have a sense of common identity based on language, religion, ethnicity, culture, or political history, and who are sometimes described as being a "nation," even though they may be widely dispersed and reside in two or more states. Likewise, states such as the Soviet Union, China, India, and Nigeria are composed of numerous nations of people. It follows that the term "nation-state" is appropriately used as a concept to refer to a sovereign political unit in which the people have developed a strong sense of community, or "nationalism." The governments of most states strive to instill and reinforce nationalistic feelings in the citizenry by means of the educational system and patriotic symbols, such as national flags, anthems, holidays and ceremonies. Finally, the term "country" refers to a geographical area, such as Great Britain or Persia, which does not necessarily coincide with the boundaries of any contemporary state (see Tivey, 1981).

The governments of states officially recognize one another as being one of their kind and in doing so create what could be called a world community of states. This recognition may be conferred both bilaterally, when two governments agree to exchange diplomats and establish embassies in the capital city of the other country, and multilaterally, when a political entity is admitted to membership in the United Nations and other IGOs. States that are recognized in this way are accorded formal legal equality in the enjoyment of the prerogatives of sovereignty and in the right to participate in international decision-making bodies.

Membership in this community has increased rapidly over the past century. During the heyday of colonialism in the nineteenth century, there were on the average only about 20 independent and sovereign states, most of which were European. The number of states grew gradually to roughly 50 by the end of World War II. But by far the most rapid increases have taken place during the last three decades as the colonial empires were dismantled. Currently, there are more than 160 independent states, all but a few of which are members of the United Nations. More than 95 percent of the world's population and territory is within the boundaries of an independent state. There are still, however, as many as 20 or 30 territories, most of a relatively small size, that could become states in the foreseeable future. The emergence of many new states has significantly fragmented political authority on a worldwide basis from what it was when a few European colonial powers controlled most of Africa, Asia, and Latin America. The large number of states has also rendered the process of making and implementing global policies much more awkward and complicated and, in some cases, completely frustrated it.

The formal legal equality that countries have as sovereign members of the community of states obscures great differences in characteristics such as territorial size, population, level of development, military power, and type of political and economic systems. The population of China, which now exceeds one billion, is more than double the total inhabitants of the 50 states of Africa. Together the United States and Soviet Union account for more military expenditures than do all of the other 160 states combined. More than 30 percent of the world's gross economic product takes place within the United States. These selected figures illustrate the fact that the community of states consists of a few very large states and numerous small ones, many of which are miniscule by comparison. The skewed distribution of states on many traits has been a source of tension in the many international policy-making arenas in which the larger states do not have votes in proportion to their size and the contributions they are called upon to make in support of international institutions and programs. Larger states are at an advantage, however, in being better equipped with the diplomatic personnel and bureaucratic support to have their interests effectively represented in the forums where policy making takes place (Gordenker, 1979, xvi).

It is tempting to think of states as being single, unified actors with the highest level officials making the final decisions on matters pertaining to international cooperation. While foreign policy making appears to be quite highly centralized in some countries, there are many others, notably the Western democracies, in which authority is divided in both a political and legal sense. Thus, while it is the administrative branch of government that normally has the primary responsibility for negotiating and voting on international policies, as well as seeing to it the state complies with them, it is not uncommon for legislative bodies to have the prerogative of ratifying treaties and deciding whether to appropriate funds for international programs. Moreover, the judiciary branch of the government may be called upon to offer judgments on how international policies, in particular those that have standing as international law, are to be interpreted and applied in specific cases. Thus, states might be more appropriately looked upon as a group of actors that are related to one another, but nevertheless can be largely autonomous in playing certain roles.

Nor should states be looked upon as unitary actors in the more limited role of representation in international policy-making bodies. To be sure, some international policy problems, such as arms control, are part of the realm of what is sometimes called "high politics" that draws the attention of the highest-level, national leaders who provide at least some guidance on the positions taken by their countries. Moreover, it is not uncommon for heads of states or foreign ministers to address the General Assembly during the "general debate" that is held at the beginning of each annual session. From a practical standpoint, however, top leaders can be expected to keep abreast of only a small proportion of the international activities involving their countries. Thus, even though foreign ministers may have the principal responsibility for the full scope of their country's foreign affairs, increasingly the negotiations and the actual decisions on matters of international public policy are falling to lower-level officials. These are often the directors of relevant ministries and agencies, who meet with their counterparts from other countries. On some technical subjects, countries are represented by experts drawn from outside governmental circles. These matters, which are normally delegated to somebody other than a high-level political leader, are sometimes described as being in the realm of "low politics."

Governments of states appoint delegates to represent them in the many bodies in which international policy-making takes place. It would appear that the more leeway the delegates are given in determining the position that their countries will take, the more likely it is that an international body will be able to reach an agreement on a global policy. There is the danger, however, that such delegates, whose perspective has been shaped by the give and take of international negotiations, will be unable to persuade their superiors back home to confirm the international agreements that have been concluded. Conversely, agreements will be more difficult to conclude when the delegates are given specific instructions and must confer with their foreign ministries before modifying these positions or reacting to new proposals. Once finalized, however, such agreements are more likely to be affirmed by the home government. Generally speaking, governments tend to supervise their delegations less closely on matters regarded to be of little consequence; for example, those taken up by the International Labor Organization (ILO) and WHO, as opposed to the weightier issues that come before the IMF, ITU, or GATT that can have a significant bearing on central economic interests. Moreover, representatives chosen for their expertise are normally given more latitude in negotiations, especially on technical matters, than those who are appointed on the basis of their political credentials. Delegates from the larger, more powerful states are usually given less autonomy than those from smaller countries, partly because more is at stake and because of the greater resources that the national bureaucracies have for monitoring issues and formulating detailed instructions (see Cox and Jacobson, 1981, p. 85).

IGOs as Policy Actors

An IGO is an international institution established with the objective of structuring communication and cooperation between member states on a continuing basis. Most IGOs are created by the joint action of two or more states that is formalized in a treaty known as a charter. States become members of these IGOs upon ratifying the charter, thereby signifying their intention to fulfill the obligations set forth in it, one of which is to contribute to the funding of the regular operations and special programs of the organization. Member states may withdraw from an IGO and, as a group, disband the organization if it no longer serves their interests or needs. Newer organizations, such as UNCTAD, came into being in a slightly different way, through creation by a resolution adopted in one of the other IGOs. An IGO is more than a congress or series of conferences by virtue of having a permanent headquarters staffed by an administrative organ, usually called a secretariat. Meetings of the policy-making organs of IGOs, in which all or a selected part of the member states are represented, are held at prescribed intervals during which decisions are made according to established procedures (Jacobson, 1984, p. 8). These international bodies are the primary arenas in which global policies are made by representatives of member states, an aspect of IGOs that will be discussed later this chapter.

In this section our concern is with IGOs as actors in their own right, a subject that is fraught with ambiguity. Should an IGO be looked upon as an actor when one of its decision-making organs adopts a resolution? Or should resolutions be interpreted as a composite of decisions made by the governments of individual states, or their representatives, in a forum that is part of the IGO? This question arises in interpreting the resolution adopted in Security Council in 1950 calling for a collective military response by the United Nations membership to protect South Korea against the North Korean invasion. Was it an act of the Security Council or a collection of individual acts of its members? This is a difficult issue to resolve. Let us assume, however, that in the case of resolutions, the IGO is simply the arena for a collaborative action by states and not an actor in its own right.

There are other circumstances, however, when it could be said that IGOs, or more specifically their officials, are international actors. The creators of an IGO may endow it with what is called a "legal personality" that permits it to exchange representatives and conclude agreements with other IGOs or with states (Levi, 1979, p. 70). Executive directors or other members of the IGO's secretariat play a variety of roles on behalf of the organization, such as by participating in international conferences or meeting with officials of other IGOs to arrange joint projects. Member governments can, of course, elect to place limits on the amount of discretion that IGO officials have in acting for the organization. Active and respected executive directors usually have considerable leeway on most matters affecting the organization. The secretariat commonly performs a variety of other roles related to the making and implementing of the policies of the IGO, such as drawing up agendas, drafting resolutions, formulating budgets, compiling and distributing information, educating broader publics, implementing programs, and monitoring violations of rules. What the secretariats accomplish can be quite remarkable given the limited resources available to them, which are miniscule in comparison to those of the larger states. The operating budget of the United Nations has yet to reach $1 billion a year while the resources available to the entire UN family of agencies amounts to about $5 billion in contrast to a U.S. federal budget that is approaching $1 trillion. The total staff of the United Nations is only 42,000 in contrast to the nearly three million employees of the United States government (Jacobson, 1984, p. 79).

The first modern IGO was the Rhine River Commission, founded at the Congress of Vienna in 1815 to regulate traffic and trade on the key international waterway of Western Europe. Few other IGOs were established until the late nineteenth century, at which time their numbers began to grow rapidly. By the beginning of World War I, the number of IGOs had swollen to 49 and, on the eve of World War II, it stood at 86. After World War II, growth sharply accelerated so that by 1980 there were more than 300 (Feld and Jordan, 1983, p. 9). By another count, which includes IGOs created by IGOs, the number of IGOs exceeds 600 (Jacobson, 1984, p. 9). There has also been a substantial and steady rise in the average number of members. Less than half of the IGOs, including most of those in the United Nations family, have potentially universal membership in the sense of being open to nearly any state that wants to be a member. The remainder are restricted to certain types of states, such as OPEC, whose membership is limited to oil-producing states, or to the states of a certain region, such as the European Economic Community (EEC). IGOs also differ considerably in the breadth of the policy problems they address. The United Nations is the most prominent example of only 18 general purpose IGOs which stand apart from the vast majority that focus on a narrow range of problem areas (Jacobson, 1984, pp. 48–49).

INGOs as Policy Actors

It was noted in the introductory chapter that non-governmental organizations (NGOs) are the primary actors in the emerging phenomenon of transnationalism, a process which some observers contend is leading to fundamental changes in the world political order. NGOs have been very active, resourceful and, in some cases, both influential and effective as participants in the development and implementation of international public policy. Countless NGOs have been organized exclusively on a national basis. Many of them attempt to influence the positions of their governments on international policies and occasionally even venture directly into international arenas. In this section, however, our primary concern is with the international variety of NGOs, or what are referred to as INGOs, whose membership is drawn from at least two countries.

The primary distinction between "governmental" and "nongovernmental" groups is to be found in their origins; the former are created by intergovernmental agreements, and the latter are not. It is also generally the case that the members of INGOs are private individuals or groups. There are, however, some INGOs which draw part of their membership from the public sector, an example being the International Air Transport Association, which counts among its members several publicly owned and operated airlines. Thus, some definitions of INGOs stipulate that the members drawn from at least some of the countries must be nongovernmental in character (Skjelsbaek, 1971, p. 422). Like IGOs, INGOs have a permanent headquarters, regular meetings, and specified rules for making decisions. Transnational corporations (TNCs) fulfill these conditions, but are usually not grouped with other INGOs because they are fundamentally different in being oriented to the profit motive. While TNCs are significantly affected by some international public policies, they normally do not play a direct role in making them, rather they seek to exert influence through national or international trade associations, which are a type of NGO.

Over the past century, growth in the number of INGOs has been even greater than that of the IGOs, while reflecting the same historical developments; in particular there have been rapid increases in response to advances in long-distance communication and travel and the disruptions of the two World Wars. The Rosicrucian Order, a fraternal organization believed by some to be the first INGO, dates back to the seventeenth century (Skjelsbaek, 1974, p. 424). Others identify either the World's Evangelical Alliance or the world Alliance of YMCAs, founded in 1846 and 1855 respectively, as the first of the modern INGOs (Feld and Jordan, 1983, p. 29; White, 1968, p. 279). On the eve of World War II, the number had grown to 330, and by 1939, it stood at 730. The proliferation of new INGOs has been phenomenal in the four decades since World War II. Estimates based on a restrictive definition of the Union of International Associations put the population of INGOs at 4,265 in 1980 (Jacobson, 1984, p. 51). It should be noted that the geographical distribution of memberships in INGOs has been highly skewed in favor of the developed countries, which has caused less developed countries to be wary of the role INGOs play in global policy making. In modern times, there has been a tendency for groups of IGOs with overlapping or complementary interests to work together as a federation or in consortia to increase their impact on international public policy. Examples of these larger umbrella organizations include the Union of International Associations and the Conference of Nongovernmental Organizations, both of which advance the cause of INGOs generally. Most focus on more specific issues, among which are the International Coalition for Development Action, the International Confederation for Disarmament and Peace, and the International Baby Food Action Network.

The contemporary population of INGOs contains a motley assortment of associations that ranges from the Women's International League for Peace and Freedom, the International Chamber of Commerce, and the World Energy Conference to the Muslim World League, the Socialist International, and possibly even the Roman Catholic Church. INGOs have been estblished to achieve a variety of objectives. Many can be described as international pressure groups that were formed to promote a specific cause, such as the International Organization for Standardization, and the International Planned Parenthood Federations, or the welfare of a specific type of disadvantaged people, such as the International League of Societies for the Mentally Handicapped and the International Union for Child Welfare (see Willetts, 1982). Organizations such as Oxfam, the International Committee of the Red Cross, and the Salvation Army dispense humanitarian assistance, in some cases that which is made available by IGOs and governments of states.

Numerous INGOs were formed to promote the special interests their members have in international policies. Among the most prominent are the international trade associations, whose memberships are drawn from corporations, many of which are transnational in their operations. Examples of this type of INGO are the International Chamber of Shipping, the International Automobile Association, the International Hotel Association, the International Federation of Agricultural Producers, and the International Air Transport Association. These industry-oriented INGOs are countered in some policy-making arenas by those that represent the interests of workers and consumers, such as the World Confederation of Labor, the World Federation of Trade Unions, and the International Organization of Consumer Unions. Professionals also organize themselves internationally, not only to promote the interests they have in international public policy, but also to further the development of their professions through cross-national contacts and exchanges of information. Approximately one thousand of what are referred to as international scientific and professional associations (ISPAs) fall into this category (Feld and Jordan, 1983, p. 245). Among these are the INGOs associated with the highly respected International Council of Scientific Unions, which has become an important source of expertise for international policy makers.

As many as 800 INGOs are accorded an opportunity to participate in an official way in international policy processes by virtue of having been awarded "consultative status" with one or more of the IGOs that bestow it, most notably the Economic and Social Council (ECOSOC) and several other U.N. specialized agencies. This designation is given to INGOs that have a legitimate interest in the activities of the IGO and have demonstrated a potential for contributing to its work. A provision for such consultations was written into Article 71 of the Charter of the United Nations, due in part to the influence of the 1200 NGOs that were in attendance at the San Francisco conference in 1945 (Willetts, 1982, p. 11). Depending upon which of several categories of consultative status that it had been granted, an INGO may have the right to receive the documents of the IGO and to circulate its own written statements to all delegations as official documents. Under certain circumstances, representatives of INGOs are given permission to deliver speeches to decision-making bodies of the IGOs.

Regardless of whether or not they have consultative status, INGOs have left their mark on international public policy, either as a result of the pressure they exert on behalf of their causes, or because of the services they offer states and IGOs. Inasmuch as they are not public organizations, INGOs can afford to be more creative and less inhibited in the policy positions they take than are other actors who much be responsive to political influences.

GLOBAL POLICY PROCESSES

Policies are made and carried out through a series of activities known as a *policy process*. While the manner in which each global policy is developed is unique in some respects, certain features are common to most policy processes. This section presents a model that contains many of the elements commonly associated with policy processes. As such, it is a reconstructed logic that describes how policies can be rationally made and implemented so as to maximize the likelihood of successfully addressing the problem at hand. Admittedly, few if any global problems are tackled in a way that fully conforms to the procedures laid out in the model and, in many cases, the reality of the process diverges substantially from the ideal. The objective in presenting the model is not, however, to describe how global policies actually come into being and are implemented; rather, it is presented as a theoretical instrument for analyzing and comparing the ways in which a variety of global policies have been addressed.

A policy process is an exercise in decision making. In this regard, the model policy process presented in this section is essentially a formula for making decisions rationally that pro-

Table 3:1   **Stages in a Rational Policy Making Process**

1. Recognition of a policy problem
2. Specification of procedures
3. Understanding on goals and principles
4. Formulation of policy alternatives
5. Consideration of policy alternatives
6. Decision on a policy
7. Implementation of the policy
8. Evaluation of the policy
9. Decision on the future of the policy

ceeds through a logical progression of the nine steps listed in Table 3.1. The first step is to identify and define the problem that is to be addressed. Then, an accommodation is necessary on the procedures that will govern the conduct of the policy effort. Having dealt with the formalities, the third step is to reach an understanding on the goals and principles that will lend a sense of direction to the policy-making endeavor. The fourth step entails formulating and proposing a set of policy alternatives that holds at least some promise for successfully addressing the policy problem. Next, the policy alternatives are thoroughly examined in an effort that includes fact finding, analysis, debate, and negotiation, which leads to the sixth step, a decision on which of the policy options to pursue. The seventh step is the implementation of the policy, which can be a formidable challenge especially at the global level. When sufficient time has elapsed to assess the success of a policy, it may be subjected to the eighth step, a review that lays the basis for the final, and ninth step, a decision on the future of the policy—whether it is to be terminated, modified, replaced, or continued.

To what extent are global problems addressed in the way prescribed by the model policy process that has just been outlined? This is an empirical question, which is addressed in each of the six case studies taken up in the latter half of this book. This chapter explores what each of these steps typically entails within the context of global policy making and the types of actors that are normally involved in them.

Recognition of a Policy Problem

A policy is a strategy devised to address a problem that is not only of concern to a community but that can also be potentially ameliorated if a suitable course of action is pursued. In the absence of such a policy problem, obviously no reason or need exists to continue further with a policy process, which is in essence a problem-solving type of activity. Thus, the first step in any policy process is to identify and examine the nature of the problems that are to be addressed, and in doing so, to draw up an agenda that contains the most serious and pressing problems that a community faces.

Some problems are manifest in ways that can hardly be ignored. The devastation of modern war led to the establishment of the United Nations as part of a strategy for preserving international peace. Likewise, few could escape the widespread economic tribulations of the Great Depression, which prompted creation of the Bretton Woods system to stabilize the international economic order. The magnitude or severity of problems such as the international traffic in drugs and the extinction of species of plants and animals in tropical rain forests are not nearly as evident to the casual observer. Tendencies toward overpopulation and the buildup of pollutants in the atmosphere are examples of the many problems that arouse little sense of urgency until data are collected and compiled that dramatize the seriousness of the situation.

Neither a troublesome set of circumstances nor an attractive opportunity that could readily be exploited is fully recognized as a policy problem until it appears on the agenda of an appropriate policy-making forum. Responsibility for drafting the agendas of the councils and assemblies of IGOs typically resides with the directors of the organization, who normally try to be responsive to the desires of the members of the organization regarding which problems they would like to have taken up. It may be necessary for the member states who are most seriously affected by a problem to persuade other members that the situation warrants serious attention by the entire organization (Mansbach and Vasquez, 1981, p. 94). One opportunity they have to do this is the "general debate" held at the beginning of the annual fall meetings of the General Assembly during which a representative from each member state has an opportunity to deliver a speech on what its delegates contend are the most pressing problems facing the international community.

Those with official roles in the recognition of global problems often become aware of them in a secondary way through the efforts of other actors. The first warnings may come from other IGOs that have collected relevant information. Often, however, the alarm is sounded by NGOs that have a special interest in a troublesome matter or that have particular types of expertise, as is true of the many ISPAs. Such was the case with the widely read reports of the Club of Rome on the limits to the natural resources of the planet, of the Stockholm International Peace Research Institute on the world arms buildup, and of a group of scientists led by Carl Sagan and Paul Ehrlich on the dangers of a "nuclear winter."

Specification of Procedures

Before any serious and organized attempt to address a policy problem can be mounted, agreement must be reached on procedural matters. Among these are rules concerning when and where meetings will be held, who will be permitted to attend them, and the rules that will apply to discussions and voting. These issues can be especially important and difficult to resolve at the international level where policy processes are generally not as well structured and routinized as they are within states.

Perhaps the most salient procedural issue in global policy making is the selection of the arena or series of arenas in which the problem will be taken up. Will it be in an already established international body, such as one of the principal organs or specialized agencies of the United Nations system? If so, there will be relatively little latitude in the designation of other procedures in that most are prescribed by the regular operating rules of the institution. Nevertheless, within these rules some options may remain, such as the timing of discussions and votes and the roles that are to be played by subsidiary bodies such as committees or working groups. Some policy problems are addressed in temporary, ad hoc arenas, such as single-issue world conferences, most of which are sponsored by an established institution such as the General Assembly. It may be necessary to resolve numerous procedural matters well in advance of the meetings. Where and when will the conference be held? Which nations, IGOs, INGOs, and other types of actors will be permitted to attend and participate in the deliberations? Who will preside over the sessions? What level officials will represent states? What preparatory sessions will be held for preliminary discussions and hammering out policy proposals? Will issues be dealt with singly or as a package? Will decisions be made by consensus or by a majority vote? Is the outcome to be in the form of a resolution or a treaty?

Procedural matters can have a significant factor in how a policy problem is addressed, if, in fact, it is addressed at all. If a stalemate develops over procedures, the policy process may proceed no further, as has been the case with the sidetracked Global Negotiations which were to have begun in 1981 as a forum for serious discussions of Third World proposals for a "new international economic order." When an accommodation is reached on procedures, the specifics of them—such as the composition of the policy-making body that is designated—can significantly shape the course of discussions and the decisions ultimately made. For example, the General Assembly, with its nearly universal membership and one-nation-one-vote form of majority rule, is a very different type of arena from the Security Council, with its limited membership and veto rights for the five permanent members. It also differs from the International Monetary Fund and World Bank, in which votes are weighted according to financial contributions. The nationality and personal leadership skills of the elected presiding officers, such as the president of the General Assembly, may be a critical factor in the effectiveness of various international bodies in addressing global problems within their domain. Where meetings are held (for example, whether in a developed country or a Third World location) can set the atmosphere for the discussions and influence the decisions that are reached, as has been the case with sessions of UNEP convened at its headquarters in Nairobi.

Ultimately, it is up to the states to decide whether to accept a proposed set of procedures, and those with an important stake in the policy outcomes can be expected to be actively involved in discussions and negotiations over them. The officials of IGOs often play a key role in proposing procedures and steering states toward an accommodation that allows the policy process to continue. INGOs have been known to take an active interest in procedural matters, in particular those that have an effect on the opportunities that they will have to influence global policy makers, such as through the exercise of the prerogatives of consultative status.

Understanding on Values

As was observed in the previous chapter, identification of policy problems presumes certain judgments about what is desirable and undesirable. Many of the same values also guide efforts to address these problems. Without a clear sense of direction based on common or compatible values, the entire policy process is likely to flounder.

Value questions influence the direction of problem solving in two ways. First, values are subsumed in the *goals* toward which the policy makers strive. These objectives may be grand and vague, such as maintaining world peace. On the other hand, they may be quite specific about achieving a desired state of affairs within a specified time frame, such as the goal of eradicating hunger in the world by 1984 that was adopted at the World Food Conference. Second, values may also be incorporated into *principles,* which can be described as the ground rules that may not be compromised or violated in pursuing those goals that have been adopted. A good example of a principle in the realm of global policy is the notion of sovereignty of states. In most cases, sovereignty would not be viewed as a goal of global policy, but rather as a prerogative of states that should not be violated by policies that are adopted. Thus, the effect of principles is to place some limits on the range of policies that can be adopted. Goals may be difficult to distinguish from principles, especially when a value such as "justice" is a goal in one context and a value in others.

Values receive ample mention in global policy-making circles. They are repeatedly mentioned in speeches delivered in international forums. Likewise, the preambles of many international documents, typically contain what can be a rather lengthy list of eloquently stated goals and principles that presumably guided its formulation. The Charter of the United Nations well illustrates such a document. Not only does it contain a preamble containing a series of aims, but its first article sets forth four "purposes" of the United Nations beginning with the objective of maintaining "international peace and security." The second article specifies seven "principles" that are to guide the work of the organization and the actions of its member states, beginning with "the sovereign equality of all members." Such statements, which are often adopted in a pro forma fashion, are typically replete with platitudinous phrases and international catchwords that convey little substance and invite a variety of interpretations. Occasionally, goals and principles become a serious topic of discussion in international forums, a noteworthy example being the United Nations Conference on the Human Environment in 1972 at which a Declaration of Principles containing 26 articles, which were to apply to the future formulation of international environmental policy, was adopted following a contentious debate.

Formulation of Policy Alternatives

The next step in an orderly and rational policy-making process is to formulate a variety of policy proposals. Most policy problems can be addressed in several ways. For example, terrorism might be tackled by preventive measures such as heightened security, by a deterrent strategy incorporating stiff punishments and international agreements providing for extradition of criminals, or by programs designed to redress some of the social grievances that have given rise to terrorism. Ideally, consideration is given to any policy option that has some potential for making progress toward achieving the goals that were decided upon in the previous step, while not violating generally accepted principles. Uninhibited brainstorming is the appropriate activity at this stage; critical analysis of the policy proposals will take place later.

Policy making is rarely undertaken in this rational a manner, especially at the global level. In actual practice, the search for policy alternatives is usually abridged in several ways. One such practice is to simultaneously consider a few, but by no means all, of the policy alternatives that hold some promise for ameliorating the problem. Thus, the World Population Conference of 1974 gave

considerable attention to two very different approaches to population pressures. The first was to reduce undesired pregnancies by
making contraceptives universally available; the second was to
emphasize economic development and enhanced opportunities
for women as ways of reducing incentives for large families. The
possibility of migrations from overpopulated to sparsely populated areas was not seriously considered. Another frequently
taken shortcut is to consider promising policy alternatives se-
quentially until one is identified that is judged to be satisfactory, at
which point no further policy proposals are considered. The concept "satisficing" was coined by Herbert Simon (1957, pp. 204–5)
to refer to this procedure of settling for a policy that will fulfill a
certain level of aspiration. Finally, efforts to formulate policies
may focus on a single draft proposal that incorporates what is
believed to be the most promising or practical approach. Policy
alternatives are then treated as amendments. Gradually, a modified policy evolves that it is hoped will have fewer weaknesses and
will encounter less resistance that the original draft. Such an
approach was taken at the most recent Law of the Sea Conference, where the chairman, at the end of each session, would
circulate a single "negotiating text" that would became the basis
for discussions at the next scheduled round of talks. While more
practical and less time consuming than a thorough search for all
plausible policy alternatives, shortcuts taken at the policy formulation stage risk overlooking what could prove to be the best
solution to the problem at hand.

Who can be looked to for policy proposals in global arenas?
Draft proposals may come from any of the principal types of
actors that participate in the policy process: states, IGOs, and
INGOs. Sometimes states work in concert with one another or
with the officials and staffs of IGOs. IGOs often draft proposals
either on their own or in cooperation with other IGOs. INGOs are
also a fertile source of policy proposals, but whether they are
taken seriously depends on the issue area and the reputation and
type of expertise the INGO has to offer. Occasionally, proposals
of INGOs will be endorsed or officially put forward by state
delegations. In other instances, INGOs will work with IGOs to
formulate joint policies, as in the case of the World Conservation
Strategy, which was a cooperative effort on the part of UNEP and
two INGOs, the International Union for the Conservation of

Nature and Natural Resources and the World Wildlife Fund. If the subject is a highly technical one, INGOs having the relevant expertise may even be commissioned by an IGO to draft up resolutions. On more highly politicized issues, such as arms control, INGO proposals are typically ignored.

Consideration of Policy Alternatives

Having expanded the range of potential policies, the next task for policy makers is to scrutinize them, and in doing so, to reduce the options under active consideration to a single policy proposal. When refined, the text of this proposal is then submitted for formal approval in the next stage of the policy process. Normally, this end product is a synthesis of the desired features of several of the policy proposals.

The policy consideration stage is in itself a two-part process. The first is to review the policy options, giving the most attention to those that hold the greatest promise for successfully ameliorating the problems of concern. Among other things, this entails forecasting the probable outcomes of the policy proposals if implemented. To what extent would each contribute toward furthering the goals of the policy makers? Moreover, what unintended consequences might there be of either a fortuitous or undesirable nature? This is also an appropriate time to raise questions about the feasibility of each proposal, such as whether enough support would be forthcoming from key actors. Numerous IGOs and INGOs are active participants in this enterprise, providing information and perspectives that may be relevant to the examination of policy alternatives. Many of the IGOs have bureaus that routinely collect information and generate statistics that can be used for this purpose; some have an in-house capacity to do research on policy options. Those that do not have been known to invite NGOs to perform a consultative role. On many matters, ISPAs are the most reliable and authoritative source of the specialized knowledge needed for evaluating policy alternatives. Moreover, it is not uncommon for INGOs to distribute unsolicited information or reports in conjunction with lobbying efforts directed at persuading national delegations to vote for the measures they are advocating.

The second part of the policy consideration stage entails discussion, debate, and negotiation. It may be necessary to strike numerous bargains and compromises if an accommodation is to be reached on a policy that is palatable to most if not all parties that will be asked to accept and support it later. A failure to do so could stymie the entire policy-making effort. In the global sphere of policy making, talks aimed at a resolution of differences can drag on for years, if not decades, as attempts are made to satisfy states with sharply divergent perspectives and interests. Whether such an accommodation is accomplished can depend in part on the personal mediation skills of the presiding officers of the international policy-making bodies, among whom are the president of the General Assembly and the chairpersons of the numerous ad hoc world conferences.

Decision on a Policy

All that has gone into the policy process thus far culminates in a decision on a policy that will be implemented to address the problem of concern. The decision may be structured as a choice between two or more policy alternatives that are still under consideration. In the international community, it usually comes down to a question of whether to accept or to reject a single policy proposal that is the product of the negotiations and compromises of the preceding step. Ideally, the policy selected is the one that offers the most favorable prospect of furthering the objectives of the policy makers. In actual practice, however, there are many factors, including political considerations, that interfere with making a purely rational decision.

The criterion for adopting a policy may be a consensus of all voting parties or, alternatively, a specified majority, usually one-half or two-thirds of those casting votes. Clearly, a consensus is more desirable in view of the breadth of support for the policy that it indicates. Policies on which a consensus is reached may, however, be so watered down with compromises that they are weak and ineffectual as solutions to the problems they address. Majority voting, on the other hand, may make it possible to adopt stronger measures, but frequently at the expense of polarizing the community. Moreover, the minority opposing the policy may include some of the key actors whose support is essential to its success.

Ultimately, the responsibility for adopting global policies resides with the states. States also have the prerogative of declining to commit themselves to comply with most of these policies. Thus, at the international level, there is a greater incentive to seek a consensus than in national legislatures where the minority must accept the will of a majority of the law makers. Striving for a consensus in international bodies in which as many as 160 states are represented is an ambitious undertaking, and one that is all too often not feasible. Furthermore, strict observance of the consensus rule would permit a few states, perhaps even a single one that is small and insignificant, to exercise a veto power that would thwart the will of the vast majority. Thus, while it may not be uncommon for international bodies with large memberships to seek a consensus, or as close to one as possible, there are usually fall-back voting procedures that permit a majority of the voting states to adopt resolutions and sometimes even drafts of treaties, both of which may contain policies. Voting in some international bodies is weighted on criteria such as the size of each country's financial contribution to the organization, as is the case with the World Bank and the IMF. Under the rules of the Security Council, five of the more powerful member states have the right to veto substantive measures.

Implementation of the Policy

In a metaphorical sense, policy makers are the architects of a strategy for addressing a problem. Those who implement policy are akin to the engineers and construction workers who take the blueprints and strive to make them a reality. Naturally, the unique characteristics of any policy dictates much of what needs to be done to carry it out. Nevertheless, there are several challenges that commonly arise in the implementation stage of the policy process that should be noted here.

The task of implementation commonly begins with the creation of the bureaucratic infrastructure that is needed to carry out the policy. At the global level, it may be necessary to establish a new international regulatory agency or commission, as specified by the policy makers. If so, arrangements must be made for a permanent headquarters, the appointment of an executive director, and the hiring of a staff. Alternatively, the task of implementing the policy is sometimes assigned to an existing institution, such as one of the specialized agencies affiliated with the United Nations, which may need to be expanded or reorganized if it is to assume additional responsibilities. Some policies entail creating communication networks between agencies in order to coordinate their separate operations in ways that contribute to a solution to the problem at hand. Funding must be secured to sustain the agency and to support any programs that the policy prescribes.

Implementation also often involves giving more specific meaning to the vague parts of policies. Constrained by time and limited expertise, it is not uncommon for policy makers simply to rough out the primary features of the policy and to delegate responsibility for fashioning the details on standards, rules, and procedures to an international agency or commission. When disputes arise, an interpretation may be needed on how a policy applies to given situation. Thus, most policies that could generate competing claims lay out a procedure for having disputes adjudicated if the parties are unsuccessful in reconciling their differences through negotiation. This service is usually performed by an international tribunal, either one that is set up to handle cases related to a particular set of policies or, alternatively, the International Court of Justice, which handles a broad range of cases although not a great number.

Finally, a major part of the task of implementing policies is to induce the cooperation of relevant actors. If some choose not to comply with regulations and obligations contained in a policy, others may follow suit, thereby diminishing the prospects for success in ameliorating the situation. In this regard, the perennial problem exists of how to cope with the "free-rider" who refuses to observe international standards or accept responsibilities, while benefiting from the compliance of others. Enforcement of rules is basically a two-step process: the first is to detect violations; and the second is to bring pressure or force to bear on the guilty parties to discourage or prevent further transgressions. Traditionally, it has been the responsibility of governments of states to insure that they and their nationals comply with international regulations. When, for whatever reasons, states fail to police their own behavior adequately, it has been primarily up to other states to apply sanctions. There has been a trend, however, for IGOs and INGOs to play a more active role in enforcing some global policies, especially in monitoring compliance with regulations.

Evaluation of the Policy

Once sufficient time has elapsed for a policy to have taken effect, the time comes to evaluate not only the policy itself but also the way in which it is being implemented. Such an evaluation should assess the extent to which progress is being made in achieving the objectives of the policy without causing other problems which were either completely unanticipated or are much more serious than had been foreseen. A policy evaluation can extend much deeper by questioning the values and principles that have given it direction, or even whether or not the problem was defined in an appropriate way, if in fact there was a serious problem to begin with. Clearly, evaluations are more meaningful and useful when conducted objectively with the realistic possibility that proposals for significant changes will result, rather than simply being an exercise in justifying or defending past policies by highlighting the positive results while ignoring or playing down the failures. A rare example of a thorough and penetrating review is the self-examination undertaken by the international disaster relief system between 1972 and 1978 that led to a candid and critical report and significant changes in policy (Stephens and Green, 1979, p. 295).

Global policies receive a considerable amount of scrutiny from a variety of sources, but often not in a systematic fashion. Some policies are assessed on a continuing basis, while serious reviews of others are undertaken only when inadequacies become readily apparent. Some policies provide for official reviews at specified times or intervals, as is the case with the five-year review conferences of the Non-Proliferation Treaty of 1968, which will be discussed in a later chapter. Anniversaries have sometimes been the occasion for an evaluation, as with the special review conference convened by UNEP in 1982 to assess the programs that had been undertaken to address environmental problems in the decade following the landmark meetings in Stockholm. Evaluations may be undertaken by the international bodies that originally adopted the policies or by the staffs of international agencies that implement them. In some cases, an independent commission of respected public figures and experts is appointed to undertake an independent review. INGOs monitor the effectiveness of some global policies either as requested by IGOs that respect their expertise and objectivity or on their own initiative in regard to policies in which they have a special interest. Sometimes states conduct their own reviews when there is doubt about whether it is in their interests to support and comply with the policy, as is being done by the Reagan administration in regard to the work of a number of the specialized agencies of the United Nations, most notably the United Nations Educational, Scientific, and Cultural Organization (UNESCO).

Decision on the Future of the Policy

Evaluations serve little purpose unless the results are taken into account in a decision about the future of the policy, the final step in model process. At this point, four basic courses of action can be taken. First, the decision may be to *terminate* the policy if it is no longer needed after having achieved the purpose for which it was instituted. Second, if the policy appears to be on track but insufficient time has elapsed for it to achieve its goals, the choice may be to *continue* the policy in its present form or to implement its later phases. Third, if the policy has been partially successful, but has shortcomings that could be corrected, the most appropriate course of action may be to *modify* it. Finally, if the policy has been largely ineffective and has had other undesirable consequences or if the goals of the policy makers have changed significantly, the only viable option may be to *replace* the policy, assuming that there is another more promising policy alternative that could be implemented. If the decision is made to substantially modify the policy or to replace it entirely, the policy process loops back to the third or fourth steps described above, which entails specifying values and formulating policy alternatives, respectively.

International bodies occasionally grapple with questions pertaining to the future course of their policies. Some consider changes on a regular basis, as frequently as annually, an example being the International Whaling Commission. Other bodies review policies at much longer intervals—twenty years in the case of some of the basic rules of the ITU whose procedures will be taken up in a later chapter. Some treaties specify a date when parties may trigger a review process to consider the future course of international policy. For example, the Antarctica Treaty provides that a review conference will be held after thirty years from the time the treaty came into effect upon the request of any of the consultative parties.

THE ARENAS OF GLOBAL POLICY MAKING

Public policy making at any level of political organization takes place in decision-making arenas. Most global public policies are made in the numerous forums associated with specific IGOs in which the members of the organization transact their business. These bodies vary in several ways, one of the most important being the matter of membership. Our primary concern is with global arenas; i.e., those international bodies in which any of the states in the world can, at least in principle, become participating members. Obviously, institutions such as the General Assembly of the United Nations with unlimited membership are properly categorized as being global. Some bodies with restricted membership, such as the fifteen-member Security Council, may also be classified as being global, but only if all major geographical regions or types of countries are represented and all states could, at least in theory, be among those selected to occupy a seat. Another important attribute of policy-making arenas is the breadth of the policy problems that are taken up in them. The General Assembly, in which virtually any issue might be considered, is the best example of a general purpose forum. Most global arenas take up a narrow range of policy problems. Each global policy-making arena has its own procedures for proposing, considering, and deciding upon policy alternatives as well as for implementing and reviewing the success of them. Each also has its own rules and practices regarding the role that INGOs and other nonofficial participants play in the policy process.

The discussion of global policy making arenas that follows draws a distinction between the regular meetings of permanent bodies as opposed to ad hoc conferences that are occasionally convened for a single, limited period. Over the years, most of the policy-making activity of the international community has taken place in the permanent bodies. In recent times, however, a substantial part of these efforts have been shifted to increasingly frequent world conferences.

Permanent Organs

The charters of IGOs provide for the regular convening of one or more permanent decision-making bodies devoted to the making and carrying out of policies. IGOs typically have two such arenas: an *assembly* that is a plenary body in which all member states are represented and a *council* in which a selected group of countries are seated. Assemblies and councils normally play quite different roles in the policy process.

Assemblies sometimes carry the official name of "conference" or "congress." Most meet relatively infrequently, but at regular intervals that are specified in the organization's charter. The General Assembly, the most prominent of the assemblies, is in session for four months each fall, which is more frequent than is the case for the plenary bodies of most IGOs. It is more common for assemblies to meet once every few years, as for example, the assembly of the UPU, which meets only once every five years. Convening these large groups more often would be costly and would strain the diplomatic resources of many of the smaller and poorer countries. In view of the amount of time that lapses between their meetings, it is not surprising that the policy-making role of assemblies is normally confined to making decisions on the general policy directions of the organization. Some assemblies, however, also have the primary responsibility for establishing budgets. Voting in assemblies is almost always on a majority basis with each nation's vote counting equally.

Foreseeing that the assemblies would not only be expensive to convene but also would be inefficient at making and implementing policies because of their unwieldy size, the drafters of most IGOs charters made provision for councils, which are sometimes called "executive boards" or "committees." Councils normally meet much more frequently than the assemblies, sometimes as often as monthly, which enables them to play a greater role in overseeing the details of the operations of the organization. Council membership is usually limited, in most cases to between 15 and 50 states. One of the largest is ECOSOC, which with 54 members is hardly an efficient decision-making body. The councils of the FAO and UNESCO are also large, with memberships of 49 and 45, respectively. The Security Council with only 15 members and the IMO with 16 are among the smaller councils. Many councils have been enlarged substantially over the years to accommodate new types of members, in particular the Third World states (Jacobson, 1984, p. 85). Voting procedures in councils vary widely, with some having weighted votes, vetoes, or qualified majorities which tend to increase the impact of major states.

States become members of councils in several ways. Seats on most councils are filled for fixed terms by elections conducted in the assemblies of the same IGOs. Charters or informal rules dictate the composition of some councils to ensure a certain type of balance, such as representation of all geographical areas. A portion of the positions on several councils are allotted to the states that have the greatest stake in work of the organization or provide it with the largest amount of its resources. Thus, six of the seats on the council of the IMO are to be occupied by the states with the largest interest in providing international shipping services, and six are to be filled by the leading states in international seaborne trade. The governing body of the ILO is to include ten of the most industrially important states. Even when such criteria do not guarantee them a seat, some of the larger states are reelected repeatedly to certain councils in deference to the importance of their support for whatever actions are taken. (Jacobson, 1984, p. 88).

Many IGOs have found it necessary to establish subsidiary bodies to do much of the spadework of policy making or to implement the programs that have already been adopted. These bodies are given a variety of names—committees, subcommittees, advisory committees, special committees, commissions, subcommissions, and working groups, to mention a few. The General Assembly has a well-established set of committees, each of which has responsibility for in-depth consideration of certain types of problems and resolutions before recommending a course of action to its parent body.

Ad Hoc Arenas

Over the past fifteen years, ad hoc arenas have become increasingly important as sites for the development of international public policy. They can be distinguished from the permanent arenas not only by their temporary nature, but also in the way in which they originate. Whereas the regular meetings of permanent bodies are usually spelled out in the charters of IGOs, the decision to hold an ad hoc conference is made in the form of resolution adopted in one of the permanent forums, often the General Assembly. The agendas of ad hoc meetings tend to be more narrowly focused, commonly on a single policy problem, such as food, technology, development, or disarmament.

Some ad hoc conferences take the form of *special sessions* of the General Assembly, which are arranged to allow several weeks for that body to concentrate exclusively on a single global problem that is thought to be particularly serious. The hope is that decisive action will be taken to address the problem. Thus far, eleven such special sessions have been held, five of which have taken place since 1973 (see Table 3.2). In addition, "emergency special sessions" of the General Assembly may be convened within twenty-four hours after being requested by a majority of its membership or by nine members of the Security Council, as provided for by the Uniting for Peace Resolution of 1950. Five of these emergency sessions were held between 1956 and 1967 and another four between 1980 and 1983 to discuss serious threats to world peace when the Security Council was immobilized by the vetoes (see Bennett, 1984).

Numerous *world conferences,* sponsored either by the General Assembly or by one of the specialized agencies, have been held in various locations around the world. During the past fifteen years, a series of major conferences were convened, some of which were extravaganzas that were major world events in their own right. Among the first were the United Nations Conference on the Human Environment, held in Stockholm in 1972, and the World Population Conference and the World Food Conference, both of which took place in 1974—in Bucharest and Rome, respectively (see Table 3.3). World conferences typically last only a few weeks, sometimes as few as two. Little could be accomplished in such a short period if it were not for the extensive preparatory meetings that take place before most of the conferences. The United Nations Conference on Science and Technology for Development held in 1979 was not unusual in being preceded by well over one hundred international conferences, seminars, symposia, and

Table 3.2   **Special Sessions of the General Assembly**

Topic	Year
Palestine	1947
Palestine	1948
Tunisia	1961
Financial and Budgetary problems	1963
Peacekeeping Operations and Southwest Africa	1967
Raw Materials and Development	1974
Development and International Cooperation	1975
Financing of UN Interim Force in Lebanon	1978
Namibia	1978
Disarmament	1978
International Economic Cooperation	1980
Disarmament	1982

workshops sponsored by a variety of groups both within and outside the United Nations system. It is at these preliminary meetings, sometimes strung out over several years in various locations, that the time-consuming tasks of debating draft resolutions and working out compromises normally take place. Thus, by the time the world conference occurs, little remains to be resolved before the resolutions are formally adopted, commonly by consensus. A notable exception to this pattern was the most recent United Nations Conference on the Law of the Sea, which entailed an extended series of meetings spread over nine years.

Almost all states send representatives to the major conferences. The delegations are typically led by directors or high-level officials of the state ministries most directly involved with the problem being discussed. Higher ranking national leaders occasionally attend; Secretary of State Henry Kissinger's presence at the World Food Conference was a noteworthy example. Representatives of IGOs whose programs have a bearing on the policy problem are usually invited to attend, and at times, they may play an active role in the deliberations. The conferences also attract participants from many NGOs as well as interested individuals.

Table 3.3:   Selected Major World Conferences

Topic	Year	City
Human Environment	1972	Stockholm
Law of the Sea	1973–82	Caracas, Geneva, and New York
Population	1974	Bucharest
Food	1974	Rome
Women and Development	1975	Mexico City
Employment	1976	Geneva
Human Settlements (HABITAT)	1976	Vancouver, British Columbia
Water	1977	Mar del Plata, Argentina
Desertification	1977	Nairobi
Agrarian Reform and Rural Development	1979	Rome
Science and Technology for Development	1979	Vienna
New and Renewable Sources of Energy (UNERG)	1981	Nairobi
Least Developed Countries	1981	Paris
Exploitation and Peaceful Uses of Outer Space (UNISPACE)	1982	Vienna
Aging	1982	Vienna
Population	1984	Mexico City
Peaceful Uses of Nuclear Energy	1986	(location to be announced)

INGOs of the pressure group variety have made a practice of organizing simultaneous "parallel" conferences or "forums" that take place simultaneously near the site of the official meetings, in which they discuss what are thought to be the "real" issues that are being ignored at the official meetings. Coalitions of INGOs can also usually be counted on to publish a newspaper that reports and editorializes on what transpires at the conference.

What purposes are served by the special sessions and world conferences? The ostensible rationale for them is that the agendas of many IGOs are so crowded that simply not enough time exists during the regular sessions for a thorough discussion of global problems that it is felt should be addressed. In contrast to regular sessions, at which the attention of delegates is fragmented among many matters, a world conference provides an opportunity for delegates to direct their undivided concern to a single problem. World conferences also heighten awareness of problems that might otherwise be obscured by the many other issues that preoccupy leaders and the public at large. It may be noted that some of the conferences attract many news media representatives, who look upon these occasions as significant international events, especially when high level officials attend. As the frequency of the global conferences increased and their novelty wore off, they began to receive less publicity.

The most important reason for the growing number of world conferences may, nevertheless, be the successes of earlier ones in initiating a global response to the problems being considered. Typically, a conference adopts a statement of goals and principles, a recommended program of action, proposals for a new fund to provide assistance for Third World countries, and sometimes a proposal for new international institutions, all which are submitted to the sponsoring organization. Many of these recommendations have been implemented. The more productive conferences, such as the Stockholm Conference on the Human Environment which led to the creation of UNEP, may later be identified as significant turning points in the evolution of the global public policy directed at a certain problem. Not all of the world conferences have had such an impact. Little if any apparent progress was made on arms control, much less arms reduction, at the two special sessions devoted to the topic of disarmament. The United Nations Conference on New and Renewable Sources of Energy also fell short of the goals of its organizers, in large part because of the reluctance of the United States to support international programs for assisting less development countries develop their fossil fuel resources or make use of renewable resources of energy.

Sequence of Policy Arenas

Efforts to address global policy problems are normally routed through a progression of arenas, each of which becomes the setting for one or more of the nine steps in the policy process model. To lay the theoretical groundwork for analyzing and comparing global policy processes, let us consider the sequence of arenas diagramed in Figure 3.1. This ordering of arenas is modeled on the path by which a number of prominent policy problems have been tackled in recent years. Naturally, the chronology of arenas differs somewhat from one global policy problem to another. Thus, action taken to address some global policy problems inevitably conforms more closely to the model than do endeavors directed at other problems.

The first step of the sequence is less well defined than the later stages. Some policy problems are initially taken up in what can best be described as exploratory meetings, a good example being the Biosphere Conference sponsored by UNESCO in 1968. The discussions among invited scientists and the conclusions they reached regarding the rapidly growing severity of ecological problems gave an impetus to plans for the Conference on the Human Environment in Stockholm in 1972, after which environmental concerns were accorded a more prominent position on the global agenda. Other problems are examined initially by representatives from a group of concerned countries that begin meeting among themselves before calling upon the General Assembly or another international body to include them on their agendas. As will be noted in Chapter 6, the basic problems addressed in Third World proposals for a new international economic order were first explored by a group of nonaligned states from Africa and Asia that first met in 1955 at Bandung, Indonesia. Numerous INGOs also hold forums in which problems are discussed and reports issued in an effort to stimulate national and international action.

The next step is for the policy problem to be acknowledged by

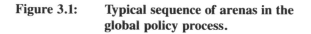

**Figure 3.1:   Typical sequence of arenas in the
global policy process.**

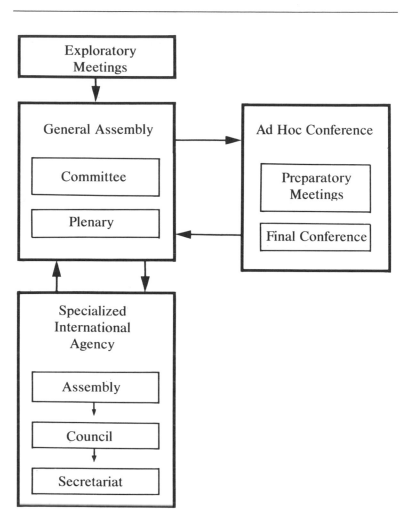

one of the international assemblies, which in the model will be presumed to be the General Assembly. At this stage, substantial work needs to be done before a decision can be made on an international policy response to it. The problem must be analyzed and policy alternatives formulated and scrutinized. These tasks may be delegated to a standing committee or to a temporary body, such as ad hoc working group. If the problem is an especially important one in which there is widespread interest and concern, a decision may be made to convene a special session or a world conference devoted exclusively to addressing that problem. If so, the date of the conference is usually set several years in the future and a series of preparatory meetings are scheduled to undertake the spadework. If the preparatory meetings successfully complete their work, draft resolutions setting forth principles and a program of action will be ready for the conference. If approved at the conference, with or without modifications, the recommendations contained in these resolutions are passed on to the General Assembly for a decision on whether to implement them. The General Assembly may, of course, adopt the recommendations, possibly in a significantly modified form, or reject them. The principal policies and actions proposed by some of the world conferences, the Stockholm conference on the environment being a notable example, have been implemented promptly; in other cases much more resistance has been encountered.

When a policy response is adopted by the General Assembly, responsibility for implementing it is commonly delegated to a specialized agency or commission. In some cases, these institutions are established solely for the purpose of carrying out the policy at hand; in other cases it is simply a matter of assigning an additional responsibility to a previously existing agency. Agencies and commissions may also have an internal sequence of arenas through which the implementation process proceeds. In the case of agencies, policies commonly are passed from an assembly, to a council, and finally to the secretariat for final action. Commissions in turn often refer matters to a network of subcommissions or working groups before taking final action. Most agencies and commissions report back to a parent body, usually the General Assembly or ECOSOC, on the progress that they have made in implementing the policy. They must also come back to the parent body for funding the programs they sponsor. In some cases, the implementing agencies also take responsibility for reviewing the success of the policies, in others this task is taken up by an independent commission or possibly even a specially convened conference. If significant changes in the policies are recommended, the matter may be referred back to the General Assembly for new policy directives.

Many policy problems are handled in different ways. The sequence of steps traced in the model perhaps reflects most closely how relatively new problems are handled. Older problems within the purview of well-established specialized agencies, such as the ILO, WHO, or ITU, are typically dealt with by that agency without receiving much if any attention from the General Assembly. And in some cases, it is the specialized agency rather than the General Assembly that sponsors a world conference.

CONFLICT IN THE GLOBAL POLICY PROCESSES

Conflict and cooperation go hand in hand in any society. One of the overriding objectives of public policy at any level of political organization is to prevent destructive forms of conflict from emerging or to manage or resolve contentious issues when they do arise. Policy processes can also be a major cause of conflict or, to put it another way, conflicts inevitably surface over the terms of any significant cooperative endeavor. Global policy making is no exception to this general rule because the decisions that are reached can have important consequences for states and other social groupings. Some policies, for example, have implications for how the wealth of the world will be distributed; others affect the security of states or the quality of their natural environment. With some exceptions, the participants in the global policy process can be expected to push for those policies from which they will derive the most benefit. In the absence of a willingness to compromise, the conflicts that arise over policy issues can delay, if not totally thwart, efforts to agree upon and implement international responses to global problems.

Policy problems are described as being *politicized* to the extent that the conflicts have evoked an intensity of emotion. Politicization is also a function of the amount of publicity that the issues have received and, thus, their salience to a broader public beyond the policy makers. Decisions on problems that are not very highly politicized, such as most of the matters before the UPU and the World Meteorological Organization (WMO), can be made in a more rational way, primarily on the basis of technical considerations. Highly politicized matters, such as arms control or Middle Eastern disputes, often require much more negotiation to arrive at a decision that will be acceptable to the many publics that have become interested in them. Some policy problems have escaped becoming very highly politicized because of their technical nature and the failure of many to realize what interests they have at stake. When such an awareness develops, as recently has been the case with the Third World in regard to Antarctica and outer space, a higher level of politicization can be expected.

Lines of Conflict

Conflict in the policy process may involve any of the types of actors identified earlier in this chapter. Naturally, the disagreements that receive most attention are those that occur between national governments, because they ultimately decide upon the policies and provide essential support for their implementation. Thus, conflicting views among states tend to be more disruptive of the policy process. IGOs may also be at odds with one another, especially those with limited, non-overlapping memberships that have incompatible interests. Issues of turf and competition for limited funding can arise among IGOs with universal membership. INGOs may support opposing causes, as is commonly the case between those representing industry, labor, and environmental groups. Nor should conflicts that surface between different types of actors be overlooked. For example, states have been uneasy at times about the role played by INGOs in the policy process, especially in monitoring their failure to comply with international policies.

The lines of conflict that are drawn between states over global public policy can be observed in the debates and votes that take place in international bodies. Some groups of states with common interests caucus regularly, so as to present a unified front that will enhance their influence. Frequently, the lines of disagreement that form are unique to a specific policy problem area or even to a single issue. There are, however, three groups of states whose interests conflict on a broad range of policy issues. The smallest and usually the most unified of these groups is the Soviet bloc or East. The largest coalition comprises the less developed countries of Asia, Africa, and Latin America—the Third World or South. Less cohesive, but nevertheless readily identifiable as a bloc, is the collection of highly developed states that have market economies and democratic political institutions, often referred to as the West. In the first two decades following World War II, the split between East and West, which has been primarily over political and security issues, was the most prominent line of conflict in international politics. In more recent decades, an even more pervasive division has emerged over economic matters, in particular the distribution of wealth in the world. Despite being labeled as the "North/South" confrontation, it is primarily a division between the West and South. The evolution of unity among the less developed states and their dialogue with the states of the West is examined in more detail in Chapter 6.

Types of Issues

Conflict occurs over issues. *Issues* are questions that arise in the policy process on which the participants have a choice between two or more positions that they can take. There is conflict when participants take diverging positions on an issue, usually in response to what they perceive to affect their interests. Issues can emerge at any stage in a policy process and jeopardize its continuation if they remain unresolved.

The most basic issue pertaining to global policy is how much of a commitment should be made to the enterprise of collaborative problem solving through international institutions and conferences. Various actors have calculated quite different assessments of the opportunities and drawbacks that are intrinsic to global, as opposed to national or regional, efforts. In recent decades, much of the support for expanding the role of global institutions has come from the small states and the less developed states, both of which are very numerous in most international institutions. Smaller states have an interest in international cooperation not only because they are less able to buffer themselves from the instabilities and uncertainties of a poorly managed international system, but also because of the benefits they derive from pooling the limited resources they have for addressing common problems. The less developed countries have seen global policy as a way of using their strength in numbers to generate the foreign assistance needed for fulfilling their development aspirations, while redressing some of the inequalities in the distribution of the world's wealth. The United States, frequently finding itself in a minority position because of both its large size and high level of development, has become a leading opponent of proposals to address many of humanity's problems in a global way. The Soviet Union and its allies have a longer tradition of resisting efforts to strengthen the role of the United Nations that dates back in its early years of the organization, when it was dominated by the Western nations.

Conflict may surface on the issue of whether certain circumstances are identified as being problematical and therefore deserving of a place on formal agendas. Naturally, those who are most adversely affected by a set of conditions can be expected to press the hardest for international corrective action, while those who derive some benefit from existing conditions will be reluctant to have them placed on international agendas. For example, fluctuating and declining prices for primary commodities are much more of a problem for the less developed countries that depend upon their export for revenue than for the countries that import these goods. Combatting terrorism is a much higher priority for the developed countries because they are frequently victimized by it while otherwise being relatively secure. Large international flows of refugees are usually more of an issue for the states to which they flee than for those they leave.

Procedures can have a significant bearing on the character of global policies and have commonly been a divisive subject. Voting rules in international bodies have been a continuing source of procedural conflict. Such was the case at the founding of the United Nations, when the question arose of whether permanent members of the Security Council should be endowed with a veto power. The large influx of small, less developed countries into many international institutions has prompted the larger developed states to question the fairness of "one-nation, one-vote" rules. Under such a procedure, a voting majority of 75 states can account for as little as 5 percent of the world's population, whereas 90 percent reside in just 12 states (Luard, 1979, p. 7). Conversely, the newly independent and less developed states have challenged the weighted voting systems that favor the larger, more developed states in forums such as the World Bank and the IMF. Once established for a particular institution, voting rules and other procedures are difficult to change because of the entrenched voting strength of the members who would stand to lose influence if the rules are modified. Thus, conflicts arising over the procedures that will apply to a particular policy-making effort often surface over which arena will be used—a council with limited memberships and in some cases weighted voting or, alternatively, an assembly open to all states, each of which has one vote.

Values are often expressed in such terms as peace, economic development, social justice, and sovereignty that are so widely embraced as to have become mere platitudes that are politically awkward to argue against. Moreover, being highly abstract and vague in meaning, they may be interpreted in many ways, sometimes ones that are even diametrically opposed. Serious disputes over the propriety of a certain value are most likely to occur when efforts are made to give them more specific definitions, as has been the case with the principles of self-determination and nonaggression and the doctrine of the common heritage of man that has been applied to the oceans and outer space. Issues pertaining to the relative priority given competing values, each of which is commendable in its own right, can also become a serious point of contention. Thus, in the preliminary meetings leading up to the Stockholm Conference of 1972, there was a marked reluctance on the part of Third World leaders to subscribe to the environmental goals and principles being promoted by the industrialized states out of concern that the international commitment to the economic development of their countries would be compromised.

Even when a widespread commitment exists to good-faith efforts to achieve certain objectives and principles, sharply opposing positions may be taken on the policy approaches that should be adopted to achieve them. These disagreements may reflect divergent assessments of the prospects for the success of the alternative problem-solving strategies. But more often, conflicts arise as each state attempts to influence the terms of international cooperation in ways that maximize the benefits that will accrue to it while minimizing the costs that they will absorb. Often this means working for policies that circumscribe the behavior of

other actors, while keeping open as many options for one's own
state or organization as possible. Such a tendency is readily
apparent in negotiations over arms control. Accommodating diverse interests may require prolonged negotiations. It is also quite
possible that the policy process will break down at this stage,
particularly if key states conclude that the benefit derived from
likely policy outcomes will not offset the sacrifices that will be
required of them. With many international programs, the states
that would gain the most immediate benefits are not the ones that
would be called upon to provide the bulk of the funding.

The potential for conflict does not end with the adoption of a
policy. Sharp disagreements may be expressed over how the policies are interpreted by states as they carry out their responsibilities or by international agencies as they give the policy more
specific meaning. What procedures are to be established for enforcing rules can be an even more contentious matter. Governments of states that make a practice of complying with
international regulations are much more likely to insist on effective international monitoring procedures than are those which fear
that detection of their continuing violations will be an embarrassment and provoke reprisals. Differences also arise over whether
economic sanctions, such as trade embargoes, should be used as
an enforcement instrument, in part because they can be very
costly to some of countries that impose them, possibly even more
so than to the target country. Whether policies are to be reviewed
and, if so, by whom and when, can also be a sensitive issue
between those who desire that they be continued without significant changes and those whose interests are best served by substantial alterations or a termination of the policy.

The specific issues over which conflicts surface and come to a
head may be a reflection of other, more basic differences. For
reasons of international image or domestic political considerations, governments are often reluctant to oppose the concept of
global problem solving or to stand in the way of other countries'
efforts to place policy problems on the agendas of IGOs. Similarly,
they may be reluctant to take issue with goals and principles that
are widely accepted in the international community or even those
policies that have been proposed for addressing them. A less
politically costly strategy may be to assume an unaccommodating
posture on the procedures that will be used in deciding the policy,

such as in selecting the arenas where the policy problem will be addressed. Another way of thwarting the intent of an international policy is to refuse to agree to strong enforcement measures on grounds that they infringe too much on the prerogatives of sovereign states.

In view of the potential for conflict at each stage of international policy processes, it seems remarkable that agreements are ever reached on strategies for addressing global problems. That they are achieved is evidence that whatever conflicts of interest have arisen over international efforts to address a problem are not perceived to be zero-sum in character. International cooperation is a realistic possibility only when all parties believe that the result will be an improvement in their situation or at least the avoidance of an undesirable turn-of-events. But even when all parties stand to derive some benefits from international cooperation, an agreement on global policies may be elusive if the distribution of benefits is perceived to be inequitable. Designing policies that the governments of all countries will conclude is not only advantageous but also fair is the preeminent challenge for global policy makers.

CONCLUSIONS

This chapter has described in very general terms the process of making and implementing global policies that address the broad agenda of contemporary problems that have been receiving worldwide attention. In doing so, the major types of actors—states, IGOs, and NGOs—have been identified along with the roles they commonly play in the policy process. The basic stages of a rational policy-making effort have been reviewed along with the permanent and temporary arenas in which they typically take place. Presented in an abstract way, the process appears to be a more orderly and rational project than is actually the case in the messy reality of the contemporary world. Global policy making is normally an awkward and protracted undertaking which undoubtedly fails far more often than it succeeds. What makes the policy process especially complicated at the global level of political organization is the need to accommodate the diverse interests of a large population of states which, being sovereign in a legal if not

economic sense, cannot be compelled to contribute con-
structively to the solution of global problems. The substance of
the global policies that are the product of this process is the
subject of the chapter that follows.

REFERENCES

Bennett, A. LeRoy (1984). *International Organizations* (3d ed.). En-
glewood Cliffs, N.J.: Prentice-Hall.
Cox, Robert W. and Harold K. Jacobson (1981). "The Decision-making
Approach to the Study of International Organization," pp. 79–104 in
Georges Abi-Saab (ed.), *The Concept of International Organization*.
Paris: UNESCO.
Feld, Werner J. and Robert S. Jordan (with Leon Hurwitz) (1983). *Inter-
national Organizations: A Comparative Approach*. New York:
Praeger.
Gardner, Richard N. (1972). "The Role of the UN in Environmental
Problems," *International Organization,* Vol. 26, No. 2, pp. 237–54.
Gordenker, Leon (1979). "Reflections on the General Assembly," pp. xii–
xx in *Issues Before the 34th General Assembly of the United Nations*.
New York: UNA-USA.
Held, David (1983). "Introduction: Central Perspectives on the Modern
State," pp. 1–58 in David Held et al. (eds.), *States and Societies*. New
York: New York University Press.
Jacobson, Harold K. (1984). *Networks of Interdependence: International
Organizations and the Global Political System* (2d ed.). New York:
Alfred A. Knopf.
Levi, Werner (1979). *Contemporary International Law: A Concise Intro-
duction*. Boulder, Co.: Westview Press.
Luard, Evan (1979). *The United Nations: How It Works and What It
Does*. New York: St. Martins.
Mansbach, Richard W. and John A. Vasquez (1981). *In Search of Theory:
A New Paradigm for Global Politics*. New York: Columbia University
Press.
Simon, Herbert A. (1957). *Models of Man*. New York: John Wiley.
Skjelsbaek, Kjell (1971). "The Growth of International Non-governmental
Organizations in the Twentieth Century," *International Organization,*
Vol. 25, No. 3 (Summer), pp. 420–42.
Stephens, Lynn and Stephen J. Green (1979). "Conclusions: Progress,
Problems, and Predictions," pp. 293–311 in Stephens and Green (eds.),
Disaster Assistance, Reform and New Approaches. New York: New
York University Press.

Tivey, Leonard, ed. (1981). *The Nation State: The Formation of Modern Politics.* New York: St. Martins.

White, Lyman C. (1968). *International Non-Governmental Organizations.* New York: Greenwood Press.

Willetts, Peter, ed. (1982). *Pressure Groups in the Global System.* London: Frances Pinter.

4 THE RESPONSE

Global Policies and Implementation

What emerges as the product of the slow and awkward global policy process described in the preceding chapter has been characterized by one prominent scholar as being "incomplete," "uncertain," and "disputed" (Luard, 1979, p. 73). A vast number and variety of global policies have been promulgated to address the entire range of problems surveyed in Chapter 2. However, many remain in a primitive state of development, and there are significant gaps to be filled by international public policies. Uncertainty prevails because global policies are often stated in vague language and, thus, are susceptible to different and sometimes contrasting interpretations. Moreover, it may be unclear whether the rules and obligations contained in the policies are binding on states. These ambiguities frequently lead to disputes over how the policies should be applied in specific contexts.

The topic taken up in this chapter is the substance of global public policies, rather the processes that brought them into being. Consideration is given not only to the types of policies that have been adopted and implemented, but also to the values that they are designed to achieve and the principles that are not to be compromised. Not to be overlooked in an examination of policies are the strategies commonly used to implement them, which entail inducing states and other international actors to conform with rules and standards as well as securing adequate funding for programs that are authorized. But before proceeding with these substantive matters, it is necessary to review the several forms that international public policies can take, which have a bearing on their legal status and, thus, whether states are bound to observe them.

THE EXPRESSION OF GLOBAL POLICIES

Global policies, as well as the goals and principles that guided their creation and the procedures spelled out for implementing them, have been expressed in several forms. The two primary ones are treaties, which are negotiated agreements, and resolutions, which are voted upon in a quasi-legislative fashion. Not only are these two types of documents adopted in dissimilar ways, but they also have different legal implications. While treaties are generally regarded as an expression of international law and therefore binding on those that become parties to them, resolutions are usually looked upon as simply being recommendations. In addition, there are several longer-standing sources of international law that under some circumstances might be classified as global policy, including customary practice, the decisions of international tribunals, general principles of law, and the writings of eminent jurists. The primary contributions to contemporary global policy from these latter sources have most frequently been general principles that are not to be compromised.

Treaties

A *treaty* is a formal written agreement that has the effect of projecting a policy into the future (McDougal, 1980, p. 270). Treaties are negotiated between interested parties, which are usually states, but occasionally includes one or more IGOs. The vast majority of the approximately 15,000 treaties registered with the United Nations as of 1980 involve a small number of international actors, frequently only two, and thus would not be regarded as an expression of policies of global scope (Bilder, 1981, pp. 6, 233). Global policies are spelled out in the much smaller number of multilateral treaties, to which all states are invited and encouraged to become parties. These latter treaties, some of which are called protocols, conventions, charters, or articles of agreement, are negotiated in the decision-making organs of IGOs or specially convened ad hoc conferences. Treaties are subject to numerous rules that evolved gradually as international customary law, which was codified by the United Nation's International Law Commission in the form of the Vienna Convention on the Law of Treaties of 1969. Under these rules, a treaty is a consensual type of commitment, meaning that states are not legally obliged to comply until they have voluntarily completed the prescribed procedures for becoming an official party.

Acceptance of a treaty by the states that negotiated it is normally a two-step process. The first is the *signing* of the document, usually by the head of each state's delegation to the negotiations, which takes place shortly after an agreement has been reached on the text. The second step is each state's formal *ratification* of the treaty in accordance with its constitutionally prescribed municipal procedures, which for many countries requires approval by one of its legislative bodies. States that did not participate in the negotiations may *accede* to the treaty using procedures that are similar or identical to ratification. There has been a tendency for governments to simplify the process of accepting treaties in view of their enhanced ability to instruct their negotiators and desire to circumvent recalcitrant legislative bodies (Akehurst, 1982, p. 124). Multilateral treaties do not officially "enter into force" until after they have been formally accepted by a prescribed number of states, commonly one-third of those participating in the negotiations. This may take years, if not decades, because of the characteristically slow pace of ratifications. A typical case is the Vienna Convention mentioned above, which was to come into effect thirty days after having been ratified by the thirty-fifth state, an event that did not occur until 1980, eleven years after its signing. However, in the time between the signing and entry into force, states are expected to refrain from acting in ways that undermine the purposes of the treaty.

Several other features of treaties have a bearing on their utility as expressions of international public policy. First, in ratifying a treaty, states sometimes attach "reservations," or "understandings," which indicate their unwillingness to be bound by certain objectionable articles. Traditionally, it has been up to the other states signing a treaty to decide whether to accept these reservations, which if allowed to stand could substantially weaken the impact of the document. Some treaties explicitly prohibit such reservations. Second, most treaties indicate a time when they will terminate, such as on a certain future date or when a specified event occurs. Prior to that time, the treaty may simply become inoperative because only a small number of states have ratified it, or because a significant number of those that formally become parties to the treaty fail to comply with its provisions. Finally, most treaties have an escape clause that permits states to withdraw their acceptance if, because of changed circumstances, it no longer serves their interests. Normally this can be done legally only when a designated period has elapsed after the state gives notice of its intention to withdraw. It is relatively rare, however, that states exercise this option (Green, 1982, pp. 137–50).

Resolutions

The international community tackles much of its agenda of global problems using procedures that have the trappings of a legislative process. These deliberations take place in the assemblies and councils of IGOs and in the numerous ad hoc conferences that are convened each year. Resolutions bearing similarities to bills taken up in domestic legislatures are introduced, debated, and finally voted upon by delegates from participating states. Whereas treaties take effect upon the consent of each of the interested parties, resolutions are adopted by the affirmative votes of a designated percentage of voting states. No further action is taken by states to officially approve a resolution after it has been voted upon. Resolutions address a variety of matters related to international public policy, such as goals and principles that guide policies, rules and standards that apply to states, various educational and assistance programs that increase capacities to deal with the problem, and budgets and operations of international agencies that carry out the policies. A few resolutions are given the title of declaration, which bestows on them a sense of solemnity and greater importance and is indicative of principles of great and lasting importance (Ramcharan, 1979, pp. 94–95).

It could be argued that resolutions should not be looked upon as legislation because normally they are not binding on states, but are merely recommendations. This observation is only partly true. To be sure, a state can avoid being bound by the resolutions of IGOs simply by declining to become a member of the organization. However, if a state elects to ratify the charter of certain IGOs, it may then be obliged to comply with the rule-creating resolutions adopted by a majority vote in the deliberative bodies of the organization. Not surprisingly, states have been reluctant to relinquish any of their sovereignty and thus resist most proposals that would delegate very many if any of their decision-making prerogatives to IGOs, except on matters that are perceived to be technical or trivial. This explains why most resolutions that set standards of behavior for states simply have the status of being recommendations.

Nevertheless, there are numerous instances in which states have agreed to be bound by resolutions, some of which are potentially significant. A notable example is the Charter of the United Nations that obliges all members to carry out the decisions of the Security Council, which could include imposing compulsory economic or military sanctions on aggressor states. However, there has been a continuing reluctance to invoke this power, which originally was to have been a key element in the collective security arrangements of the United Nations. Some of the resolutions adopted in the General Assembly are also binding on the United Nations membership, such as those which establish the assessments to be paid by each nation. Likewise, the membership of several of the specialized agencies, including the UPU, ITU, ICAO, and WHO, are expected to observe rules spelled out in resolutions adopted by majority vote. It is less clear what is implied by the charter of WHO which states that members are "to do their utmost" to carry out the decisions of the organization's congress. Some of the agencies permit states to "opt out" of the provisions of resolutions, but only for legitimate reasons during a limited period following the vote, after which the resolution is inalterably binding. States can, of course, excuse themselves from observing binding rules and responsibilities by withdrawing from the IGO, but most have been reluctant to take such a drastic step in view of the other benefits they derive from membership (see Luard, 1977, pp. 288–98).

Customary Practice and Other Sources of International Law

Rules or principles take other forms that under certain circumstances might be looked upon as international policies. The most noteworthy of these is *customary law, which is composed* of norms of behavior that have been observed over an extended period by most states, as manifested in their laws, treaties, and actions. To be considered customary law, such a practice must also be widely believed to be a legal obligation of states (Nardin, 1983, p. 167). Customary law is generally conceded to be binding on all states without their consent except, for those that took an attitude of persistent opposition before the custom became crystallized (Virally, 1968, p. 137). Nor can states abrogate the responsibilities they have under customary law. Unlike treaties and resolutions, which are formally stated in official documents, customary rules represent an unwritten form of law, although written interpretations can be found in the decisions of tribunals and the writings of respected legal scholars.

Is customary law properly categorized as a form of international public policy? Obviously, it does not originate in a structured decision-making process of the type described in the previous chapter. Nor is customary law similar to treaties and resolutions in being the product of a deliberate and coordinated effort among states and other international actors to devise a strategy for addressing a particular policy problem. Rather, customary practices evolve in a gradual, informal, and haphazard manner over an undefined period (Henkin, 1979, p. 34). Nevertheless, once these norms are widely recognized and respected, it is not uncommon for them to have much the same effect as the explicitly stated policies in serving as guides for behavior. Some customs have evolved as ways of addressing a continuing problem or preventing one that could arise in the future. This was the case with the practice of granting diplomatic immunity to the ambassadors of foreign states to prevent harassment of them that could ultimately lead to a breakdown of communication between governments. Such customs might be considered international public policy if the definition of the latter is not restricted to a consciously designed course of action laid out by specific policy makers in designated arenas.

Other potential sources of international law and global policy are of lesser importance. Among these are judicial decisions, including those of the International Court of Justice (ICJ), which bind only those countries that have agreed to accept them. While it could be argued that these judgments simply interpret customary norms of behavior, treaties, or other sources of international law, domestic and international courts have occasionally gone beyond this role in making decisions that set forth new legal principles. Another potential source of law mentioned in the statutes of the ICJ is what is known as "general principles of law," which are basic doctrines, such as justice and equity, that have become an integral part of the legal systems of states. These principles, some of which are based on Roman law, have sometimes proved to be useful in filling the gaps in other types of law (Akehurst, 1982, pp. 34–35). The appropriateness of applying principles drawn from domestic law to the international context has been challenged on grounds that the legal systems at these two levels are fundamentally different and separate from one another. Finally, there have been circumstances in which the writings of noted legal scholars have had a pronounced impact on international law and public policy, a prominent example being the seventeenth-century treatises of Hugo Grotius, which left a mark on the traditional law of the sea. Here again, it is appropriate to ask whether those writings are an independent source of international rules rather than simply being interpretations of customary practice or general principles.

Treaties, resolutions, and customary law each have certain advantages and drawbacks as instruments for expressing global policy. Customary laws have the unique virtue of being binding on all states in almost all situations. The one exception are states that stake an objection to a norm as it becoming a legal custom while refusing to follow the example of other states in abiding by it. It is generally understood that new states are bound by customary law that exists when they become a member of the international community, even though they were not in a position to object to it (von Glahn, 1981, p. 23). Nevertheless, customary law has perhaps the most significant shortcomings from a policy perspective, which stem from its vagueness. Because it is not written down in specific language, its tenets are frequently shrouded in ambiguity and are more prone to conflicting interpretations. Moreover, there is no definitive way of determining whether a specific rule of behavior has been observed by a sufficient number of states for a long enough period to have acquired the status of customary law. The great increase in the number of states in recent decades has added further to the complexity of making such a judgment. It is also questioned whether new states are obliged to comply with the customary law that was in effect at the time of their independence, since obviously they could not play a role in its evolution. Finally, in view of the required test of time, customary law would appear to be ill-suited to managing contemporary international affairs when the pace of change is rapid, as it is in so many aspects of the highly complex, modern world.

Treaties have several significant advantages over customary law as a way of expressing international public policy. Being written documents, the content of treaties can be stated with much more precision and detail than is possible with unwritten customary laws. This is not to say, however, that treaties are usually free of ambiguities. It is not uncommon for vague language to be inserted into the text to gloss over conflicts, where an unequivocal statement might cause some states to reject the treaty. Treaties can also be more flexible instruments for responding to rapidly changing circumstances because they can be used to prescribe rather abrupt changes in the behavior of states. By contrast, customary law has an inherent bias toward continuity in accepted behavior. Not to be overlooked, however, are drawbacks of treaties that do not apply to customary law. One such limitation is the prerogative that states have to choose whether to be bound by the provisions of any treaty. But even on this point, there is a school of thought which contends that a treaty can be binding on nonparties if it has been accepted or observed by a large enough proportion of countries to be construed as an expression of what has become customary law (see D'Amato, 1971).

Recently, there has been a growing tendency to express global public policies in the form of resolutions. Because they can usually be debated and voted upon in a matter of days or even hours, resolutions are sometimes described as being an "instant" form of policy. Rarely does consideration of a resolution take more than a month or two. In contrast, treaties normally come into effect only upon the completion of a protracted process that can drag on for decades. Furthermore, negotiating multilateral treaties has become ever more cumbersome as the number of participating states has grown. The resolution route to the adoption of global policy is not, however, without significant disadvantages. Many resolutions have little if any affect on the behavior of states because they are regarded as nothing more than recommendations. This is especially true of resolutions which were opposed by a determined minority that included the very states whose cooperation is most needed to carry out the intent of the document. For example, even when passed by overwhelming majorities, resolutions on nuclear arms control typically have no perceivable consequence because they lack the support of the superpowers.

It should not be inferred, however, that there are not any circumstances in which resolutions have a significant impact on the behavior of states. The influence of resolutions is derived less from any legal status ascribed to them as from the political and moral force they generate, which is generally greater for those that were adopted by a vote that approaches being a consensus. Furthermore, as with treaties ratified by large numbers of countries, at least one school of thought contends that an overwhelming majority of states voting in favor of a resolution is evidence that it expresses broadly accepted norms that might qualify as legally binding, customary law (Humphrey, 1979, p. 30). A conspicuous example of such a resolution is the Universal Declaration of Human Rights adopted by the General Assembly in 1948, the impact of which will be discussed further in Chapter 7. Not surprisingly, the most enthusiastic advocates of the legislative method for creating what has been called "new international law" can be found among the newly independent, less developed countries, who have frequently been able to marshal large majorities in favor of resolutions of special interest to them.

This section has alluded to an evolution taking place in the ways international public policies are set forth. Traditional sources of international law, such as customary practice and judicial decisions, have proved to be too vague or incomplete to govern the affairs of a rapidly changing and increasingly interdependent world. The initial shift was to a greater reliance upon treaties, which spell out what is expected of international actors in much greater detail than does customary law (Coplin, 1966, p. 11). Thus, the International Law Commission of the United Nations has been assigned the task of codifying customary law on important aspects of interstate relations, such as military aggression, use of the seas, and diplomatic relations, in the form of treaties that would substantiate as well as override the original customary law. More recently, there are signs that the preeminence of treaties as a way of setting forth global policies may be declining somewhat in favor of resolutions adopted by majority vote, which can be used to react to policy problems much more quickly, albeit less authoritatively.

VALUES AND GLOBAL POLICY

Values are an integral part of global policy. This is apparent from the fact that the text of virtually every international policy-setting document, regardless of whether it is a resolution, a treaty, or a charter of an IGO, begins with a series of lettered phases, typically fifteen or twenty, which lay out the goals and principles to be promoted or preserved by what follows. These statements usually are neither given much attention nor become the subject of serious controversy, in part because it is customary to express them in abstractions or platitudes that obscure what can be sharp and deep differences over values. Occasionally, resolutions are adopted in the early stage of policy development with the exclusive purpose of specifying the goals and principles that will guide decisions on a future course of action. Two examples are the Declaration of Principles on the Development of the Seabed Beyond the Limits of National Jurisdiction, which was adopted by the General Assembly in 1970, and the Text of Environmental Principles, which was approved at the Stockholm Conference in 1972.

Global Goals

Global policy is directed toward the achievement of the goals of the world community, as opposed to aspirations that are specific to certain states or to other types of the actors, either as individuals or groups of limited membership (see Chittick, 1981). The tensions that sometimes arise between the interests of the community and the individual is illustrated by Rousseau's allegory of the stag hunt in which a group of hunters have encircled a deer in a forest that, if killed, will provide enough meat to feed their entire village. However, as the hunters close in for the kill, one of them leaves the circle to snare a hare for his own dinner. In doing so, he enables the deer to escape, much to the chagrin of the others. There are many goals of the world community that are analogous to capturing the deer, among which are the survival of the human species, world peace, a prosperous and orderly world economy, preservation of the natural environment, the establishment of global transportation and communications networks, and the eradication of contagious diseases. The ambitions of a state to increase the territory and resources under its control, or to acquire nuclear weapons in order to gain a military advantage over their enemies, parallel the self-serving motivations the single hunter has for capturing the hare (Johansen, 1980, pp. 17–18). Firm support for global cooperation can be expected only from those international actors who perceive that their individual interests are not incompatible with, but are clearly advanced by, progress on the goals and principles of the larger community. Stated in terms of Rousseau's allegory, the individual hunter will be committed to the group's goal if his share of the deer contains more venison than would be provided by the entire hare (Levi, 1979, p. 4).

Goals at all levels, the global level being no exception, should not be viewed as separate, parallel tracks that never converge or intersect. Rather, goals are related to one other in ways that have a greater resemblance to the root structure of a tree that leads up to a single trunk. Most global goals are *instrumental,* or intermediate, in the sense of contributing to the achievement of a higher goal, which in turn facilitates the fulfillment of even higher order objectives. At the top of the hierarchy of goals are the *ultimate,* or terminal goals, that are pursued because they are intrinsically desirable, not merely because they are a way of accomplishing other values. Thus, rather than being means to other objectives, ultimate goals are ends unto themselves (Kim, 1984, p. 22).

Can such a hierarchy of values be constructed from the goals that embellish the innumerable international documents that are adopted each year? Let us begin to consider this question by looking at the Charter of the United Nations. Meeting in San Francisco during the waning stages of World War II, the framers of the Charter directed their efforts toward creating a global institution that would further the goals of "international peace and security" for all states. Convinced that peace could be preserved only by ameliorating the conditions that lead to war, the framers charged the United Nations with promoting social progress and better standards of life as well as respect for fundamental human rights. Thus, economic and social objectives were looked upon as being instrumental to the ultimate objective of saving future generations from the scourge of war. It could also be argued that peace, when defined as the absence of war, is in turn an intermediate goal that contributes to the achievement of values that are even more fundamental, namely survival, a decent quality of life, and a sense of human dignity for all of humanity. What constitutes an acceptable quality of life is not an easy question to answer. By one definition, it entails a world in which individuals are able to achieve their full potential as human beings (Galtung, 1969, 167–69).

Most of the goals that are bandied about in international circles are directly or indirectly instrumental to this ultimate objective of enhancing human welfare. Several general goals could be placed at a second level, including international peace and security, a robust and stable world economy, satisfaction of basic human needs, respect for human rights and the attainment of social justice, and preservation of the natural environment. Each of these second-level goals is actually an umbrella concept that encompasses a cluster of objectives. Thus, basic human needs implies certain values, such as adequate food, shelter, clothing, literacy, water and sanitation for all people. Preservation of the natural environment entails the conservation of nonrenewable resources including fossil fuels, preservation of renewable resources such as soil and forests, prevention or reduction of pollution of the ecosystem, and saving the genetic diversity of life forms on the planet.

Other global goals can be positioned at lower levels of a value hierarchy. The bold and idealistic objective of general and complete disarmament was promulgated in a resolution adopted by the General Assembly in a 1959 resolution as a means to the achievement of international peace and security. Reducing the rate of population growth, especially in Third World regions where it has been especially rapid, is viewed as a means to ensuring that the basic needs of the entire world's population can be satisfied without ravaging the natural environment. Chains of values can be identified which extend downward several levels. For example, the vitality of the world economy depends upon the achievement of a number of other goals, one being a high level of international trade, which in turn is possible only if several other objectives are being realized, including a reduction of import restrictions and nontariff barriers to trade, sufficient international liquidity, and an efficiently operating global transportation network.

The structure of global goals should not be envisioned in a

vertical direction only. There are numerous horizontal relationships between the various roots of the value hierarchy described above. In fact, it appears that progress on each of the second-level goals would contribute to the fulfillment of most of the others. For example, peace, which implies the prevention of a nuclear war that could trigger a "nuclear winter," is clearly instrumental to the value of preserving the natural environment. Similarly, the environmental goals of maintaining the fertility of agricultural land and of preventing pollution are prerequisite to the satisfaction of basic human needs, most notably the elimination of hunger and the prevention of diseases, such as cancer. The relationship between many of these second-level objectives is reciprocal. Consider the relationship between human rights and economic development. Most historical evidence suggests a tendency for basic human rights to be respected to a significantly greater degree in states that have achieved a relatively high level of economic development. Conversely, the elimination of arbitrary forms of discrimination that result in the underutilization of human abilities, such as a caste system, can contribute significantly to the economic advancement of a country.

It would be naive to assume, however, that all global goals are fully compatible with one other, in which case what is done to further one objective may detract from progress toward the realization of others. Incompatibilities between goals may simply stem from a need to divide scarce resources between two competing priorities, such as stimulating long-term industrial growth as opposed to a direct attack on the problem of poverty. A more serious problem arises if two objectives are diametrically opposed in the sense that strategies used to pursue one tends to undermine progress toward the other. For example, efforts to control population growth may be implemented at the expense of freedoms of the individual, in this case the right to determine the size of his family, which is recognized in the Universal Declaration of Human Rights. Perhaps the most discussed of the apparent incompatibilities between global goals is the case of economic growth and development, on the one hand, and environmental preservation, on the other. Efforts to limit pollution and conserve resources have been seen as antithetical to the goal of maximizing the growth of agricultural and industrial production. Third World countries threatened to boycott the Stockholm Conference in 1972 in order to underscore their concern that policies prompted by the growing environmental fervor in the industrial world might lead to the creation of barriers that would hinder their development plans.

Apparent incompatibilities between competing or conflicting goals are not necessarily irreconcilable. For example, it may be possible to increase the resources available to pursue competing goals in order that both can be fully achieved. Tensions between conflicting objectives may be more difficult but not impossible to resolve. One potential strategy is to reconsider the goals and attempt to redefine them in ways that are not inconsistent with the achievement of other priorities. Or it may be possible to devise new strategies for achieving one or both of the goals that will reduce the incompatibility. Further reflection and research that takes into account the longer term consequences of policies may reveal that the values are not as much in conflict with one another as was first believed. Finally, if all of these possibilities fail to reconcile conflicting values, it may be necessary to work out a trade-off, or compromise, between them. All of these strategies have played a part in efforts to harmonize aspirations for economic development in a way that does not take a heavy toll on the environment, which has led to the coining of the concept "eco-development."

Global Principles

In the preceding chapter, principles, were defined as ground rules that limit the range of acceptable policy options. In contrast to goals, which in most cases are specific to efforts to address a single policy problem, principles such as sovereignty, nonintervention, equity, proportionality, and the peaceful settlement of disputes are potentially applicable to a wide range of global policies. Other concepts are more limited in their relevance, as has been the case with the "common heritage of mankind" doctrine, which has been applied to the use of the seabed, outer space, and the airwaves as well as to the preservation of endangered species of plants and animals and of the treasured cultural artifacts of previous generations and civilizations. Finally, there are many principles that are specific to a single problem, such as the original commitment of the International Monetary Fund to fixed exchange rates. Another example, is the long-standing cannon of the Universal Postal Union that the territory of all member states constitutes a "single postal territory" for purposes of setting postal charges.

Even though principles are normally listed in international documents along with goals, their origins may be quite different. To be sure, some principles are the product of a conscious decision in much the same way that goals and policies are normally formulated. Thus, prior to the Stockholm Conference of 1972, widespread agreement was reached on the principle that global environmental objectives should not be pursued by strategies that retard the economic development of Third World countries. Similarly, it was decided within the context of WHO that the goal of preventing the spread of diseases should not be tackled in ways that would impose unnecessary restrictions on international trade and the movement of people across national boundaries. By contrast, some principles gradually became tenets of international customary law, among which are the doctrines of nonaggression, self-determination, and freedom of the seas. Custom is most often the origin of the principles that are more generally applicable. In more recent times, many of these principles have been given more specific definition in resolutions adopted in the General Assembly, most notably the Declaration on Principles of International Law of 1970.

Of the numerous principles that have a bearing on global policy, the one that clearly appears to have had the greatest and most widespread impact is the doctrine of state sovereignty. As defined in the previous chapter, sovereignty implies that a government is vested with the supreme authority to make and implement policies which apply to the territory of a state and people, both nationals and nonnationals, who reside within its borders. A corollary to sovereignty is the principle of nonintervention, which prohibits outside actors from intervening in the internal affairs of a sovereign state. The latter principle has been repeatedly violated by the major powers. Nevertheless, these principles have been a major obstacle to the establishment of the strong international institutions and policies needed to effectively respond to many global problems. However, as will be noted in examining international public policy on human rights, a growing tendency has evolved to viewing sovereignty as not being an absolute value, but rather one that must be defined and redefined in response to changes in national and international interests (Perkins, 1981, p. 63). Recognizing the many ways that interdependence dictates international cooperation, some states have elected to exercise their sovereign authority by yielding portions of their decision-making prerogatives to international bodies.

Equity, which connotes justice or fairness, has been described as a spirit or attitude that pervades all law (Levi, 1979, p. 43). It appears that with the passage of time, equity has been on the rise as a standard used to appraise the validity of policies. As with sovereignty, the principle of equity is applicable as a ground rule for most efforts to establish global public policies, if it is not in fact one of the primary goals. Policies can be expected to receive little, if any, support from states that consider them to be unjust. Third World countries are especially vocal in challenging the equity of international laws and policies on matters as diverse as trade and monetary order, international shipping, telecommunications, and the use of the seabed and outer space. Their case is based partly on the grounds that many of the international policies and procedures they are questioning were established before they were independent and could represent and lobby for their interest. The impact of these efforts of the Third World to increase the salience of the equity issue have been described by one observer as the "fairness revolution" (Cleveland, 1977, p. 49).

The many, varying interpretations of equity—some of which are almost diametrically opposed to others—have been the subject of intense debate in international policy-making circles. It is tempting to define equity in terms of equality, either regarding opportunity or treatment, or in terms of the distribution of rewards. Legally, states are sovereign equals, which means that all have the same rights to be free from outside interference in their domestic affairs; thus an equality of opportunity. It is further argued, particularly by spokesmen for smaller countries, that the doctrine of sovereign equality implies that each state be allowed one, and only one, vote in international assemblies. However, the cause of justice is not always served by treating all states equally. For example, it would hardly be fair for all members states to pay the same assessment for the support of the United Nations regardless of the size of their population and economy. On similar grounds, the larger states, which pay much larger assessments to the support of international institutions, question the fairness of the one-

nation, one-vote rule. On a different front, the demands of the
Third World for a new international economic order presume that
justice dictates policies that will reduce gross imbalances in the
distribution of the world's wealth, thereby, achieving greater
equality of result. Fairness in this sense might require unequal
treatment, such as special trade preferences to less developed
countries that would otherwise be unable to compete with the
industrialized countries for a more equitable share of the world's
exports. Fairness might also entail special assistance programs for
the poorest countries whose development would otherwise be
stymied.

Principles are not always in harmony with one another, and in
numerous cases, might actually appear to be at odds with the
achievement of global goals. The doctrine of national sovereignty
makes it possible for the highly developed states to thwart efforts
of the poorer majority to bring about a more equitable distribution
of the world's wealth in much the same way that inequalities in
incomes within states have been reduced. Sovereignty is also
antithetical to vigorous international policies designed to heighten
respect for human rights, to curb transboundary pollution, or to
limit the growth of the world's population. While equity, defined in
terms of equality of result, is consistent with satisfying the basic
needs of the poorest classes of people, it is often not compatible
with achieving the most efficient use of resources, and thus the
most rapid rate of economic growth. Moreover, equity of result
could have disastrous implications for the environment, particularly in the exhaustion or destruction of natural resources, if it
is achieved by dramatically increasing the material consumption
of the poor (see Hardin, 1974). On the more positive side, justice
may be an important precondition for the maintenance of a stable
world peace.

POLICY RESPONSES

As defined previously, a policy is a purposeful course of action
that has been adopted to address a problem preferably in ways
that achieve the objectives of its makers without violating principles they feel committed to respect. Numerous global policies
have been adopted in the many IGOs having unrestricted mem-

bership. Some are the narrowly focused instruments of international regulatory agencies in fields as diverse as aviation, shipping, food, fisheries, health, nuclear energy, meteorology, and intellectual properties. Others are elements of grandiose packages of policies, or "action plans," examples of which are the International Development Strategy and the World Conservation Strategy, that address much broader global policy problems. This section identifies several types of policies that have been adopted to address the global agenda, with a basic distinction being drawn between regulations, which are directed at the behavior of states or other international actors, as opposed to programs, which make certain services available. Frequently, these two types of policies are interrelated parts of a larger strategy for coping with a problem.

Regulations as Global Policy

Most global problems are at least partly a consequence of human actions, in particular those of the governments of states or their nationals. The solutions to these problems are often to be found in the behaviors of these actors. Thus, many policy responses incorporate regulations which discourage conduct that is troublesome for other actors, while inducing constructive actions that contribute to the welfare of the larger community. At the global level, some regulations are mandatory, or binding, while most are merely recommendations for voluntary action. Even when rules are technically not binding, there may be a strong expectation that states will comply. Normally, governments of states have the responsibility of ensuring that not only their own behavior is in conformity with international regulations, but also that of their nationals, including private individuals as well as group or corporate actors based in their countries. There is one notable case in which individuals are also directly accountable for actions that violate international law. Soldiers are expected to refrain from acts that constitute crimes of war even if ordered to do so by their commanders, as set forth in the judgment of the Nuremburg Tribunal, which heard the cases of the accused Nazi war criminals after World War II.

Most regulations can be classified as one of four basic types. First, there are *restrictions* that place bounds on the range of permissible behavior. Some restrictions prohibit certain actions altogether, whereas others limit them in some way, such as in frequency or in the circumstances under which they are committed. One of the most prominent prohibitions that applies to the behavior of states is contained in Article 2 of the Charter of the United Nations, under which all members are to refrain "from the threat or use of force against the territorial integrity or political independence of any state." Arms control agreements also take the form of restrictions, either on the number or types of weapons that can be deployed or used or on where they may be located. For example, treaties ban the development, production and stockpiling of biological weapons as well as the testing of nuclear weapons in the atmosphere and the positioning of them on the seabed, in Antarctica or in outer space. In a very different domain of global policy, there is a convention that prohibits states from importing specimens of endangered species or products derived from them. As a conservation measure, limits have been placed on the harvests of selected species of fish and whales in the oceans.

Obligations are a second type of regulation, which spell out behaviors that are expected of actors in positive way. Thus, states violate obligations when they fail to act in a prescribed manner. For example, under the terms of Article 37 of the United Nations Charter, member states have the duty to refer to the Security Council any dispute that threatens international peace and security, which cannot be settled by negotiation or other peaceful means of conflict resolution. States are also obliged to pay assessments to finance the operations of the United Nations and other IGOs of which they are members. They have the responsibility to ensure the safety of foreign diplomats assigned to their country and to grant asylum to political refugees from other nations. International health codes require that states provide timely information on the outbreak of communicable diseases within their boundaries and the measures that have been taken to prevent their spread. Many obligations have been written into the rules of the UPU, one of which is the mandate that states will expedite the transfer or delivery of mail that originated in foreign countries. One last example is the responsibility that a state has to compensate victims of other countries for damage caused when space vehicles it launched fall back to earth.

The distinction between obligations and *standards,* a third type of regulation, is not always a clear one. Standards are codes designed to achieve either a degree of uniformity or a minimum level of performance among states, often in the interest of safety or the coordination of international activities or transfers. To promote safety, UNESCO has drawn up a set of symbols for highway signs in different countries and has promoted the adoption of similar traffic rules; the ICAO has set minimum qualifications for airline pilots and has routinized landing procedures used at airports throughout the world; and the WHO has established common names for drugs and standards for their purity. Weights and measures have been standarized to facilitate international trade and classification scheme has been adopted to achieve cross-national consistency in reporting trade and industrial output. To improve weather forecasting, WMO has detailed procedures and timing for the collecting of weather data at stations on land and at sea throughout the world. The UPU has established specifications for letters and packages that facilitate the efficient transfer of mail between countries.

Finally, rather than specify what actors must or must not do, some regulations spell out what they have a *right* to do or to expect. For example, in becoming members of the United Nations, states do not relinquish the right to use military force in self-defense, either individually or collectively, if subjected to an armed attack. Under the recently concluded law of the sea, convention vessels of all states are entitled to make use of international straits, subject to the conditions of "transit passage." All states have the right to conduct scientific research for peaceful purposes anywhere on the continent of Antarctica and to make use of the resources of outer space and celestial bodies. In their demands for a modified international economic order, the countries comprising the Group of 77 have asserted the right to choose their own economic system and to assert control over their natural resources. While most rights spelled out in global policies reside with states, there is an important group of entitlements known as human rights that apply to individuals, a subject that is taken up in Chapter 7.

With the exception of rights, regulations can be a nuisance for states. Why then are states so often willing to accept treaties and resolutions that impose limits on the behaviors that are permissible for them? The answer lies in the belief that greater benefits will be enjoyed as a result of the reciprocating compliance of other states, such as in refraining from committing violent acts against noncombatants during times of war. Furthermore, establishing the rights that states enjoy normally requires the adoption of restrictions or obligations that apply to other states. For example, the right of nations to security within their borders implies a prohibition on armed aggression by other states and an obligation of third states to come to their assistance if such an attack occurs, as provided for in the Charter of the United Nations. The numerous regulations that are a part of global policies testify to the fact that most national governments perceive that their interests are better served in a world in which the behavior of other states is more orderly and predictable.

This explains why regulations are a major part of policies that address problems that are transboundary in character or involve the use of international commons that are beyond the territorial jurisdiction of any state. Where there are international interactions or transactions, especially ones on which states and their citizens have become dependent—as is the case with trade and the flow of mail—regulations become an instrument for making them more routine and reliable. Likewise, restrictions and obligations are a critical part of policies designed to cope with problems that can have serious consequences for states other than those in which they originate, as is true of contagious diseases. In regard to international commons, there is a role both for a statement of rights that explains what uses states and their nationals are allowed to make of these areas and for restrictions that limit the extent to which the various users interfere with one another. Regulations can be expected to play a less central role than programs in international responses to the global problems that are contained within the boundaries of countries.

PROGRAMS AS GLOBAL POLICY

Programs providing for some type of service or assistance to states or their populations are the principal international policy response to many problems appearing on the global agenda. This is especially true of policies that address what are essentially domestic problems experienced by countries that are unable to take corrective action that is both effective and efficient. When an internal situation is of special concern to the outside world, as could be the case with the imminent extinction of localized species or the deterioration of an important cultural artifact, the rationale for an international program may be a more equitable sharing of the costs of preservation among the larger, interested community. Programs may also be a key ingredient in strategies designed to address potential transboundary problems—in particular those of a spillover variety, such as epidemics, air pollution, and overpopulation—that could not otherwise be contained by the country in which they originate.

The money expended on internal programs that address global problems is very modest, especially in comparison with the budgets for comparable programs of the larger countries. Annual expenditures for the operating budget of the United Nations and its specialized agencies, as well as for all of the programs that they sponsor, is approximately $5 billion in contrast to a Federal budget of the United States that approaches $1 trillion a year (Jacobson, 1984, p. 79). The expenditures of the City of New York alone are more than three times the size of the budget of the United Nations system. As a result, most international programs have been designed to stimulate, facilitate, or coordinate action by states and NGOs, which also sponsor a wide variety of related projects of their own. If used efficiently in these ways, limited funds can have a considerable catalytic effect that results in an observable improvement in conditions.

Most international programs offer some type of *multilateral assistance* that is channeled through international institutions as an alternative to the more numerous bilateral programs that often come with overt or implied political conditions. Much of the multilateral assistance is of a financial nature that is provided in the form of grants or loans. Financial assistance may be granted in a lump sum that a state can use at its discretion, but is more frequently provided for a specific use or project. The loans made by the IMF to assist countries faced with balance of payments problems are of the general purpose variety, although stringent conditions are sometimes imposed on the recipient to correct the conditions that led to the imbalance. On the other hand, most of the funds dispensed by the United Nations Development Programme (UNDP) are tied to specific projects sponsored by the specialized agencies. For example, with funds provided by UNDP, the FAO has promoted national efforts directed at land reform, nutrition, education, irrigation, and fishery conservation. UNESCO has sponsored projects that assist countries in conducting scientific research on subjects such as natural resources, the ecology of natural disasters, and the use of arid zones, as well as in establishing education programs designed to reduce illiteracy or offer advanced training in science and engineering. Likewise, the money made available to countries through the United Nations Fund for Population Activities is earmarked for specific projects, many of which facilitate family planning. UNICEF dispenses funds for projects in the countries that establish health centers, provide basic education, combat diseases, and improve nutrition.

Multilateral assistance offered as a part of global policies is not exclusively of a financial form. Some programs provide impoverished people living on the margins of survival with the basic necessities of life. The World Food Program was established by the General Assembly in 1961 to dispense emergency food assistance. WHO conducts vaccination campaigns against communicable diseases. Refugees have been the recipients of relief services provided by either the United Nations Relief and Works Agency for Palestine Refugees or the United Nations High Commissioner for Refugees. Victims of natural disasters, such as typhoons, earthquakes, tidal waves, and volcanic eruptions, receive basic provisions from several international agencies and private sources, most notably the League of Red Cross Societies, whose efforts are coordinated by the Office of United Nations Disaster Relief Coordinator.

Technical forms of assistance are often better adapted to limited budgets of international agencies that social programs in view of the potential multiplier effect in the results. Technical assistance is available through muiltilateral channels on matters as diverse as applying fertilizers, planning public health systems, developing nuclear power, setting up vocational training programs, providing essential services in murshrooming municipal areas, and managing wildlife preserves. Expertise is shared in a variety of ways. One is through experts that are recruited and assigned to work in countries that need technical assistance. Demonstration projects can also be an effective way of conveying technical knowledge.

Knowledge on a wide variety of subjects is disseminated by means of hundreds of short courses, seminars, and technical conferences sponsored annually by IGOs. Scholarships are made available to students and officials from less developed countries to study at foreign locations, in some cases at institutes sponsored by IGOs. The ILO, for example, offers courses on social and labor policy for government and industry leaders at its International Institute for Labor Studies, which was founded in Geneva in 1961, and on technical and vocational training at another center that was established in Turin, Italy, in 1965. The IMO has opened the World Maritime University in Malmo, Sweden, to assist Third World countries in the field of shipping.

Technical assistance programs are also an example of a second broad category of programs of IGOs, which can best be described as *information and research services*. These programs include such activities as gathering, processing, compiling, registering, generating, and disseminating information. A distinction can be drawn between those projects in which IGOs actually collect raw data or conduct basic researcher as opposed to simply performing a coordinating role as a repository, compiler, or clearing house for information or knowledge generated by others. In many cases the IGO compiles data gathered by a network of monitors using procedures it has prescribed. Such is the case with the World Weather Watch of WMO that receives weather data from cooperating weather stations around the world and the Epidemiological Intelligence Network established by WHO for the rapid receiving and reporting of information on outbreaks of contagious diseases anywhere in the world. Another example is the Trade Information Center run jointly by UNCTAD and GATT. Agencies also are sometimes called upon to serve as centralized registries for items as diverse as ratifications of treaties, potentially conflicting uses of common resources such as the oceans and outer space, and environmental preserves.

Increasing knowledge through research is often an essential part of the larger strategy that is devised for addressing global problems. As a matter of public policy, research is handled in several ways. Projects on a wide range of subjects are undertaken in-house by IGOs, including many of the specialized agencies, the United Nations Institute for Training and Research, and the newly formed United Nations University, which is to become a geographically dispersed network of international centers for re-search and training headquartered in Tokyo. IGOs also often lend their financial support to the research activities of a variety of outside groups that have expertise to the problems that they address. Meetings of experts are convened by IGOs as a way of bringing the latest scientific findings and insights to bear on a subject of interest and of stimulating new research efforts that might result in significant breakthroughs. Finally, it is not uncom-mon for international agencies to serve as a clearinghouse that keeps records on where research is being conducted on a specific topic. Those who are interested in certain types of scientific knowledge can then be referred to the research institutes available to provide it.

The dissemination of information and research findings is also an integral part of the many of the programs of IGOs. Each year the United Nations family of organizations produces a blizzard of publications that include numerous statistical series, summaries of agency activities, research reports, bulletins, periodicals, and bibliographies. These publications are designed not only to satisfy the needs of the international community for reliable information on a broad range of subjects but also to educate leaders and the international public as a whole on the nature and severity of the problems they face as well as the progress that has been made in addressing them.

Some problems have been addressed by programs of a very different nature. Among the more interesting of these are efforts directed toward keeping the peace in a number of international trouble spots, which, unfortunately, have been of only limited success. The services of a mediator, such as a special envoy or even the Secretary General of the United Nations, and special fact-finding committees have been made available to assist states in resolving peace-threatening disputes. At the request of dispu-tants, the United Nations has sent contingents of peace-keeping forces composed of forces from neutral or nonaligned states into as many as fifteen locations—Kashmir, West Irian (Indonesia), Cyprus, the Sinai (Egypt), the Golan Heights (Syria), and south-ern Lebanon, to mention a few—where they perform tasks such as observing boundaries, supervising cease fires, and facilitating evacuations. Most of these forces have been very small and intro-duced at the invitation of one or more of the disputants, including the one on whose territory they are stationed. Thus, their role has normally been limited to a passive one of providing a neutral presence where belligerents are distrustful of one another. In a few cases peace-keeping forces have been more actively involved in determining the outcome of a conflict, most notably in the Congo (now Zaire) in behalf of the besieged government of the newly independent state threatened by the secession of one of its key provinces. A much larger, collective security force was mounted to confront North Korea's armed aggression against South Korea in 1950. The permanent armed force that the Security Council was to have under its control, as provided for in Article 46 of the United Nations Carter, has never been assembled. Thus, it has been necessary to organize peace-keeping forces on an ad hoc basis.

IMPLEMENTATION OF POLICIES

The treaties or resolutions in which global policies are expressed are often impressive documents that hold substantial promise for ameliorating the problems they address. These documents are, however, simply the blueprints of strategies for tackling policy problems, which will have little if any impact unless vigorously carried out. As we shall see, international policies are implemented in ways that are quite different from the manner in which the domestic polices are put into effect. Furthermore, it appears that obstacles to successful implementation of policies are greater at the international and global levels, although this is an arguable point. In this secion we will focus on how two of the primary challenges that arise at implementation stage of the policy process are normally dealt with at the international level: the first is to induce compliance with regulations; the second, to secure adequate funding for programs.

Compliance with Regulations

The enforcement of rules and obligations is usually envisioned in the context of a vertically structured legal order that is found in most modern nation-states. Such a system has a hierarchy of authorities that stand above the general population—police forces, prosecutors, judges, and corrections officials—who have responsibility for detecting violations of regulations and bringing the guilty parties to justice. By contrast, the international community has a horizontal structure of authority in which there is no higher political authority that can compel the obedience of the members of a society. Being at the top level of the international authority structure, states not only are formally autonomous, but also legally equal. Not even the largest, and most powerful states stand above the smallest ones in legal authority. Thus, whatever inducements there are for compliance with rules and obligations in the community of states must be of a fundamentally different nature from those employed within national societies (see Falk, 1962, pp. 353–63; Barkun, 1968, p. 16).

The rate of compliance with international regulations is higher than might be expected in view of the absence of a higher authority empowered to enforce them. One scholar of the international legal system observed "that it is probably the case that *almost all nations observe almost all principles of international law and almost all of their obligations almost all of the time"* (Henkin, 1979, p. 46). Naturally, there is a greater expectation that states will conform to the provisions of treaties that they have formally accepted, and thus have assumed a legal responsibility to observe. Nevertheless, it is not uncommon for states to honor the terms of multilateral treaties that they have not ratified, and therefore are not obliged to respect. Likewise, most states act in accordance with the rules that have been adopted in the specialized agencies, regardless of whether they are legally binding, as well as with the basic principles of customary law. Recommended norms of behavior that are written into resolutions and declarations adopted in general purpose forums such as the General Assembly are less likely to be heeded.

The rate of compliance with some regulations is much higher than for others. The rights and immunities of foreign diplomats are routinely respected by most countries, although there have been flagrant exceptions, one being the American diplomats held hostage in Teheran for more than a year. Most states are reasonably diligent in fulfilling their responsibilities to forward international mail. International rules applying to use of airspace are rarely violated intentionally. Even on the subject of arms control, most countries, the superpowers included, have refrained from violating the terms of the treaties in force as they continued developing and deploying weapon systems not prohibited or limited. For half a century there were no documented violations of the 1925 protocol banning the use of chemical weapons in warfare. On the other hand, while most countries have refrained from committing acts of armed aggression against their neighbors, there are numerous exceptions, two well publicized examples being Iraq's invasion of Iran in 1980 and Argentina's seizing of the Falkland Islands in 1982. Human rights is one of the few examples of a group of standards enshrined in declarations and treaties that have been consistently and blatantly violated by many countries, including a substantial number that have officially accepted them. Why human rights has been such a notable exception to a general pattern of compliance with international regulations will be considered in Chapter 7.

Why do most states make a practice of complying with international regulations that they are not compelled to accept? The answer seems to lie in a perception that their interests are more favorably served by observing international rules than by violating them. Compliance is likely when there is little to be gained from violating international rules, such as by stationing weapons of mass destruction on Antarctica, the seabed, or outer space, when other potential sites have greater strategic value, such as on submarines plying the oceans. In some cases, significant perils inherent in noncompliance may be readily apparent to potential violators. For example, unauthorized use of airspace by planes or sea lanes by ships increases the risk of collisions, which if they were to occur could be far more costly than whatever advantages there may be from ignoring the applicable international rules. Another illustration of what one observer has described as compliance because of "automatic self-interest" is the 1972 treaty prohibiting the development, stockpiling, or use of biological weapons in view of the possibility that a state's own population may inadvertently become the victims of its own germ warfare program (see Fisher, 1981, pp. 127–29).

Obeying rules or living up to obligations often entails costs and lost opportunities. However, the sacrifices associated with compliance must be weighed against the consequences that violations might have, particularly on the behavior of other states. Most governments subscribe to the principle of reciprocity in their dealings with one another. Consequently, a government desiring to have other states observe international rules to its benefit must demonstrate its willingness to abide by the same rules to the benefit of others. To do otherwise might provoke what could become a costly succession of tit-for-tat reprisals. Thus, a state that abuses the rights of foreign diplomats assigned to its capital risks having its own diplomatic personnel stationed in the offended country treated in like fashion or perhaps even being expelled if diplomatic relations are broken off. Likewise, disregard for the rules of war by one party to an armed conflict, such as mistreatment of prisoners or the use of chemical weapons, will quite likely provoke reprisals in kind and possibly at an escalatory level. Flaunting provisions of an arms control agreement frees other parties from their obligations to comply. As more countries violate a rule, it will be respected less by other states who will question whether they too should continue to feel bound by it. Thus, to derive the benefits of the law, it may be necessary for a state to conform to it (see Henkin, 1979, p. 54; Perkins 1981, p. 37).

The tendency for states to comply with international regulations is reinforced by several other considerations. Governments are usually sensitive to the impact that a blatant disregard for international regulations would have on their reputation for being responsible and law-abiding. The community of states is not so large that a nation's pattern of breaking international rules will go unnoticed. States known for a repeated failure to honor their international commitments and responsibilities risk becoming an international pariah with whom other governments are reluctant to enter into agreements. Domestic considerations might also be a factor in a decision to abide by international rules. If not deterred in the first place, democratic governments may be persuaded to cease violating international standards of behavior, particularly in a blatant way, in the face of a strong negative, reaction from important national constituencies (Henkin, 1979, pp. 60–68). Such was the case with the protests from congressman, international legal authorities, and concerned citizens in the United States to the illegal covert involvement of agents of their government in the mining of Nicaraguan harbors in 1984. Violations of duly ratified international regulations may also be contrary to the laws of a nation, even its constitution.

Violations and Enforcement Strategies

In view of the many reasons for states to conform to international rules, why are they sometimes violated? It is possible that governmental officials are simply unaware of the rules their country is violating or that they have misinterpreted them. Nor is it uncommon for poorer countries to lack the technological or financial means necessary to comply with international standards or to have more pressing demands on their limited resources. A government may also lack the capacity to monitor what its nationals are doing in violation of international law, as in the conduct of military personnel on battlefields. Willful violations of international rules must be explained in other ways. For instance, a nonconforming government may have concluded that there is little likelihood that its transgressions will be detected and thereby become a source of embarrassment. Then, there are circumstances in which the rule-abiding behavior of other states presents opportunities that are too attractive for less inhibited, irresponsible countries to pass up. Some states are successful in attracting foreign investments by presenting themselves up as havens from international standards. Finally, situations arise in which interests that would be sacrificed by obeying international regulations are of such great consequence that a government sees no alternative but to disregard them; for example, if its security would be jeopardized by faithfully observing the restrictions contained in arms control agreements.

How to increase the rate of compliance with regulations is a challenge frequently encountered by international policy makers. In some cases an enforcement strategy is spelled out that in effect becomes an extension of the policy. At a minimum, it may be a scheme for making governments more conscious of what they need to do to fulfill the obligations that are set forth in the policy. This might be accomplished by requiring states to submit periodic reports to an international commission on what is being done to conform to specific international standards. In the case of states that lack the technological or financial means to comply with what is expected of them, it may be necessary for more advanced nations to offer appropriate forms of assistance, such as relevant expertise or the equipment that is prescribed by international standards. The more significant challenge, however, is posed by states that ignore international regulations out of what they perceive to be their self-interest. What can be done to induce them to become more cooperative and responsible members of the international community?

The challenge of dealing with willful violators of international regulations can be taken up by other states, IGOs, or even INGOs, acting on their own or in consort with one another. In horizontal structures of authority, the primary burden of enforcement resides with the actors at the same level as the potential violators. This being the case with the international system, it is primarily up to states to deal with other states that demonstrate an unwillingness to comply with regulations that are a part of global policies. The roles played by IGOs is usually tightly limited by the states that created them, reflecting both a reluctance on the part of states to compromise on their prerogatives of sovereignty and an anxiety that sometime they might be in the embarrassing position of having an IGO use its enforcement powers on them. INGOs have greater freedom of action, but can exert little leverage over states and thus normally play no more than a secondary role in inducing compliance with international rules.

Rules normally will not be taken seriously unless there is a realistic chance that violations will be detected and brought to light with some undesirable consequences for the guilty party. Thus, a major issue in the negotiation of arms control agreements is how compliance is to be verified. Will there be on-site inspections? If so, by whom and under what circumstances? Or is it sufficient to rely upon "national means of verification," such as satellite surveillance and other types of intelligence operations? With any international policy, the question arises of what sources of information on violations will be accepted. It is customary to acknowledge allegations of noncompliance that are made by states that are a party to the treaty and to expect the accused state to respond satisfactorily to the charges. Some IGOs, notably those in the technical fields, are responsible for monitoring compliance with global policies. But it may be INGOs or individual victims that are the most fertile source of information on transgressions of some international policies, such as those in the field of human rights and the environment. States have been relatively slow to accept the legitimacy of complaints forwarded directly from these nongovernmental sources, who are not subject to the political inhibitions that have a moderating effect on accusations of states and IGOs. Governments anticipate that calling attention to the violations of foreign states will jeopardize other aspects of their relations with those states and cause their own record to be scrutinized more closely. IGOs must weigh the consequences of antagonizing the very governments that established them and are depended upon for financing.

A number of the IGOs have assumed the role of receiving complaints of infractions and investigating them to determine their veracity. It is quite possible that the accusations have little or no basis in fact, but have been put forward to embarrass a country for political reasons. Likewise, judicial organs of IGOs are frequently called upon to interpret regulations that it is alleged are not being observed. Some IGOs compile the results of their investigations in reports. Merely issuing such a report may cause sufficient embarrassment to a government to prompt it to take steps to improve its performance in observing the international regulations in question. Stronger forms of pressure are, however, often necessary.

Several types of action can add to the pressures on states to compliance with international rules. One approach is to mobilize world opinion by calling attention to an offense, condemning it, and calling upon the guilty party to alter its behavior. Denunciations stated in the form of resolutions can be a strong inducement to a violating state to alter its behavior, especially if adopted by large majorities that include allies. Both the Security Council and the General Assembly have made a practice of condemning acts of aggression and calling upon their perpetrators to halt them. A resolution calling for "the immediate and unconditional withdrawal of all foreign troops" from Afghanistan, which was adopted by the General Assembly in 1980 by a vote of 104 to 18, sent a resounding message of disapproval to the Soviet Union for its military intervention in Afghanistan. This and other United Nations resolutions have had little apparent impact on the Soviet military presence in Afghanistan. Nevertheless, the unexpectedly strong international reaction may have a deterrent effect on the Soviet Union or on other states contemplating aggressive actions elsewhere. Some NGOs have also attempted to mobilize opinion as a way of influencing states that are lax in conforming with international regulations that are of particular interest. An environmentally oriented group named Greenpeace is noted for its daring open-seas tactics designed to call attention to whaling operations of states that refuse to comply with the regulations of the Internationa Whaling Commission (see Mandel, 1980).

Stronger pressure may be exerted on rule breakers in the form of sanctions. Nations can penalize offending states either by acting on their own or in support of a collective action decided upon in an IGO. Among the more frequently applied sanctions are breaking diplomatic relations, cutting back or suspending assistance programs, terminating trade perferences or declaring an embargo on all trade, restraining investments of multinational corporations, denying access to exclusive fishery zones, and refusing to engage in international athletic competition. IGOs have the prerogative of withholding the services they provide to their member countries and of suspending voting rights and even membership in the organization. Even NGOs have gotten into the act of imposing sanctions, one of which is to organize boycotts on the products of offending countries or corporations. As employed by an alliance of NGOs, this may have been a significant factor in Nestlé Corporation's decision to comply with WHO's recommended procedures for the marketing of infant formulas in the Third World.

The record of sanctions has hardly been auspicious in persuading countries to cease some of their more blatant violations of international rules. Whether such penalties have a deterrent effect on other potential noncompliers is difficult if not impossible to observe because few governments will admit to being influenced by fear of becoming a target of sanctions. Moreover, the usefulness of sanctions as a strategy for implementing international policies is often limited by several other considerations. First, the consequences of the sanctions may not fall as heavily on the decision makers who are responsible for the violations as on other sectors of their national populations; frequently the disadvantaged ones, whose conditions the policy may have been designed to improve. Second, sanctions usually exact a toll on those who impose them, such as lost exports in the case of trade embargoes. States not participating in the sanctions are often quick to take advantage of the possibilities that have been opened and in doing so undermine whatever impact the sanctions might otherwise have had. In some contexts, the lack of cooperation of a few states can thwart the efforts of a vast majority of countries that are willing to impose penalties that have been agreed upon.

The ultimate tactic for enforcing regulations is compulsion by means of physical force, which is practiced more regularly in vertical as opposed to horizontal legal systems. In the horizontally ordered international system, force is usually not an option for rule enforcement. None of the IGOs have a standing military capability that could be used to confront states endowed with even the most modest of armed forces. On the rare occasions when force has been applied in support of global policy, it has been that of states either acting on their own or as part of joint force legitimized and coordinated by the Security Council or the General Assembly. Such an armed response may have widespread approval when circumstances warrant it, as in the event of military aggression. However, most states are reluctant to commit their own military personnel to such ventures unless important, immediate interests are at stake. Moreover, the potential utility of force to compel compliance with international regulations is limited to action against smaller, less well-armed states without militarily powerful allies that will back them. Using force against any of the major military powers that have violated international rules is clearly impractical. Thus, barring the creation of a strong international armed force coupled with a dismantling of the military establishments of states, a very unlikely scenario indeed—it would appear that compulsion will continue to be rarely used strategy of enforcement.

The purpose of sanctions at the international level is quite different from the rationale for punishments meted out by courts to individuals who have violated domestic laws. A fine or a prison sentence that a government levies on convicted criminals is simultaneously intended as a retribution for a past transgression and a deterrent to other potential violators. The objective of most enforcement actions taken at the international level is to elicit cooperation from a state that has been flaunting international rules. Once the desired behavior is forthcoming, the sanctions normally are discontinued. Consequently, international sanctions are generally less of a deterrent to other would-be violators and, thus, to elicit what has been described as "first-order compliance." Rather they are a course of action that can be used as leverage to alter the behavior of those who have already been determined to be in violation of international regulations, or what could be termed "secondary compliance" (Fisher, 1981, pp. 20–33).

Financing Global Programs

With few exceptions, the governments of states have been the primary, if not the exclusive, source of financial resources used to implement global public policies and operate IGOs that sponsor them. This money has been provided in two ways, one being the payment of *assessments* to IGOs, which are the international equivalent of a tax that states are obligated to pay as a condition of membership. The other entails *contributions* to funds, which are voluntary grants that are akin to gifts given voluntarily to charitable causes. Assessments are used primarily to pay the operating expenses of IGOs. In doing so, they cover many of the costs of administering international programs. Assessments have also been used to finance some programs, among which were several of the peacekeeping forces. Contributions are a supplemental form of funding used primarily to fund international programs that are not supported fully by assessments. The money provided through assessments and contributions has rarely been very adequate in view of the objectives of global policy, nor has it been very stable from one year to the next. Ironically, some of the larger and wealthier states, the United States included, have been especially parsimonious in their contributions to these programs. This lack of generosity is hardly attributable to financial hardship, because the amounts requested are quite small relative to their national budgets. It is more a reflection of misgivings over how the money is to be used and the way the assessment are apportioned to the member states.

Under an assessment scheme, each member of an IGO is expected to provide an assigned percentage of the budgeted funds. Normally each country's share is calculated using a formula that takes into account such factors as population and national income, which reflect its size and ability to pay. Maximum and minimum amounts may also be set. Thus, under the current assessment schedule of the United Nations, which dates back to 1978, no state contributes more than 25 percent nor less than .01 percent of the budgeted funds. Seventy-five members pay the minimum figure, an additional 10 members pay only .02 percent. The fairness of the allocated shares has been a subject of seemingly endless dispute, with the smallest states arguing that the minimum assessments require them to pay a disproportionately large share of their national income. The larger states complain that their share of the votes in IGOs with a one-nation, one-vote system is ridiculously small in view of the heavy financial dependence of the organizations on them. In the General Assembly more than 50 percent of the votes can be cast by countries whose combined assessments amount to only 1 percent of the United Nations budget (Bennett, 1984, p. 89).

Normally, states pay their assessments to the United Nations and other IGOs which they have joined, although not always in a timely fashion. The reasons they meet their obligations are similar to those that lead them to comply with other obligations. Perhaps the most important of these is the perception that the benefits derived from the organization more than compensate for the expenses. Falling behind in payments could subject them to the sanction of losing the privileges of membership in an IGO. Members of the United Nations who fall in arrears in an amount that exceeds their combined assessments for the previous two years risk losing their vote in the General Assembly, unless the reasons for nonpayment are beyond their control. Keeping up with assessments is also a way of nurturing a reputation for being a respectable member of the international community.

Nevertheless, states occasionally have refused to pay all or part of what is assessed them. The Soviet Union and France balked at paying special assessments to cover the expenses of United Nations peacekeeping forces stationed in the Middle East from 1956 to 1967 and in the Congo from 1960 to 1964. The United States has refused to pay for United Nations activities that involve the Palestine Liberation Organization and the South West Africa People's Organization. Recently, Poland declined to pay its assessment to the ILO. The combined backlog of unpaid regular and special assessments to United Nations now approaches $700 million, which exacerbates the severe financial strains on the organization (Puchala et al., 1984, pp. 159–60). There has been, however, a reluctance to suspend the voting rights of these countries for fear of provoking the withdrawal of important members of the organization.

A gradual tendency can be noted toward a greater reliance on voluntary contributions of states as a means of financing international programs. This trend is evident in the proliferation of special funds over the past decade. Presently, there are more than 25 United Nations programs or funds that receive part if not all of their revenues from voluntary contributions (see Table 4.1 for a partial listing). Such funds have been established to provide financial support for programs with causes as diverse as children, refugees in general, Palestinian refugees in particular, food, agricultural development, the environment, population, human settlements, and science and technology for development. The largest recipient is the UNDP, which in 1984 took in more than $400 million from 98 governments. This fund is the primary source of money for projects and programs sponsored by the specialized agencies, which, with few exceptions, do not have a separate fund. UNICEF, which also solicits private donations, and the United Nations Fund for Population Activities (UNFPA) are also among the leading recipients of contributions.

Table 4.1:   Funds and Programs Financed at Least in Part by Contributions

U.N. Development Programme
U.N. Children's Fund
U.N. Fund for Population Activities
U.N. Fund for Drug Abuse Control
International Fund for Agricultural Development
U.N. Institute for Training and Research
Voluntary Fund for Women
Habitat and Human Settlements Foundation
U.N. Industrial Development Fund
U.N. Environment Programme
U.N. High Commissioner for Refugees
U.N. Financing System for Science and Technology
     for Development

The amounts contributed to various funds fluctuate from one year to the next, occasionally very sharply. Moreover, some funds are much more successful than others, as measured by the percentage of the targeted figure that is donated to them. This irregular pattern is not surprising because contributions remain subject to the whims of governments, including legislative bodies, whose willingness to provide money often reflects economic and political trends and developments in their countries. The level of contributions may be part of a strategy to influence the policies and activities of international agencies. At the 1984 World Population Conference in Mexico City, the United States threatened to suspend contributions to the UNFPA to protest the support it gives NGOs that either perform or support abortion. In an effort to make the contribution process more systematic, pledging conferences are convened at which countries pledge amounts of money to replenish the various funds sponsored by the organization and its specialized agencies.

What accounts for the increasing reliance on contributions as the primary source of revenue for international programs, when assessments would seem to promise a more predictable and perhaps larger amount of revenue? The answer lies in the greater political resistance that is encountered in establishing or expanding programs financed by assessments, which states are obliged to pay to IGOs to remain a member of good standing. Normally, fewer votes will be cast against a program if the governments of states retain the right to decide how much, if any, money they will contribute to its support. Thus, it is possible to launch a greater variety of international projects if the funding is to come from contributions. Moreover, even if there are enough votes to initiate a program through assessments, it is not unlikely that some of the states that opposed it will withhold a portion of their assessment in protest, thereby challenging the authority of the organization and jeopardizing its financial solvency, as was the case with the peacekeeping forces (Luard, 1979, pp. 120–21).

In recent years, the limits of the generosity of the principal contributors to international organizations and programs has been seriously tested. Increasingly, the developed countries, the United States and Soviet Union included, are taking the position that there should be no growth in the size of the United Nations budget beyond the rate of inflation (Puchala et al., 1983, p. 150). Donor fatigue among those states which are repeatedly called upon to provide the bulk of the funding is also apparent in increasing resistance to the growing numbers of funds and escalating target figures. As a result, the danger exists that various funds will be impoverished by competition among themselves for the limited amount of money that states are willing to donate. Among the many programs already jeopardized are the action plans of the UNEP on regional seas, environmental education, tropical forests, desertification, and soil loss, and the International Fund for Agricultural Development which is directed to the needs of small farmers and the rural landless people.

SUMMARY

This chapter briefly reviewed the typical products of the global policy process that was analyzed earlier. Global policies are expressed in written form in treaties that are negotiated by representatives of interested states or resolutions adopted in a quasi-legislative fashion by majority vote. Treaties are binding on states that ratify or accede to them whereas resolutions normally are regarded as merely being recommendations, except in some specialized agencies where compliance is expected of all members. Some customary law can also be looked upon as a form of global policy even though it is not written down and evolves in a slow, haphazard manner, rather than being deliberately devised to address a specific policy problem. Gradually, customary law is being superseded by treaties which articulate policies in a more detailed and less ambiguous way. More recently, however, the awkwardness of the process of negotiating multilateral treaties among upwards of 150 states has prompted a greater reliance on resolutions, which are a more flexible although less authoritative way of expressing global policies.

The substantive elements of global policies address three questions. First, what values in the form of goals and principles are to be pursued or respected? Goals can be arranged in a hierarchy in which some are instrumental to the achievement of others, with the ultimate objective being to enhance human welfare. Second, what policies are to be adopted that will address the problems of concern to the policy makers? Most global policies can be categorized either as regulations that spell out what states and other international actors may or are may not do or as programs that provide a service to the community of states. The objective of regulations is a more orderly and predictable world in which states display a respect for the rights and interests of one another. Programs serve a variety of purposes, among which are allowing countries, especially the smaller ones, to enjoy some of the advantages of scale and the poor countries to receive economic and technical assistance. Third, what strategies will be used to implement the policy responses? In the case regulations, the primary task is to induce compliance through monitoring that detects violations and exertion of pressure on violators to reform their behavior. The primary challenge in administering programs is to secure adequate financing, either through assessments or voluntary contributions from governments or private sources.

REFERENCES

Akehurst, Michael (1982). *A Modern Introduction to International Law* (4th ed.). London: George Allen and Unwin.

Barkun, Michael (1968). *Law Without Sanctions: Order in Primitive Societies and the World Community.* New Haven, Conn.: Yale University Press.

Bennett, A. LeRoy (1984). *International Organizations* (3rd ed.) Englewood Cliffs, N.J.: Prentice-Hall.

Bilder, Richard B. (1981). *Managing the Risks of International Agreement.* Madison: University of Wisconsin Press.

Chittick, William O. (1982). "Macromotives and Microbehavior: A Prescriptive Analysis," pp. 205–229 in Gary K. Bertsch, *Global Policy Studies.* Beverly Hills: Sage Productions.

Cleveland, Harlan (1977). *The Third Try at World Order: U.S. Policy for an Interdependent World.* New York: Aspen Institute for Humanistic Studies.

Coplin, William D. (1966). *The Functions of International Law: An Introduction to the Role of International Law in the Contemporary World.* Chicago: Rand McNally and Company.

D'Amato, Anthony (1971). *The Concept of Custom in International Law.* Ithaca, N.Y.: Cornell University Press.

Falk, Richard A. (1962). "The Reality of International Law," *World Politics,* Vol. 14, pp. 353–63.

Fisher, Roger D. (1981). *Improving Compliance with International Law.* Charlottesville: University Press of Virginia.

Galtung, Johan, (1969). "Violence, Peace, and Peace Research," *Journal of Peace Research,* Vol. 6, pp. 167–90.

Green, N. A. Maryan (1982). *International Law: Law of Peace* (2nd ed). London: MacDonald and Evans.

Hardin, Garrett (1974). "Living on a Lifeboat," *Bioscience* Vol. 24, pp. 5651–68.

Henkin, Louis (1979). *How Nations Behave: Law and Foreign Policy* (2d ed.) New York: Columbia University Press.

Humphrey, John P. (1979). "The Universal Declaration of Human Rights: Its History, Impact, and Juridical Character," pp. 21–37 in B. G. Ramcharan, *Human Rights: Thirty Years after the Universal Declaration.* The Hague: Martinus Nijhoff.

Jacobson, Harold K. (1984). *Networks of Interdependence: International Organizations and the Global Political System* (2d ed.) New York: Alfred A. Knopf. Westview Press.

Levi, Werner (1979). *Contemporary International Law: A Concise Introduction.* Boulder, Co.: Westview Press.

Luard, Evan (1979). *The United Nations: How It Works and What It Does.* New York: St. Martin's Press.

Mandel, Robert (1980). "Transnational Resource Conflict: The Politics of Whaling," *International Studies Quarterly,* No. 24, No. 1 (March), pp. 99–128.

McDougal, Myres S., Harold D. Lasswell, and Lung-chu Chen (1980). *Human Rights and World Public Order: The Basic Policies of an International Law of Human Dignity.* New Haven, Conn.: Yale University Press.

Nardin, Terry (1983). *Law, Morality, and the Relations of States.* Princeton, N.J.: Princeton Universtiy Press.

Puchala, Donald J., ed. (1983). *Issues Before the 38th General Assembly of the United Nations.* New York: UNA-USA.

Ramcharan, B. G. (1979). "Standard Setting: Future Perspectives," pp. 93–107, in Ramcharan (ed.), *Human Rights: Thirty Years After the Universal Declaration.* The Hague: Martinus Nijhoff.

Virally, Michel (1968). "The Sources of International Law," pp. 116–74 in Max Sorensen (ed.), *Manuel of Public International Law.* New York: St. Martin's Press.

von Glahn, Gerhard (1981). *Law Among Nations* (4th ed). New York: Macmillan.

| Part 2 | **CASE STUDIES IN GLOBAL POLICY** |

5 NUCLEAR PROLIFERATION

Preventing a Threat to World Peace

On May 18, 1974, India's Prime Minister Indira Gandhi received a coded message stating "the Buddha is smiling," which informed her that her country had successfully tested a nuclear "device" underground in the Rajasthan Desert. In announcing the achievement, the Indian government insisted that the test was undertaken solely for peaceful purposes, such as mining, oil and gas exploration, finding underground water, river diversion, and earth moving, a contention that India still maintains is its nuclear policy. Technically speaking, however, a peaceful explosion is indistinguishable from a weapons-related test.

All nuclear explosives or bombs are not of equal political importance. A country's first explosion, regardless of its announced purpose, is given far more weight internationally than subsequent tests and the nuclear weapons that are constructed later (Nye, 1981, p. 35). The fact that India was the first country to join the "nuclear club" following the adoption of an international non-proliferation policy in 1968 added more to the perceived significance of the event. Thus, it was that India's explosion triggered especially harsh international condemnation, which paradoxically was stronger than the criticism directed at China and France for a series of weapons-related, nuclear tests in the atmosphere that caused widespread radioactive contamination (Thomas, 1981, p. 60). Moreover, India's blast, despite not immediately followed by a weapons program, has perhaps had a greater impact in shaping international public policy on nuclear weapons than have the hundreds of nuclear tests conducted by the United States and the Soviet Union during the 1970s or the addition of thousands of nuclear warheads to their arsenals which can be delivered internationally with ever increasing accuracy.

Since the building of the first atomic bombs and their use against Japan by the United States toward the end of World War II, nuclear weapons have been treated as a forbidden fruit internationally. India was only the sixth nation to set off a nuclear explosion, having been preceded by the United States (1945), the Soviet Union (1949), the United Kingdom (1952), France (1960), and China (1964). In addition, it is widely believed that Israel and South Africa have clandestinely developed nuclear weapons that have not yet been tested or could assemble them quickly as circumstances dictate. Argentina, Brazil, Libya, Iraq, Pakistan, South Korea, and Taiwan lead a list of potential future proliferators which in the foreseeable future will have the technical means and weapons-grade materials needed to produce nuclear bombs as well as an apparent motivation for doing so.

PROLIFERATION AS A GLOBAL POLICY ISSUE

The freedom to take whatever defensive steps are believed necessary to maintain the physical security of its population and territory is one of the most jealously guarded prerogatives of sovereign states. If it were possible for all states to achieve a sense of security through the buildup of armaments, there would be no need to address security problems internationally. Not even the superpowers, however, have the technological and economic means to fully defend their citizens against modern weaponry. Thus, the security of states depends not only upon their defensive preparedness, but also upon developments beyond their borders. The acquisition of new weapons by other states, even with the purest of defensive motives, is often perceived as a serious threat to the security of one's own country. Thus, encouraging other countries to exercise restraint in developing new weapons systems can contribute significantly to a sense of national security, perhaps even more than a costly arms buildup that diverts resources away from other national priorities.

The danger of nuclear war is a subject of serious worldwide concern because the catastrophic consequences of such an occurence would not be limited to the states that are directly involved in the hostilities. Among these would be the health-threatening effects of radioactive fallout carried indiscriminately across national boundaries by the prevailing winds. In addition, large quantities of smoke and dust emitted into the atmosphere could have widespread climatic effects and disrupt agriculture over large regions. Recent calculations of scientists reveal that a major exchange of weapons could quite possibly plunge much of the world into a frigid "nuclear winter" that would kill off many species of plant and animal life (see Ehrlich et al., 1984). Environmental effects aside, uninvolved states might also have to contend with economic problems following destruction of the industrial societies, such as those stemming from a disruption of trading relationships, the international banking system, multinational business enterprises, and development assistance programs. The security of many states might also be seriously undermined by a breakdown in the international political order.

There are two dimensions to the nuclear proliferation problem. One is the rapid increase in the arsenals of the states already possessing nuclear weapons, or what is often called *vertical* proliferation. The analysis that follows concentrates on the second dimension, *horizontal* proliferation, which refers to the potential acquisition of nuclear weapons by additional states. More headway has been made toward establishing global policies on the horizontal aspects of the proliferation problem, perhaps because it would be virtually impossible for the international community to exert effective pressure on the superpowers to reduce their arsenals. In contrast, most of the states aspiring to join the nuclear weapons club continue to require varying amounts of outside assistance in order to acquire the fissionable materials, technology, and expertise needed to produce nuclear weapons. Thus, there is reason for hope that the further spread of nuclear weapons can be slowed if the advanced nuclear countries act together and resist the temptation to undercut each other to curry political favors or commercial advantages with weapons aspirants.

International efforts to halt or at least to slow the rate of horizontal proliferation presume that the probability of a catastrophic nuclear war increases sharply with growth in the number of states possessing nuclear weapons. It is not, however, an anxiety based exclusively on numbers of nuclear states. Established members of the nuclear club who have spearheaded the development of international policies on nuclear proliferation have expressed concern that some states on the threshold of having nuclear weapons are politically unstable and therefore cannot be counted upon to have responsible leadership. It is also feared that some of these threshold countries have deficient command-and-control procedures which may not be able to prevent unauthorized use of nuclear weapons by overzealous military personnel or theft by dissidents or terrorists (Wohlstetter et al., 1979, p. 132). The potential problem is compounded by pressures to be able to launch their nuclear weapons quickly on warning in view of the vulnerability of a small, newly acquired arsenal to preemptive attack by other countries. Nor is it reassuring to note that some of these threshold states are parties to intense regional conflicts, which have led to repeated hostilities and wars with neighboring states. The worst fear is that the superpowers would feel compelled to come to the support of allies threatened by a new nuclear state, which could trigger a series of events that would bring them to the brink of a nuclear confrontation of far greater consequence (Dunn, 1982, pp. 85–87).

PEACEFUL APPLICATIONS AND THE POTENTIAL FOR PROLIFERATION

The task of preventing the further proliferation of nuclear weapons has been complicated by a simultaneous commitment over the past three decades to promote peaceful applications of the atom, in particular for generating electricity, by all interested countries, including those without nuclear weapons. The large escalations in oil prices engineered by the OPEC countries during the 1970s, coupled with the temporary Arab embargo on oil exports to selected supporters of Israel, sparked a worldwide surge of interest in nuclear power as a way of achieving greater self-reliance in energy. During the 1970s the amount of electricity generated by nuclear reactors increased seven fold (Potter, 1982, p. 1). By 1982 there were 279 nuclear power reactors and at least 323 additional research reactors operating in 54 countries (Sivard, 1982, p. 20). The technologies, expertise, and fissionable materials developed in conjunction with these programs bring additional countries closer to having the ability to produce nuclear bombs. Thus, it has been estimated that as many as 36 states have achieved the technical and economic prerequisites of a "latent" capability to produce nuclear weapons (Meyer, 1984, pp. 40–42). To prevent, deter, or discourage them from joining the nuclear weapons club is a major challenge for international policy, an understanding of which requires a brief digression on the nuclear fuel cycle.

Barring an unusual opportunity to purchase, borrow, or steal nuclear weapons, governments or other groups intent on acquiring them must contemplate the possibilities of building a bomb on their own or in concert with other nonweapons states. To do so requires a level of scientific and technological expertise which is well within the reach of countries that have achieved a moderate level of technological development. There are numerous opportunities for training nuclear engineers at foreign universities, and most of the required technical information can be gleaned from published sources. Securing a sufficient quantity of weapons grade material, either highly enriched uranium or plutonium, is a more formidable challenge for the would-be nuclear weapons states (Gilinski, 1978, p. 84).

The uranium needed to fuel most of the research and power reactors is unsuitable for the production of bombs because of its relatively low content of the highly fissile isotope U235, which can be split to release neutrons and great amounts of energy. Most reactors use uranium that has been enriched from a .7 percent concentration of U235 to a 2 to 4 percent level. This slightly enriched uranium falls far short of containing the 20 percent concentration of U235 that is necessary to build even the crudest of nuclear bombs. Uranium enriched to a level of 90 percent or higher is preferred for the production of nuclear weapons. Only a few types of reactors used primarily in research require uranium that is highly enough enriched to be fabricated into bombs.

The process of enriching uranium has been beyond the means of all but the largest and most advanced nuclear nations because of the high cost, technological complexity, and prodigious energy requirements of the gaseous diffusion technique, which has been used to produce almost all of the enriched uranium for reactors and weapons to date (Potter, 1982, p. 71). Thus, most countries have been dependent on foreign sources for the enriched uranium needed to fuel their reactors, and in so doing, must accept the conditions imposed on its use by the suppliers. Up until the mid-1970s, the United States had a virtual monopoly as a supplier of enriched uranium for the noncommunist world. Since then the United States has lost much of its market share, first to the Soviet Union and, more recently to two European-based consortia: Urenco, which is a joint project of British, Dutch, and West German interests and Eurodif, a creation of the French government along with Belgium, Spain, Italy, and initially Iran. New methods of enrichment are being developed using centrifuge, aerodynamic, and laser isotope separation technologies on a small scale that will be less complex and costly and therefore within the reach of larger numbers of states that desire to develop their own means for producing highly enriched uranium (Potter, 1982, pp. 72–73; Neff, 1984, pp. 19–21).

Plutonium, the fissionable substance used in the initial tests of five of the six countries that have exploded nuclear devices, is a byproduct of the operation of nuclear reactors, which accumulates in the fuel rods as the uranium is irradiated, or "burned." An average power plant produces enough plutonium to manufacture 20 to 25 bombs each year (Potter, 1982, p. 2.). Before being fabricated into a bomb or recycled for use as a reactor fuel, the plutonium must be chemically separated from left-over uranium and other highly radioactive wastes in a process that is known as reprocessing. Because reprocessing facilities require less sophisticated technologies than enrichment plants and can be constructed at much less cost, the plutonium route to a supply of highly fissile materials has fewer impediments for an aspiring nuclear weapons state. Moreover, the reprocessed plutonium is in a form that could be handled by nonstate actors, such as terrorist groups seeking to manufacture a bomb. India's nuclear device was constructed using plutonium separated from the spent fuel extracted from a reactor supplied by Canada. Nevertheless, the cost and technical difficulty of reprocessing is sufficiently high to be beyond the means of most countries and probably all terrorist groups. France, Japan, and the United Kingdom have been gearing up to offer commercial reprocessing services. Several other countries, including potential proliferators, have plans to build smaller reprocessing facilities. It is estimated that, within a decade, more reprocessed plutonium will be produced from spent fuel from nuclear power plants than is contained in the combined nuclear weapons stocks of the United States and Soviet Union (Levanthal, 1985, pp. 12–13).

Plutonium will play a more central role in a new generation of nuclear power plants known as fast breeder reactors. An advantage of the breeder reactor is its capacity to generate as much as 40 percent more fissile material in the form of plutonium than is orginally fed into the reactor. As a result, the breeder process can extract upwards of 70 times as much energy from a given amount of natural uranium than the widely used light water reactors of the previous generation (Potter, 1982, p. 16) This explains why the breeder reactor was looked upon as an especially attractive possibility amid pessimistic projections made in the mid-1970s that known world reserves of uranium would be depleted in two or three decades unless technologies were developed that could make better use of them. Widespread use of the breeders would, however, greatly increase the amount of weapons-grade plutonium in circulation, thus complicating the task of curbing the proliferation of nuclear weapons. Thus far, France and the United Kingdom have been leaders in the commercial development of the breeder. West Germany, Japan, the Soviet Union, and the United States have also invested heavily in the technology. Among the less developed countries, India also has a breeder project under way.

Some argue that the ostensibly "peaceful" applications of nuclear technologies, such as power-generating facilities, do not increase the probability of proliferation. A nation bent on fabricating nuclear weapons would presumably use smaller scale "research" or "production" facilities designed to produce the needed quantities of weapons-grade, fissionable materials much more efficiently and cheaply than would the commercial reactor programs. This in fact was the route used by all of the states that have acquired nuclear weapons thus far. Another school of thought contends thay any nuclear facilities, regardless of the reasons they were acquired, are an ever present temptation to a government that would not have deliberately set out to develop the capability to produce nuclear armaments. Should circumstances become more threatening, a beleaguered government may decide to exercise the option its peaceful programs provide for developing nuclear bombs. Thus, caution is called for in supplying nuclear materials and technologies available to any additional states. This latter view has been the more influential in the evolution of international policy on proliferation.

In any event, the nuclear fuel cycle is very much an international process, since no region, with the exception of North America, has a uranium supply that will meet its anticipated demand. Moreover, because optimally sized enrichment and reprocessing plants could service many power plants, it is much more economical for all but the countries with the largest nuclear programs to contract for these services abroad, even if they can afford the large investments that would be required.

THE MAKING OF NONPROLIFERATION POLICY

Which states should participate in designing international policies on the horizontal proliferation of nuclear weapons? How this question is answered has a bearing on which arena is selected for the task. One possibility is a forum where states which both possess and do not possess nuclear weapons collaborate in negotiating a policy that is acceptable to both. Second, it is conceivable that the advanced states which can supply other nations with what is needed for producing nuclear bombs would agree among themselves on a nonproliferation policy and impose it on the nonweapons states without their consent. In doing so, they risk antagonizing the nonweapons states and may even provoke them into seeking nuclear weapons. Finally, groups of nonweapons states could pledge among themselves to keep nuclear weapons out of their region, thereby establishing what is known as a "nuclear-weapons-free-zone." Over the past two decades, the proliferation issue has been discussed in all three of these types of forums with mixed results.

The proliferation issue has been considered extensively in bodies in which nations that both do and do not have nuclear weapons are represented. It has repeatedly been on the agendas of the General Assembly, not only for the regular annual sessions, but also for the two Special Sessions on Disarmament held in 1978 and 1982. But the most intensive discussions on a wide range of arms control issues, including nonproliferation, take place in what is now the 40-member United Nations Conference on Disarmament, a body that has been expanded, reorganized, and renamed several times since it came into being as the Eighteen Nation Disarmament Committee (ENDC) in 1961. ENDC was the setting for negotiations on the Treaty on the Non-Proliferation of Nuclear Weapons, commonly referred to as the Non-Proliferation Treaty or simply the NPT. Since coming into effect in 1970, just two years after it was adopted by the General Assembly and opened for signing, the NPT has been the core document in international policy on preventing the spread of nuclear weapons. At the insistence of the nonweapons states, a provision was inserted calling for periodic review conferences if requested by a majority of the ratifiers of the treaty. Review conferences held in 1975, 1980, and 1985 were contentious affairs in which the nonweapons states raised hard questions about whether the nuclear powers were living up to certain of their treaty commitments. The proliferation issue was also a central topic of discussion at major United Nations conferences on New and Renewable Sources of Energy (1981) and Nuclear Energy (1983).

The Vienna-based International Atomic Energy Agency (IAEA) is another important locus of decision-making in which both weapon and nonweapon states can participate. Established in 1957, the IAEA has grown in membership to 114 states with the entry of China in 1984. As spelled out in its charter, the agency is to accelerate and enlarge the contribution of atomic energy to "peace, health, and prosperity throughout the world," while implementing safeguard procedures that would detect the diversion of nuclear materials to weapons production. In undertaking the latter, the IAEA becomes an actor in its own right rather than simply being a policy arena. The European Atomic Energy Agency (EURATOM) has a mission that is similar to those of the IAEA, but with responsibilities that are regional in scope.

The advanced nuclear supplier states have not been content to rely exclusively on the forums open to nonweapon states. In an effort to standardize their nuclear export policies, they began meeting in a group known as the Zanggar Committee, having assumed the name of the Swiss professor who chaired the sessions. India's test explosion in 1974 spurred the United States into convening another series of meetings, to which the six other major nuclear supplier states—Canada, France, West Germany, Japan, the United Kingdom, and the Soviet Union—were invited.

Later, eight other minor or potential suppliers were summoned to join the discussions. This second group has been called the London Group in reference to the location of its series of secret meetings beginning in the fall of 1974.

While construction proceeded on commercial breeder reactors and reprocessing plants in Europe and Japan, President Carter persuaded the Western leaders meeting at the London Economic Summit in 1977 to participate in another series of meeting called the International Nuclear Fuel Cycle Evaluation (INFCE), which lasted until 1979. The objective was to study, but not to negotiate, possible ways of meeting energy needs without the use of technologies that would involve handling large amounts of plutonium, or what pejoratively has been called the "plutonium economy." But this time the meetings were not limited to the supplier states, in part because of the protests of importing states to the secret deliberations of the London Group. The 519 experts participating in the conference represented five IGOs and 46 countries comprising a cross-section of levels of nuclear development (Nye, 1981, p. 25). Even several of the threshold states which have not accepted the NPT took part in the discussions.

Nuclear-weapons-free-zones have been discussed by non-weapons states in several regions—Scandinavia, Africa, the Middle East, and South Asia, to mention a few. The most promising achievement thus far has been made by the Latin American states, twenty-two of which have fully accepted the 1967 Treaty of Tlatelolco that would keep the area completely free of nuclear weapons. Four key countries of the region—Argentina, Brazil, Chile, and Cuba—have not become full parties to the treaty. Argentina has announced its intention of ratifying the treaty, but has reservations about provisions pertaining to safeguards and peaceful explosions. Brazil and Chile are withholding final approval until the other holdouts have ratified it. The agreement is being implemented by a regional organization called OPANAL, the acronym for its Spanish name (see Redick, 1981, Spector, 1984).

Nuclear issues have attracted feverish activity by nongovernmental organizations, but by and large they have focused on the vertical proliferation of arms by NATO and the Warsaw Pact. Prominent among the NGOs concerned about the spread of nuclear arms are associations of scientists, such as the Pugwash

Movement and the Union of Concerned Scientists; groups of physicians anxious about their lack of capacity to render aid to victims of nuclear war, or what some of them call the final epidemic"; and religious groups such as the World Council of Churches and the National Conference of Bishops, who have moral reservations about nuclear weapons and the policies related to the possible use of them. Several associations have formed the NGO Disarmament Committee, which monitors discussions of the issue in United Nations bodies. Various groups opposed to nuclear power and in favor of alternative, or "appropriate," technologies that have cropped up in many countries have had the most active interest on the horizontal dimension of the proliferation problem. Such groups have little direct influence on international policy, although it is conceivable that they could have an indirect impact on national governments by raising issues and mobilizing public opinion. On the other side of the issue are trade associations, most notably the Atomic Industrial Forum, which represent the interests of a nuclear industry that has come upon hard times in recent years and has looked to exports to the Third World to take up the slack from a badly depressed market for reactors in the industrialized countries.

THE NON-PROLIFERATION TREATY AND SAFEGUARD PROCEDURES

The framework of international policy on the proliferation of nuclear weapons continues to be the Non-Proliferation Treaty (NPT), which came into force in 1970 after having been ratified by 40 states. The ostensible objective of the treaty was to minimize the likelihood of nuclear war by holding down the number of states having access to nuclear weapons, hopefully to the five that had manufactured and exploded a nuclear device prior to 1967. The designers of the treaty assumed that the only effective strategy for denying additional countries nuclear weapons would be to prevent them from achieving the *capacity* to produce them. The goal of nonproliferation was not to be achieved, however, at the expense of peaceful applications of the atom, which were then believed to hold great promise for meeting the world's future energy needs.

The NPT is composed of a few strenuously negotiated tradeoffs between several of the nuclear weapons states and a much larger group of nations that have not acquired such a capability. Under the terms of the treaty, the nuclear-weapons states are not to transfer nuclear weapons or explosive devices to any non-nuclear-weapons states nor to assist or to encourage them to manufacture their own nuclear weapons. Parties to the treaty which do not have nuclear weapons previously agree not to acquire them in the future, either by obtaining them from other states or by manufacturing them on their own. Taken in isolation, these two provisions establish a double standard which would give countries that had tested nuclear explosives by the end of 1967 a permanent monopoly over what are by far the most potent weapons. Several other articles were added to the NPT to compensate for this rather gross inequity in order to make it more palatable to the non-nuclear-weapons states. First, countries foregoing nuclear weapons are guaranteed the right to use nuclear energy for peaceful purposes and to participate in the "fullest possible" exchange of equipment, material, and technology for such programs, including useful byproducts of the text explosions conducted by the nuclear-weapons states. Second, the nuclear-weapons states are expected to make good faith efforts toward bringing an early end to the vertical arms race among themselves and eventually to achieving nuclear disarmament, thereby diminishing the military disadvantages of the states willing to forswear nuclear weapons. Finally, any state may withdraw from the treaty ninety days after issuing a statement showing how further compliance with the treaty in the face of "extraordinary event" jeopardizes its "supreme interests."

Concerned that the nonweapons states would be tempted to take advantage of the opportunities for the manufacture of bombs that are inherent in civilian nuclear power programs, the designers of the NPT were not content to make the commitment of these countries not to acquire nuclear weapons a matter for self-enforcement. Rather, it was agreed that nuclear materials would not be supplied to a nonweapons state that is party to the treaty unless it was willing to submit to international safeguards implemented by the IAEA. The objective of these safeguard procedures is to detect diversions of nuclear materials, including enriched uranium and plutonium, to the production of nuclear weapons or

other explosive devices. Most earlier transactions of nuclear materials were also subject to these safeguards. The NPT went one
step further, however, in requiring that the importing states agree
to "full-scope" safeguards, meaning that all of their nuclear activities would come under IAEA inspections, not simply the ones
that would be making use of the internationally transferred materials.

As planned, the safeguards would provide for the "timely detection" of any disappearance of fissionable materials in quantities
sufficient to build a nuclear explosive. In this context, "timely"
implies a monitoring system that will uncover any irregularities in
the handling of nuclear materials in less time than would be
needed by would-be proliferators to convert the materials into a
nuclear explosive (Moglewer, 1981, p. 24). IAEA procedures rely
on a detailed accounting of nuclear materials by operators of
civilian facilities which are later scrutinized by IAEA personnel
who are empowerred to make on-sight inspections and conduct
tests to verify the accuracy of the reports. The physical inventory
of fissile materials is compared with the amount that was originally made available for use in reactors, with the difference being
labeled MUF, which stands for "material unaccounted for." A
MUF figure greater than what would be expected in the normal
operation of a reactor is considered to be evidence of a possible
misuse of the fuel. In some case, the IAEA buttresses its accounting procedures with physical safeguards, such as remote control
television systems for on-sight surveillance and seals on con-
tainers of spent fuel, which if broken or tampered with is reason to
conclude that an illegal diversion of nuclear materials has taken
place (see Von Baeckmann, 1979, pp. 184–85). By 1980, the IAEA
had assumed responsibility for safeguards on some 700 nuclear
facilities around the world and was annually making more than a
thousand inspections in as many as fifty countries (Moglewer,
1981, p. 24; Schiff, 1984, p. 107). In requiring detailed international
on-sight inspections of a highly sensitive type of activity, these
safeguard procedures are an affront to the national sovereignty
that is unique among global policies (Schiff, 1984, p. 97).

It should be kept in mind that the IAEA's safeguard procedures
are not designed to prevent, but merely promptly to *detect*, illegal
transfers of fissile materials to military uses. In the event a significant diversion were uncovered, the IAEA is instructed to file a

report with the Security Council, a procedure that as yet has not been invoked. Those contemplating a diversion of fissile materials for weapons use may anticipate that detection could trigger a strong international reaction, including sanctions imposed by the nuclear supplier states acting on their own or collectively through the IAEA. A likely sanction would be to suspend further shipments of nuclear materials to the state guilty of violating the treaty. The possibility of having their civilian nuclear program crippled by international sanctions may be sufficient to deter a government from giving in to the temptation to use materials from safeguarded facilities to produce nuclear bombs.

The NPT is the most widely supported arms control treaty, having been ratified by 125 nonweapons states and three of nuclear weapons states—the United States, the Soviet Union, and the United Kingdom. France refuses to ratify the treaty, but has indicated it would comply with its provisions. Although initially critical of the treaty, China has shown no inclination to assist other countries to develop nuclear weapons. While most nonweapons states are among the ratifiers, it is significant that India and several of the threshold states having the greatest apparent interest in acquiring nuclear weapons have declined to become parties, namely Israel, Argentina, Brazil, Pakistan, and South Africa. Some, but not all, of the nuclear facilities of these countries have, nevertheless, been subjected to IAEA safeguards as a conditions for being supplied nuclear fuel. The Nuclear Nonproliferation Act adopted by the United States in 1978 denies nuclear exports to any nonweapons state that is unwilling to agree to full-scope safeguards on its peaceful nuclear activities, including those that have refused to accept the NPT.

BUTTRESSING THE NONPROLIFERATION REGIME

India's nuclear blast shook whatever complacency remained about the possibility of further proliferation of nuclear weapons in the aftermath of the NPT coming into effect in 1970. Hard questions were asked about the adequancy of the treaty and the effectiveness of the safeguard procedures of the IAEA. The United States, persistently among the most anxious about the spread of nuclear weapons, was instrumental in convening the London Nuclear Suppliers Group in 1974 to discuss how the international nonproliferation regime, which it considered to be very shaky, could be reinforced to prevent other countries from following India's path to devising a nuclear explosive.

One glaring shortcoming of the NPT was the absence of specific crtiteria for deciding which technologies and nuclear materials contribute to a country's ability to manufacture nuclear explosives and, therefore, should be subject to safeguards, as provided for in the treaty. Soon after adoption of the NPT, disagreements arose over the proliferation dangers of a growing list of items sometimes described as being in the nuclear "gray area." The situation was further complicated by swift increases in the world's nuclear trade and the emergence of new suppliers anxious to capture a share of the international reactor market. As international competition became more intense, exporters were tempted to be less strict in requiring safeguards on gray area items in order to gain competitive edge on rival suppliers (Potter, 1982, p. 109). To avoid having the NPT undermined by competition among suppliers for limited markets, it became imperative that nuclear exporters agree on a common policy regarding what types of purchases would be subjected to international safeguards.

The task of drawing up a set of guidelines for exporters was undertaken, first by the Zanggar Committee shortly after the NPT came into effect, and later by the London Group. In 1974, after several years of deliberations, the Zanggar Committee announced a "trigger list" of nuclear materials and technologies that should be delivered to nonweapons states only if provisions were made for the application of international safeguards to the facilities that would make use of them. Arrangements also were made for the supplier countries to report regularly to one another on their nuclear exports to nonweapons states so as to make it possible to detect combinations of purchases from several exporters that could be used to manufacture nuclear explosives (See Kapur, 1979, p. 58).

The London Group then took up the subject and in 1976 disclosed an export policy which included a more extensive trigger list. A slightly modified list was made public in 1978 after a series of meetings attended by an expanded group of suppliers. The

London Group's code of conduct for nuclear exporters is more significant, however, for its provision that "restraint" should be exercised in the sale of certain "sensitive" technologies, such as enrichment and reprocessing plants, that are considered high risks for proliferation because they produce weapons-grade materials and would be difficult to safeguard adequately. Moreover, the motivations for acquiring these types of facilities usually are suspect because their scale and cost renders them ill-suited to the nuclear power programs of most threshold states, who could contract for these services much more economically abroad. Thus, a supplier state would presumably exercise restraint by refusing to sell a sensitive technology unless it could be shown to be necessary for civilian programs and be subjected to ample safeguards.

During the Carter administration, the United States tried to convince the other advanced nuclear nations to proceed cautiously, if at all, on their own development of the components of the plutonium economy. If the advanced countries denied themselves these technologies, so it was argued, they would not be transferring large amounts of plutonium that could be converted to bombs in a matter of weeks, if not days. Moreover, they could withhold these proliferation prone breeder reactors and reprocessing plants without violating the NPT guarantees of a free flow of technologies useful in civilian programs. To set an example that he hoped other countries would follow, Carter announced that the United States would put a hold on further construction of its commerical reprocessing plant at Barnwell, South Carolina, and pilot breeder program at Clinch River, Tennessee.

These efforts were not successful in persuading other advanced countries to alter their plans. These states were willing, however, to participate in the International Nuclear Fuel Cycle Evaluation, which was convened to assess the possibility that modified or alternative fuel cycles may be less prone to diversions of weapons-grade materials. The report on the evaluation, issued in 1979, was a disappointment to Carter for its failure to conclude that breeder reactors, and the reprocessing done in conjunction with them, pose a greater proliferation danger than programs based on other fuel cycles. The report did suggest, however, that breeders are not appropriate for countries with small nuclear programs, and that reprocessing was not necessary for the safe storage of spent fuel, one reason or excuse often cited by threshold states for acquiring a reprocessing facility.

CONFLICT BETWEEN THE NUCLEAR "HAVES" AND "HAVE-NOTS"

Despite the technical nature of the nuclear subject, it was inevitable that the proliferation issue would from the beginning be a highly politicized one. Not only does the issue significantly affect the security interests of nations, but it is also intricately linked to strategies for meeting energy needs critical to their economic growth and development. The most conspicuous line of conflict over proliferation policy is between what for lack of better terms will be referred to as nuclear "have" and "have-not" states, or what is basically a North/South split between developed and less developed countries. On some issues, the division is more precisely between the states that possess or do not possess nuclear weapons; on others, disagreements arise between the nuclear supplier and importer states. The other prominent line of conflict, has arisen among the group of advanced nuclear states, with the United States, the dominant supplier, frequently being at odds with Japan and the European countries, which are simultaneously both suppliers and importers of nuclear products. Remarkably, proliferation has not been a significant bone of contention between the United States and the Soviet Union. It is noteworthy that the two superpowers frequently presented a united front in the negotiations leading up to the NPT, even to the point of submitting identical draft proposals. They have continued working together in the implementation of the treaty through regular exchanges of information.

From the list of more than one hundred parties to the NPT, it appears that most states, regardless of whether they possess nuclear weapons, perceive a common interest in preventing further proliferation. Within the group of nonweapons states, however, are many that have reservations about the double standard which allows the superpowers and other nuclear-weapons states to maintain what from their perspective is a nuclear hegemony over countries that have accepted the NPT prohibition on owning nuclear weapons. During the negotiations leading up to the NPT, representatives of the nonweapons states pushed hard for provisions that would obligate the nuclear powers to reduce and eventually to eliminate their nuclear arsenals, which in effect would make the nonproliferation treaty a step toward a larger goal of worldwide disarmament (SIPRI, 1979, p. 76).

Toward this end, the nonweapons states pushed for specific commitments from the nuclear powers that would be difficult for them to disregard in the future. One such possibility was a comprehensive test-ban treaty that would prohibit all nuclear tests, including those conducted underground, which were exempted from the Limited Test Ban Treaty of 1963. Other proposals included a ban on the production of new nuclear waspons and delivery systems and a substantial reduction in existing weapons stocks (SIPRI, 1979, p. 82). When it became apparent that the resistance by the United States and the Soviet Union to making specific commitments could jeopardize prospects for a nonproliferation treaty, delegates from the nonweapons states resigned themselves to accepting a vaguely worded promise from the superpowers to negotiate agreements aimed at nuclear disarmament, with no specified time limit. The nonweapons states continued to insist, however, on periodic reviews of compliance with the NPT and the right to withdraw from it if circumstances dictated. Implicit in the review process was the threat that an inability or unwillingness of the superpowers to make significant progress toward nuclear disarmament might cause the nonweapons states to reassess their commitment to the NPT. By making the treaty less durable, the nonweapons states believed they could put more pressure on the nuclear powers to honor their commitments (SIPRI, 1979, p. 122).

The nonweapons states have used the three NPT review conferences and the Special Sessions on Disarmament in 1978 and 1982 to direct sharp criticisms at the superpowers for their continued buildup of nuclear arms and the slow pace of arms control negotiations. At the 1975 review conference, the superpowers could point to the SALT I agreements freezing the number of land and submarine-based launches while constricting the deployment of ABM systems as being evidence of good faith efforts to carry out their treaty obligation to control nuclear arms. Having just failed to ratify the SALT II agreement, the United States could not make a similar claim convincingly at the 1980 review conference. Delegates to the 1982 Special Session on Disarmament could argue that the superpowers should accept widely discussed proposals for a mutual freeze on the testing, production, and deployment of new nuclear weapons as a way of demonstrating the sincerity of their intentions to comply with their NPT commitments on nuclear disarmament (Epstein, 1982, p. 4). The position of the superpowers was even less defensible at the 1985 review conference of the NPT given the suspension of arms control talks and their failure to sign any new agreements, while adding substantially to their nuclear arsenals.

India has been especially outspoken in criticizing the NPT, not only for the inequities, but also because of where it draws the line on proliferation. Under the terms of the treaty, any nuclear explosion is considered tantamount to possessing nuclear weapons. India's position is that the two are different, since even after a test explosion, which may be necessary for legitimate peaceful applications of the atom, a major policy decision must still be made on whether to go ahead with the manufacture of nuclear weapons. Furthermore, from the Indian perspective, the threat to exercise an option to build nuclear weapons, as demonstrated by a successful test explosion, is one of the few ways the nonweapons states can put pressure on the nuclear powers to seriously consider reducing their arsenals (Kapur, 1979, p. 146). Ironically, the failure of international policy makers to distinguish between test explosions and a nuclear weapons capability means that once a country such as India has tested an explosive device, it has little more to lose from exercising its option to develop a nuclear arsenal.

Nuclear trade policies have also been a subject of contention between the nuclear haves and have-nots. Some nonweapons states call attention to the promise of guaranteed access to the technology and materials needed for civilian nuclear programs as an inducement for them to accept the NPT and, thus, to forgo nuclear weapons. Having become parties to the treaty, they are disturbed that the nuclear suppliers have shown little inclination to give them preferential treatment over the nonratifiers in their export policies. A curious feature of the NPT is its failure to require that "full-scope" safeguards be applied to transfers of nuclear material to the nonparties among the nonweapons states, whereas those which are parties to the treaty are obligated to accept them. As a result, some critics complain that nuclear materials and technology have been supplied even more generously to nonparty states and with only limited safeguards being required (Beres, 1980, p. 231). Unless the nuclear trade with the nonratifiers is restricted, the ratifiers derive no advantage from their willingness to comply with international policy and may be tempted to withdraw from the treaty (Greenwood and Haffa, 1981, p. 24).

The importing states argue that they have been betrayed by the efforts of supplier states to agree on the conditions and restrictions that will apply to trade in the nuclear field. The fact that meetings of the London Group were closed to outside scrutiny gave them reason to accuse the supplier states of acting as an exporters' cartel (Khan, 1982, p. 57). From the perspective of the importers, any refusal to sell "sensitive" facilities, such as reprocessing plants, violates the NPT guarantees of full access to the technologies needed for peaceful applications of atomic energy, so long as they submit their facilities to international inspections. Furthermore, they contend that restrictive export policies perpetuate their dependence on sometime unreliable foreign sources of fuel. Thus, not only would the nuclear powers enjoy a monopoly on the armaments, but also on other advanced civilian technologies (Imai and Rowan, 1980, p. 23). In recent assessments of the NPT, the importing states of the Third World have insisted that they should have a greater role in any decisions about modifying the nonproliferation regime (Scheinman, 1981, p. 101).

Underlying these disagreements between the nuclear have and have-not nations are different perceptions of the NPT. The have-nots look upon the treaty as a negotiated package of trade-offs between nuclear weapons and nonweapons states expressed in the form of a contractual obligation that is to be taken literally as the last word on nonproliferation. The nuclear haves—especially those with nuclear weapons—interpret the treaty more flexibly, arguing that changing circumstances and new dangers dictate adjustments. To the advanced nuclear states, nonproliferation measures compromise the core of the treaty, whereas the other articles are of only secondary importance. Included in this second category are guarantees that the nonweapons states will have access to nuclear materials and technology and the commitment of the nuclear powers to reduce their armaments. The nuclear have-nots consider it unfair that their commitments are viewed as being irrevocable, while the nuclear haves have been allowed to reinterpret their obligations (Kapur, 1979, p. 86). The have states rationalize these apparent inequities by arguing that all states, including those without nuclear weapons, have a stake in preventing proliferation by whatever means are necessary (SIPRI, 1979, p. 128).

TENSIONS AMONG THE SUPPLIER STATES

The nuclear have-not states have been frustrated by the unity of the technologically advanced supplier countries, especially when they met clandestinely as the London Group. From the perspective of the supplier states, however, the discord among them on nuclear issues at times has been more apparent than their common interest in containing proliferation. During the Ford and Carter administrations, the United States was sharply at odds on nuclear issues with several of its Western allies which had been investing heavily in the nuclear field, namely France, West Germany, the United Kingdom, and Japan. Canada and Australia, both of which, like the United States, are significant suppliers of natural uranium ore, generally have been more in agreement with American policies.

Trading policies in the nuclear field have been one major point of contention among the Western supplier states. In the aftermath of India's successful test, the United States was alarmed at the willingness of several European countries to sell what it regarded to be proliferation-prone technologies to nonweapons states, some of which for political reasons were thought to be high political risks for manufacturing nuclear weapons. Of particular concern to the United States were French plans to sell reprocessing plants to Pakistan and Korea, neither of which were cost-effective additions to civilian programs, and a reactor requiring highly enriched uranium fuel suitable for explosives to Iraq. The United States was also sharply critical of a German contract with Brazil to provide both enrichment and reprocessing facilities, despite its provisions for strict safeguards approved by the IAEA. Subsequently, South Korea gave in to pressure from the United States to cancel its purchases from France, which in turn was eventually persuaded to revoke its sale to Pakistan. West Germany and Brazil were not, however, willing to renegotiate their contracts. The more flexible export policies on these "sensitive" technologies enabled the European suppliers to "sweeten" the deals they offered potential importers in hopes of wresting away a share of limited international market over which American firms have traditionally enjoyed a virtual monopoly. Foreign sales have been important to new reactor suppliers as a way of reducing unit costs which otherwise would be prohibitively large given the small size of their domestic markets.

The wisdom of proceeding with the plutonium economy was a second major issue that split Western supplier states. The Carter administration took the position that the breeder fuel cycle was so risky for proliferation that the advanced nuclear nations would be prudent to deny it even to themselves. The European and Japanese governments were far more committed to the breeder reactor and reprocessing and had fewer qualms about the extent to which such facilities would increase the risk of proliferation. To them, outlawing plutonium would be like throwing away vitally needed energy (Meller, 1980, p. 103). Being much more reliant on imports of fossil fuels than the United States, they looked to nuclear power as a way of becoming less dependent on OPEC for critical energy resources. Here again in the case of reactor fuel they were in a situation of dependency, but this time on the United States. The United States was not perceived as a reliable source following a surprise announcement in 1974 that it could not enter into any new long-term contracts to supply reactor fuel. Having been encouraged earlier by the United States to reprocess the spent fuel to make better use of what were then believed to be scarce reserves of uranium, the American allies embarked on a strategy to become more nearly self-reliant in nuclear fuels, which included going ahead with the plutonium economy (Brenner, 1981, pp. 14–17). Germany's deal with Brazil was also a way of lessening its dependence on the United States as a source of uranium and enriched reactor fuel.

This issue was brought to a head by the 1978 Nuclear Non-Proliferation Act of the United States which its allies looked upon as an unwelcomed attempt to interfere with their nuclear policies. The strongest protests were raised against the strict "end use" restrictions on all reactor fuel supplied by the United States, even on that which came from the other sources, but was used in equipment imported from the United States. Such fuel was to be reprocessed or transferred to a third country only with the consent of the United States. The members of EURATOM were exempted from the restrictive policy, but even they were concerned that the United States would decide to curtail the flow of spent fuel from other countries, thereby undermining the profitability of the large investments made by France and the United Kingdom in commercial reprocessing facilities. The Japanese resented the way the act applied uniformly to all nonweapons countries, thus putting advanced nuclear countries, which had long since rejected nuclear weapons, in the same category as less advanced countries, such as Pakistan, that appear to be strongly motivated to acquire a bomb (Foch, 1980, p. 126). To its allies, it appeared as if the United States was making a last ditch effort to reestablish its eroding dominance in the nuclear field by thwarting their efforts to free themselves from a dependence on its exports of reactor fuel. In recent years, tensions have lessened among the supplier states, as the Reagan administration adopted a more relaxed policy that poses fewer obstacles to the plans of the other nuclear supplier states to engage in plutonium reprocessing.

PREVENTING VERSUS DISCOURAGING PROLIFERATION

There are two basic policy approaches to forestalling further spread of nuclear weapons. One tries to *prevent* proliferation by making it as difficult as possible for additional states either to obtain nuclear weapons from foreign sources directly or to assemble what is needed to manufacture nuclear explosives themselves. The other approach seeks to *discourage* proliferation by influencing the decisions that governments make on whether to seek nuclear weapons. Preventing proliferation is largely a technical problem requiring the advice of experts on what should not be exported to nonweapons states and how to erect obstacles to the use of their civilian nuclear programs for military purposes. (Military force can also be used to prevent proliferation, as was demonstrated by Israel's attack on Iraq's Osirak reactor in 1981.) Discouraging proliferation poses more of a political challenge involving incentives or sanctions as instruments of influence. The existing nonproliferation regime, featuring IAEA safeguards and restraint on the export of sensitive technologies by the London Club, is weighted toward prevention. It is buttressed, however, by the threat that new entries into the nuclear weapons club will be condemned and be subjected to stiff sanctions. Moreover, the NPT offers a carrot to states willing to deny themselves nuclear weapons in the prospect of international assistance on the peaceful applications of nuclear power.

Can the preventive capacity of the existing nonproliferation regime be enhanced? One approach simply would strengthen the current safeguard procedures of the IAEA by increasing the frequency and thoroughness of inspections by an enlarged staff. Other possibilities have been proposed by those who consider the nuclear industry, as it is currently being developed, to be impossible to adequately safeguard. For example, it may be feasible to reduce the presence of pure plutonium or highly enriched uranium in the fuel cycle by the co-location of plants for reprocessing and fuel fabrication. Spiking fissile materials with highly radioactive substances might effectively protect them from diversion. Denaturing them with nonfissile isotopes would retard their explosive potential. Other strategies involve investments in new technologies, such as fueling reactors with thorium, which produce power from alternative nuclear fuel cycle that do not use or generate weapons-grade materials. Unfortunately, it may be two or three decades before such options could be made operational (Hildenbrandt, 1980, p. 103). These were among the potential "technological fixes" that were considered at INFCE, but none of them were found to be fully adequate to prevent proliferation without significantly hindering plans for the development of nuclear power.

Another strategy for preventing proliferation would "internationalize" the links in the nuclear field cycle that involve handling weapons-grade materials. Clustering these facilities in special internationally operated nuclear parks would make surveillance easier and reduce the risks inherent in transporting dangerous substances (Meller, 1980). Such a proposal was first offered by the United States in the form of the Baruch Plan when it enjoyed a nuclear weapons monopoly at the end of World War II. How serious the United States was about having nuclear power and weapons controlled internationally was never put to a test because of the quick rejection of the plan by the Soviet Union. Concerns about the plutonium economy have sparked renewed interest in the possibility of internationalizing sensitive facilities. Proponents hoped that international ownership and management of enrichment and reprocessing services would be looked upon as being sufficiently reliable and free of political encumberments to dissuade individual countries from investing large amounts of capital in their own facilities.

Advocates of the prevention approach believe that it is still possible to erect adequate impediments to proliferation and that without such safeguards there is little prospect of stemming the spread of nuclear weapons. In other circles, however, there is a growing sense of resignation that it may be impossible over the long run to prevent determined countries from joining the nuclear club. Not only that, but the prevention policies may have the undesired effect of spurring the threshold states into trying to become self-reliant in nuclear materials and technology and, in doing so, to develop a capacity to produce nuclear weapons. If this is the case, the best nonproliferation strategy may be not to rely on safeguards, but to fall back on ways of persuading coutries not to exercise an option to build nuclear weapons.

Proliferation can be discouraged by emphasizing the disadvantages of joining the nuclear weapons club. The prospect of strong penalties imposed by other members of the international community acting unilaterally or as a group may be enough to deter a decision to acquire nuclear weapons. Aside from a cut-off of technical assistance and trade in the nuclear field, the sanctions might include a reevaluation of security guarantees or alliance relationships, a denial of loans from the World Bank, or an expulsion from a key international agency (Dunn, 1982, p. 108). There is often, however, a reluctance to apply strong penalties, especially if other foreign policy objectives are at stake or if the penalties would be costly to the countries being asked to impose them. Moreover, some countries are much better able to withstand sanctions than others and are less likely to give in to international pressures.

Reducing the insecurities that prompt the interest of states in nuclear weapons would be a more positive way of discouraging proliferation. Insecure states could, for example, be offered more conventional arms as an alternative to nuclear weapons for satisfying their defensive needs. This strategy has the drawback of posing what has been called the "dove's dilemma" in that it might fuel conventional arms races, which can be as serious a threat to world peace as the spread of nuclear weapons (Dunn, 1981). Some states might take advantage of the situation by threatening to manufacture nuclear weapons as bargaining leverage for obtaining conventional weapons that would otherwise be unavailable to them. It should also be kept in mind that several of the most insecure, threshold states are political "pariahs" in the international community, namely Israel, South Africa, South Korea, and Taiwan, which most governments would be reluctant to help arm. Finally, there is no guarantee that a country buttressed with conventional weapons would not later decide to add nuclear weapons to its arsenal. The anxieties of nonweapons states might also be allayed by a commitment of the militarily powerful to come to their defense in the event they are attacked. This policy option has little appeal to potential defenders that are reluctant to become entangled in regional conflicts on the side of countries they would not otherwise be inclined to support.

The nuclear powers have been called upon to take steps to reduce the threat that their weapons pose to other countries as a way of discouraging proliferation. Promises could be made never to use nuclear weapons against states that agree to forgo them, a commitment that the superpowers have been reluctant to make on an unconditional basis (Myrdal, 1982, p. 182). The United States views its nuclear weapons as a deterrent to attacks by countries, such as those of Eastern Europe, that have threatening conventional capabilities. Interest in joining the nuclear club could perhaps also be held down if the superpowers were to refrain from flaunting their advantage in nuclear weapons and play down their usefulness as an instrument of foreign policy (Quester, 1981, p. 226). Also, by way of example, the nuclear-weapons states could agree to a comprehensive test ban that would hinder further development of nuclear weapons. The ultimate step would be to reduce significantly their nuclear arsenals, thereby complying with their responsibilities under the NPT. A decision by the nuclear powers to diminish their nuclear advantage could backfire, however, if the threshold states were to conclude that smaller arsenals would be more influential in a world in which military power is less centralized (Nye, 1981, p. 36; Quester, 1981, p. 218).

Thus, paradoxically, it may that vertical proliferation dampens incentives for horizontal proliferation (SIPRI, 1979, p. 27).

A third school of thought places little stock in either preventing or discouraging proliferation as long as a major commitment remains to the continued development of nuclear power. From this perspective, the best chance of preventing proliferation lies with a complete shutdown of the nuclear power industry, which it is contended is not only not needed, but also has become so expensive that it is losing out in the market to other energy sources. The demand for nuclear power can be reduced further both by using electricity only where it is needed—substituting more efficient, primary energy sources elsewhere (as in space heating) and by investing in techniques of conserving energy. Bombs could, of course, be produced using materials generated in research or production facilities, but without the cover of a civilian nuclear power program, the military motivations for operating them would be all too apparent to the international community which could make the would-be proliferator pay a heavy political price (Lovins et al., 1980, p. 1147).

ASSESSMENT AND PROSPECTS

Taking the most obvious criterion of effectiveness, stability in the number of nuclear weapons states, the nonproliferation regime appears to be remarkably successful. Despite the spread of the nuclear power industry into as many as forty countries, there continue to be only five states that are acknowledged to have nuclear weapons, the same number as when the negotiations on the NPT began two decades ago. The proverbial dam may be ready to break, however, as more countries become able to produce nuclear explosives, including some that have chosen not to accept the NPT. A successful test explosion by one or two additional countries could trigger an "if them, then us," type of chain reaction as other threshold states try to match the accomplishment for reasons of security or prestige. It may be more realistic to ask *when* the dam will break and in what fashion rather than *if* it will break (Potter, 1982, p. 11).

Quite possibly, additional countries will, in the short run, assume an ambiguous posture on nuclear weapons. Some may follow the lead of India in establishing a "nuclear option" based on a demonstrated capacity to manufacture bombs if circumstances dictate. Others may elect to build nuclear bombs secretly and not to acknowledge their existence, as may already be the case with Israel and the Republic of South Africa. Neither strategy is as likely to trigger as strong international condemnation and sanctions as a straightforward announcement that nuclear weapons have been acquired. Moreover, rumors of the availability of nuclear weapons can prove to be almost as effective a deterrent to would-be attackers as confirmed possession of them.

Many doubts have been expressed about whether the nonproliferation regime is equal to its task in view of changing circumstances and tensions that have been building in recent years. The rapid growth of the nuclear industry worldwide has stretched the limited resources the IAEA has to implement its safeguard procedures which, even under the best of circumstances, may be incapable of a reliable and timely detection of the misuse of fissionable materials. The growing impatience of the nonweapons states over the failure of the United States and the Soviet Union to limit their vertical arms race and discontent over the export policies of supplier states were evident in the failure of the 1980 NPT Review Conference when the participants did not agree on a final statement similar to the one five years earlier in reaffirming a "strong common interest" in averting the further proliferation of nuclear weapons. Nevertheless, so far no country has renounced its commitment to the treaty, which may be evidence that the norms or practical disadvantages against proliferation are still strong. The sharpest conflict arises over the strategy for slowing the spread of nuclear weapons.

In dwelling on the NPT's frailties, the danger exists of exaggerating the role of the formal international regime in containing the spread of nuclear weapons. The decision of several countries with advanced nuclear technologies—Canada, Switzerland, Sweden, West Germany, Italy, and Japan—to pass up opportunities to acquire nuclear weapons would appear to be less a result of the NPT and its safeguards than a calculation of whether nuclear weapons would enhance their security or, alternatively, might even increase their insecurity by attracting preemptive attacks from other countries. The governments of some countries, Japan and Norway being notable examples, are unlikely to seek nuclear weapons in the face of stiff political opposition that is independent of international influences. Thus, there is reason for guarded optimism that a further weakening, or even a complete breakdown of the nonproliferation regime, would not necessarily be followed by additions to the nuclear weapons club.

The depressed condition of the commercial nuclear industry may also have an impact on the longer-range prospects for proliferation. The grandiose projections of the amount of nuclear power that would be generated at the turn of the century, which were issued at the time of the "energy crisis" of the mid-1970s, have been revised downward. Since then, orders for new reactors in the industrialized world have plummeted, and many previous orders have been cancelled or deferred, largely because of the spiraling costs of construction accompanied by a leveling off of energy demand during a period of slower economic growth. The exceptions to this trend have been France and the Soviet Union where the nuclear industry is owned and controlled by the central government which is less sensitive to the large economic risks than are private owners (Potter, 1982, p. 102–4). With fewer reactors than were predicted and alternative sources of enriched uranium, there is less reason to invest in the components of the plutonium economy. Moreover, if the nuclear route does not appear to be the answer to the energy needs of the highly developed countries, then Third World states would be less likely to invest their scarce capital in expensive nuclear projects that would contribute to a nuclear weapons option.

The task of keeping weapons grade material away from states committed to producing their own bombs has become more complicated with the breakdown of the monopoly maintained by the United States and Soviet Union on the supply of enriched uranium. In the 1970s, European corsortia became an alternative source of supply for nuclear materials and technology. Now there is the prospect of so-called "second tier" states, such as China, Argentina, Brazil, India, Spain, and South Africa, entering the nuclear market. As competition for a dwindling market shares intensifies, some of these states may give into pressures to be lax on requiring safeguards as a way of attracting customers.

In any event, the international community would be well advised to prepare for additions to the nuclear club, keeping in mind that the ultimate objective of international nonproliferation policy is to reduce the likelihood of nuclear war. In the event there are more nuclear weapons states, the challenge will be to prevent the use of nuclear weapons by design, miscalculation, or accident (Dunn, 1982, p. 150–51). The established nuclear weapons states should be prepared to advise any new members of the club on what can be done to reduce the likelihood of a nuclear war, such as the adoption of fail-safe procedures to guard against accidental or unauthorized uses or the refinement of strategies for rationally managing crises. Nuclear proliferation may even induce governments to behave in a more responsible fashion, although few in the international community would like to put this proposition to a test.

REFERENCES

Beres, Louis René (1980). *Apocalypse: Nuclear Catastophe in World Politics.* Chicago: University of Chicago Press.

Brenner, Michael J. (1981). *Nuclear Power and Non-Proliferation: The Remaking of U.S. Policy.* Cambridge: Cambridge University Press.

Dunn, Lewis A. (1981). "Some Reflections on the 'Dove's Dilemma'," *International Organization,* Vol. 35, No. 1 (Winter), pp. 181–92.

Dunn, Lewis A. (1982). *Controlling the Bomb: Nuclear Proliferation in the 1980s.* New Haven: Yale University Press.

Ehrlich, Paul R., Carl Sagan, Donald Kennedy, and Walter Roberts (1984). *The Cold and the Dark: The World after Nuclear War.* New York: W. W. Norton.

Epstein, William (1982). "For a Mutual Nuclear Freeze," *Disarmament Times,* Vol. 5, No. 19 (July 7), p. 4.

Foch, René (1980). "European Views on Nonproliferation," pp. 121–32 in Eberhard Meller (ed.), *Internationalization: An Alternative to Nuclear Proliferation?* Cambridge, Mass.: Oelgeschlager, Gunn & Hain.

Gilinski, Victor (1978). "Nuclear Energy and Proliferation of Nuclear Weapons," pp. 83–91 in Albert Wohlstetter, Victor Gilinski, Robert Gillette, and Roberta Wohlstetter, *Nuclear Policies: Fuel Without the Bomb.* Cambridge, Mass.: Ballinger, 1978.

Greenwood, Ted, and Robert Haffa, Jr. (1981). "Supply-Side Non-Proliferation," *Foreign Policy,* No. 42 (Spring), pp. 125–40.

Hildenbrand, Gunter (1980). "Nuclear Energy, Nuclear Exports, and the Nonproliferation of Nuclear Weapons," pp. 83–108 in Eberhard Meller (ed.), *Internationalization: An Alternative to Nuclear Proliferation?* Cambridge, Mass.: Oelgeschlager, Gunn & Hain.

Imai, Ryukichi and Henry S. Rowen (1980). *Nuclear Energy and Nuclear Proliferation: Japanese and American Views*. Boulder, Co.: Westview Press.

Kahn, Munir Ahmad (1982). "Nuclear Energy and International Cooperation: A Third World Perception of the Erosion of Confidence," pp. 48–67 in Ian Smart (ed.), *World Nuclear Energy: Toward a Bargain of Confidence*. Baltimore: Johns Hopkins University Press.

Kapur, Ashok (1979). *International Nuclear Proliferation: Multilateral Diplomacy and Regional Aspects*. New York: Praeger.

Levanthal, Paul (1985). "Flaws in the Non-Proliferation Treaty," *Bulletin of the Atomic Scientists,* Vol. 41, No. 8 (September), pp. 12–15.

Lovins, Amory B., L. Hunter Lovins, and Leonard Ross (1980). "Nuclear Power and Nuclear Bombs," *Foreign Affairs,* Vol. 58, No. 5, 1137–1177.

Meller, Eberhard (ed.) (1980). *Internationalization: An alternative to Nuclear Proliferation?* Cambridge, Mass.: Oelgeschlager, Gunn and Hain.

Meyer, Stephen M. (1984). *The Dynamics of Nuclear Proliferation*. Chicago: University of Chicago Press.

Moglewer, Sidney (1981). "IAEA Safeguards and Non-proliferation," *Bulletin of the Atomic Scientists,* Vol. 37, No. 8 (October), pp. 24–29.

Myrdal, Alva (1982). *The Game of Disarmament*. New York: Pantheon Books.

Neff, Thomas (1984). *The International Uranium Market*. Cambridge, Mass.: Ballinger.

Nye, Joseph S. (1981). "Maintaining a Nonproliferation Regime," *International Organization,* Vol. 35, No. 1 (Winter), pp. 15–38.

Potter, William C. (1982). *Nuclear Power and Nonproliferation: An Interdisciplinary Perspective*. Cambridge, Mass.: Oelgeschlager, Gunn & Hain.

Quester, George H. (1981). "Preventing Proliferation: The Impact on International Politics," *International Organization,* Vol. 35, No. 1 (Winter), pp. 213–40.

Reddick, John P. (1981). "The Tlatelolco Regime and Nonproliferation in Latin America," *International Organization,* Vol. 35, No. 1 (Winter), pp. 103–34.

Scheinman, Lawrence (1981). "Multinational Alternatives and Nuclear Nonproliferation," *International Organization,* Vol. 35, No. 1 (Winter), pp. 77–102.

Schiff, Benjamin N. (1984). *International Nuclear Technology Transfer: Dilemmas of Dissemination and Control*. London: Rowman & Allanheld.

Sivard, Ruth Leger (1982). *World Military and Social Expenditures 1982*. Leesburg, Va.: WMSE Publications.

Spector, Leonard S. (1984). *Nuclear Proliferation Today.* New York: Vintage Books.

Stockholm International Peace Research Institute (SIPRI) (1979). *Postures for Nonproliferation: Arms Limitation and Security policies to Minimize Nuclear Proliferation.* London: Taylor and Francis, Ltd.

Thomas, Raju G. C. (1981). "The Nuclear Club and Affirmative Action," *Bulletin of the Atomic Scientists,* Vol. 37, No. 5 (May), pp. 60–63.

United Nations (1980). *Nuclear Weapons: Report of the Secretary General.* Brookline, Mass.: Autumn Books.

Von Baeckmann, A. (1979). "IAEA Safeguards Technology," pp. 179–86 in SIPRI, *Postures for Nonproliferation: Arms Limitation and Security Policies to Minimize Nuclear Proliferation.* London: Taylor and Francis, Ltd.

Walker, William (1984). "Proliferation and Nuclear Trade: A Look Ahead," *Bulletin of the Atomic Scientists,* Vol. 40, No. 4, pp. 29–33.

Wohlstetter, Albert (1979). *Swords from Plowshares: The Military Potential of Civilian Nuclear Energy.* Chicago: University of Chicago Press.

6 ECONOMIC DEVELOPMENT

Addressing the Needs of the World's Poor

In a speech in Nairobi in 1973, Robert McNamara, then president of the World Bank, observed that as many as 650 million people live in "absolute poverty," which he defined as being "conditions of deprivation that fall below any rational definition of human decency" (quoted in Clark, 1981, p. 177). Many of these people can be found living in the cramped and squalid conditions of shanty towns that spring up daily in the mushrooming Third World metropolises, but the vast majority reside in austere villages scattered about the countryside, the greatest concentrations being in South Asia and sub-Sahara Africa. With their meager capacity to produce or purchase food, most of the absolute poor suffer from malnutrition. The water they drink, which for many can be obtained only at great effort, is often contaminated, in part because there are no facilities for the sanitary disposal of human waste. Even though people are more prone to illnesses under these conditions, there are few doctors, clinics, and hospitals to which the poor can turn for medical care. The toll in human lives is evident in high infant mortality rates, stunted growth, mental retardation, low levels of energy, and shortened life expectancies. Having had no opportunitites for education, most adults among the absolute poor are illiterate and unskilled; thus, there is little hope of escaping the grinding proverty into which they are born.

The living conditions of the "absolute poor" are not much worse than those of the rest of the poorest half of the world's population. Nor are they unlike the standard of living endured by all of but the smallest of elites during preindustrial times. Their plight, however, stands in stark contrast to the comfortable existence of nearly all of the 30 percent of world's population living in countries that are called "developed," which have undergone an industrial and technological revolution over the past century and a half. Some have become welfare societies which have virtually eliminated poverty by guaranteeing all citizens enough income for basic necessities of life, as well as education, medical care, and retirement security. The most advanced of the developed countries have become "post-industrial" societies in which consumers, satiated with material possessions, use an increasing share of their incomes for services. Detractors put these countries in an "overdeveloped" category, in view of their ostentatious consumerism which to them seems inappropriate given the poverty that so much of humanity continues to endure and the unnecessary depletion of scarce, nonrenewable resources.

A few selected statistics portray vividly the differences between living conditions in the world's poorest and richest societies. Let us begin by comparing figures on GNP, a widely used but admittedly imperfect indicator of what a country produces and, thus, the general level of economic well-being of its citizens. It is remarkable that the developed countries, in which less than one-quarter of the world's population resides, account for more that three-quarters of the world's GNP. In contrast, the poorest fifth of humanity receives only 2 percent of the world's income (Sivard, 1982, p. 5). The GNP/capital of most of the highly developed countries of western Europe and North America had surpassed $10,000 compared to a mean of less than $300 for the more than two billion in thirty-four of the lowest income countries (World Bank, 1984, pp. 218–19). Figures on energy consumption are often used as an alternative to GNP as an indicator of industrialization. Here too the differences are especially striking. In the United States the average citizen annually consumes an amount of energy that is equivalent to what is contained in more than 11,000 kilograms of coal whereas the average citizen of India uses the energy equivalent of only 237 kilograms of coal (Sivard, 1981, pp. 37–39).

The contrast in living standards can also be seen in statistics on social conditions. The average caloric intake of food in the developed countries was 3,426 in 1980, half again as large as the 2,360 figure for the Third World. Virtually all citizens of the developed regions have access to clean water, compared to fewer than half in the less developed countries, and only 11 percent in

Nepal. The consequences are apparent in infant mortality rates, which are less than 20 per 1000 live births for most developed countries, far fewer than 96 figure for the Third World as a whole and the one in every five infants that dies in some African countries. Likewise, literacy is almost universal in the developed world compared to less than 60 percent of the adult population of the Third World that has even the most basic of skills in reading and writing. In Afghanistan, the literacy rate is only 20 percent, in Somalia it is a dismal 6 percent (Sivard, 1983, pp. 36–41).

The prevalence of poverty in the world along with the highly skewed distribution of the world's wealth has become one of the most prominent topics on the agendas of many international institutions. Initially, the task for the international community was seen as one of helping the poorer countries to quicken the pace of development that had transformed Europe and North America into highly industrialized societies. The less developed countries would be advised on how to use their natural and human resources most effectively and limited amounts of economic assistance would be given to start the development process. As their societies developed, citizens of the Third World countries would benefit from a general enhancement of their living conditions and fewer would live in poverty. Over the past two decades, a more radical outlook on the nature of the development problem has been pushed to the forefront by Third World leaders. Contending that the international economic order that has prevailed since World War II not only hinders but even thwarts their development efforts, they have proposed fundamental reforms which became known as the "new international economic order," or the NIEO for short, when brought before the General Assembly as a package in 1974. Since then, the possibility of implementing parts of the NIEO has been the subject of an extensive series of discussions and negotiations between developed and less developed countries in a variety of international forums, which is informally called the "North-South dialogue."

DEVELOPMENT AS A GLOBAL ISSUE

Is it appropriate that development should have become such a prominent item on global agendas? Several reasons can be cited for answering this question in the affirmative. What first comes to mind is the natural tendency for human beings to have compassion for the suffering of other human beings, regardless of their nationality or country of residence, especially when the means are at hand for improving the life circumstances of the poor. These humanitarian tendencies also underlie efforts to promote human rights which, as interpreted in the Universal Declaration on Human Rights, have been extended to include "positive" rights to the basic necessities of life. Development is also an international issue by virtue of the pervasiveness of poverty in three-quarters of the world's states, many of which have made very little progress in improving living standards. Thus, even if development is looked upon as essentially a domestic problem, much can be learned by sharing the extensive expertise and experience that is available on how less developed countries can most effectively use their limited means to realize their economic objectives. And, for many of these countries, the only hope for breaking the grip of poverty on their population lies with assistance from outside.

A more compelling reason for global policies on development is the inability of all nations in an interdependent era to divorce their economic destinies from the outside world. This is especially true of the less developed countries whose fragile economies have been highly susceptible to outside disruptions. Some of the current difficulties they encounter are the legacy of a previous era during which their labor and natural resources were ruthlessly exploited by colonial rulers who displayed little apparent concern for the welfare of the societies they controlled. As colonialism waned, newly independent, underdeveloped countries had to contend with an international economic order that often stymied their ambitions for development. The prices paid on international markets for the primary products that many Third World nations depend upon for exports fluctuate, sometimes wildly. When averaged out, the prices have not kept pace with the increasing costs of the technology, capital goods, and petroleum that developing countries need to import. Efforts to diversify their economies have been hindered by trade barriers that prevent their manufactured goods from entering the large markets of the developed countries. In recent years, the tight monetary policies of the industrialized countries, in particular the United States, have led to a significant reduction in Third World exports, while driving up the interest rates on the money they borrow internationally to finance their development plans.

Transnational corporations, most of which are based in the advanced Western countries, are also a major outside factor in the development prospects of Third World states. They often make significant and unique contributions to the industrialization of less developed host countries by offering large amounts of capital, advanced technologies, and access to markets that would otherwise not be available to them. It is also apparent, however, that the investments can be inappropriate and exploitative and, consequently, distort more than facilitate the economic development of the host country. Self-defeating competition among less developed countries for private investment permits the transnational corporations to play one against another in negotiating concessions. As a result, the investments of the foreign-based firms may be very profitable, but contribute little to the economy of the host.

Should the development of the Third World be of concern to the rich, industrialized countries, so much so that they should be willing to make significant contributions to the process? One consideration is the significant impact of the developing countries on the world economy. In recent years they have been the destination of nearly one-quarter of the exports of the industrialized, Western nations (Sewell and Mathiason, 1982, p. 60). Thirty-six percent of the exports of the United States in 1983 went to developing countries, a greater share than the combined purchases of Japan and the European Common Market (see Tucker, 1985, pp. 182–84). Recently, the Third World has accounted for 45 percent of the exports of Japan (Wallace, 1982, p. 208). As repayment of the rapidly mounting international debts takes a greater share of the export revenues of leading Third World importers, such as Brazil and Mexico, their ability to import goods is likely to decline sharply, resulting in less economic growth and employment in the developed world. Thus, rather than being viewed simply as objects of aid and charity, the developing countries should be looked upon as important participants in an increasingly interdependent, international economic system (Cassen et al., 1982, p. 1). Some economists maintain that the best if not the only hope for stimulating the stagnating economies of the industrialized countries lies in the growth of the relatively less saturated markets of the developing countries. Thus, the Third World could become the "engine of growth" for the entire world economy (Sewell, 1979, pp. 71–73).

The underdeveloped condition of much of the Third World has numerous other international implications which can affect even the richest of countries. For example, widespread poverty amid frustrated hopes for a better life is a principal contributor to revolutions and other forms of political instability that jeopardize the foreign investments of firms based in the industrialized countries. Unemployment and economic misery occasionally trigger migrations from poor lands which heavily tax the social services of the neighboring countries, a prime example being the large, uninvited flow of people from Mexico and the Caribbean that enter the United States illegally to seek work and a better life. Societies with low average income tend also to have high population growth rates, which put pressure on global food supplies and cause the overuse of agricultural land. The poor also often lack the resources to preserve or protect the environment, as is the case with impoverished rural villagers who strip forested areas for firewood because they cannot afford other fuels. Scientists fear that the cumulative impact of deforestation throughout the Third World may be widespread climate changes that would affect agriculture on a global scale. Hard pressed to satisfy immediate needs of their citizens, governments of less developed countries are reluctant to invest their meager resources in controlling pollution which can have broader international consequences when it enters the atmosphere, river systems, and the oceans. These are but a few of the many reasons why the highly developed nations cannot afford to ignore the economic problems of the Third World.

THE MAKING OF INTERNATIONAL
DEVELOPMENT POLICY

In contrast to international discussions of most other policy issues which are confined to one or two international forums, economic development and the NIEO have been such pervasive issues on international agendas that it is difficult to identify very many global arenas in which these subjects haven't received at least some attention. Thus, it will be not be possible to offer a comprehensive accounting of the large number of arenas that address issues related to development. Instead, this section will identify a few of the focal points of policy making on development in which both developed and less developed countries participate. Some of these arenas have been taking up development questions in a general way while others have been preoccupied with the North-South dialogue that has been taking place over Third World proposals for an NIEO.

While the United Nations was created primarily to keep peace in the world, much of the activity of the organization has been directed toward economic problems, especially the development of the Third World. This concern with development reflects an assumption by its creators that economic problems are a major threat to international peace and, in more recent times, the influence of the large influx of newly independent, less developed members for which economic development is the overriding priority for international action. Much of the available time in the regular sessions of the General Assembly is taken up with development matters, high points of which were the declarations of the 1960s, 1970s, and 1980s as the First, Second, and Third Development Decades and the adoption of International Development Strategies for the latter two of these decades. ECOSOC, another of the central organs of the United Nations, devotes an even greater proportion of its agenda to the economic problems of the Third World and oversees a number of the development programs of the United Nations. Numerous United Nations sponsored conferences have addressed issues related to development, noteworthy examples being the World Food Conference (1974), the Conference on Science and Technology for Development (1979), the World Conference on Agrarian Reform and World Development (1979), the Conference on New and Renewable Sources of Energy (1981), and the Conference on the Least Developed Countries (1981).

Several of the specialized agencies affiliated with the United Nations are not only arenas for formulating policies that have a bearing on development, but are deeply involved in addressing development problems as actors. Such is the case with the FAO, which as one of its primary missions is to assist less developed countries increase their food production through the application of modern agricultural practices. The World Bank, in making decisions on which loan applications by less developed countries to fund, is in effect implementing a development policy. The IMF, though it was not set up as primarily a development agency, has a major role to play in helping Third World countries cope with balance of payments problems that jeopardize their capacity to import what is necessary for their development programs. Among the other specialized agencies that are active on development projects are the WHO, UNESCO, and the ILO.

While issues related to the NIEO have occasionally been a topic of discussion in the international bodies mentioned above, the most intensive talks on basic reforms to the world economic order have taken place at other locations, some specifically established for this purpose. The first such arena was the United Nations Conference on Trade and Development (UNCTAD), which held its initial meetings in 1964. UNCTAD was formed as an organ of the General Assembly at the request of less developed countries to be a forum in which their specific trade problems would be addressed more directly than they have in the GATT rounds of multilateral trade negotiations, which have primarily been a vehicle for reducing trade barriers among the advanced industrial countries.

The six major conferences of UNCTAD held thus far at four-year intervals, the most recent having taken place in Belgrade in 1983, stand out as major events in the continuing North-South dialogue. Acting on a recommendation made at UNCTAD I in 1964, the General Assembly established the United Nations Industrial Development Organization (UNIDO) to assist in the development of the new international economic order by promoting the growth of industry in the Third World. UNIDO's general conferences, held every fifth year, have been among the more contentious meetings between North and South on development issues. Recently, UNIDO became the sixteenth of the United Nations' specialized agencies.

Some of the most intensive discussions of the NIEO took place in a series of ad hoc arenas, beginning in the mid-1970's with the tumultuous Sixth Special Session of the General Assembly on the topic of "raw materials and development," which was held in April 1974 in the wake of OPEC's trade embargo and quadrupling of oil prices. After acrimonious debate, documents were approved that contained the demands of the less developed countries for a

NIEO which were the basis for the Charter of Economics Rights and Duties of States that was adopted by the General Assembly at its regular session later in the year. Talks aimed at implementing the provisions of the Charter, which is viewed as the definitive statement on the NIEO, began in the more restrained atmosphere of the General Assembly's Seventh Special Session on "development and international cooperation" held in 1975. There a decision was made to convene the Conference on International Economic Cooperation (CIEC), which met outside the context of the United Nations from 1975 to 1977 in Paris. Twenty-seven countries representing the industrialized world, the oil exporting states, and the other less developed countries were chosen to attend the CIEC, which it was hoped would be a more conducive setting for reaching agreements than the politically charged General Assembly with its unwieldy numbers.

Frustrated with what little progress was being made in implementing the NIEO, Third World leaders attempted to revitalize the floundering North-South dialogue by proposing a major series of international meetings which would address the problems their countries face in trade, energy, raw materials, development, and money and finance. In 1979 the General Assembly adopted a resolution calling for such a series of meetings to be called Global Negotiations. Specific plans were to be worked out at the Eleventh Special Session of General Assembly, which had already been scheduled for 1980 to review the NIEO. The Global Negotiations were to have commenced in 1981, but a continuing impasse on their format and agenda has led to indefinite postponements and doubts that they will ever be held. In the meantime, some of the issues to be discussed in the Global Negotiations were taken up briefly at a summit conference of twenty-two heads of state from both North and South, which was held at Cancun, Mexico, in October 1981, but again without breakthroughs on making the NIEO a reality (see Bhagwatti and Ruggie, 1984).

PARTICIPANTS IN THE NORTH-SOUTH DIALOGUE

The national governments participating in the making of international development policy, including the dialogue over the NIEO, have coalesced into three major groupings—the North, the

East, and the South—which have displayed a surprisingly high degree of unity in their bargaining positions. In some contexts, the label "North" is used to refer to the group of all developed countries in view of their location in the Northern Hemisphere to the north of most less developed nations. A few developed countries are exceptions, notably the Oceania states of Australia and New Zealand. The "North" in the so-called "North-South dialogue" is composed of smaller group of highly industralized democracies of Europe, North America, and Oceania, as well as Japan, the only Asian nation in the group, all of which have markets economies and foster private enterprise. It is to this economically dominant group of countries, led by the United States by virtue of its overwhelming size, that the less developed countries, the "South" in the development dialogue, have directed their requests for assistance and demands for international economic reforms. Most of the countries in the Southern group are located in Africa, Asia, and Latin America. The third major grouping of states on development issues is the Soviet bloc, known as the "East," which includes the socialist countries of Eastern Europe. The Soviet bloc has been on the sidelines of development debates expressing sympathy for the less developed countries whose problems they blame on exploitation by the capitalist countries. The bloc does not, however, have the apparent inclination or economic strength to offer much assistance to the Third World in pursuing its objectives for development.

These three groups of states meet frequently among themselves to coordinate their bargaining positions prior to major negotiating sessions between the blocs. The North has done much of its caucusing on development issues in the 24-nation Organization for Economic Cooperation and Development (OECD), which was established in 1961. Within the OECD is a group called the Developed Assistance Committee through which the major donor nations attempt to coordinate their policies on economic assistance. Reacting to the oil prices rises of 1973–74, many of these same countries, being heavily reliant on petroleum imports, formed the International Energy Agency (IEA) to counter the bargaining leverage of OPEC. In the mid-1970s the North attempted to link whatever concessions it would make on the NIEO to the willingness of OPEC to take steps to enhance the security of supply of oil and to moderate the price increases. Economic policies toward the Third World have also been on the agendas of the annual Economic Summits of the seven major Western economic powers, which began in 1974. Members of the European Economic Community worked out joint trade policies that affect the development plans of Third World countries, including special trade preferences granted to a group of former colonies known as the African, Caribbean, and Pacific (ACP) countries. Members of the Soviet bloc have formulated their posture on development-related issues in the Committee for Mutual Economic Assistance (CMEA), which in some respects is an Eastern equivalent of the OECD and the EEC.

It is remarkable that the states of the Third World have also been able to organize and present a cohesive front in the North-South dialogue. Not only do their large numbers—now approaching 130—work against unity, but also their differences in geographical size, population, level of economic development, type of economic development, type of economic and political systems, international alliances, and language and culture. Within the South are the desperately poor countries, including 31 that have been recognized as being "least developed," which have especially great needs for foreign assistance. States that are land-locked, located on islands, newly independent, or have chronic food deficits are also sometimes categorized as being especially disadvantaged (Lewis, 1982, p. 114–15). At the other extreme are the newly industrialized countries, known as NICs, whose dynamic economies have already been overtaking some of the lagging Northern countries in per capita GNP and the oil-rich OPEC countries which accumulated huge surpluses of foreign currencies following the price increases of the 1970s. A common antipathy for colonialism and the cause of self-determination initially brought the Third World states together in the period after World War II. Since the early 1960s, following the dismantling of the colonial empire, the basis for Southern unity shifted to common economic problems and the perception that a minority of wealthy states were controlling an economy that was keeping the majority of countries poor.

The coalition of Third World states, which has become such a major force in world politics, has it origins in a 1955 conference held at Bandung, Indonesia. It was attended by representatives from 29 invited African and Asian states, including several of influential Third World leaders of the era—Nehru, Chou En-lai, Nasser, and Sukarno, to mention a few. Six years later another meeting was held in Belgrade under the leadership of Tito, Nasser, and Nehru. The 26 countries that were invited to send delegations were selected for their refusal to align militarily with either of the superpowers, a criterion which excluded nearly half of the states that participated in the Bandung meetings (see Mortimer, 1980, pp. 6–13). This group of states, which has become known as the Non-Aligned Movement (NAM), has grown in numbers while maintaining its identity through periodic meetings, including summit conferences normally held at three year intervals.

The fourth summit of the group, convened in Algiers in 1973 and attended by delegations from 75 countries that included 50 heads of state, was especially notable for a new, higher level of unity among the NonAligned states that was reflected in a consensus on Algerian drafted proposals for a NIEO, which were presented to the Sixth Special Session of the General Assembly. The seventh and most recent summit of NAM, held in New Delhi in March 1983, was a comparatively subdued gathering attended by leaders from 101 of Third World countries as which the chairman, Indira Gandhi, attempted to move the association back to a neutral position following the efforts of Cuba's Fidel Castro to steer it toward the Soviet bloc when he hosted the sixth summit in Havana in 1979 (see Jackson, 1983).

The Non-Aligned Movement is only one of two associations used by the Third World nations to present a unified front on world issues. The second came together at the first meetings of UNCTAD in 1964, an organization which was initially proposed at the 1961 Belgrade meetings of the Non-Aligned. The organizers of UNCTAD I divided the countries attending into four lists for purposes of achieving a geographical balance in smaller groups. The countries on two of the lists—List A, which included the African and Asian states, and List C, comprising the Latin America nations—combined to form a caucusing group that became known as the Group of 77, in reference to the total number of countries on the two lists that year. The highly industrialized members of OECD appearing on List B and the Soviet bloc on List D have continued to negotiate in UNCTAD as separate groups.

The Group of 77 has maintained a relatively high degree of

unity, not only in UNCTAD, but also at many other arenas within the United Nations, including the headquarters in New York City and most of the specialized agencies, especially the World Bank, IMF, UNIDO, FAO, and UNESCO. Its presence has been felt in the United Nations Environment Programme as well as many of the megaconferences, including the Conference on the Law of the Sea. Though the name of the group has not changed, its membership had grown to 125 by 1982, which if its votes as a bloc, forms a three-fourths majority in many United Nations bodies. The Group of 77 has been meeting with ever-increasing frequently to discuss its negotiating positions, the most important ones being occasional ministerial gatherings prior to meetings of UNCTAD.

The relationship between these parallel tracks of Third World unity is an ambiguous one. Most less developed countries are members of both organizations, although roughly twenty members of the Group of 77 have not joined NAM. NAM is sometimes characterized as having more of a political emphasis in taking up issues such as the legitimacy of certain governments and the threat the nuclear arms race poses for the Third World, whereas the Group of 77 directs most of its energies more narrowly to economic issues, in particular to the NIEO. It could also be said that NAM is more included to politicize larger issues, and in doing so to generate controversey and dissension, whereas the Group of 77 tends to concentrate on specific, concrete matters that are being negotiated on a day-by-day basis in various United Nations bodies (Sauvant, 1981a, p. 5). Neither group has been able to assemble a very elaborate headquarters, and rather than maintaining a substantial permanent staff of its own, the Group of 77 has relied heavily on the secretariat of UNCTAD for the support of its activities, while NAM has looked to its chairing country to provide logistical support or the group.

Nongovernmental groups have also been active, and in some cases influential, participants in the North-South dialogue. Two are especially noteworthy, both of which are based in developed countries, but have lent considerable support to the cause of the South. Since it was established in 1969, the Overseas Development Council, most recently chaired by Robert McNamara, has done much to increase awareness of North-South issues in the developed countries, particularly in the United States, and to persuade Americans of how their destiny is intertwined with the

Third World in an era of economic interdependence. The other is the Independent Commission on International Development Issues organized and chaired by former West German Chancellor Willy Brandt. The so-called Brandt Commission published major reports in 1979 and 1983 which lend strong support to the Third World call for a NIEO. The first of the reports (Brandt Commission, 1979) was circulated widely and is credited with revitalizing the North-South dialogue at the time and setting in motion the plans for the Cancun summit meeting in 1981.

GROWTH AND BASIC NEEDS AS GOALS OF DEVELOPMENT POLICY

As with many other frequently used terms, the concept "development" has been defined in many different ways. All of these definitions of development have one thing in common, however; they imply an improvement in the quality of life and, thus, an interpretation of the "good life" that philosophers have attempted to describe for millennia. Furthermore, most would agree that development is a process through which people achieve a greater degree of their "potential as human beings," to borrow a phase from Mahatma Gandhi. To do so implies not only access to the basic necessities of life—in particular food, water, clothing, shelter, and medical care—but also satisfying social relationships, intellectual fulfillment through educational opportunities, a sense of self-esteem as a contributing member of one's society, and a degree of control over one's own destiny. At a societal level, development usually involves major changes in traditional values and beliefs, in the distribution of income and economic rewards, in types of employment, in social relationships including those of the family, and in governing institutions. Development is sometimes used interchangeably with the term "modernization," which more approrpiately refers to the adoption of the contemporary practices and lifestyles of the trend-setting societies, in this era the advanced industrialized societies of the West. Whether modernization, defined in this way, is a necessary or sufficient condition of development is a question on which there is sharp disagreement (Bryant and White, 1982, pp. 14–15).

In recent years considerable disagreement has arisen over what the immediate goals of international development policy should be. Traditionally, the emphasis has been on increasing the rate of *economic growth,* which is usually measured in GNP. Targets for annual growth in the GNPs of the less developed countries of 5, 6, and 7 percent were set for the first three Development Decades, respectively, up to half of which is taken up by the rapid rates of population growth that prevail in the Third World. Furthermore, it has been widely assumed that the most promising, route to economic growth is through rapid industrial growth following the example of the most advanced Western nations. Thus, the goal of an 8 percent annual growth in manufacturing output was set for the Second Development Decade; and UNIDO, meeting in Lima in 1975, set a goal of increasing the the Third World share of the world's industrial production from its current 9 percent to 25 percent by the year 2000. Industrial growth requires large amounts of capital most of which must be generated domestically through savings and reinvestment of profits. This can take place only when the gratification of desires of a society for consumer goods is postponed in the interests of building up an industrial base that promises to generate more for consumers in the future. Moreover, private investment is likely to be highest when the income and wealth of the society is concentrated so that the wealthier classes will have surplus income to use for this purpose. Eventually, if all works as predicted by economic theories, the fruits of growth will "trickle down" to the poorest classes, which will then be better off than if their immediate needs and desires had been addressed.

The apparent failure of economic growth to relieve the suffering of very poor, even where it has been most spectacular in the newly industrializing, or middle income, countries, has triggered a reassessment of the objectives of international development policy. To monitor more directly the living conditions of the poorer classes, the Overseas Development Council introduced the physical quality of life index (PQLI), which locates countries on a 100 point scale on the basis of statistics reported on infant mortality, life expectancy, and literacy. The developed countries uniformly have PQLI scores in excess of 90 which are consistent with their high GNP per capita. In the case of the less developed countries, however, major discrepancies can be observed in the two measures of development. For example, in 1982 Brazil and Mexico, two of the leading examples of newly industrialized countries, reported GNP per capitas in excess of $2000, yet had PQLI scores that were only in the mid-70s, which are similar to those of China and Sri Lanka, two countries that have GNP per capitas of barely over $300. Iraq, which reported a GNP per capita of $3000, had a PQLI score of only 51; Saudi Arabia with a GNP per capita of more than $16,000, which ranks up with those of the most highly developed countries of the West, has a PQLI figure of just 45, which is on a par with many of the poorer nations of the world (Tucker, 1985, pp 218–19).These statistics reveal in a rather dramatic way that growth measured in GNP per capita does not necessarily translate into an adequate standard of living for the poorest classes, which is an essential outcome of the process of development.

These discrepancies between economic growth measured in GNP per capita and basic social welfare did not escape the attention of international policy makers, including Robert McNamara, who is 1972 began calling attention to the "bottom 40 percent" of less developed societies who were not touched by growth (Clark, 1981, p. 173). The next break with an exclusive emphasis on growth and industrialization came in a resolution adopted at the 1976 World Employment Conference suggesting that *basic human needs* should be addressed as an integral part of development strategies (see Ghai et al., 1977). Since then, the goal of ensuring that the "basic needs" of all human beings will be satisfied, by the end of century has become a widely accepted objective of international development policy (see Ghosh, 1984). Under McNamara's direction, the World Bank began assessing the impact that impending loans would have on the conditions of the poorest classes of the recipient countries. Similarly, the expectation that the conditions of the poor would be improved was written into the foreign assistance legislation of the United States.

An emphasis upon satisfying basic needs implies some major changes in strategies of development. For one thing, the traditional policies designed to maximize economic growth are not directed at any special group, but at the society as a whole, in contrast to the basic needs approach which is targeted specifically at improving the standard of living of the underprivileged, preferably by increasing their income through new employment opportunities. Secondly, the usual emphasis of the growth strategies on industrialization tends to favor the large cities over rural areas. By contrast the basic needs approach would concentrate on rural areas where upwards of 85 percent of the absolute poor live (Loup, 1980, pp. 128–34). Finally, whereas the dynamics of the free market most effectively allocate a society's resources for economic growth, they tend to price the poor out of the market for food, shelter, and the other basic necessities of life. Thus, some government intervention in the economy may be necessary if the basic needs of the poorest classes are to be effectively addressed. Decisions must be made on what needs will be satisfied for which people and by what means. To meet the needs of the poor, major changes may be required in what a country produces and how what it produces is distributed.

ECONOMIC ASSISTANCE AS INTERNATIONAL DEVELOPMENT POLICY

The role to be played by outside economic assistance has been the leading issue in international development policy. In the aftermath of World War II, the United States, the sole major developed country to come through the war largely unscathed, was the only potential donor of substantial amounts of development assistance. At that time, however, the United States was not very receptive to requests for economic assistance from the less developed countries, even though it was willing to contribute heavily to rebuilding the war ravaged countries of Europe through the Marshall Plan. Likewise, the World Bank, as it was initially established, made loans almost exclusively for reconstruction of war damage despite the efforts of what was then a relatively small number of independent Third World countries to make economic development an equally important mission of the bank. With little international public assistance, the Third World countries were left to generate capital for development either from domestic sources or from private, foreign investors. The only concession the North was willing to make was a promise to reduce trade barriers that would open their markets to what was produced by the developing countries (Spero, 1985, p. 180).

Fearing the spread of communist influence in the newly independent, less developed regions, the United States and its allies quickly became more interested in the Third World. Beginning in the late 1950s, numerous international assistance programs were set up which offered less developed countries a variety of sources of modest amounts of outside public funding for their development programs. As of 1980, bilateral assistance programs, which channel funds directly to recipient countries, have been established by 30 donor countries, among which are 17 members of the OECD and 8 members of OPEC, as well as the Soviet Union (Camps, 1981, p. 273). Numerous multilateral channels have also been established, but they dispense less than half as much assistance as flows through the bilateral channels. The greatest sources of multilateral funding are the four major development banks: the World Bank and three regional development banks—the Inter-American, the Asian, and the African. Most of the technical assistance programs sponsored by the specialized agencies affiliated with the United Nations, such as FAO and WHO, are funded through the United Nations Development Programme (UNDP), which was established in 1965. Several other United Nations funds have been set up independent of the UNDP, including UNICEF, the World Food Program, and the International Fund for Agricultural Development. Multilateral assistance is also channeled through the European Common Market.

Despite being limited almost exclusively to funding the reconstruction of the war-torn countries after it came into existence in 1946, the World Bank has been the primary multilateral source of development funds. It has grown into a collection of three lending institutions now known as the World Bank Group. The original bank, the International Bank for Reconstruction and Development (IBRD), was designed to be a break-even operation that would loan money at interest rates comparable to those offered by private lenders. Because of these "hard" terms, a large proportion of the 1,700 loans made by IBRD to nearly 100 countries up to 1980 went to middle income countries which were thought to be good credit risks. Most of the $50 billion the IRBD had lent in this way was raised in the world's private capital markets with the backing of the bank's capital stock contributed by its 140 members, which by 1980 has grown to $35 billion. In 1956 a subsidiary of the IBRD was set up called the International Finance Corporation (IFC), which as of 1980 had distributed $10 billion in loans to private companies in less developed countries. In response to criticisms that the World Bank's lending policies effectively ruled out loans to the least developed countries, a third lending "window" was opened in 1960 called the International Development Association (IDA). By 1980 it had made $15 billion available to 50 of the poorest countries on "soft," or "concessional," terms. No interest is charged on IDA loans and 50 years is allowed for repayment of the principal, with a 10-year grace period before any payments are due. Even then, it is doubtful whether many of these loans will be repaid (Plano and Olton, 1982, pp. 133–35).

One of the objectives of the three United Nations development decades was to encourage a flow of financial resources to the less developed countries of at least one percent of the GNP of the developed countries. Seven-tenths of this amount was to be "official development assistance" from governments, dispensed through bilateral or multilateral channels, while the remainder would be private investments. Only the Netherlands, Norway, and Sweden among the seventeen OECD donors have achieved this .7 percent level for official assistance. Over the past decade, the economic aid program of the United States, which has not agreed to the target figure, has amounted to less than .30 percent of its GNP. Ironically, the development assistance of the OECD countries as a group declined from .51 percent of their combined GNPs in 1960 to .34 in 1970. Since then the percentage has edged up very slightly. Following, the oil price rises of 1973–74, several of the OPEC countries began to offer foreign assistance to a selected group of countries, which in 1975 was a relatively generous 2.9 percent of their combined GNP. The figure for the Arab members of OPEC was an even higher 5.7 percent. OPEC's percentages have fallen off considerably since then, but are still substantially higher than those of the OECD members (World Bank, 1984, pp. 252–53). In contrast, the assistance programs of the Soviet bloc have amounted to only .12 percent of its GNP (Wallace, 1982, p. 233).

In 1983 the OECD countries contributed a total of $27.5 billion in official development assistance to which the OPEC countries added nearly $7 billion and the Soviet bloc $2 billion (World Bank, 1984, p. 253). How significant is this level of assistance to the development programs of the Third World countries? The combined aid figures have been roughly comparable to private investments in the developing countries from the OECD countries during the early 1980s (Tucker, 1985, p. 238). Exports, however, are a much more important source of foreign revenues for the less developed countries. In 1983 their combined exports exceeded $500 billion, slightly less than half of which came from the non-OPEC countries in the group (see Tucker, 1985 p. 214–15). Thus, foreign assistance is a relatively insignificant source of funds for the Third World as a whole. Nevertheless, it can be a critical factor in the development plans of the least developed countries which have difficulty attracting private investments and competing in international markets (Lewis, 1982, p. 102). Unfortunately, the distribution of international assistance has been determined more by political considerations than the economic need of the potential recipients. Thus, Israel, hardly a less developed country, and Egypt have been the leading recipients of economic assistance from the OECD countries. Syria and Jordan have received more than half of OPEC's foreign assistance (Wallace, 1982, p. 240). Meanwhile, the assistance provided to the heavily populated countries, such as India, has in no way corresponded to their share of the population of the Third World, which is reflected in very small amounts received per capita.

THE NIEO AS A MORE RADICAL DEVELOPMENT STRATEGY

The international development strategies adopted in conjunction with the three United National Development Decades, which by and large have been accepted if not fully supported financially by the developed countries, can be implemented without major changes in the economic relationships between the North and South. Third World leaders have contended that these traditional approaches have failed and will continue to fail because they do not remove obstacles to economic development that are inherent in the prevailing international order, which was in place before many of their countries achieved independence. Viewing this existing economic order, which they did not participate in designing or creating, as being prejudicial to their interests, they proposed some basic reforms in what became known as the NIEO. These proposals for a NIEO, which have become the credo for a crusade by the Third World for greater economic justice, can be looked upon as a more radical international approach to development.

The NIEO is difficult to summarize, not simply because of the number and diversity of the proposals it encompasses, but also because the proposals have undergone considerable change since they were first presented. Among the principal issues the NIEO addresses are the prices of the commodities that many less developed countries rely heavily upon for export revenues, trade barriers that restrict access to the markets of the developed countries, the role of the International Monetary Fund in international finance, the funding of economic assistance programs, the investment practices of multinational corporations, agricultural modernization and food security, and the development of domestic energy resources. In advancing their proposals for a NIEO, Third World leaders have had several overriding economic and political goals. The economic goals are, first, accelerated growth and, second, a greater share of the world's income. These economic goals would be achieved, not by a massive redistribution of the wealth that has been accumulated by the developed countries, but by greater opportunities for the less developed countries to grow economically in the future (ul Haq, 1975, p. 158). Politically, the less developed countries desire to exercise more control over their own economic destiny and to participate on more equal terms with the industrialized countries in decisions that affect the international economic order.

Sharp fluctuations and a long-term decline in the prices of several key food stuffs, minerals, and other primary commodities on international markets have been a continuing source of frustration for many Third World countries which depend on them for export revenues. Encouraged by the success of OPEC in dictating high oil prices and resentful and pressures from the United States on some of its members to withdraw from the cartel, the less developed exporters of several commodities successfully pushed for a provision in the 1974 declarations on the NIEO that recognized the right of all states to form or join international producer associations without retaliation. Of greater importance, however, is an agreement reached at UNCTAD IV in 1976 calling for the establishment of the Integrated Programme for Commodities designed to stabilize the prices of primary products at a level that would be "fair" to both producing and consuming states. The program would manage prices and supplies in two ways. First, a "common fund" would be set up to purchase "buffer stocks" of the principal primary commodities to prevent a significant decline in prices should there be an oversupply on international markets. During periods of scarcity relative to demand, some of the stocks would be released to dampen price rises for the benefit of consumers. A 1980 agreement authorizing a modest Common Fund of $750 million still lacks 11 of the required ratifications. Second, agreements would be negotiated between the producers and consumers of 18 major commodities that would stabilize prices and index them to reflect changes in the prices of a representative group of manufactured goods. In return, the producers would guarantee importers an adequate supply of the commodities. In 1984, only five such agreements were in effect, specifically on sugar, coffee, cocoa, tin, and natural rubber. The future of even these few agreements is in serious doubt (see Puchala et al., 1984, p. 87).

Attempts by Third World countries to sell processed or manufactured goods in the larger markets of the developed world have often been frustrated by tariffs, quotas, and other protective import restrictions. The governments of less developed countries contend that the trade talks sponsored by GATT are unsuitable for negotiating reductions of these barriers because of two of the organization's guiding principles, "reciprocity" and "nondiscrimination." Complying with the principle of reciprocity would open their domestic markets to imports from the developed world, which may be too much competition for their fledgling industries. Moreover, they contend that for the manufactured goods produced in their countries to penetrate the markets of the developed nations, they must be subject to less stringent trade restrictions than are competing exports from other developed countries, which would be a clear violation of the principle of nondiscrimination. Thus, Third World states favor UNCTAD to GATT as a forum for discussing trade with the industrialized countries. Here they have pushed for unilateral tariff concessions in the form of a "generalized system of preferences" that would give their manufactured and semimanufactured exports an edge over industrialized competitors for the markets of developed countries. Preferences of this type were first extended on a temporary basis by the European Economic Community to its former colonies beginning in 1971 and shortly thereafter by Japan and the United States to all less developed countries. In recent years the less developed countries have asked that these preferences be made permanent and applicable to a broader range of goods (Loehr and Powelson, 1983, p. 38).

Proposals that would make more financial resources available for development have also been an integral part of the NIEO. The developed countries have been urged to meet if not exceed the standard for economic assistance that was set for the Development Decades, that being .7 percent of their GNPs. More of the assistance would be funneled through multinational as opposed to bilateral channels in order that it be allocated on economic criteria rather than on the basis of special political relationships and, moreover, that there be no stipulations on where the money may be spent. Beyond that, it is hoped that assistance programs could be funded on an automatic basis so that they would be "predictable, assured, and continuous" rather than being dependent on annual appropriations that fluctuate with the political whims of the legislative bodies of the donor states (Sauvant 1981b, p. 101). It has also been suggested that international sources of funding for assistance programs should be developed that would be independent of national donors, possibilities being international taxes on the use of the oceans for fishing, deep sea mining, and even navigation.

Another focal point of the Third World attack on the existing economic order has been the powerful IMF, which has the task of facilitating trade by stablizing the value of national currencies and by helping countries cope with temporary balance of payments deficits. Increasing the quotas contributed by the member countries has been proposed as a way of expanding the funding base of the IMF in proportion to the great growth in world trade over the past two decades and the mounting international debt of many less developed countries. A case has been made for the IMF to create more of its own currency called Special Drawing Rights (SDRs) and for a greater proportion of the SDRs to be allocated to loans to deficit-plagued, less developed countries. Finally, there have been appeals for an easing of the strict conditions that the IMF has imposed on the economies of recipient states to bring their exports and imports into balance and enable them to repay the loans. The economic austerity mandated by the IMF, it is argued, adds to the hardships of the poor in the borrowing countries and on several occasions has even touched off violent political reactions.

Finally, multinational corporations have been the subject of a litany of Third World complaints. Among the practices of the corporations in less developed countries that it is alleged hinder their development are wages rates that are a small fraction of what is paid for comparable work in the home country, a failure to reinvest the large profits earned in the Third World, the acquisition of capital locally in competition with domestic firms, the charging of excessive prices for technologies that are inappropriate in the host country, and the undervaluing of the contributions of the host country to the final product (Loehr and Powelson, 1983, pp. 63–94). The NIEO would give host governments more authority over the multinational corporations operating in their countries, including the right to "nationalize" foreign property and to determine themselves how much compensation will be paid to the previous owners. A more important feature of the NIEO, however, is the proposal for an enforceable, international "code of conduct" designed to ensure that multinational corporations operate in ways that are fairer to Third World host countries and contribute more to their economic development. Negotiations on such a code have been taking place in a special working group of the United Nations Commission on Transnational Corporations, which was established in 1976. A separate code of conduct on the transfer of technology is being negotiated elsewhere.

Numerous Western economists have questioned whether the NIEO would have the result desired by its proponents if fully implemented (see Bauer, 1981; Thompson, 1983; Loehr and Powelson, 1983). More specifically, there is skepticism that the NIEO would enhance the living conditions of the world's poorest people because several of its key provisions, in particular those pertaining to trade, would probably benefit the newly industrializing countries far more than those in the least developed category. Moreover, there is concern that the increased flow of money into the Third World countries as a result of the NIEO would be siphoned off by the modernized classes that are already comparatively well-off, rather than reaching the people with the lowest living standard. Other questions have been raised about the economic wisdom of the NIEO, including charges that it would create an environment that would be less conducive to Third World development than the existing one. For example, codes of conduct for multinational corporations could so undermine their profitability as to discourage future foreign investments. If the Integrated Programme for Commodities works according to plan, it would increase the price many less developed countries would pay for the primary goods they need to import while further enriching developed countries that export the same commodities. More flexibility in the monetary policies of IMF could trigger more inflation both within countries and internationally. Finally, any slowdown in the growth of the economies of the developed countries caused by the NIEO is likely to diminish foreign markets so essential to Third World development plans.

THE POLITICS OF INTERNATIONAL
DEVELOPMENT POLICY

As with any issue involving the distribution of wealth, it was perhaps inevitable that international policies on economic development would become highly politicized. Moreover, it was also predictable that development would be a much more salient issue for the Third World where poverty is prevalent and the current distribution of the world's wealth is believed to be unjust. It was not, however, until the mid-1960s, after most of the former colonies had achieved independence, that economic development replaced self-determination as the major international preoccupation of the Third World. Until then development was primarily a subject of "low" politics to be dealt with by technical ministries. The rise of the development issue to the realm of "high" politics began with the early meetings of NAM and the Group of 77. Then, with the adoption of the "Charter of Algiers" at the First Ministerial Meeting of the Group of 77 in 1967, Third World leaders initiated a concerted effort to draw the attention of their counterparts in the industrialized world to their proposals for international economic reforms (Sauvant, 1981a, pp. 3–4). They were not fully successful in doing this until the dramatic actions of OPEC in 1973–74 and the Sixth Special Session of the General Assembly of 1974. Since then development and the NIEO have been subjects of high politics for the advanced industrialized countries as well, as is apparent from the inclusion of these topics on the agendas of the annual Economic Summits of the major Western countries and from the attendance of President Reagan and several other Western heads of state at the North-South summit at Cancun, Mexico, in 1981.

Relations between North and South have vacillated between extremes of contentiousness and constructiveness. At times it appeared that the South was making the highest common denominator demands while the North the lowest common denominator offers (Lewis, 1982, p. 97). Such was the case at the General Assembly's special session and regular annual meetings of 1974 at which the major documents outlining the NIEO were debated and adopted, despite the strong opposition of the United States and other key developed countries. The ability of OPEC to turn the tables on the North in dictating oil prices gave a boost to the confidence of the South, which was reflected in the new assertiveness with which it pushed its demands for international economic reforms. A conciliatory period followed as the North displayed a willingness to discuss the NIEO and the south withdrew or modified some of its more radical demands. The South in effect acknowledged that strong language and overwhelming voting majorities in world assemblies do not compel the North to take the steps that are necessary to implement the NIEO. Toward the close of the decade, the South, impatient with what appeared to be procrastination in the negotiations on the part of the North, again began to press harder for the commencement of the Global Negotiations. In the more recent meetings, such as UNCTAD VI convened in June 1983, the delegates from the South have again adopted a more moderate and pragmatic strategy, apparently having concluded that it would be futile and probably counterproductive to push the North for significant concessions, given the seriousness of its own economic problems.

The Northern and Southern blocs have not been without internal conflicts, but these have been secondary to the struggle between the blocs. The United States, the leading Northern actor, has generally taken more of a "hard line" on development assistance and proposals for international economic reform than have several of the European countries, most notably the Netherlands and the Scandinavian nations (see Olson, 1981). The potential for intra-bloc conflict is much greater in the South with its many more states with widely diverging economic conditions and levels of development. For example, the vast majority of Third World states, being oil importers, have seen their limited export earnings consumed by the increased price of petroleum charged by the OPEC countries, which are also members of the Southern caucusing groups. Thus far, the possibility that the OPEC countries would use their leverage with the North for concessions on the NIEO along with their foreign assistance programs have kept them from becoming ostracized from the rest of the Third World. States that depend heavily on the export of primary resources stand to benefit from a stabilizing and indexing of prices of these commodities, but at the expense of the many resource-poor, less developed countries which would pay more for their imports. Similarly, the needs of the newly industrializing countries are very different from those of the least developed countries. To the former, access to the markets in the developed world is a paramount objective; to the latter a greater flow of development assistance is more important. The unity of the Third World can also be strained by the preferential treatment that some less developed countries have enjoyed with developed countries, in most cases their former colonial ruler. Finally, differences in economic and political philosophies have led to disputes. Cuba's attempts to orient the NAM toward the Soviet bloc when the group met in Havana in 1979 were resisted by a moderate majority that desired to keep the organization truly "non-aligned" (see Jackson, 1983, pp. 37–54).

International development policies affect groups within countries in different ways. Certain exporting industries in the industrial world stand to gain from the expanded markets generated by economic assistance to Third World countries as well as by more rapid growth in their economies generally. Other industries would face stiffer competition for domestic markets if trade restrictions are lifted on manufactured goods from less developed countries where much lower wage rates prevail. Who in the Third World countries will derive the greatest benefit from international development policies depends upon whether they are designed to stimulate industrialization and economic growth, in which case it would be the modernized sectors of the societies, which are concentrated in urban areas, or, alternatively, to satisfy "basic needs," in which case it will be the very poor, most of whom, live in rural areas. This perhaps explains in part why many Third World leaders have not been very enthusiastic about the increasing emphasis of a number of aid-granting institutions on addressing the problems of the absolute poor.

ASSESSMENT AND PROSPECTS

By several measures the Third World has made substantial economic progress over the past quarter century. The annual growth in its GNP between 1955 and 1980 averaged out to more than 5 percent, which was the goal of the First Development Decade, but was below the 6 and 7 percent targets that were set for the next two Development Decades, respectively. Over the same period the per capita GNP for the less developed countries, calculated in 1980 U.S. dollars, more than doubled from 340 to 730. The fact that the economies of less developed countries on the average grew at a higher percentage rates than did those of industrialized Western countries is reflected in a slight increase in the Third World's share of the world GNP (World Bank, 1982, pp. 21–22). There have also been improvements in social indicators. Between 1950 and 1979, life expectancy in the less developed countries grew from 43 to 58 years, the literacy rate increased from 33 to 56 percent, and the mortality rate for children aged 1 to 4 dropped from 28 to 12 per thousand (World Bank, 1982, p. 24).

These growth figures for the Third World as a whole conceal great differences between countries in their progress toward development. While the economies of the so-called "middle income" countries, which include most members of OPEC along with the newly industrializing countries, grew at very impressive rates, those of many of the poorest countries were stagnant. Annual growth in GNP for the World Bank's group of 33 "low-income" countries, when India and China are excluded, was only 2.7 during the 1970s (World Bank, 1982, p. 21). Because population increased at about the same rate, there was no increase in the low average income of the citizens of this group of states. The GNP per capita actually declined in eighteen of these states, most of which are located in sub-Sahara Africa. Despite the lack of economic growth in the poorest countries, steady improvements were recorded in life expectancy, infant mortality, and literacy, but on this score also they lag far behind the rest of the Third World.

The prospects for the foreseeable future are not very promising in view of several recent trends. The rate of growth of the world economy has slowed, especially since 1979, the year of the second major round of increases in the price of oil. Recession and stagnation in the economies of the developed world have softened the market for the primary products of the Third World, causing the prices for some of them to drop to the lowest levels in decades. It has also strained the generosity of the major donor countries, in particular the United States which cut by one-third its contributions to the IDA, the primary source of concessional aid to the least developed countries. Unusually high unemployment rates in the industrialized states have prompted the imposition of new trade restrictions to protect jobs jeopardized by imports, especially on manufactured goods from the Third World (Brandt Commission, 1983, p. 107). Finally, the credit-worthiness of even the most successful of less developed countries has been undermined by their mounting debts.

The "North-South dialogue" is at a low ebb and the prospects for its revival do not appear to be very promising. As was mentioned above, the documents containing the blueprint for the NIEO were adopted in 1974 over the objections of some of the countries whose cooperation was most needed to bring it into being. What earlier willingness there was on the part of the governments of the United States and the other major industrialized countries to discuss the NIEO seriously, as was apparent at the Seventh Special Session, may have been a startled reaction to OPEC's display of economic power and concerns that OPEC would apply its newly discovered leverage on behalf of Third World interests more generally. Recently, the leaders of the industrialized countries seem to have assumed a more defensive posture in discussions over the NIEO, agreeing verbally with the overall objectives of development while procrastinating on concrete commitments, as was apparent in the breakdown in the talks over the arrangements for the Global Negotiations. They apparently have not been persuaded that the progress of the Third World in fulfilling its development objectives is crucial to the recovery and vitality of their own economies. They have acted promptly, however, when the interests of their countries or influential nationals in the Third World are in clear and immediate jeopardy. Such has been the case in new loan packages arranged through the IMF to avert the threatened default of heavily indebted countries, such as Mexico, on previous loans that were extended by private banks based in the developed world.

In proposing the NIEO, the Third World leaders emphasized international solutions to their development problems. Having been frustrated in doing this, they may have no other alternative but to shift more of their attention inward to what can done domestically to cope with poverty and achieve a better life for the people of their country. This may entail a politically difficult decision to alter a highly skewed distribution of income in many less developed countries and to reduce coercively the high fertility rates that have been causing population to mushroom in some countries. There has also been considerable discussion among the NAM states and the Group of 77 about "collective self-reliance," or "South-South" relations, by which the Third World countries would work among themselves to further their common objectives for development. Neither of these possibilities, however, warrants much optimism, especially in the case of the poorest countries. Thus, most of the world's poor are unlikely to see significant improvements in their living conditions during their lifetimes and it is not unlikely that their numbers will swell as the population of the Third World continues to grow.

REFERENCES

Bauer, P. T. (1981). *Equality, the Third World, and Economic Delusion.* Cambridge, Mass.: Harvard University Press.

Bhagwati, Jagdish N. and John Gerard Ruggie, eds. (1984). *Power, Passions, and Purpose: Prospects for North-South Negotiations.* Cambridge, Mass.: MIT Press.

Brandt Commission (1979). *North-South: A Program for Survival.* Cambridge, Mass.: MIT Press.

Brandt Commission (1983). *Common Crisis: North-South Cooperation for World Recovery.* Cambridge, Mass.: MIT Press.

Bryant, Coralie and Louise G. White (1982). *Managing Development in the Third World.* Boulder, Co.: Westview Press.

Camps, Miriam (1981). *Collective Management: The Reform of Global Economic Organizations.* New York: McGraw-Hill.

Cassen, Robert (1982). "Overview," pp. 1–40 in Robert Cassen, Richard Jolly, John W. Sewell, and Robert Wood (eds.) *Rich Country Interests and Third World Development*. London: Croom Held.

Clark, William (1981). "Robert McNamara at the World Bank," *Foreign Affairs*, Vol. 60, No. 1, pp. 167–84.

Ghai, D. P., A. R. Khan, E. L. H. Lee, and T. Alfthan (1977). *The Basic Needs Approach to Development*. Geneva: International Labor Office.

Ghosh, Pradip K., ed. (1984). *Third World Development: A Basic Needs Approach*. Westport, Conn.: Greenwood Press, 1984.

Jackson, Richard (1983). *The Non-Aligned, the UN, and the Superpowers*. New York: Praeger.

Leipzinger, Danny M. (1981). "The Basic Human Needs Approach and North-South Relations," pp. 255–77 in Edwin P. Reubens (ed.), *The Challenge of the New International Economic Order*. Boulder, Co.: Westview Press.

Lewis, John P. (1982). "Development Assistance in the 1980s," pp. 96–128 of Roger D. Hansen (ed.), *U.S. Foreign Policy and the Third World: Agenda 1982*. New York: Praeger.

Loehr, William and John P. Powelson (1983). *Threat to Development: Pitfalls of the NIEO*. Boulder, Co.: Westview Press.

Loup, Jacques (1980). *Can the Third World Survive?* Baltimore: Johns Hopkins University Press.

Mortimer, Robert A. (1980). *The Third Word Coalition in International Politics*. New York: Praeger.

Olson, Robert K. (1981). *US Foreign Policy and the New International Economic Order: Negotiating Global Problems, 1974–1981*. Boulder, Co.: Westview Press.

Plano, Jack C. and Roy Olton (1982). *The International Relations Dictionary* (3d ed.). Santa Barbara, Calif.: ABC-CLIO.

Puchala, Donald J., ed. (1984). *Issues Before the 39th General Assembly of the United Nations: 1984–5*. New York: United Nations Association of America.

Sauvant, Karl P. (1981a). *The Group of 77: Evolution, Structure, Organization*. New York: Oceana, 1981.

Sauvant, Karl P. (1981b). "The NIEO Program: Reasons, Proposals, and Progress," pp. 41–77 in Karl P. Sauvant (ed.), *Changing Priorities on the International Agenda: the New International Economic Order*. Oxford: Pergamon Press.

Sewell, John W. (1979). "Can the North Prosper Without Growth and Progress in the South?" pp. 45–76 in Martin M. McLaughlin (ed.), *The United States and World Development: Agenda 1979*. New York: Praeger.

Sewell, John W. and John Mathieson (1982). "The United States and the Third World: Ties That Bind," pp. 41–93 in Robert Cassen, Richard

Jolly, John W. Sewell, and Robert Wood (eds.), *Rich Country Interests and Third World Development*. London: Cromm Helm.

Sivard, Ruth Leger (1981). *World Energy Survey*. Leesburg, Va.: World Priorities.

Sivard, Ruth Leger (1982). *World Military and Social Expenditures—1982*. Leesburg, Va: World Priorities.

Sivard, Ruth Leger (1983). *World Military and Social Expenditures—1983* Leesburg, Va.: World Priorities.

Spero, Joan Edelman (1985). *The Politics of International Economic Relations* (3d ed.). New York: St. Martin's Press.

Thompson, W. Scott (1983). *The Third World: Premises of U.S. Policy*. San Francisco: Institute for Contemporary Studies.

Tucker, Stuart K. (1985)."Statistical Annexes," pp. 147–233 in John W. Sewell, Richard F. Feinberg, and Valeriana Kallab (eds.), *U.S. Foreign Policy and the Third World: Agenda 1985–86*. New Brunswick, N.J.: Transaction Books.

ul Haq, Mahbub (1975). "Negotiating a New Bargain with the Rich Countries," pp. 157–62 in Guy F. Erb and Valeriana Kallab (eds.), *Beyond Dependency: The Developing World Speaks Out*. Washington, D.C.: Overseas Development Council.

Wallace, James R. (1982) "Statistical Annexes," pp. 129–246 in Roger D. Hansen (ed.), *U.S. Foreign Policy and the Third World: Agenda 1982*. New York: Praeger.

World Bank (1982). *World Development Report 1982*. New York: Oxford University Press.

World Bank (1984). *World Development Report 1984*. New York: Oxford University Press.

Wriggins, W. Howard and Gunnar Adler-Karlsson (1978). *Reducing Global Inequities*. New York: McGraw-Hill.

7 HUMAN RIGHTS

Promoting Civil and Political Freedoms

History is blemished with countless incidents of peoples suffering at the hands of other human beings. Over the centuries, there have been numerous cases of a populace being treated in a brutal and arbitrary way by foreign invaders or colonial powers, but it has perhaps been more tragically common for people to be killed, tortured, or persecuted by other members of their own society. Ironically, some of the most inhumane acts, including those of a genocidal character, have been committed—or at least condoned or tolerated—by those who govern the victims. Such was the case with three particularly tragic episodes of modern times: the massacre of two million of the three million Armenians living in Turkey prior to and during World War I, Stalin's political purges and forced collectivization of agriculture which together claimed the lives of tens of millions of Russians during the 1930s, and the Holocaust during which upwards of six million European Jews were systematically exterminated in Nazi concentration camps during the era of World War II (Rubinstein, 1983, pp. 12–27).

A disturbing number of atrocities have taken place in more recent times. In Indonesia, half a million are believed to have been executed in 1965–66 as the armed forces of the country attempted to annihilate the communist party whose leaders were alleged to have participated in a plot to overthrow President Sukarno. In Burundi, at least 80,000 people, mostly of the numerically larger Hutu ethnic group, were killed during May and June 1972 by government forces dominated by the Tutsi minority in reaction to an unsuccessful rebellion. In Kampuchea, hundreds of thousands lost their lives as a result of the forced relocations of urban populations to rural areas and of the extensive purges of "counterrevolutionaries" and other "undesirable elements" conducted by the Khmer Rouge after it came to power in 1975 (Amnesty International, 1983, p. 24). While none of these examples of large-scale cruelty, or the numerous other recent incidents that could be cited, have been of the magnitude as the purges and pogroms of Stalin and Hitler, they have exacted a devastating impact on the countries in which they took place.

Genocide and other mass killings are among the most extreme of the many ways in which governments have mistreated citizens and other residents of their countries. More limited and selective executions of actual and potential political adversaries by the army, police, or special "death squads" at governmental direction continue to occur in numerous countries. Many of the same governments have arrested and imprisoned hundreds, if not thousands, of alleged political opponents and dissidents, often without benefit of even the most cursory and unfair of trails and, in some cases, even without charging those who are imprisoned with any specific crime. While incarcerated, political prisoners often must contend with excruciating forms of physical and psychological torture, which are administered either to extract information or "confessions" or simply to dissuade them from future activities that the leaders consider a threat to their rule (see Amnesty International, 1984). Some governments attempt to conceal the scope of politically motivated killings and imprisonment by making arrests covertly and then refusing to acknowledge them, in which case the victims are said to have "disappeared," with little regard given to the emotional agony that this practice causes for relatives and friends.

States have also come under heavy criticism for blatant, discriminatory treatment of segments of their populations on the basis of such inappropriate criteria as race, sex, religion, age, and ethnicity. The Republic of South Africa is regarded as an international pariah for its apartheid system that strictly segregates its population on racial lines and perpetuates the political control of the white minority. Women in many cultures continue to be treated as second-class citizens in matters such as wages, property rights, voting franchise, social privileges, and educational opportunities. Numerous ethnic, linguistic, religious, or other social minorities in countries throughout the world have been subjected to discrimination: the untouchables in India, blacks and native Americans in the United States, foreign guest workers in Europe, the Asian population of Uganda, Jews in the Soviet Union, Catholics in Northern Ireland, Molluccans in Indonesia, Chinese in Vietnam and much of Southeast Asia, the Palestinians in the occupied West Bank, and Tamils in Sri Lanka, to mention only a few.

These practices are but a few of the more obvious violations of what have become known as human rights. Put simply, a human right is something any person is entitled to expect from his society (Henkin, 1978, p. 2). Human rights are not simply gifts or favors for which one should be grateful, but claims against society, as represented by its government, which may be demanded or insisted upon without embarrassment (Feinberg, 1973, pp. 58–59). Among the widely recognized human rights are not only freedoms from certain types of mistreatment, such as being subjected to arbitrary arrest or torture, at the hands of any actor, including one's government; but they also entail what a society is expected to provide for its individual members in a positive way to the fullest extent possible, such as the satisfaction of certain basic needs. Human rights are considered to be universal in the sense that all people are entitled to enjoy them, irrespective of characteristics such as their race, religion, sex, nationality, social class, political beliefs, occupation, education, physical handicaps, or talents and accomplishments. Moreover, human rights cannot be transferred or reliquished, nor can they be forfeited for failure to be exercised (Henkin, 1978, p. 3). Historically, human rights have often been looked upon as being part of a natural or "higher" law that should guide human action, believed by some to be of divine origin, which are not to be overridden by man-made laws or customs.

Concern over the protection of human beings from the tyrannies of governments can be traced back over millennia to the great religions of the world, as well as to the political traditions of the ancient Hebrews, Greeks, and Romans. Of greater relevance to contemporary policies on human rights, however, were the dramatic developments in political thought taking place in the West several centuries ago, beginning with the Enlightenment. During that era, belief in the "divine right of kings"—the doctrine that monarchs derive their authority from God—gave way to the contract theory of authority expounded by seventeenth-century philosopher John Locke, which posited that the authority of governments came not from divine sources but from the people. Thus, under terms of the contract, a government was to serve the interests of the people, as defined by the people, and could be removed by the people if it failed to meet their expectations (Hurwitz, 1981, pp. 16–17). Locke's theories are at least partly credited for inspiring the great political documents of the Western world, beginning with the English Bill of Rights of 1688, the American Declaration of Independence of 1776, the Constitution of the United States of 1789 and its supplemental Bill of Rights, and the French Declaration of the Rights of Man and the Citizen (1789). In modern times, the constitutions of most states affirm the human rights enunciated in these documents.

Traditionally, human rights have been treated exclusively as a domestic issue between governments and the people under their jurisdiction. Reverence for the principles of state sovereignty and nonintervention discouraged outside efforts to intervene on behalf of populations victimized by even the most cruel and tyrannical of rulers. This type of thinking has been increasingly challenged during the twentieth century, especially in the aftermath of revelations of the horrors of the atrocities committed by the Nazis against the Jews during World War II, which led many commentators to conclude that state sovereignty is not an absolute principle, but rather was subject to certain limitations in regard to human rights. Human rights came of age as an international issue with the adoption of the Declaration of Human Rights by the General Assembly in 1948, and since then it has occupied a prominent placc on the agendas of a number of international institutions.

HUMAN RIGHTS AS A GLOBAL ISSUE

At first glance, it appears that the protection of human rights is strictly an issue between individuals and their governments, and thus one that is neatly confined within the borders of states. Why is it then that human rights should become a subject of intensive international discussion leading to policies which, if fully implemented, would impose significant limitations on the sovereignty of governments over what has traditionally been thought to be within the domain of domestic affairs?

The United Nations took up the cause of human rights ostensibly to fulfill its primary objective of preserving world peace (Humphrey, 1967, p. 39; Henkin, 1979, p. 94). The World War II experience with the aggression of Hitler's Germany and Mussolini's Italy led to a widespread belief that states which blatantly violated basic human rights posed a serious threat to the security of others. It was assumed that leaders who were unprincipled in governing their own people could not be counted on to act responsibly in their international dealings. Moreover, authoritarian leaders have at times yielded to the temptation to manipulate the information which their populations receive in ways that arouse fear and hatred of foreign societies as a tactic to divert attention away from frustrating domestic conditions, which include the repressive practices of the government. This explains in large part why the Western European countries limited their plans for economic integration to states with well-established, democratic political systems. This type of thinking also underlay the Western insistence that certain human rights standards be written into the Final Act of the Helsinki Conference on Security and Cooperation in Europe of 1975, which was negotiated with the objective of reducing tensions between East and West in Europe.

There are more immediate and concrete reasons why human rights is a legitimate subject of international public policy. When war breaks out between states, soldiers taken prisoner are vulnerable to being tortured and civilians frequently become victims of the indiscriminate violence wrought by opposing military forces. During times of peace, large numbers of diplomats, laborers, journalists, businessmen, performers, students, researchers, and tourists travel internationally and, as they do, encounter the risk of being mistreated by the government or society of those countries that host them. This possibility was dramatically illustrated by the attack on the American embassy in Teheran in 1979, and the holding of its diplomatic personnel as hostages for fourteen and one half months. Human rights also becomes an international issue when governments enact measures to restrict the civil liberties of their nationals living in foreign countries in ways that violate the protections afforded to aliens by the laws of the host countries. Some governments have stationed agents in foreign countries to monitor the activities of their fellow citizens and intimidate them into not speaking out in ways that would be embarrassing to their leaders (Vogelgesang, 1979, p. 218). Death squads have been used to execute political opponents living abroad, as in the case of the 1976 assassination of Chilean exile Orlando Letelier in Washington, D.C., an act which was committed by hired Americans at the explicit direction of Chile's secret police.

Gross violations of human rights within a country become an international "spillover" problem when they trigger a flow of political refugees seeking asylum in foreign countries that are ill-prepared to care for them even temporarily or to absorb them permanently into their societies. Having experienced intense persecution in several European countries, Jewish people migrated to Palestine in large numbers where they established the state of Israel in 1948. Violence and warfare at that time caused an estimated one million of the original Arab inhabitants of the area to flee their homeland. The continuing plight of these Palestinian refugees in neighboring countries lies at the heart of tensions that persist in the Middle East. In 1971 India was confronted with the enormous task of feeding and sheltering upwards of ten million Begali refugees from East Pakistan who fled the brutality of government forces during the Pakistani civil war. More recently, hundreds of thousands of "boat people" seeking to escape the reprisals and repression of the governments of Vietnam and Haiti have posed serious resettlement problems for the states in which they seek asylum, as have the nearly one million Kampucheans seeking sanctuary in Thailand from the brutality of the Pol Pot regime and later his Vietnamese conquerors.

Human rights is inherently an international issue for several other quite different reasons. For one, outside support is often critical to the survival of an oppressive regime. Thus, it could be argued that, foreign governments, even those with exemplary domestic records on human rights, become accomplices in the violations of the authoritarian regimes they supply with the military means necessary to stay in power (van Boven, 1979, pp. 83–89). Such a charge was leveled by Khomeini and his followers against the United States for its support of the despotic regime of the former Shah. Of particular relevance are programs for foreign military officers and policemen that include training in paramilitary and counterinsurgency techniques for dealing with civil unrest. Foreign economic aid, trade, and investments may also contribute to the tenacity of governments that treat their people badly, as would seem to be the case with the Republic of South Africa. The decision of corporations to invest in foreign countries may even be influenced by opportunities for higher profits in states with governments that are lax in the defense of labor rights, such as those pertaining to the safety of work places and the freedom to form unions and bargain collectively. This practice suggests another reason why human rights is intrinsically as international issue. By failing to recognize and implement human rights that are observed in other countries, a state can sometimes achieve important advantages over them; it may be able to sell its goods on international markets more cheaply; it may be more successful in attracting investments of multinational corporations; or it may achieve a higher level of military preparedness. Thus, in the absence of international standards which all states are committed to uphold, competitive pressures may erode whatever inclinations a government might otherwise have to improve its performance on the protection of human rights.

Finally, the sense of identity human beings have for one another that transcends national boundaries also underlies international concern for human rights. It is not uncommon for people to develop a strong sense of empathy for those who suffer hardships, either as a consequence of natural disasters or intentional acts of cruelty at the hands of their governments or other members of their societies (Falk, 1979, p. 211; McDougal et al., 1980, p. 47). International concern can be especially strong among those who have irredentist bonds based on a common history, religion, or ethnicity with the victims of discrimination or persecution in foreign countries. Thus, it is understandable that the Nazi genocide against the European Jewish population was not looked upon as being simply an internal matter, but was widely regarded as a crime against Jews throughout the world and an affront to humanity as a whole or, in the words of the Nuremberg judgments, as a "crime against humanity." Knowledge that atrocities of this magnitude have taken place without prompting an intervention from outside, and could occur again in the future, contributes to the insecurity of all people who could become the victims of such a regime. Lacking any prospect of protection or relief within their own countries, actual or potential victims of cruel and tyrannical governments can only look to foreign countries or to the international community as a whole for support.

THE MAKING OF HUMAN RIGHTS POLICY

Were it not for the repeated references to human rights in the United Nations Charter, it is possible that the issue would have declined in international importance as the intense revulsion to the Nazi Holocaust gradually faded into history. The most straightforward among seven references to human rights in the Charter is Article 55, which charges the United Nations with promoting "universal respect for, and observance of, human rights and fundamental freedoms for all without distinction as to race, sex, language, or religion" (Humphrey, 1967, p. 41). In carrying out these responsibilities, the United Nations became the central arena of international policy making on human rights, a function which it continues to serve although significant efforts have been made in the field by several regional organizations. Within the United Nations, the General Assembly, and its Third Committee, stand at the apex of the policy-making pyramid on most human rights questions from where it receives and acts upon reports and recommendations submitted by an extensive network of commissions, subcommissions, and working groups, many of which are routed through the Economic and Social Council.

The United Nations body having the most important role in formulating international policy in the field is the Commission on Human Rights, one of two commissions that report to ECOSOC, the other being the Commission on the Status of Women, which has a narrower focus. The Human Rights Commission was constituted in 1946 by ECOSOC as provided for in Article 68 of the United Nations Charter. The initial task of the Commission was to draw up an international bill of rights which would give more specific meaning to the references in the Charter to human rights. Later, the Commission began to play an active role in the promotion and enforcement of human rights, but not to the exclusion of continuing efforts to draft additional international standards. Over the years, the Commission has been expanded from 18 to 43 members who are appointed by ECOSOC to 3-year terms after having been nominated by their governments. The commissioners are expected to play a dual role of representing their country on the panel while at the same time promoting human rights throughout the world (Hoare, 1967, p. 62).

The Commission depends on temporary and permanent groups for spadework on various issues. The most notable of these is the Subcommission on Prevention of Discrimination and Protection of Minorities, which was established by ECOSOC at the request of the Commission at its session in 1947. Members of the Subcommission are appointed by the Commission on the basis of their expertise and are expected to act as individuals who are not beholden to any government (Hoare, 1967, p. 71). As a result, these experts tend to be less inhibited by political considerations in making their recommendations than are the members of the Commission, who think of themselves as being representatives of their countries. Most of the other panels reporting to the Commission concentrate either on a specific type of human right, such as the working groups on "enforced or involuntary disappearances" and "indigenous populations," or on the situation in a specific country, examples being the ad hoc working groups on Chile and South Africa.

Several of the specialized agencies of the United Nations have been working independently on human rights questions related to their responsibilities. The ILO was a pioneer in international efforts to define and protect human rights during the era of the League of Nations. Its numerous and widely ratified conventions address issues such as collective bargaining, forced labor, discrimination in employment, and working conditions. UNESCO has had a long-standing interest in reducing discrimination in education and recently has been embroiled in the Third World's call for a "new information and communication order." Critics contend the proposal is an attempt at news management that would be a significant obstacle to press freedom and the international flow of information, which in the West are looked upon as being among the more fundamental civil and political rights. In recent years discussions have been taking place in the WHO on the subject of medical ethics, such as the role of health personnel in the practice of torture.

Discussions of international public policy on human rights have also occurred at numerous world conferences. One that stands out was a meeting convened in Teheran in 1968 to review the progress that had been made in protecting human rights in the 20 years since the General Assembly adopted the Universal Declaration of Human Rights. Racism and colonialism were among the issues receiving special attention at this meeting. Also notable are the International Labor Conference of 1976 and a series of United Nations Congresses on the Prevention of Crime and Treatment of Offenders. Other conferences have been held in conjunction with special decades declared to heighten awareness of specific human rights problems. For example, the first United Nations Women's Conference, which was held in Mexico City in 1975, launched the United Nations Decade for Women. A second conference was held in Copenhagen in 1980 and a third in Nairobi in 1985 at which the accomplishments were reviewed. In 1978 a World Conference to Combat Racism and Racial Discrimination was held in conjunction with a decade dedicated to those problems which began in 1973.

Uneasiness over the impact that human rights violations could portend for nearby states has prompted groups of countries with similar political traditions to work together on a regional basis to establish minimum standards and procedures for enforcing them. In 1953, the Council of Europe adopted the European Convention on Human Rights and established a special commission and court to carry out its provisions, which is generally conceded to be the most advanced system for the the protection of human rights internationally (Forsythe, 1983, p. 16). In 1975, the 35 Eastern and Western countries represented at the Helsinki conference declared their intention to observe certain human rights, including the reuniting of families and a freer flow of information between the two blocs, in what has become known as "basket three" of the Final Act of the meeting. The failure of the Soviet bloc countries to observe these rights has been a central item on the agendas of the follow-up conferences of the Helsinki nations that took place in Belgrade and Madrid. In 1969, the Latin American countries reached agreement on a human rights convention, which came into force in 1978, and the members of the Organization of African Unity in 1982 adopted the Banjul Charter of Human and People's Rights.

Nongovernmental organizations have had more of an impact on

international human rights policy and its enforcement than on the policy responses to most other global issues. For more than a century, the International Committee of the Red Cross (ICRC) has been actively involved in framing rules on the treatment of victims of war and has an officially recognized role in implementing them. The ICRC has been a recipient of the Nobel Peace Prize and a winner of the United Nations Prize for Human Rights (Forsythe, 1983, p. 51). The Anti-Slavery Society was the primary force behind the adoption of the a 1926 treaty banning slavery. Later, intensive lobbying by 42 private organizations invited to participate in the 1945 San Francisco conference by the United States was crucial to the inclusion of strong human rights provisions in the United Nations Charter (Humphrey, 1967, p. 40; McDougal et al., 1980, p. 260).

In recent decades, a veritable explosion has occurred in the number of NGOs in the human righs field. In 1974, sixty of the INGOs, often referred to as the "human rights industry," formed the Non-Governmental Organization Committee on Human Rights to coordinate their activities and pool scarce resources in an effort to compound their influence on the proceedings of the Human Rights Commission in Geneva. The most prominent of these INGOs is the London-based Amnesty International, which in 1977 received the Nobel Peace Prize for its work on behalf of persons imprisoned for political reasons, or what the association refers to as "prisoners of conscience." Since being formed in 1961, Amnesty International has grown to an organization of more than 200,000 individual members from 95 countries, many of whom participate in 2671 local groups that have been organized in 53 countries (Ennals, 1982, p. 66; Amnesty International, 1982, p. 7; see also Power, 1981). Two other INGOs that are highly respected for their work on behalf of human rights are the International Commission of Jurists, which is committed to the observance of the rule of law and due process, and the International League for Human Rights, which has promoted the establishment of a broad variety of international standards on human rights. Also on the roster of INGOs active in the human rights field are religious associations, such as the Roman Catholic Church, the World Council of Churches, the World Jewish Congress, Bahai International, and the World Muslim Conference; women's groups, such as the International Council of Women; labor bodies such as the

World Federation of Trade Unions and the World Conference of Labor; and professional associations, such as the International Press Institute and PEN, the latter being concerned with the protection of writers (McDougal et al., pp. 174–75; Rodley, 1979, p. 138).

THE INTERNATIONAL BILL OF RIGHTS

The comprehensive international bill of rights, which the Commission on Human Rights was assigned the task of developing, was to specify the type of treatment people were entitled to expect from their governments. There were several precedents for international standards on human rights, one being the long-standing principle of international common law which obliges states to provide "extraordinary" protection to diplomats and minimum standards of justice to aliens (Henkin, 1979, p. 229). The 1864 Geneva Convention on the treatment of victims of armed conflict was perhaps the earliest formal treaty in the field of human rights. It has been followed by a series of treaties designed to make war more humane for both combatants and civilians, the most recent having been adopted in 1977 which extends certain protections to insurgent forces. Also notable is a 1926 convention which outlaws the practice of slavery. And finally, while no mention of human rights is made in the Covenant of the League of Nations, treaties were adopted under its auspices that provided for the protection of certain European minorities whose mistreatment had been among the causes of World War I. Some protections were also provided to people living in the mandate territories under the League's jurisdiction (Falk, 1979, p. 212).

The international bill of rights eventually took the form of three documents, the first being the Universal Declaration of Human Rights, which was adopted by the General Assembly on December 10, 1948, without a dissenting vote, but with the abstentions of the Soviet bloc along with Saudi Arabia and South Africa. The Declaration, which was drawn up with dispatch by the Commission on Human Rights, gives more specific meaning to the rather vague references to the protection of rights that were contained in the Charter. As a resolution of the General Assembly, the document has only the status of a recommendation and is, therefore, not even legally binding on the governments that voted for it. Declarations are, however, considered to carry more weight than other resolutions. Thus, there is a stronger expectation that states will give serious consideration to complying with them (Humphrey, 1967, p. 55). Over the years the Declaration has grown substantially in stature. Not only has it become a landmark in international public policy on human rights, but it also ranks among the most significant actions in the history of the General Assembly. Its principles have been incorporated into numerous international treaties as well as the constitutions of many newly independent states, leading some legal scholars to argue that it is an expression of the customary law of the international community, which is binding on all states (McDougal et al., 1980, p. 274).

Described by one observer as a "masterly blend of Western libertarianism and welfare state principles," the Declaration proceeds from the premise that all human beings are born free and equal in dignity and rights and are to enjoy the right to life, liberty, and security of person regardless of race, color, sex, language, religion, or political belief (Henkin, 1979, p. 231). In regard to civil rights, it provides that no person should be subjected to slavery; to torture or to cruel, inhumane, or degrading treatment or punishment; to arbitrary arrest, detention, exile; or to interference with privacy, family, or home. People charged with crimes are to be presumed innocent until proven otherwise by an independent and impartial tribunal and to have professional help in preparing a defense. Numerous freedoms are to be protected, including those of thought, conscience, and religion, as well as the rights to express opinions openly, to receive and to impart information freely through any media, to assemble peacefully, to join associations and trade unions, to marry and to form a family, and to own property. Each individual has the right to a nationality and should be allowed to move freely within any country, to leave any country including his own, to return to his country, and to seek and enjoy asylum from persecution for political reasons in other countries. In the political realm, the Declaration affirms the democratic right to take part in the government of one's country, directly or through freely chosen representatives. The authority of the government is to be the will of people as expressed in periodic and genuine elections in which all citizens have an equal vote that is cast secretly.

In addition, the Declaration identifies several economic and social rights. All people are entitled to enjoy a standard of living that is adequate for their health and well-being, which includes food, clothing, housing, and medical care, with special provision being made for mothers and children. Everyone is to have an opportunity for free education, with primary schooling being compulsory and with higher education being accessible to all on the basis of merit. There is also the right to employment of the individual's choosing and protection against unemployment. Wages are to be equal for equal work and to be adequate to support a family in dignity. Workers are entitled to rest and leisure, reasonable limitations on working hours, and even to periodic paid holidays (see Kartaskin, 1982).

At the time of its adoption, the Declaration was looked upon as being simply a recommendation that would probably have little impact on the performance of governments in protecting human rights. Thus, even before the document was voted on by the General Assembly in 1948, the Commission on Human Rights began to incorporate its provisions into a multilateral treaty. All states would be encouraged to ratify the treaty and, upon doing so, would be legally bound to implement the rights that were spelled out in it. Early in the process it was decided that two separate treaties should be created: an International Covenant on Civil and Political Rights and an International Covenant on Economic, Social and Cultural Rights. The Commission completed its drafts of the Convenants in 1954, but it was not until 1966 that the General Assembly gave them its unanimous approval after more than a decade of debate in its Third Committee. Ten additional years elapsed before the documents had received the 35 ratifications required to come into effect. By 1982, the list of countries that had become parties to the Covenants had grown to 70.

Sometimes referred to as the "children" of the Declaration, the Covenants reaffirm and refine many of the rights identified in the parent document (Henkin, 1981, p. 26). Thus, rather than reviewing what the Covenants have in common with the Declaration and Covenants, let it suffice here to mention a few of the key differences. The right of peoples to self-determination appears for the first time in both of the Covenants along with their right to freely dispose of their natural wealth and resources and not to be deprived of their means of subsistance. Whereas almost all of the other rights spelled out in the international bill of rights refer to what individuals are entitled to claim from their governments, self-determination is a right that applies to social groups. Its inclusion in the Convenants was a concession to the intense campaign of the Third World during the 1950s and 1960s to bring about an end to colonialism. This principle of self-determination can, however, have serious drawbacks for new states if their numerous ethnic minorities make use of it to legitimize their demands for political autonomy. Another significant addition is the controversial provision of the Covenant on Civil and Political Rights permitting governments to declare a "public emergency" when circumstances threaten "the life of the nation," during which it may temporarily suspend many of the rights spelled out in the document. It was feared that this provision could become a major loophole that would be used habitually by repressive governments to weaken the force of the document. After extensive discussion, the right to own property and not to have it arbitrarily taken away was omitted from the Covenants due to the persistent opposition from socialist states.

The three core documents of the international bill of rights have been supplemented by numerous other declarations, resolutions, and conventions—fifty by one count—which define more detailed standards on specific human rights issues (Sohn, 1979, p. 187). Some focus on certain types of practices that are contrary to the enjoyment of basic human rights, such as genocide, slavery, forced labor, racial discrimination, apartheid, and unnecessary violence in warfare, whereas others key in on categories of people who are often victims of discrimination and other forms of unfair treatment, such as women, workers, refugees, stateless people, or prisoners of war. The process of defining these specific rights continues, sometimes very slowly. After two decades of negotiation, a declaration concerning intolerance and discrimination based on religion was adopted by the General Assembly in 1981. Work continues on a convention that would ban torture and other cruel, inhumane, or degrading forms of punishments and on documents aimed at the special problems of children, migrant workers and their families, indigenous propulations, and people belonging to national, religious, and ethnic minorities.

MONITORING THE PERFORMANCE OF STATES

Establishing global standards on such a broad array of human rights was a remarkable series of accomplishments for international policy makers. These efforts will be to little or no avail, however, unless they lead to substantial improvement in the way people are treated by their governments. As with other international laws, each state has an option on whether or not to accept the numerous international treaties on human rights. Having formally accepted any of them, a state is obliged to make good faith efforts to ensure that its population enjoys those rights. Unfortunately, many states have refused to make a commitment to observe the standards that have been set internationally. But perhaps even more disconcerting to the promoters of human rights are those governments which applaud and ratify the principal international documents on human rights, but continue to treat their populations in a brutal or repressive manner in blatant disregard for the commitments they have made to act otherwise.

Anticipating that governments could not be counted upon to be diligent in the protection of human rights, several international institutions have been charged with monitoring and issuing reports on their performance. The United Nations Commission on Human Rights and its assortment of subcommissions and working groups perform this role when there is reason to suspect that a consistent pattern of serious violations of human rights has been taking place in a country. Several of the treaties call for the creation of new commissions or committees to review the extent to which the parties are following through on their commitments. Such is the case with the 1966 Covenant on Political and Civil Rights which provided for the establishment of a new international body called the Human Rights Committee to be formed of eighteen individuals "of high moral character and recognized competence in the field of human rights" who are nationals of states that have ratified the document. These individuals were to be elected by secret ballots cast by the parties to the treaty

(Robertson, 1981, p. 337). Panels of this type, whose members serve in the capacity of individuals selected for their competence and experience rather than as appointed representatives of their governments, are less likely to be swayed by political considerations and therefore can be expected to more rigorously scrutinize the performance of governments on the basis of whatever information is available (Forysthe, 1983, pp. 45–48).

One source of information commonly used in monitoring the human rights performance of states is the self-assessments of their governments. Several of the major treaties, including the Covenant on Civil and Political Rights, obligate each party to report periodically on what if any steps it has taken to uphold the provisions of the treaty. Clearly, it would be naive to expect that most national governments would be straightforward in calling international attention to deficiencies in their human rights records. It is more likely that governments will attempt to conceal the extent of their violations as they try to present the most favorable image they can as protectors of the rights they have committed themselves to observe. Nevertheless, the exercise of preparing these self-evaluations may have the positive effect of making some states more aware of international standards and of deficiencies in their performance that they would be willing to correct. Moreover, in the interests of maintaining their credibility, governments may be more objective in their self-evaluations if they anticipate that their reports will be thoroughly scrutinized by an international panel that will confront their representatives with embarrassing questions based on contradictory information received from other sources.

The ease with which evidence of violations can be collected from alternative sources varies considerably from one country to the next. In the more open societies, an independent news media can be a useful source of information. Outside observers can gain access to the alleged victims of human rights abuses or to their lawyers and can attend their trials, which are normally open to the public. The political opposition will be all too willing to share what knowledge it has of violations. Closed societies in which governments use modern technology to maintain a tight reign on the flow of information, including control or censorship over all types of media and restrictions on international and domestic travel, pose a more formidable challenge for outside investigators.

But even in the case of the strictest totalitarian regimes, word of mistreatment of certain individuals leaks to the outside world in the form of letters from the victims themselves or from relatives or friends who know something about their whereabouts and condition (Ullman, 1979, p. 4). The reliability of this type of information can often, however, be challenged on the grounds that it may have been fabricated or exaggerated by the opponents of a government to embarrass and weaken it politically. Verifying allegations can be difficult if not impossible, especially when electrical or psychological techniques of torture are used which leave no visible mark that corroborates the story of the victim (Dominguez, 1979, p. 93).

Should testimony about human rights violations from these unofficial sources be taken into account by the relevant international bodies as they monitor the compliance of states with international standards? This has been a major issue in the evolution of international human rights policy. Initially, it was considered inappropriate for most international bodies to review the multitude of complaints forwarded to them by private individuals and groups. Instead, the recognized procedures has been for states to complain about the violations taking place in other states, using whatever information they had, in accordance with the principle that each party to a treaty has the right to demand compliance from other parties and to take appropriate action if they fail to comply (Henkin, 1978, p. 102). Several conventions specify an existing tribunal, such as the International Court of Justice, or set up a new one to render judgments on the disputes that arise between states in this way. It should be noted that parties to the 1966 Covenant on Civil and Political Rights have the option of whether to expose themselves to allegations of noncompliance coming from other states and, thus far, only a few states have declared their willingness to permit such allegations. But even where this state-to-state procedure for complaints is permitted, it has been used infrequently. Not being the direct victims of human rights abuses, states lack a strong incentive for pointing out violations taking place in other countries; moreover, a potential accuser may be deterred by the expectation that its own less than perfect human rights record will in turn be publicized internationally by the governments that are the target of its allegations. Finally, governments may anticipate that their complaints against other states will be dismissed as simply being politically motivated propaganda.

Recognizing the inadequacies of the state-to-state complaint system for monitoring human rights violations, some international human rights panels have been authorized to receive testimony from INGOs having consultative status, and in a few cases, from individuals directly. Not being encumbered by extraneous political considerations that inhibit foreign governments, INGOs have proven to be a much more fertile source of evidence on human rights abuses. Especially notable contributions are made regularly by Amnesty International, which for more than twenty years has worked painstakingly to gather and verify information on individuals, who there is reason to believe, have been imprisoned for political reasons. Amnesty International is often able to persuade governments, which are sensitive to accusations that they have something to hide, to allow its representatives to make on-site investigations, to observe trials, or to visit and interview specific individuals whom they have designated as being "prisoners of conscience." Amnesty International's reputation for thoroughness and impartiality in researching complaints from private sources has lent considerable credibility both to the testimony it presents to international human rights commissions and to its annual reports which detail the plight of political prisoners in as many as a hundred countries. The ICRC and the International Commission of Jurists Red Cross are two other highly respected INGOs which engage in similar monitoring activities, the latter particularly in regard to the conditions in which prisoners of war are being detained.

The issue of whether international institutions should be permitted to review communications received from individuals complaining of mistreatment at the hands of their governments has been especially controversial. There has been a gradual trend toward a greater receptivity to these types of complaints, but only after those involved have exhausted all national rememdies without success. The Trusteeship Council and General Assembly have a long-standing practice of considering petitions from individuals residing in non-self-governing territories (Sohn, 1979, p. 202). Likewise, refugees have been permitted to address their grievances directly to the United Nations High Commissioner for Refugees. The Commission on Human Rights refused to consider communications from individuals until 1970 when it was authorized by ECOSOC to examine them if there was a possibility of "gross violations of human rights and fundamental freedoms." The Commission responded by instituting a cumbersome process for reviewing individual complaints. But because of the Commission's stringent rules on the type of information that is admissible, only about 10 percent of the tens of thousands of communications it receives each year can qualify for consideration. The rules of some international panels restrict the consideration of petitions from individuals to those coming from countries that have formally agreed to the procedures, as is the case with the European and Inter-American human rights systems. An optional protocol was appended to the Covenant on Civil and Political Rights which authorizes the Human Rights Committee to review and investigate complaints it receives from individuals living in the states that have ratified it, which by 1982 numbered only 22.

Gathering information on the performance of governments is a critical first step in achieving the objectives of the international bill of rights. The capacity of international institutions to play this role is enhanced when they are allowed to receive the testimony of INGOs and the complaints received directly from individual victims.

INDUCING COMPLIANCE WITH HUMAN RIGHTS STANDARDS

Detecting human rights violations alone will not bring an end to harsh and arbitrary treatment of people by their own societies. The more difficult challenge for the international community is to encourage those states that have been revealed as persistent violators of human rights to improve their records to be in compliance with the international standards set forth in the international bill of rights and the numerous supplementary resolutions and conventions on specific types of rights. This task has been taken up not only by international institutions, but also by foreign states acting on their own and by nongovernmental organizations that actively gather information on human rights violations. The strategies employed in these endeavors have ranged from relatively gentle attempts at private persuasion to forceful military interventions. None of these strategies has been effective in all types of situations, although each has the potential for some success under certain circumstances.

The least coercive of these international enforcement strategies is "quiet diplomacy," which entails private discussions with the governments that have been shown to be deficient in their protection of human rights. Several international commissions hold such talks in conjunction with the regular reports that governments must submit as required by treaties they have ratified. This procedure is also used by some nongovernmental organizations, a notable example being the ICRC, which shares the results of its investigations on the treatment of prisoners of war exclusively with the government that is holding them. Likewise, the United States and other major countries frequently choose confidential channels for prodding their allies into tempering their repressive practices. These efforts at quiet diplomacy are unlikely to yield significant results unless the targeted government is genuinely committed to maintaining a good record on human rights, but has misinterpreted international standards or has been blind to shortcomings in its own performance. Such a regime may be more receptive to outside suggestions to improve its human rights records if it is spared the embarrassment of appearing to have buckled under to international pressures (Vogelgesang, 1979, p. 229). These gentle efforts are, however, unlikely to induce major changes in the behavior of governments that rely upon repression for maintaining political control of their societies, unless there is the concomitant threat of stronger, public forms of international pressure to follow if the behind-the-scenes efforts fall short of reforms.

If quiet persuasion fails, outside pressure on a state to uphold international standards on human rights can be increased by publicizing its record of serious violations. This strategy, sometimes described as the "mobilization of shame," presumes that a favorable international image will be so important to a state that it will be more conscientious in upholding human right in order to avoid having its reputation tarnished by embarrassing revelations of how it mistreats its population. Amnesty International relies heavily on publicity, much of which is generated by local chapter, in its efforts to win freedom for the "prisoners of conscience" it identifies. The tactic seems to have been quite successful judging an estimate at one time that 50 percent of the prisoners it works for have been released within a fairly short time (Joyce, 1979, p. 80). Public disclosure of serious violation is also part of the enforcement arsenal of international institutions, including the Commission on Human Rights, which each year issues special reports and adopts resolutions calling attention to the countries it concludes are especially lax in protecting human rights, among which have been South Africa, Israel (in the occupied West Bank), Argentina, Chile, Guatemala, Bolivia, Afghanistan, Kampuchea, Poland, and Paraguay. The Commission has been criticized for its reluctance to investigate and issue a report on many of the countries identified by its subcommission as serious violators of human rights (Rodley, 1979, pp. 170–71).

Stronger measures have occasionally been employed against some of the more serious and blatant violators of human rights both by international institutions and by foreign countries. In 1968 the Security Council imposed a mandatory embargo on trade with Rhodesia to put pressure on Ian Smith's white minority government to transfer political power to the black majority. Likewise, the Security Council in 1977 adopted a mandatory embargo on arms shipments to the Republic of South Africa coupled with a ban on nuclear collaboration in an effort to induce the regime to alter its policies of strict racial segregation known as apartheid. Acting on its own, the United States in 1974 adopted legislation that would terminate military assistance to states that were guilty of a continuing pattern of gross violations of basic human rights and the next year extended the policy to economic assistance. The United States, under the terms of the Jackson-Vanik Amendment of 1974, withheld "most favored nation" trading status from the Soviet Union as long as it imposed emigration taxes that thwarted the ambitions of some of its Jews to leave. The United States has also advocated that the World Bank, IMF, and other international lending agencies take human rights performances into account when making decisions on loan applications, but was unable to overcome the reluctance of these institutions to mix political and economic considerations (Forsythe, 1983, p. 106).

Neither mobilizing shame nor economic sanctions can be counted upon to significantly alter the record of states in the field of human rights. Governments are likely to react to negative publicity as a public relations problem rather than as a reason for basic reforms in their human rights policies. Damage to their international reputations can sometimes be effectively lessened by fervently denying the charges, by questioning the political motives of their accusers, or by arguing that they have been unfairly singled out for international scrutiny when other states with comparable or worse records receive little attention. Highly visible, symbolic actions, such as the freeing of prominent prisoners whose cases have been the object of international concern, can also be used as image-enhancing ploys while cruel and repressive policies quietly continue. Then there are some states— South Africa and Israel being leading examples—which seem resigned to being type-cast as international pariahs and therefore perceive that they have little more to lose from being the target of additional adverse publicity. Economic sanctions often have little impact because they are not universally observed. What is denied a country from states participating in an embargo may be readily available from others who are willing to set aside human rights considerations in their economic dealings. Thus, the economic assistance denied to Argentina and Chile by the United States during the late 1970s was more than compensated by loans from multinational institutions and private banks (Forsythe, 1983, pp. 106–8). Moreover, all too often other foreign policy considerations interfere with the willingness of states to apply sanctions to the countries whose friendship is valued because of security interests or investment opportunities.

The method of last resort for bringing an end to serious human rights violations is the use of military force in accordance with the principle of "humanitarian intervention." There is a long history of such practices in the defense of coreligionists that have been seriously mistreated in foreign states (Henkin, 1978, p. 89). Examples in modern times include India's intervention in the Pakistani civil war in response to atrocities taking place in Bengal, Tanzania's attack on Uganda to bring down its leader Idi Amin, and Vietnam's invasion of Kampuchea ostensibly to end the inhumane policies of the Pol Pot regime. When interventions are undertaken unilaterally by neighboring states, especially by a traditional adversary, as was the case in the examples just cited, there are frequently grounds for questioning whether the action was motivated purely by humanitarian concerns or, on the contrary, that a deplorable human rights record was used as an excuse for pursuing other aggressive ambitions (Falk, 1979, p. 208). Furthermore, regardless of the motivation, the cost of military interventions can be high in loss of life and suffering and is a realistic option only against small, relatively weak states.

THE NEW POLITICS OF HUMAN RIGHTS

International human rights standards generate relatively little controversy when stated in vague and lofty language, and when they are interpreted as long-range goals rather than immediate expectations. Thus, the Universal Declaration on Human Rights was drawn up rather quickly by the Commission on Human Rights and adopted in the General Assembly without a dissenting vote. Human rights become a highly politicized issue when negotiations take place to give them more specific meanings, and strategies are being considered and implemented which put pressure on states to promptly comply with them. While there is little disagreement that murder, torture, slavery, and detention without trial are gross violations of basic human rights, arguments have arisen over the freedom of speech and assembly, the right to own property, and the requirements of a democratic system (Buergenthal and Torney, 1979, p. 325).

The most basic line of conflict that emerges over international human rights policy naturally occurs between those states which have a long-standing tradition of observing a wide range of civil and political rights and those which have chronically violated them. Thus, pressure for rigorous standards and strong international mechanisms for enforcing them comes largely from states with stable, democratic political systems that have good, if not perfect, records in the protection of civil liberties. For the most part, these are the Western nations which have also achieved a high level of economic development. Resistance to the active international enforcement of these rights comes mostly from the authoritarian regimes of Soviet bloc or the Third World which fear that any easing up on their repressive tactics would unleash political forces that could seriously undermine their authority and perhaps lead to their overthrow (Ullman, 1979, p. 1).

The tendency for international human rights policy to become a polarized North-South issue, with the East joining in with the

South, is sometimes referred to as the "new politics" of human rights. Third World critics of the international bill of rights, especially those parts that pertain to civil and political rights, contend that it is grounded in the Western political tradition, with key elements being alien to the cultures of societies in other regions of the world. Thus, whereas Western thinking emphasizes rights, individual interests, and freedom from despotism, Third World cultures have tended to place more importance on obligations, collective goals, and perpetuating tradition (Said, 1978, p. 2). The perceived Western bias implicit in the Universal Declaration is explained by the fact that few African and Asian states were among the 50 charter members of the United Nations that participated in the drafting of the document (Vogelgesang, 1979, p. 229; Zvobgo, 1979, pp. 94–95).

The overriding issue of the new politics of human rights is one of priorities, with Third World leaders taking the position that economic and social rights should take precedence over most civil and political liberties. This type of thinking is illustrated by the following statement of Jahangir Amuzegar (1978), an Iranian official during the repressive reign of the Shah.

In the third world countries, suffering from poverty, widespread illiteracy, and a yawning gap in domestic distribution of incomes and wealth, a constitutionally guaranteed freedom of opposition and dissent may not be as significant as freedom from despair, disease, and deprivation. The masses might indeed be much happier if they could put more in their mouths than empty words, if they could have a health-care center instead of a Hyde Park corner—if they were ensured gainful employment instead of the right to march on the capital. . . . To champion the cause of human rights is an admirable pursuit. But let us not forget that empty heads and empty stomachs may find the due process also frightfully empty.

It is further argued that economic and social development is a precondition of the democratic freedoms that are widely enjoyed in the industrialized West (Moskowitz, 1979, pp. 112–14). Consider the following quotation from an unnamed African president.

Imperialists talk about human rights, drinking tea or sipping champagne. They can afford to—after all, they have it made.

If we had had slaves for 200 years to build our roads, build our homesteads, sow our fields; if we had had multinationals for 300 years looting wealth from other people's lands; if we had literate, healthy, well-fed citizens—if we had a diversified economy and people had jobs—we too could talk about human rights from our air conditioned offices and homes. But we can't do it; we have nothing (quoted in Zvobgo, 1979, p. 93).

This argument, that economic development is a precondition for the observance of political and civil liberties, has been used by authoritarian regimes of the Third World to argue against strict international enforcement of human rights standards. It has also underlain their efforts to link the human rights issue to their proposals for a new international economic order. They have sought to shift the onus for their failures to protect civil and political rights to the injustices they allege are inherent in the existing international economic system and the unresponsiveness of the developed countries to their repeated calls for reforms (Donnelly, 1981, p. 640).

The notion that economic and social entitlements should have priority over democratic liberties has also been a serious point of contention between East and West. In contrast to the West with its capitalistic inclinations to preserve choices and freedoms for the individual, socialist states subscribe to the Marxist dictum that the individual is relatively unimportant compared to the advancement of the goals of the society as a whole (McDougal et al., 1980, p. 77; Falk, 1981, p. 2). From the socialist perspective, the observance of certain of the civil liberties that are honored in the West, especially economic freedoms, would interfere with efforts to plan rationally the use of the resources of a country to optimize economic growth while achieving its other social objectives. Thus, in forums such as the meetings held to review compliance with the Helsinki accords, Eastern delegates, when confronted with Western protests over Soviet restrictions on such matters as immigration, treatment of dissidents, and press censorship, counter with the observation that the communist systems have a more admirable record in satisfying the basic economic and social needs of all of their people than have the capitalist states, most notably the United States, where large numbers are malnourished, unemployed, and without access to medical care despite the general material abundance of the nation.

The Third World, with the encouragement of the Soviet bloc, has taken advantage of its swelling majority in the General Assembly to shift international attention to economic and social entitlements, largely at the expense of the civil and political rights (Donnelly, 1981). This call for a revision in the prevailing United Nations policy on human rights was first apparent at the Teheran conference of 1968. The proclamation adopted at this conference is notable for the provision that "since human rights and fundamental freedoms are indivisible, the full realization of civil and political rights without the enjoyment of economic, social, and cultural rights is impossible." The relationship between the two types of rights was again taken up in 1977 by the General Assembly which adopted what has become a controversial, but nevertheless influential, resolution that establishes guidelines for future international efforts to promote human rights. Commonly referred to by its number 32/130, the resolution passed by a vote of 123 to 0, with abstentions from 15 states including most of the Western democracies. Its text reinforces the Teheran proclamation on the "indivisibility and interdependence" of civil and political freedoms, on the one hand, and economic and social needs, on the other, and goes further to pronounce that the realization of the New International Economic Order is essential to the promotion of human rights (see International Commission of Jurists, 1981).

For the most part the West has stuck to its doctrine of human rights which calls for the observance of democratic freedoms regardless of the level of economic development, although a few countries, the Scandinavian ones in particular, have expressed views similar to those of the Third World leaders (Donnelly, 1981, p. 642). Claims that economic and social advancement are a precondition for political liberties are looked upon as a convenient excuse for governments that lack the political will to dispense with their repressive policies and to address the injustices that spark unrest. It is observed that such countries as India, Sri Lanka, Venezuela, Costa Rica, Botswana, and Ghana demonstrate that it is possible for less developed countries to recognize political and civil rights (Forsythe, 1981, p. 441). Furthermore, while there is evidence that political repression can facilitate economic growth measured in GNP, it is also apparent that authoritarian regimes are often less successful in taking care of the basic needs of their populations, as measured in the Physical Quality of Life Index (Hewlett, 1979, p. 472).

The politics of the implementation of human political and civil liberties is also played out over specifically which countries become the subject of scrutiny and condemnation by international bodies such as the Commission on Human Rights and the General Assembly. What indignation has been expressed in the Third World over violations of civil and political rights has been concentrated on two countries: South Africa and Israel. South Africa has been castigated for the blatant racism of its apartheid system and continuing colonialist control of Namibia in defiance of a 1966 General Assembly resolution terminating its trusteeship over the area and declaring its further occupation illegal. Israel repeatedly comes under attack for its refusal to return the territories it conquered from neighboring Arab states in 1967 and the alleged ill-treatment of the Arab population of these territories. The tolerance of Third World spokesmen for the excesses of black, native governments—most notably the unusually cruel regimes of the Tutsi minority in Burundi, of Idi Amin in Uganda, Macias Nguema in Equatorial Guinea, and Bokassa in the Central African Empire—has been challenged by the United States, which also attempted to draw attention to human rights violations committed by the Soviet Union and by the governments it supports in Afghanistan, Poland, Nicaragua, Cuba, Ethiopia, and Vietnam (in Kampuchea). The United States has also been critical of what it considers to be the excessive amount of attention being given to the excesses of the right-wing dictatorships in Latin America that it supports, which have been harshly criticized by the Soviet bloc.

ASSESSMENT AND PROSPECTS

The provisions of the United Nations Charter which called for the promotion of human rights triggered what has now been four decades of persistent, and at times concerted, efforts to establish and implement international policies designed to improve the way people are treated by their government and societies as a whole. The first major task was to define what human rights are and which ones should be protected so as to establish standards against which the performance of governments can be assessed. In spite of the ideological diversity of the world's societies, international policy makers have been remarkably successful in identifying an extensive variety of universal human rights and giving them more specific meaning, as is evidenced by the virtual consensus that were initially reached on the core documents of the international bill of rights. While the difficult initial step in defining international standards is nearly complete, it appears likely that thinking about human rights will continue to evolve, and expand possibly in new directions such as environmental rights, medical ethics, and communications, in part as a response to technological advancements that pose new ethical questions.

Having established a set of international standards, the next task has been to induce governments to accept and comply with them. Toward this end, significant progress has been made over the past two decades in setting up procedures through which international commissions and committees can monitor how well the performance of governments measures up against the international expectations. The effectiveness of these bodies in scrutinizing the human rights records of states has been enhanced by their greater openness to information on violations that is supplied by individual victims and their relatives and associates and by INGOs such as Amnesty International. The international community has not progressed very far, however, in devising effective ways to put pressure on recalcitrant regimes that are undeterred by verbal condemnations of the abusive or repressive ways in which they have been treating elements of their populations.

How widely have these standards and enforcement procedures been accepted by governments? The act of ratification is one indication of a state's acceptance of a treaty and intentions to comply with its provisions, albeit not always a reliable one. Thus far the record of ratifications of human rights treaties is mixed. For example, the 1949 Geneva Convention on armed conflict by 1980 had been accepted by 145 of 152 eligible countries. In contrast, only 6 countries have acceded to Article 41 of the 1966 Covenant on Civil and Political Rights, which authorizes the Human Rights Committee to consider adverse allegations that are forwarded by other states that have also declared their acceptance of the article (Forsythe, 1983, p. 21). Figures of this type can be misleading, however, because some states habitually ratify treaties but have no apparent intention of complying with the rights set forth in them, examples being the Soviet Union, Poland, and Chile. Conversely, the failure to accept the treaties formally does not necessarily imply a reluctance to respect the rights spelled out in them, a case in point being the United States which, despite periods of international activism in the field and admirable domestic record, has yet to ratify several of the principal conventions, including the two covenants of 1966 and the earlier treaty banning genocide.

Ultimately, the effectiveness of international policy on civil and political rights must be assessed not by the number of ratifications of the core treaties, but on the actual performance of governments in protecting basic liberties. So far the record has not been very encouraging, for it appears that governments have fewer qualms about violating human rights standards than the international law on most other subjects. Amnesty International's 1982 report documents significant violations of a variety of political and civil rights in 121 countries. This pattern is borne out by the 1982 world survey conducted by Freedom House which found that only about 35 percent of the world's population lives in countries categorized as being "free," as opposed to 42 percent living in countries listed as "not free," with the remaining 23 percent residing in "partly free" states. Over the past two decades, little change is evident in the percentages, except for 1975 and 1976 when India was moved from the free to partly free category due to the "emergency" declared by Indira Gandhi (Gastil, 1985, p. 5). What is especially distressing is the blatant nature of the violations in numerous countries which have become integral instruments of political control by governments that lack strong public support (Falk, 1979, p. 267).

International standards on civil and political rights, and economic and social ones as well, are far ahead of the norms of behavior of most states. In fact, no states, even the economically advanced Western democracies, have fully implemented all of the rights contained in international bill of rights, much less all of the other international documents that have been adopted over the past forty years. Critics have suggested that because international standards on human rights are so unrealistically high, they are not taken seriously and are violated with impunity. Governments that flagrantly violate them can take the sting out of international criticisms by pointing to the human rights skeletons in the closets of even the most respected countries. Moreover, it can be argued that setting high standards is a futile exercise until the conditions of underdevelopment that give rise to repressive, authoritarian regimes are alleviated. This claim highlights the essence of the position taken by some Third World leaders that economic and social entitlements should be given priority over the recognition of civil and political liberties, and that the reform of the international economic order must be part of any strategy to promote human rights. On the other hand, international standards can be looked upon as goals which offer a clear sense of direction on how political systems should be humanized. International declarations and covenants can be cited by those who champion human rights within countries to add legitimacy to their demands for the protection of basic liberties. Furthermore, foreign states or the international community as a whole will have grounds for taking action against governments that have treated elements of their populations especially badly.

Just as it has taken centuries for the Western democracies to implement many of the basic rights contained in their great historical documents, a task which as yet is not complete, it should be expected that the progress in the new, less developed countries— many of which are plagued by political instability—will also be a long-term process. Setbacks will take place in some countries, but over the long run it is likely that the flurry of international activity in the human rights field since World War II will continue to be a force for improvements in the treatment of individuals by their governments. Of broader significance, however, is the impact that human rights policies have had in undermining the preeminence of the traditional notions of state sovereignty and nonintervention which have held sway for centuries.

REFERENCES

Amnesty International (1982). *Amnesty International Report 1982*. London: Amnesty International Publications.
Amnesty International (1983). *Political Killings by Governments*. London: Amnesty International Publications.
Amnesty International (1984). *Torture in the 1980s*. London: Amnesty International Publications.

Amuzegar, Jahangir (1978). "Rights and Wrongs," *New York Times,* January 29, p. 17.

Buergenthal, Thomas and Judith V. Torney (1979). "Expanding the International Human Rights Research Agenda," *International Studies Quarterly,* Vol. 23, No. 2 (June), pp. 321–35.

Dominguez, Jorge (1979). "Assessing Human Rights Conditions," pp. 19–116 in Jorge I. Dominguez, Nigel S. Rodley, Bryce Wood, and Richard Falk, *Enhancing Global Human Rights.* New York: McGraw Hill.

Donnelly, Jack (1981). "Recent Trends in the UN Human Rights Activity: Description and Polemic," *International Organization,* Vol. 35, No. 4, (Autumn), pp. 633–57.

Ennals, Martin (1982). "Amnesty International and Human Rights," pp. 63–83 in Peter Willetts (ed.), *Pressure Groups in the Global System: The Transnational Relations of Issue-Oriented Non-Governmental Organizations.* London: Frances Pinter.

Falk, Richard (1979). "Responding to Severe Violations," pp. 207–57 in Jorge I. Dominguez, Nigel S. Rodney, Bryce Wood, and Richard Falk, *Enhancing Global Human Rights.* New York: McGraw Hill.

Falk, Richard (1981). *Human Rights and State Sovereignty.* New York: Holmes & Meier Publishers.

Feinberg, Joel (1973). *Social Philosophy.* Englewood Cliffs, N.J.: Prentice-Hall.

Forsythe, David P. (1982). "Socioeconomic Human Rights: The United Nations, the United States, and Beyond," *Human Rights Quarterly,* Vol. 4, No. 1 (Spring), pp. 435–49.

Forsythe, David P. (1983). *Human Rights and World Politics.* Lincoln: University of Nebraska Press.

Gastil, Raymond D. (1985). "The Comparative Survey of Freedom 1984," *Freedom at Issue.* No. 82 (January–February), pp. 3–15.

Henkin, Louis (1978). *The Rights of Man Today.* Boulder, Co.: Westview Press.

Henkin, Louis (1981). "Introduction" in Louis Henkin (ed.), *The International Bill of Rights: The Covenant on Civil and Political Rights.* New York: Columbia University Press.

Hewlett, Sylvia Ann (1979). "Human Rights and Economic Realities: Tradeoffs in Historical Perspective," *Political Science Quarterly,* Vol. 94, No. 3 (Fall), pp. 543–73.

Hoare, Samuel (1967). "The UN Commission on Human Rights," pp. 59–98 in Evan Luard (ed.), *The International Protection of Human Rights.* New York: Praeger.

Humphrey, John P. (1967). "The UN Charter and the Universal Declaration of Human Rights," pp. 39–58 in Evan Luard (ed.), *The International Protection of Human Rights.* New York: Praeger.

Hurwitz, Leon (1981). *The State as Defendent: Governmental Accountability and the Redress of Individual Grievances*. Westport, Conn.:
Greenwood Press.

International Commission of Jurists, ed. (1981). *Development, Human
Rights, and the Rule of Law*. New York: Pergamon Press.

Joyce, James A. (1979). *New Politics of Human Rights*. New York: St.
Martins.

Kartashkin, Vladimir (1982). "Economic, Social and Cultural Rights,"
pp. 111–34 in Karel Vasak (ed.), *The International Dimensions of
Human Rights*, Vol. I. Westport, Conn.: Greenwood Press.

McDougal, Myres S., Harold D. Lasswell, and Lung-chu Chen (1980).
*Human Rights and World Public Order: The Basic Policies of an
International Law of Human Dignity*. New Haven: Yale University
Press.

Moskowitz, Moses (1979). "Implementing the International Covenants on
Human Rights," pp. 109–30 in B. G. Ramcharan (ed.), *Human Rights:
Thirty Years After the Universal Declaration*. The Hague: Martinus
Nijhoff.

Power, Jonathan (1981). *Amnesty International: The Human Rights Story*.
New York: McGraw-Hill.

Robertson, A. H. (1979). "Human Rights: A Global Assessment," pp. 5–
28 in Donald P. Kommers and Gilburt D. Loescher, *Human Rights and
American Foreign Policy*. Notre Dame, Ind.: University of Notre Dame
Press.

Rodley, Nigel S. (1979). "Monitoring Human Rights Violations in the
1980s," pp. 119–51 in Jorge I. Dominguez, Nigel S. Rodley, Bryce
Wood, and Richard Falk, *Enhancing Global Human Rights*. New York:
McGraw-Hill.

Rubenstein, Richard L. (1983). *The Age of Triage: Fear and Hope in an
Overcrowded World*. Boston: Beacon Press.

Said, Abul Aziz (1979). "Pursuing Human Dignity," pp. 1–21 in Abdul
Aziz Said (ed.), *Human Rights and World Order*. New Brunswick, N.J.:
Transaction Books.

Shue, Henry (1980). *Basic Rights: Subsistence, Affluence, and U.S. Foreign Policy*. Princeton, N.J.: Princeton University Press.

Sohn, Louis B. (1979). "The Improvement of the UN Machinery on
Human Rights," *International Studies Quarterly*, Vol. 23, No. 2 (June),
pp. 186–215.

Ullman, Richard H. (1979). "Introduction: Human Rights—Toward Inter-
national Action," pp. 1–18 in Jorge I. Dominguez, Nigel S. Rodley,
Bryce Wood, and Richard Falk, *Enhancing Global Human Rights*.
New York: McGraw-Hill.

van Boven, Theo C. (1979). "The United Nations and Human Rights," pp. 17–37 in Barry M. Rubin and Elizabeth P. Spiro (eds.), *Human Rights and U.S. Foreign Policy.* Boulder, Co: Westview Press (reprinted from *Bulletin of Peace Proposals,* Vol. 8, No. 3, 1977).

Vogelgesang, Sandy (1979). "Diplomacy and Human Rights," *International Studies Quarterly,* Vol. 32, No. 2 (June), pp. 216–45.

Zvobgo, Eddison J. M. (1979). "A Third World View," pp. 90–106 in Donald P. Kommers and Gilburt D. Loescher (eds.), *Human Rights and American Foreign Policy.* Notre Dame, Ind.: University of Notre Dame Press.

8 OCEAN RESOURCES

Negotiating a New Law of the Sea

Terrestrial creatures that we are, most of us have difficulty comprehending the vastness of ocean areas. That the seas predominate over land on the surface of our planet is apparent from the fact that all the land masses, which cover only 30 percent of the earth's surface, would fit within the broad expanses of the Pacific Ocean (Walsh and Keach, 1979, p. 1). Nor should we overlook the vertical dimension of these areas. The ocean itself, or what is known as the water column, averages 12,000 feet in depth and, concealed by the opaqueness of the waters, is the irregular seabed, which is traversed by long, high ridges and by deep rifts and valleys that divide the earth's crust into six huge plates.

Ocean areas contain immense quantities of natural resources. The waters are home to species of fish and marine mammals that have been a bountiful source of protein for the world's rapidly growing human population, either by being consumed directly or by being fed first to livestock. The continental shelves, the geological prolongations of the land masses that underlie approximately 15 percent of the seabed, contain many resources found in terrestrial regions, including subsurface deposits of coal and iron ore and reserves of oil and natural gas. Oil is being produced off the coasts of 85 nations, and exploration has taken place near 25 others (Walsh and Keach, 1979, p. 15). Enormous quantities of minerals have been found lying on the ocean floor that were washed down with the runoff from the continent to form placer deposits, were welled up from the subsurface of the ocean floor by thermal activity, or precipitated through the waters forming potato-sized nodules.

With the exception of navigation and fishing, which has taken

261

place since prehistoric times, man has been slow to discover and utilize what the oceans have to offer. As recently as a century ago, the first major scientific exploration of the oceans was undertaken by a British team using a wooden steamship named the H.M.S. *Challenger.* Knowledge of the ocean areas increased dramatically in recent decades with the availability of submersibles that have taken scientists to great depths for direct visual observations, sonar technology that can be used to plot the terrain of the seabed, robots that take pictures of the ocean floor and gather samples, drilling devices that can bore the rock of the subsoil, and space satellites that can detect subtle surface variations in water temperatures and concentrations of organic substances.

Development of the ocean's wealth has been made possible by other technological advancements. Far greater quantities of fish can be harvested using larger nets made of strong, synthetic fibers. Helicopters, radar, sonar, and other electronic gear assist in locating concentrations of fish. Floating factory ships that process fish make it possible for fleets to operate in distant, highly productive waters. Gigantic floating platforms can be used to drill for oil and gas in the continental shelves under hundreds of feet of water in areas with harsh weather, such as in the North Sea. Equipment has been developed for dredging the floor of the deep seas and lifting the mineral rich materials through thousands of feet of water to surface vessels for transport to coastal processing facilities. In the latter case, the challenge has been one of not only overcoming the physical obstacles, but doing so in a way that is economically competitive with land-based operations.

The resources of the ocean regions have been a subject for global policy primarily because they are beyond what has been traditionally recognized as the territory of states. Thus, the ocean and seabed have been regarded as a commons that all states could make use of for virtually any purpose, including the harvesting of fish and other natural resources. Free and unlimited access to the natural wealth of these areas was appropriate during earlier eras when relatively little use was made of the oceans. The more intensive exploitation of marine resources in recent decades has led to two problems. One is the depletion of scarce resources, which is readily apparent in the demise of several of what had been the world's most productive fisheries under circumstances that parallel Hardin's "tragedy of the commons." The other is the

prospect of heightened conflict among competing users of resources of the seas which have come to a head as coastal states
unilaterally extend their claims to ocean areas off their shores. In
the words of former President Richard Nixon, the question is one
of "whether the oceans will be used rationally and equitably and
for the benefit of mankind or whether they will become an arena
of unrestrained exploitation and conflicting jurisdictional claims
in which even the most advanced states will be losers" (quoted in
Buzan, 1976, p. 113).

OCEAN RESOURCES AS A GLOBAL PROBLEM

The analysis of ocean resource issues that is presented in this
chapter is limited to two of the principal types: living resources
including fish and marine mammals and seabed mineral deposits.
Both have received considerable attention from international policy makers in large part because of great economic stakes that are
involved. They are also of particular interest because of the contrasting challenges that they pose for policy makers. Whereas
most of the commercially viable fisheries are located within 200
miles of land masses, which has subjected them to the claims of
adjacent coastal states, the richest mineral deposits are found in
the deeper, more distant reaches of the oceans beyond what could
reasonably be claimed by the nearest coastal states. Furthermore,
in the case of living resources, the preeminent policy problem is
to preserve a scarce, renewable resource that is susceptible to
depletion from overfishing. By contrast, the seabed minerals are
found in great abundance, which if they were to be mined on a
major scale, could flood the mineral markets to the chagrin of
land-based producers. Finally, while fisheries have been harvested
for millennia and there is an extensive history of national and
international management of them, in the case of the seabed
minerals policy makers are dealing with an untrapped resource
and thus have had a rare opportunity to work with a relatively
clean slate as they formulate an international legal regime that will
govern the future exploitation of them. Let us turn first to the
policy problems related to ocean fisheries.
The oceans contain a great variety of plant and animal species
that form a complex food chain. At the bottom end are micro-

scopic phytoplankton; at the upper end are the bigger species of fish and marine mammals, including the blue whale, which has been known to reach 100 feet in length and 150 tons in weight, and is the largest animal species known to have inhabited the planet. Most fisheries are found in a relatively small proportion of the vast ocean areas. Coastal areas rich in nutrients that have washed or blown off the land support the growth of phytoplankton and thus are a more suitable habitat for many species of fish. Some of the greatest concentrations of marine life are found where there is an upwelling of nutrients from the ocean depths, such as takes place off the coasts of Peru, California, southwest and northwest Africa, and certain regions of the Indian Ocean. Latitude is also a factor. While the warm tropical waters support a greater abundance of species, because of their intermixing, commercial harvesting is more difficult and less efficient than in temperate regions where prodigious numbers of fewer species are found. For these reasons, only about 10 percent of the ocean's area has the potential for being moderately productive as fisheries, and only 0.1 percent hold potential for being highly productive (Knight, 1977, p. 349).

A small proportion of the more than 14,000 species of marine fish are harvested commercially, either to be consumed directly by human beings or to be ground into fish meal for feeding livestock and poultry, the combination of which accounts for 15 percent of the human consumption of animal protein (Eckert, 1979, p. 16). Each species has a unique combination of traits with implications for how it is harvested and the type of management that is needed. Lobsters and oysters, for example, are known as "localized stocks" which are either sedentary or move only short distances and, thus, live their lives off the coast of a single state. By contrast, "highly migratory" stocks, such as skipjack tuna and some species of whales, range over large areas of the oceans and cross through the coastal jurisdictions of several states and the high seas as well. There are a few anadromous species, the best example being the salmon, that live most of their lives in the oceans—sometimes quite far out from shore—but return to freshwater rivers to spawn, where their movement may be obstructed by dams and other man-made impediments.

While man has been fishing for food since prehistoric times, it is only in the twentieth century and especially since World War II that fishing has been a major industry. Largely due to the technological advances, the world catch of fish more than tripled between 1950 and 1970, climbing from 21 million tons to 70 million tons, most of which comes from the oceans. Since 1970 the catch has leveled off despite even greater investments in fishing operations, a tell-tale sign that at least some of the fisheries are being depleted because too few fish are left to regenerate the stock to its previous level (Gulland, 1980, 367). Among the species for which there have been dramatic drops in the harvest are cod, haddock, halibut, herring, California sardine, and anchovy. Whales have also been particularly susceptible to overharvesting because, being mammals, they have few offspring. The bigger species of whales have been the first to decline rapidly in numbers. It is estimated that only 10,000 blue whales remain, a scant 6 percent of the virgin stock, a figure that lies dangerously close to extinction. The humpback whale has been similarly depleted. Overall, it is believed that the world's whale population is only about one-half of its virgin number (Payne, 1979, pp. 15–16).

The depletion of some of the most valued fisheries is a classical illustration of Garrett Hardin's (1968) "tragedy of the commons." Most of the rich fish beds are located in what until recently was considered to be international waters. As the reputation of highly productive areas attracted more operators, the catches eventually reached the point that the remaining stock could not regenerate itself. The large fleets with modern fishing techniques and floating factories for canning the catch can cause a significant depletion of a fishery within a few years. The individual operators have little incentive for limiting catches to conserve a fishery in international waters because of the "fugitive" character of fish; a country cannot reserve a school of fish for a future catch. If the school is passed up, it is likely to end up in the nets of fishermen from other countries. Thus, there is competition to catch the fish before others do by making greater investments in fishing fleets. As this happens, more vessels catch fewer and fewer fish, and fishing becomes less efficient and profitable for all (Eckert, 1979, p. 118).

The world's catch of living resources from the oceans could be increased by harvesting species which in the past have been largely ignored. It is estimated, for example, that more than 100 million tons of Antarctic krill could be taken annually, which would be more than double the current world fish catch. While such a catch is possible, it is doubtful that it would be commercially profitable in view of the expensive ships that would be necessary for a product that would not command a very high price (Gulland, 1980, p. 377). Moreover, intensive krill fishing would put man in competition with other animals that feed on them, including species of fish, whales, seals, squid, and birds. Another possibility is to reduce the wasting of commercially less desirable species which have previously been discarded when caught up in the nets along with the sought after types of fish. But, even if these opportunities are exploited, it is unlikely that the supply of protein from the oceans will keep pace with the continuing, rapid increases in the world's population.

The mineral deposits that have attracted the greatest interest are found in the form of manganese nodules that were first noticed lying on the floor of the deep seas by the *Challenger* expedition more than a century ago. Black or brown in color, the nodules are soft and crumbly and average about four inches in diameter. They are apparently formed when minerals in the ocean water accrete to small volcanic rocks or calcium compounds, such as a shark's tooth or a fish bone, and slowly precipitate to the ocean floor. The nodules have been found over large areas of the Pacific, Atlantic, and Indian oceans, with the greatest concentrations being located where the waters are between 12,000 and 20,000 feet deep and the seabed is broken up by deep canyons and by hills and mountains with steep irregular slopes. Mining companies have been attracted to especially dense deposits of high grade nodules located in a band in the Pacific Ocean between Hawaii and Central America that is 1500 kilometers long and 200 kilometers wide (Eckert, 1979, p. 217).

It is estimated that there are 1.5 trillion tons of nodules on the floor of the Pacific Ocean alone, which makes them the richest mineral deposit on the planet (Barkenbus, 1979, p. 5). While upwards of thirty different minerals have been detected in varying amounts in the nodules, only four—manganese, nickel, cobalt, and copper—have attracted much commercial interest. Manganese, cobalt, and nickel are used in specialty steels; copper is used extensively in wiring because of its electrical conductivity. Manganese is the most plentiful, comprising an average of about 24 percent of the weight of the nodules, while each of the other three minerals of commercial interest accounts for less than 1 percent of the weight. A United Nations study estimated that seabed reserves would sustain several hundred thousand years of current levels of consumption of manganese, cobalt, and nickel and 6,000 years of copper consumption, compared to less than a 100-year supply in the land-based reserves (quoted in Luard, 1977, p. 150). Because of high costs of mining and refining the nodules, only a small proportion of them may prove to be economically recoverable (Goldwin, 1983, p. 63).

In the early 1960s several companies began studying the technological feasibility and economic viability of mining the deep-sea nodules. Preparation for commercial mining has included extensive prospecting and the development of mining systems. Sizable investments have been made in designing, building, and testing special dredgeheads that are adaptable to the irregular terrain of the ocean floor and equipment for pumping or vacuuming the dredged material to large surface mining vessels that will separate the nodules from water and other materials and convey them to large ore carriers for transport to special coastal processing facilities (Barkenbus, 1979, p. 14–15). Most of the technological obstacles to deep-sea mining have been surmounted. Early investigations predicted that these operations could prove to be less expensive than the terrestrial competition, even by as much as 25 to 50 percent (Luard, 1977, p. 190).

There are now, however, serious doubts about whether such ventures can be profitable in the foreseeable future that may deter would-be miners and their bankers from investing the immense amounts of front-end capital that would be required, $425 to $600 million by one estimate (Barkenbus, 1979, p. 21). An additional consideration is the concurrently depressed market for minerals and the prospect that seabed mining would add significantly to the oversupply, causing prices to plunge even further (Goldwin, 1983, pp. 64–66). Outstanding legal questions and the potential for international conflict also add to the riskiness of deep-sea mining.

Recent explorations of the ocean depths have revealed that nodules are not the only important type of mineral deposit on the seabed, and thus have rekindled interest in seabed mining. In the late 1970s, scientists in small submersibles located polymetallic-sulfide deposits that are formed where hot springs, sometimes described as "black smokers" carry molten rock from the earth interior and spread them across the ocean floor. The extent of these deposits has not been determined because only a very small proportion of the ocean rift systems has been explored. Iron and copper are found in the greatest concentrations in these deposits, in addition there are traces of zinc, vanadium, silver and lead. Even more recently, scientists have also discovered cobalt-rich manganese crusts on the flanks of volcanic islands and sea-mounts, volcanoes that have not broken the surface of the water. Both of these types of deposits are found at lesser depths than the nodules and in many cases within 200 miles of islands and continents in areas that can legitimately be claimed by coastal states (see Cooke, 1984).

THE LAW OF THE SEA CONFERENCES

The basic questions of international ocean policy have been addressed in a series of three United Nations Conferences on the Law of the Sea—often referred to by the acronym UNCLOS—and in the extensive preparatory meetings that preceded them. This undertaking began three decades ago and only in 1982 was brought to a conclusion with the signing of a treaty embodying a new law of the seas. The objective of this series of conferences, attended by nearly the entire membership of the United Nations, has been to draft treaties that will govern all major activities that make use of the ocean areas including navigation, overflight, communication, disposal of wastes, and marine research, as well as the harvesting of living and nonliving resources.

The first two conferences were the culmination of a project begun in 1950 by the International Law Commission, a group of 15 legal experts which had been established by the General Assembly. Its assignment was to codify the customary laws on the use of the oceans that had evolved over the centuries and to contribute to the development of all aspects of ocean law with special emphasis on the nature and extent of coastal state jurisdiction over offshore areas (Hollick, 1981, p. 140). Following up on the work of the commission, delegations from 84 countries attending UNCLOS I in 1958 adopted separate treaties on the territorial seas and contiguous zones, the continental shelves, the high seas, and fishing and the conservation of living resources. UNCLOS II, attended by 88 states, was an unsuccessful attempt to reach agreement on several key issues that had eluded resolution at

UNCLOS I two years earlier, the most important being the width of territorial waters that could be claimed by costal states and the outer boundary of the continental shelf. The unresolved issues diminished significantly the impact of the treaties, which is reflected in the failure of any of the four to be ratified by even one-third of the community of nations.

Credit for triggering the next stage of the UNCLOS process is frequently given to Dr. Arvid Pardo, a delegate to the United Nations from the Mediterranean island nation of Malta. In one of the most memorable speeches ever delivered to the General Assembly, Pardo in 1967 called attention to the inadequacies of the 1958 ocean treaties in view of plans being developed for exploiting the mineral wealth of the deep seabed. Persuaded that the problem warranted further attention in view of the prospects for serious international conflict and pollution if such operations were not subject to international regulation, the General Assembly established a special 35-member Sea-Bed Committee, first on an ad hoc basis in 1968, then a year later as a permanent body. In 1970, the General Assembly adopted a resolution calling for the convening of a UNCLOS III to consider not only the issues upon which the Sea-Bed Committee had focused, but also a full range of other ocean issues, as had been done at UNCLOS I. The Sea-Bed Committee was given responsibility for drafting treaties for UNCLOS III, which began in 1973 with a procedural session in New York.

UNCLOS III consisted of a series of twelve sessions spread out over nine years, each lasting several weeks in one of three location—Caracas, Geneva, and New York City. The length of the conference is attributable to the immense task that lay before the delegates. For beginners, the agenda was unwieldy, consisting of 105 separate items grouped into 25 principal issues. Then, because of the inability of the Sea-Bed Committee to complete its work in the allotted time, negotiations began without the benefit of a working text. Adding to the challenge was a "gentleman's agreement" that a consensus would be sought among all states, 149 at the beginning, each with its unique combination of interests. It was remarkable that agreement was reached on most of the 446 articles of the 200-page treaty without invoking the formal voting procedure under which each state was allowed one vote, with a two-thirds majority of all states present and voting being needed to adopt each article. In the end a vote was taken at the insistence of the United States delegation which desired to record its opposition to the certain provisions on deep-sea mining which most countries had accepted and were unwilling to modify further. The tally was 130 countries in favor, 4 opposed (including the United States), and 17 abstaining. The treaty was signed by 117 states on the first day it was opened for signature, December 10, 1982, and will officially come into effect when ratified by 60 countries, probably within the decade.

The positions taken by governments have often been the product of intensive lobbying by domestic groups that make use of the oceans and would be affected by international law. This is especially true of the principal maritime states, whose citizens make multiple uses of the oceans. The defense ministries of the major powers, for example, have a vital interest in the mobility of their armed forces and are, therefore, concerned about navigational rights for submarines and surface vessels and overflight privileges for their aircraft. Coastal fishermen desiring to exclude foreign fleets from nearby waters are often at odds with operators of distant water fleets, as well as some of the major food processors. The latter are concerned that policies designed to protect coastal fishing interests would reduce their access to fisheries located off other countries' coasts. Consortia of companies with large investments in deep-sea mining, have had an active interest in the negotiations on the future seabed regime.

Numerous international organizations have either responsibilities or interests in ocean resources and the UNCLOS process. FAO has a special interest in fish as a protein source and has worked with the United Nations Development Programme to assist Third World countries in managing fisheries off their coasts. In 1983 FAO sponsored the World Fisheries Conference which drew representatives from 121 countries and 30 international organizations to discuss fisheries management. The International Oceanographic Commission, which is affiliated with UNESCO, has sponsored extensive research on the living resources of the oceans. Among regional groups, the EEC has been perhaps the most active in managing the marine resources off the coasts of its members. The Organization of African Unity and the conferences of the Non-Aligned Movement have been forums for discussion of UNCLOS issues among Third World countries. Turning to nongovernmental organizations, the Scientific Committee on Ocean Research, which is affiliated with the International Council of Scientific Union (ICSU), is a respected source of expert information on marine matters. The Pacem in Maribus group has been a strong proponent of a new ocean law, and the Costeau Society is but one of many associations concerned with the conservation of the resources of the seas.

THE EXPANDING JURISDICTION OF COASTAL STATES

Who has the right to make use of ocean areas and to exploit their natural resources? Historically this has been the fundamental issue addressed by international policy on the seas. In examining it further, it is important to distinguish *coastal margins* over which the adjacent coastal state has traditionally enjoyed special privileges, the focus of this section, from *international waters,* otherwise known as the "high seas," which lie beyond the jurisdiction of coastal states."

The notion that nation-states may assert some control over a band of adjacent waters has been a basic tenet of customary international law for several centuries. When these rights of coastal states were initially recognized for purposes of national defense and protection of offshore fisheries, they were limited to a zone of three nautical miles, the distance that could be defended by shore batteries of the late seventeenth century. This principle evolved into the concept of "territorial waters" over which the coastal state could exercise most prerogatives of sovereignty, including control over the ocean floor and air space. An exception was the right of vessels from other countries to navigate the zone under the doctrine of "innocent passage." In a limited area just beyond the territorial waters, known as a "contiguous zone," coastal states have been permitted to act in the interests of national security or to enforce national laws pertaining to matters such as customs, health and sanitation, immigration, and environmental protection.

What had been a long-standing consensus on a 3-mile width of territorial waters broke down during the mid-twentieth century as a succession of coastal states unilaterally increased the breadth of their jurisdictions. Until 1945 these claims were modest, in no cases more than 12 miles. In September 1945 President Truman proclaimed that the United States had jurisdiction over the resources of the subsoil and seabed of contiguous continental shelves even where they extended beyond its territorial waters. The action, which was prompted by the discovery of vast amounts of oil and natural gas in the Gulf of Mexico, was seized upon by other coastal states, particularly Latin American ones, as a precedent for extending their control over offshore resources, including fisheries (Knight, 1977, p. 50). The boundaries of some of these claims were defined simply as a distance from the shoreline, usually 12, 50, or 200 nautical miles; others have taken into account the depth of water or the contour of the ocean floor. Some claims are extensions of territorial waters; others are limited to exclusive rights to fisheries or other resources of the coastal margin beyond more narrowly defined territorial waters. By 1980 more than 100 coastal states had broadened their jurisdiction beyond the traditional 3-mile limit (Barkenbus, 1979, p. 29). In numerous cases these claims have gone well beyond the technological and economic means of coastal states to exploit the resources of the area; some have preceded concrete evidence of resources.

Neither UNCLOS I or II were successful in reaching a consensus on the breadth of coastal jurisdictions. On the issue of the width of territorial seas, an irresolvable deadlock developed between advocates of 3- and 12-mile limits. The Convention on Fishing and Conservation of the Living Resources on the High Seas (1958) permitted coastal states to adopt conservation measures unilaterally, but subject to the ambiguous condition that negotiations with other nations harvesting the fisheries in question had failed (Alexander, 1980, p. 6). Exploitation of the resources of the continental shelf also proved to be a sticky issue. The compromise that was finally hammered out for inclusion in the Convention on the Continental Shelf gave the coastal state exclusive jurisdiction over seabed resources to a depth of 200 meters or "beyond that, to where the depth of superadjacent waters admits of the exploration of the natural resources." This open-ended provision imposes no boundaries on what part of the continental shelf could be claimed by coastal states having access to the new technologies for deep-sea mining.

The issue of the breadth of coastal state jurisdictions was again tackled at UNCLOS III. This time, however, a consensus was reached on a band of territorial waters 12 nautical miles in width, beyond which would be a contiguous zone seaward to 24 miles and an exclusive economic zone (EEZ) out to 200 nautical miles. Within its EEZ, a coastal state would have sovereign rights for the purpose of exloring, exploiting, conserving, and managing both the living and nonliving resources of the waters, seabed, and subsoil of the area, but would not be permitted to exercise other prerogatives of sovereignty, such as the control of navigation, communications, and overflight. In cases where the continental shelf extends beyond 200 miles, coastal states may also lay claim to its resources out to the drop-off called the "continental margin," but must contribute a small percentage of the value of mineral production to an international fund to be distributed to the parties to the treaty, particularly the less developed countries. If EEZs or continental shelves of coastal states overlap, those states are to agree to an equitable dividing line in accordance with established international law. Under these provisions of the new law of the seas, coastal states will gain exclusive control of as much as 40 percent of the ocean space, which includes 90 percent of the commercially exploited living resources and all known sites that are suitable for commercial energy production (Pardo, 1983, pp. 19–20).

FROM THE FREEDOM OF THE SEAS TO THE COMMON HERITAGE OF MAN

Traditionally, the "high seas," those areas of the oceans lying beyond the territorial waters of coastal states, have been open to use by all members of the international community. This doctrine of customary law, known as the "freedom of the seas" can be traced to a legal treatise entitled *Mare Liberum,* published in 1609 by the Dutch legal scholar Hugo Grotius. In it he challenged the 1493 Treaty of Tordesillas, which divided the Atlantic Ocean along a longitude lying 1000 miles west of the Cape Verde Islands, granting exclusive navigational rights to Spain to the west and to Portugal to the east. Concerned that the treaty interfered with the development of Dutch commercial interests throughout the world, Grotius contended that no state should be permitted to appropriate any part of the oceans beyond a narrow coastal margin and that the vessels of all states had an equal right to make use of the high seas, including the freedom of navigation for its vessels. This doctrine became a guiding principle of international ocean law for more than three centuries, during which it was reaffirmed by an unbroken chain of national and international court cases. Even as recently as 1958, the "freedom of the seas" was a guiding principle of the Convention on the High Seas adopted at UNCLOS I, which provides that the high seas, or any part of them, may not be claimed by any state, but are available to all nations for activities such as navigation, fishing, laying of submarine cables and pipelines, and overflight, if undertaken with reasonable regard to the interests of other states excercising their rights to use the high seas.

The "freedom of the seas" was a product of historical circumstances, having gained wide acceptance when the oceans were thought to be virtually limitless and inexhaustible, such that the activities of a relatively small number of users would not seriously interfere with one another (Christy, 1975, p. 698). The resources of most interest were the living ones, which were thought available in such abundance that they would be adequate to satisfy the harvesting capacity of all states without being depleted. Thus, there was little need for international institutions to referee use of the high seas, nor was there much reason for users to stake claims to any part of them. Whatever additional economic revenues would result from exclusive use of claims would be insignificant compared to the cost of protecting them, assuming that the user had the means to do so.

The principle came under attack, however, as the oceans were used more intensively, especially in the period following World War II. The extended claims of coastal states significantly impinged on the amount of area falling under the high seas designation. Companies interested in deep-sea mining argued that their operations could be commercially profitable only if they were granted exclusive rights to specific seabed plots rich in mineral nodules. Avid Pardo, in his 1967 speech to the General Assembly, warned that the existing law of the seas would permit coastal states to divide up the entire seabed without any further serious international discussion, a development that would have serious implications for his country and many others. He proposed that not only should the permissible claims of coastal states to the seabed be more clearly defined, but also that the remaining seabed should be treated as the "common heritage of man." (Pardo, 1979, p. 138).

The "common heritage" concept is a major departure from the "freedom of the seas" principle in that it would treat the seabed as if it were the joint property of all states. As envisioned by Pardo, all states in their role of being part owners of the seabed would have a right to participate in decisions about how the seabed resources would be developed and to share in the benefits derived from harvesting them. This privilege would be extended to the landlocked states and those with little if any prospect of exploiting deep-sea minerals on their own. The area would be reserved for peaceful purposes and its resources conserved in the interests of future generations. Some interpretations of the common heritage doctrine suggested, furthermore, that the seabed should be developed largely for the benefit of the poorer members of the international community. In so doing, the proceeds from a nonnational area could become a new form of development assistance, which would not require a transfer of any of the present wealth of the industrial world. To implement such a regime, a need was foreseen for a new international agency which presumably would be open to the membership of all countries.

Pardo's proposals were debated intensively in the deliberations of the Sea-Bed Committee, which led first to a 1969 General Assembly resolution declaring a moratorium on any future claims to the seabed or the development of its resources while an international regime was being established. The following year, the common heritage notion was incorporated into the General Assembly's 1970 Declaration of Principles Governing the Seabed . . . Beyond the Limits of National Jurisdiction. Because the declaration was adopted unanimously, save for fourteen abstentions, it has been widely viewed as an expression of newly evolving international common law. Since then, the common heritage concept has guided negotiations at UNCLOS III where unsuccessful efforts were made by some delegations to extend its applicability to the water and air space above the international parts of the seabed, or what has been called the "creeping vertical jurisdiction" of the international community (Barkenbus, 1979, p. 146).

MANAGEMENT OF OCEAN FISHERIES

Few would deny the need to bring ocean fisheries under some form of management; however, there has been no consensus on how the fisheries should be managed. Of the many issues that have arisen over international policy on ocean fishing, the most basic one is how to divide responsibility between coastal states and international institutions.

Historically, management of ocean fisheries beyond a narrow band of territorial waters has been performed in a fragmented way by a score of international regulatory bodies known as fishery commissions, most of which have come about since World War II. Some of these commissions were established at the instigation of the FAO, which facilitates their work through its Committee on Fisheries. The commissions are voluntary associations of states varying in size from as few as two to as many as thirty members that have common interest in harvesting a fishery and keeping it productive. A majority of the commissions concentrate on a specific species, sometimes within a certain region, examples being the International Whaling Commission, the North Pacific Fur Seal Commission, the International Pacific Salmon Fisheries Commission, and the Inter-American Tropical Tuna Commission. Others manage a variety of commercial stocks in a geographically defined region as do the North-East Atlantic Fisheries Commission, the Indian Ocean Fisheries Commission, and the newly formed South Pacific Forum. Some are limited by their charters to conducting research and making recommendations, while others are empowered to adopt rules and enforce them on their members (see Johnston and Enomoto, 1981).

The domain of the international fishery commissions has been encroached upon by the expanded claims of coastal states over nearby fisheries, commonly proclaimed on the grounds that the commissions have been ineffective in preventing overfishing. When the 200-mile EEZs come into effect, most of the ocean fisheries will be under the sole control of coastal states. The new law of the seas also gives coastal states exclusive rights to harvest anadromous species that spawn in their freshwater streams, but spend much of their life span in the open seas beyond the boundaries of the EEZs. There continues to be a need for the nations that catch species which populate the high seas or migrate across the boundaries of national EEZs to prevent overfishing by agreeing upon some form of international management.

Both national and international fishery policies have been guided by three complementary goals. The first is to conserve the fishery, thereby averting a collapse that could occur if the resource is treated as an unregulated commons. Conservation in turn is essential to achieving the other two goals: maximizing not only the long-term catch but also the profitability of the fishing industry. A widely used standard for setting the annual catch at a level that would best realize these goals is known as the "maximum sustainable yield" (MSY), a concept that was written into the 1958 Convention of Fishing and the Conservation of the Living Resources of the High Seas, adopted at UNCLOS I. The MSY is the largest annual catch that can be taken without diminishing the stock (Klemm, 1981, p. 80) levels. Thus, the fisheries are conserved in order that over the long run they may make the greatest possible contribution to satisfying the growing world demand for animal protein. Advocates of a somewhat different standard would maximize the profitability of the world's fishing industries, rather than the biological potential of the resource, by setting limits somewhat below the MSY on the grounds that fish can be harvested more efficiently when stocks are maintained at high levels (Young, 1979, pp. 115–19).

Translating the MSY of a fishery into a concrete figure known as the "total allowable catch" requires fairly accurate estimates of the size of the stock, as well as familiarity with the biological traits of the species being harvested, in particular the rates of reproduction and interaction patterns with other species. The previous performance of a fishery, including trends in the annual catch, remains the most readily available type of data for calculating a MSY. Caution should be used in interpreting these figures, however, because significant fluctuations in the harvest may reflect not only the size of previous catches, but also natural factors, such as shifts in ocean currents. The International Council for the Exploration of the Sea, established in 1902, was the pioneer in research on fish stocks. It continues to conduct research on fisheries in the North and Baltic Seas and advises several of the international fishery commissions with responsibilities in the area. Other fishery commissions conduct research and collect data on catches with widely differing degrees of proficiency.

Having determined how large a catch may be allowed, the next challenge is to devise a strategy to keep the catch within a desirable range. One approach is to impose rules designed to reduce the take of fishing fleets. A "closed season" may be declared during which fishing is not permitted. Alternatively, restrictions may be imposed on the type of equipment that may be used, such as specifications on the minimum size of mesh permitted in nets, the purpose being to allow smaller specimens to escape, mature, and reproduce. Such rules have not always been effective, however, because they often do not make it impossible or even illegal to catch an excessive amount of fish, only more difficult and costly. For example, fishing operators can circumvent a closed season by investing in larger, more efficient fleets, enabling them to catch more fish during the shortened open season, but less profitably.

An alternative approach would dispense with rules on the conduct of fishing in favor of simply setting ceilings on the quantity of fish that may be taken annually. A single limit, known as a "global quota," may be imposed on the combined catch of all countries. Fishing takes place on a "first-come, first-served basis" until the limit is reached, after which it is prohibited until the next open season. Such an arrangement, which has been adopted by the International Whaling Commission in its efforts to conserve species of whales showing signs of depletion, requires frequent reports on the catch taken by the vessels of all countries working a fishery so that the accumulated catch can be updated. Unfortunately, global quotas encourage a competitive scramble among fishing operators, each trying to maximize its share of the allowable catch before the limit is reached, after which the fishermen and their equipment may be idle for extended periods. The competitive excesses can be avoided by assigning an individual quota to each nation desiring to work a fishery, which it may take at its leisure. International fishery commissions have set these national quotas on the basis of such criteria as the proportion of the catch each country has historically taken, its population, proximity to the fishery, and investments in fishing fleets. Conflicts often arise over the size of the quotas with the possibility that dissatisfied states will ignore the limits, prompting others to do likewise.

Coastal states have used a variety of strategies of managing

fisheries located in their territorial waters and unilaterally declared exclusive fishery zones. A few coastal states reserve the
total allowable catch for themselves. Others have agreed to permit
foreign fleets to operate in these zones, as some have done for
decades and even centuries, but subject to fees and licensing
procedures and to limits on the catch and other restrictions, such
as limits on the season. The United States occasionally suspends
the fishing privileges of certain countries in the 200-mile fishery
zone it legislatively enacted in 1976 as a sanction for unrelated
disapproved actions, cases in point being the Soviet intervention
in Afghanistan and imposition of martial law in Poland. In the
EEZs that will be established by the new law of the sea, coastal
states are obligated not only to conserve the living resources in
zone, but also to promote their "optimal utilization." This latter
provision means that a coastal state which does not harvest the
entire allowable catch, which it is privileged to set, should allow
foreign vessels to take the remaining surplus, with priority being
given to neighboring landlocked or geographically disadvantaged
countries. Coastal states, however, are not prevented from avoiding this responsibility by setting a lower allowable catch than
would be necessary to maintain the optimal productivity of a
fishery.

Enforcement of limits is a more complicated task for international fishery commissions that for coastal states, most of which
have developed the means for patrolling their exclusive zones.
Moreover, coastal states may make the licensing of foreign vessels
contingent on the acceptance of stiff enforcement procedures.
Rules pertaining to fishing on the high seas have been more
difficult to enforce because, under the "freedom of the seas"
principle, vessels in these areas are subject to no authority other
than the government whose flag they fly. Therefore, most fishery
commissions have relied on self-enforcement which depends both
on the willingness and capacity of nations to monitor their operators. In some cases, they have been able to reach agreement on
international monitoring procedures which provide for onboard
inspections by foreign personnel, either on a spot or continuing
basis or when there is reason to suspect violations. The primary
sanction for violations is the prospect of eroding the willingness of
other countries to comply with the limitations, which would un-

dermine the very viability of the commission and any future prospect for conserving the fishery upon which they have come to depend.

MANAGEMENT OF SEABED MINING

Given the abundance of mineral riches of the deep-sea, conservation has not yet become a serious consideration in international policy on the seabed in the way it has for depleted fisheries. The ostensible goal of international deep-sea policy is to facilitate the orderly development of those resources for the benefit of humanity. Such an objective could be interpreted to mean maximizing extraction of the minerals in the most efficient way, which is the aim of the profit-seeking mining interests based in the developed world. Countries not technologically equipped to engage in deep-sea mining endorse such activity only to the degree to which the profits are distributed in what to them seems an equitable way, along the lines of their interpretation of the common heritage principle. States which produce the same minerals from land-based operations have argued that the deep-sea should be mined only to the extent to which markets can absorb a greater supply of minerals without a significant drop in prices. Some concerns have also been expressed about the need to ensure that the mining of the seabed is conducted in ways that do not cause significant environmental damage.

Goals and principles aside, the fundamental question of international seabed policy is who will be permitted to mine the area. Initially, two types of proposals, which in some respects are polar opposites, were offered at UNCLOS III. One would leave the mining entirely to nation-based companies which could either privately or publicly owned and operated, including the corporations that have already invested heavily in mining technologies and prospected extensively for promising seabed sites. The other would grant exclusive development rights to a new internationally owned venture, known as the Enterprise, which would be a commercial arm of an International Seabed Authority that would be established to manage the non-national regions of the ocean floor. The Enterprise would carry out seabed mining, including processing and marketing of the minerals, with the objective of making profits that would be distributed to the international community as a whole. As the negotiations at UNCLOS III proceeded, a general consensus was reached on a compromise, initially proposed by Henry Kissinger, which would have it both ways by allowing simultaneous mining by national and international concerns (Nye, 1983, p. 117). This so-called "parallel" system was incorporated into the new law of the sea treaty.

The new ocean law will significantly alter the conditions under which nationally based enterprises may mine the ocean floor. Under the long-standing principle of "open access," corporations would have been permitted to help themselves to any nodules they dredged up, just as fishermen may keep the fish they catch in their nets, but would not be allowed to claim permanent rights to unmined deposits (Eckert, 1979, p. 240). The mining companies did not find this arrangement entirely satisfactory because it did not allow them to record internationally recognized claims to areas they wished to mine to ensure that they would have some protection against claim jumpers who might try to take advantage of the sizable investments that had been made in prospecting. Under the terms of the new treaty, it is possible for miners to secure an exclusive right to explore and mine a specified area of the seabed for a fixed period, but subject to several important conditions. First, the mining company must be "sponsored" by a state that is a party to the treaty. Second, two potential mining sites must be proposed, one to be chosen by the International Seabed Authority on a "you cut, I choose first" arrangement to hold in reserve for its own mining operations. Exclusive rights to develop the remaining site will then be awarded to the applying company. Third, the mining will be subject to "production authorizations" that limit the total amount of minerals that may be mined from the seabed during any given period in order to protect land-based producers. Fourth, a specified percentage of the value of what is produced or alternatively of the profits that are generated is to be paid to the International Seabed Authority to cover its administrative costs, with any surplus being distributed to the less developed countries. Finally, the company must be willing to sell the types of technologies it uses at the site to the Enterprise at reasonable commercial rates (Oxman, 1983, pp. 156–57).

Early in the negotiations on the new ocean law it became apparent that new international institutions would be needed to oversee the development of deep-sea resources. Thus, the treaty provided for the International Seabed Authority to be a policy-making and administrative agency and for an International Tribunal that could be used to resolve disputes pertaining to the law of the sea. Reaching agreement on the specifics of the Authority was one of the most arduous tasks encountered at UNCLOS III. Among the issues that were difficult to resolve were the range of its responsibilities, who would be represented on its decision-making bodies, the procedures that would be used in voting, and how it would be financed. What emerged after extensive negotiation was a blueprint for an IGO that, like many others, has an Assembly in which all parties to the treaty are represented, a Council having limited membership, an Enterprise as a mining appendage, and a Secretariat. The composition of the Council, which is to have extensive authority over mining rules, environmental restrictions, and amendments to the treaty, was a particularly contentious issue. It was finally agreed that the Council would have 36 members drawn from among the parties to the treaty, which would always include 4 of the largest consuming states, 4 of the states having the largest land-based production of the same minerals mined on the seabed, and 4 of the states whose nationals had made the largest investment in deep seabed mining. A compromise was also reached on the division of the seats between the Soviet bloc, the West, and the Third World and, as a concession to induce the acceptance of the Reagan administration, a seat was guaranteed to the largest consumer of the minerals in question, which would presumably always be the United States. The most important decisions will be made by consensus, others by a two-thirds or three-quarters majority. The $1 billion of capital needed by the Enterprise, the mining arm of the Authority, to develop one mining site would come equally from commercial loans extended by private sources and from interest-free loans provided by the states that become parties to the treaty (Oxman, 1983, pp. 157–58).

THE POLITICS OF INTERNATIONAL OCEAN POLICY

Given the scope of the UNCLOS III agenda and the tremendous stakes involved for such a large group of nations, it was inevitable that numerous and significant conflicts of interest would arise. Spirited negotiations took place between the several groupings of states that had formed around common interests, which made the process of arriving at a new ocean law long and arduous. Remarkably, the conflicts did not prove to be irreconcilable until an eleventh-hour reassessment of the United States position by the Reagan administration upon coming into office in 1981 (see Laursen, 1983, 136–48). What seems to have made such a broad consensus possible was a general conviction that a new ocean law was badly needed to avoid a breakdown of international public order in the use of the seas. This end could be achieved only if all parties to the negotiations were willing to compromise on some of their preferences in return for concessions by other countries.

Many of the conflicts reflect the different geographical characteristics of the countries participating in the negotiations. Coastal states have an interest in extending their jurisdiction to incorporate off-shore fisheries and to adjacent continental shelves rich in petroleum and natural gas. Countries with archipelagoes or coastlines indented with bays and fjords benefit from having straight baselines used for drawing the boundaries of their coastal zones, rather than a baseline that closely follows the irregularities of their shorelines. Nations bordering straits desire greater latitude in controlling shipping traffic in the interests of security, safety, and avoiding environmental damages. In contast, approximately one-third of the states represented at UNCLOS III are either land-locked or fall in the category of being geographically disadvantaged in view of their relatively short coastlines (Luard, 1977, p. 199). Their interests lie in securing access to a portion of the resources found in the more ample coastal zones of nearby states and a share of the wealth of international regions to which they contend they are entitled under the common heritage principle.

The extent to which the nationals of a state make use of the broad expanse of the oceans is another factor in the positions that were taken on many of the issues at UNCLOS III. The major maritime states, such as the United States, Japan, the Soviet Union, and several of the Western European countries, send out large number of merchants vessels, fishing fleets, naval forces, and research expeditions that operate in distant regions of the oceans, sometimes in close proximity to the coasts of foreign countries, and make heavy use of key international straits. They are also the home of the companies that have developed the technology and assembled the capital for seabed mining operations. In the interests of continuing and expanding these activities, the major maritime states, all of which are developed countries, have favored ocean policies which maximize their freedom to operate on the oceans without being encumbered by restrictions imposed either by coastal states or by the international community.

The freedom of the seas principle is not as attractive to less developed countries, for whom UNCLOS III became another forum for pursuing a new international economic order. Noting that the freedom of the seas became a tenet of customary international law when much of the Third World was under colonial domination, the doctrine from their perspective is looked upon as one of many instruments used by the rich and powerful nations to achieve and maintain their global domination. (see Anand, 1983, pp. 230–31). An Indonesian delegate to UNCLOS III observed that Grotius originated the concept at the request of the East India Company to facilities Dutch colonialization of Indonesia more than 300 years ago (Djalal, 1980, p. 22). Looking to the future, there is concern in the Third World that the rich, industrialized countries, which have the technology and capital needed to profitably exploit the wealth of the oceans, would be the only ones to benefit from a policy of free access. To achieve what they consider a more equitable distribution of the proceeds from the development of marine resources, the delegates from the Third World pushed on two issues. First, they were instrumental in the adoption of 200-mile EEZs, which would permit them to reduce the competition from developed countries to resources in areas off their coasts or, alternatively, to regulate and tax foreign activities in these areas. Second, by promoting the common heritage principle as an alternative to the freedom of the seas, they attempted to establish a legal right to share in the benefits from developing the resources of the seabed in areas beyond the jurisdiction of coastal states.

In the case of fishing, one conflict between maritime and coastal states has been especially salient. The countries which concentrate their efforts in nearby waters, such as Peru, Ecuador, and Iceland, contend that they have been besieged by the distant-water fishing fleets of Japan, the Soviet Union, the United States, and several of the Eastern European countries. Thailand, Taiwan, and South Korea are among a growing number of less developed countries engaged in distant-water fishing. With their modern equipment and factory vessels, which enable them to catch and process great quantities of fish efficiently, distant-water fleets can move into the waters off the coasts of other states and, within a few seasons, deplete a fishery to the degree that its productivity falls off sharply on a temporary or possibly a permanent basis, before moving on to another promising area. Coastal fishermen, whose reliance on traditional methods restricts their efforts to regions near their home ports, are left with a badly diminished resource. The desire to protect these nearby fisheries upon which their people have in some cases depended upon for centuries explains why some states have unilaterally claimed exclusive rights to the living resources in adjacent waters and pushed for 200-mile EEZs, which would give them a legal basis for regulating, if not excluding, foreign fleets. In contrast, owners of the distant-water fleets feared the profitability of their large investments will be jeopardized if they are forced out of the rich offshore fisheries or are required to pay high fees for the privilege of harvesting what traditionally was free for the taking.

Interests also diverge in the case of fisheries that are not contained within the boundaries of the exclusive zone of a single coastal state. Such is the case with migratory and high seas species, an example being the heavily fished tuna in the Eastern Pacific, and where coastal zones are shared, as is done by the members of the European Economic Community. Owners of large, mechanized fleets have an interest in being allowed to harvest fish as rapidly as possible on a first-come, first-served basis until the combined take of all operators reaches the total allowable catch or global quota. Countries whose fishermen use traditional techniques prefer to be guaranteed a share of the catch which can be harvested at a rate that their technology permits. When allocations are made to individual countries, disagreements frequently arise over the criteria to be used in setting each nation's share. Historically, heavy users of a fishery are at odds with newcomers desiring to expand their operations to get what they consider to be a more equitable share of the allowable catch (Joseph and Greenough, 1979, p. 26). Several of the the Latin

American coastal states have argued that their geographical proximity to the migratory routes of the Pacific tuna entitled them to preferential allocations, which is a criterion taken into account by several of the regional fishery commissions. Similarly, the United States and Canada, which host the spawning of large numbers of salmon in their freshwater streams, have argued that coastal states should be given special consideration in harvesting anadromous species. Otherwise, the coastal state would have little incentive for preserving the freshwater habitat essential to the survival of these species.

Perhaps the most contentious issue of international ocean policy involves rights to mine the deep seabed. Failing to negotiate what it considered a suitable arrangement for private mining companies, the Reagan administration refused to sign the new ocean law even though all of the other provisions of the treaty were found to be acceptable and indeed some of them to be important to United States interests. The United States has subsequently declined to attend or pay assessments for the Preparatory Commission that was given the task of implementing the treaty.

Throughout UNCLOS III, the United States has favored what could be described as a "frontier mining code" that would recognize claims of mining companies to specified seabed plots on a first-come, first-served basis and confer on them exclusive rights to develop the resources found on them. International regulations, such as limits on production and the payment of royalties, which would jeopardize the profitability of mining ventures, were also opposed. From the perspective of the United States, seabed mining is not only an economic opportunity, but also a potentially more secure source of strategically needed minerals that otherwise must be imported from politically unreliable, land-based suppliers. Thus, American delegates vehemently opposed early proposals that would have granted a monopoly over deep-sea mining to an international enterprise over which the United States might have little influence. The "parallel" system permitting both national and international mining ventures was accepted by the Carter administration as a necessary compromise, but without much enthusiasm, especially the provisions for the transfer of the mining technologies. The prospective competition of the Authority's Enterprise combined with production limits and international taxes raised skepticism about whether private mining ventures would be economically viable. Beyond the question of profitability of deep-sea mining, concerns have been expressed that establishment of an international enterprise for exploiting the resources of the seabed will be seized upon by Third World countries as a precedent for the development of other "nonnational" resources, such as those of Antarctica and outer space.

States having little immediate prospect of developing their own capacity for seabed mining would gain little from the open-access policy favored by the United States. Looking upon themselves as common owners of the seabed resources under the common heritage principle, they in effect have been saying to the mining companies, "touch the nodules at the bottom of the sea and you touch my property. Take them away and you take away my property" (Pinto, 1980, p. 32). Caucusing as the Group of 77, they have taken the position that equity rather than production and profits should be the primary goals guiding the seabed regime (Barkenbus, 1979, p. 105). From their perspective, equity could be best achieved by a strong international seabed authority operating an international company that would mine the wealth of the ocean depths with the profits being distributed on the basis of economic need, thus in effect becoming a new form of economic assistance for the less developed countries. Moreover, an international enterprise would enable all countries to participate in the development and use of mining technologies, rather than falling further and further behind the advanced states. While less developed countries would prefer that all mining be done by an international enterprise, they were practical enough to realize that the developed countries would not accept a treaty which failed to allow state-based mining companies to assume part of the action and, furthermore, they appreciated that these companies would be an essential source of mining technology. The Group 77 insisted, however, that the mining done by these companies should be regulated closely by the International Seabed Authority to ensure that it is undertaken in a manner consistent with the interests of the broader international community and that it not jeopardize, but enhance, the viability of an international enterprise engaging in parallel operations.

The interests of the prospective marine mining countries would undoubtedly have fared better if issues pertaining to the seabed had been dealt with separately in a forum limited to themselves, perhaps along the lines of the negotiations undertaken by the Antarctic Treaty Consultative Parties, which are restricted to the sixteen states that have conducted substantial scientific research activities on the continent. This in fact is what the United States has attempted to do in its efforts to get the nations whose firms have already invested in deep-sea mining ventures to agree to a "mini-treaty" that would be an alternative to the new law of the sea which it finds so objectionable. Preliminary agreements were reached in 1982 and 1983 among a group of countries, including the United States, United Kingdom, Canada, France, Japan, Belgium, Italy, West Germany, and the Netherlands, that no party would license operations in areas that had previously been licensed by the other states. While the mini-treaty provides miners some protection against encroachments or interference of other parties, it offers no security against such actions by other states. Moreover, the future of these agreements is in doubt in view of the reluctance of several of the countries to make any commitments that would prejudice their position on the more comprehensive law of the sea treaty.

ASSESSMENT AND PROSPECTS

The adoption of the new law of the sea treaty in 1982 was the climax of a long, and often tedious and frustrating, effort to create an international regime to govern the use of ocean areas. UNCLOS III, which dragged on for nine years, has been described as the most important international law-making conference ever held (Dolman, 1980, p. 39). If the product of the UNCLOS effort is accepted by most states and proves to be an effective framework for managing the use of the oceans—including the development of its resources—the experience will lend a big boost to the confidence of the global community in its capacity to work together to resolve the major policy problems that confront it. Alternatively, its failure would be a major blow to the international policy process that would prompt skepticism about whether it can bring about meaningful agreements that justify the investments that have been made in it thus far.

The impact of the new ocean law will depend in large part upon its acceptance by the nations that negotiated it. The willingness of more than 130 states to sign the treaty is reason to believe that it will receive the sixty ratifications required for it to come into effect within the decade. So far, the rate of ratifications has been a slow trickle, but the pace could quicken if a few key become parties. If this occurs, the effectiveness of the treaty could be seriously undermined by the continued opposition of the United States, given its heavy and varied use of the oceans and leading role in the international community generally. Future United States administrations may look upon the treaty more favorably, especially if its Western allies ratify it, thus thwarting efforts to establish a "mini-regime" among the potential seabed mining states which would incorporate agreements to respect each other's claims. It is also possible that the seabed provisions of the treaty which triggered American opposition will recede in importance with waning economic prospects of profitable deep-sea mining even under the most favorable legal circumstances (Goldwin, 1983, p. 67). The larger consideration for the United States is whether it will be able to enjoy the numerous advantageous provisions of the treaty, such as the liberalized right of transit passage through straits and uncontested jurisdiction over the resources of its coastal zone, without accepting the whole package of ocean law (Ratiner, 1982, p. 1006–7). Thus, the future of the treaty may come down to a question of whether the treaty is more important to the United States than the United States is to the successful implementation of the treaty by the remainder of the international community.

The issue of American participation aside, what will be the probable impact of the new law of the seas on the use of ocean resources, particularly in regard to the goals of production, equity, and conservation? Keep in mind that the treaty combines two very different approaches to resource management. It puts the immense quantities of the readily available natural resources located in the coastal margins under the jurisdiction of the adjacent coastal states, a very decentralized approach to management. Thus, it legitimizes the claims to extended coastal zones that coastal states had been making for several decades. In contrast, the management of the riches of the deep seabed is to be entrusted to the new International Seabed Authority which would be a bold experiment in the centralized, supranational control of an important natural resource. Its mining arm, the Enterprise, would be an unprecedented experiment in the international development of a resource, or what is in effect an international form of socialism.

The provisions for the EEZs hold considerable promise for the conservation of living resources concentrated in the coastal margins, but do not ensure that they will be harvested to their full potential, much less that the catch will be equitably distributed among nations. Having the exclusive right to exploit nearby fisheries, the coastal states will also absorb all of the costs of their depletion through overharvesting and will, therefore, have greater incentives for conserving them than was previously the case when they were treated as international, public resources. It is for this reason that exclusive zones of this type embody Hardin's preferred strategy for averting a tragedy. While it is still possible that some states lack the means or inclination to manage fisheries effectively, the past experience with unilaterally declared fishing zones has been a recovery of overexploited stocks. While this is occurring, there may be a significant underutilization of the fishery due to conservative estimates of the allowable catch by the coastal states and a reluctance to share "surplus" fish with foreign countries.

In any event, the EEZs will be a bonanza for a relatively small number of coastal states. More then three-quarters of the total area encompassed by the exclusive zones will be under the jurisdiction of just 25 states. Access to more than 50 percent of the area, including many of the world's most productive fisheries, would be controlled by only 13 states, with the United States, Australia, New Zealand, Canada, the Soviet Union, and Japan being the biggest winners, while upwards of 80 states would gain virtually nothing under the EEZ arrangement (Dolman, 1981, p. 236). Part of the explanation lies in the fact that the states most generously endowed with offshore fisheries also send out large distant-water fleets. Paradoxically, most of the major benfactors are highly developed states, even though it was the less developed coastal states that were the primary advocates of the exclusive zones.

The greatest unknown in the future development of ocean resources is how the seabed regime will work out. The parallel system of national and international mining of the mineral nodules represents a compromise between efficiency of production and equity of benefits, but there is reason to believe that it will achieve neither. Allowing private mining firms to operate on the ocean floor offers some prospect of efficient production, but international rules might so seriously diminish the anticipated profitability of them that the companies will be reluctant to make the necessary investments. The international enterprise has a potential for equitably distributing deep-sea resources; nonetheless little reason exists to believe that its operations would be very efficient and profitable, if viable at all, given the political pressures that would be brought to bear on it and its dependence on private firms for the needed technologies. In the final analysis, competition between the national and international companies for a limited mineral market may doom both of them to failure in what is likely to be an economically risky venture under even the best of circumstances.

REFERENCES

Alexander, Lewis M. (1980). "The New Geography of the World's Oceans Before and After the Law of the Sea," *Columbia Journal of World Business,* Vol. 15, No. 4 (Winter), pp. 6–15.

Anand, R. P. (1983). *Origin and Development of the Law of the Sea.* Boston: Martinus Nijhoff Publishers.

Barkenbus, Jack N. (1979). *Deep Seabed Resources: Politics and Technology.* New York: Free Press.

Buzan, Barry (1976). *Seabed Politics.* New York: Praeger.

Christy, Francis T. (1975). "Property Rights in the World Ocean," *National Resources Journal,* Vol. 15 (October), pp. 695–712.

Cooke, Robert (1984). "Metals in the Sea," *Technology Review,* Vol. 84, No. 3, pp. 61–66.

Dolman, Antony (1980). *Global Planning and Resource Management: Toward International Decision Making in a Divided World.* New York: Pergamon Press.

Djahal, Hasjim (1980). "The Developing Countries and the Law of the Sea Conference," *Columbia Journal of World Business,* Vol. 15, No. 4, (Winter), pp. 22–29.

Eckert, Ross D. (1979). *The Enclosure of Ocean Resources: Economics and the Law of the Sea.* Stanford, Calif.: Hoover Institution Press.

Goldwin, Robert A. (1983). "Common Sense vs. 'The Common Heritage'," pp. 59–78 in Bernard H. Oxman, David D. Caron, and

Charles L. O. Buderi (eds.), *Law of the Sea: U.S. Policy Dilemma.* San Francisco: ICS Press.

Gulland, J. A. (1980). "Open Ocean Resources," pp. 347–78 in Robert T. Lackey and Larry A. Nielson (eds.), *Fisheries Management.* New York: Halstead Press.

Hardin, Garrett (1968). "The Tragedy of the Commons," *Science,* Vol. 162 (December 13), pp. 1243–48.

Hollick, Ann L. (1981). *U.S. Foreign Policy and the Law of the Seas.* Princeton, N.J.: Princeton University Press.

Klemm, Cyrille de (1981), "Living Resources in the Ocean," pp. 71–192 in Douglas M. Johnston (ed.), *The Environmental Law of the Sea.* Berlin; Erich Schmidt Verlag.

Knight, H. Gary (1977). *Managing the Sea's Living Resources: Legal and Political Aspects of High Seas Fisheries.* Lexington, Mass.: Lexington Books.

Johnston, Douglas and Lawrence M. G. Enomoto (1981). "Regional Approaches to the Protection and Conservation of the Marine Environment," pp. 285–386 in Johnston (ed.), *The Environmental Law of the Sea.* Berlin: Erich Schmidt Verlag.

Joseph, James and Joseph Grenough (1979). *International Management of Tuna, Porpoise, and Billfish.* Seattle: University of Washington Press.

Luard, Evan (1977). *The Control of the Seabed: Who Own the Resources of the Oceans.* (rev. ed.) London: Heineman.

Laursen, Finn (1983). *Superpower at Sea: U.S. Ocean Policy.* New York: Praeger.

Nye, Joseph N., Jr. (1983). "Political Lessons of the New Law of the Sea Regime," pp. 113–26 in Bernard H. Oxman, David D. Caron, and Charles L. O. Buderi (eds.), *Law of the Sea: U.S. Policy Dilemma.* San Francisco: ICS Press.

Oxman, Bernard H. (1983). "A Summary of the Law of the Sea Convention," pp. 147–64 in Bernard H. Oxman, David D. Caron, and Charles L. O. Buderi (eds.), *Law of the Sea: U.S. Policy Dilemma.* San Francisco: ICS Press.

Payne, Millie (1979). "The Status of Whales," *The Living Wilderness,* Vol. 43, No. 147, pp. 16–17.

Pardo, Arvid (1979). "Law of the Sea Conference: What Went Wrong?" pp. 137–48 in Robert L. Friedheim (ed.), *Managing Ocean Resources: A Primer.* Boulder, Co.: Westview Press.

Pardo, Arvid (1983). "An Opportunity Lost," pp. 13–26 in Bernard H. Oxman, David D. Caron, and Charles L. O. Buderi (eds.), *Law of the Seas: U.S. Policy Dilemma.* San Francisco: ICS Press.

Pinto, M. C. W. (1980). "The Developing Countries and the Exploitation of the Deep Seabed," *Columbia Journal of International Business,* Vol. 15, No. 4 (Winter), pp. 30–41.

Ratiner, Leigh S. (1982). "The Law of the Sea: A Crossroads for American Foreign Policy," *Foreign Policy,* Vol. 60, No. 5 (Summer), pp. 1006–21.

Walsh, Don and Donald L. Keach (1981). "Science and Engineering in the Ocean," pp. 1–25 in Robert L. Friedheim (ed.), *Managing Ocean Resources: a Primer.* Boulder, Co.: Westview Press.

Young, Oran (1977). *Resource Management at the International Level.* New York: Nichols Publishing Co.

9 POLLUTION

Keeping House on a Planetary Scale

A widespread recognition of the potential dangers of pollution was prompted by several widely publicized environmental calamities during the 1950s and 1960s: episodes of intense, "killer" smog that threatened human health in New York and London: mercury poisoning from contaminated seafood in the Japanese communities of Minamata and Niigata; the disappearance of species of birds attributable to pesticides such as DDT; the "death" of Lake Erie through the process of eutrophication; and a massive oil spill from the grounding of the *Torrey Canyon,* the third largest supertanker of the day, in the English Channel in 1967 (Holdgate et al., 1982, p. 5). Without such highly visible incidents, it would be easy to overlook the potential dangers of pollution that often build up so gradually that they do not command much attention at any single time.

Pollutants pose a diverse group of problems for policy makers. They originate from many human activities—agriculture, power generation, refining, industrial production, transportation, and normal life processes, to mention a few. They are of several different forms—gasses, liquids, and solids—some of which are quite visible, while others cannot be readily detected by human senses. Pollutants are introduced into several mediums—the various layers of the atmosphere, the rivers, lakes, oceans, and aquifers of the hydrosphere, and the surface and subsurface of the land masses, which are known as the lithosphere. There is a seemingly endless variety in the chemical composition of pollutants, among the most toxic of which are heavy metals, chlorinated hydrocarbons, PCBs, and radioactive substances. Pollutants can also have a whole array of undesirable consequences, including human

294

health problems such as cancer and respiratory illnesses, the contamination of food sources, the extinction of animal species, changes in climate, and the corrosion of building surfaces, bridges, and railroad tracks in addition simply to being unpleasant.

POLLUTION AS AN INTERNATIONAL AND GLOBAL PROBLEM

Pollution is a problem that must be dealt with internationally, because air currents and river systems carrying harmful substances move unimpeded across international frontiers from one country to another. As a result, the quality of the environment of countries may depend in large part upon the effectiveness of the anti-pollution policies of neighboring states. The widespread potential for transboundary water pollution is apparent from the fact that there are 214 river or lake basins in the world that are shared by 2 or more countries. The basins of 9 of these are shared by 6 or more countries, including the Danube, Niger, Nile, Zaire, Rhine, Zambezi, Amazon, and Mekong river systems and Lake Chad (Biswas, 1982, p. 13). These rivers are commonly used for the disposal of untreated sewage and industrial wastes and carry agricultural runoffs that include fertilizers and pesticides.

Pollutants emitted into the atmosphere drift in whatever direction the winds blow them. While most air pollution problems tend to be localized near the source of the emissions, there are some that have taken on global proportions. The phenomenon of "acid rain" occurs when oxides of sulphur and nitrogen, which are spewed into the air from such sources as coal-fired power plants, smelting operations, and automobile exhaust, undergo a complex chemical change upon exposure to water vapor and sunlight. The result is an acidic solution that falls to the ground with rain or snow, which has been linked to the disappearance of aquatic life in freshwater lakes and the stunting or killing of trees. Recently, the destruction of forests has been taking place at an especially alarming rate in Central Europe (see Wetstone and Rosencranz, 1983, pp. 32–33). While the impact of acid precipitation on agriculture has not been fully assessed, research suggests that it stimulated some types of crops and damages others. The acids have also taken a toll on paint, exposed metals, and building stone, including those of such historic structures as the Parthenon, the Colosseum, and the Taj Mahal.

The transnational scope of acid rain has been enlarged by the extensive use of tall smokestacks, some as high as 500 feet, which were built to comply with national laws requiring the dispersal of pollutants that would otherwise be concentrated at dangerous levels in localized areas. As a result, acidic precipitation can fall hundreds if not thousands of miles away from the source of the pollution. To a large extent, Canada's serious problems with acid precipitation are caused by sulfur emissions from power plants in the United States, while the death of fish in lakes in Sweden and Norway is attributable to pollution from the heavily industrialized areas of the British Isles and continental Europe (Likens et al., 1979, pp. 39–47).

Two other types of air pollution have received considerable attention from scientists. One is the buildup of carbon dioxide in the atmosphere, a substantial proportion of which results from the burning of fossil fuels, especially coal. Higher levels of carbon dioxide may be contributing to a "greenhouse effect," in which the radiation of heat from the earth is retarded, causing a gradual warming of the atmosphere and accelerated melting of the polar icecaps. As a consequence, coastal areas might be submerged by rising oceans, and the climate in key food growing regions could be significantly altered (UNEP, 1980, pp. 2–6). The other concern is the possibility that chlorofluoromethanes (commonly known as CFMs or fluorocarbons) from aerosol sprays and refrigeration and exhausts from aircraft, among other pollutants, are thinning out the ozone layer of the stratosphere. If such an eventuality were to occur, the greater penetration of ultraviolet-B radiation reaching the surface of the planet would increase the incidence of skin cancer in human beings as well as adversely affect other species of animals and plants, including many of the basic food crops (see Stoel et al., 1980, pp. 11–13). Recent scientific evidence suggests that the ozone in the stratosphere is being diminished at a much slower pace than was once feared. There is the new concern, however, that the ozone levels in the lower atmosphere are increasing in a way that could reinforce the "green house" effect (UNEP, 1985, p. 2).

Pollution is also an international problem when it contaminates areas that do not fall within national boundaries. Most attention has been given to the oceans, which have long been the sink of last resort for the disposal of many of humanity's wastes. There is a growing awareness that two other nonnational areas are susceptible to pollution: Antarctica, where increased human activities threaten its fragile ecosystem, and outer space, where debris from previous space ventures poses a hazard for newer satellites that continue to function. Contaminants are deposited in the oceans from a variety of sources. The polluted waters of river systems eventually flow into the oceans forming plumes, which in the case of the Amazon extends out to 2000 kilometers from the mouth of the river (Holdgate et al., 1982, p. 79). Some wastes are discharged directly into the seas from the coastal outfalls of cities and industries. The oceans have also been used as a repository for waste dumped from vessels, including sludge and such highly toxic substances as radioactive wastes and discarded chemical and biological weapons. Less often recognized is the large volume of pollutants that precipitate into the seas from the atmosphere, including metals and synthetic chemicals.

Until relatively recently, it was believed that the oceans were vast enough to disperse and neutralize all wastes. This complacency is no longer warranted in view of growing evidence of significant damage to the ocean environment from pollutants, such as the contamination of fish and other marine life. The most serious problems occur in coastal areas, especially near urban concentrations, and in the relatively self-contained waters of gulfs and regional seas, which exchange their polluted waters with the oceans at a slow rate. Among the most heavily polluted bodies of water are the Mediterranean, the Baltic, and the Red seas and the Persian Gulf. Unfortunately, the most heavily polluted waters are in some cases the same ones that support the world's most productive fisheries (Holdgate et al., 1982, pp. 92–98).

Over the past two decades, perhaps the most significant threat to the marine environment has come from petroleum and other oily substances. The magnitude of the problem grew as substantial increases in the consumption of energy since World War II led to a flourishing trade in petroleum, most of which has been transported by the world's fleet of supertankers, which grew in numbers to upwards of 7,000 vessels (Schneider, 1982, p. 7). Some are of gargantuan proportions—one exceeds 1500 feet in length, widths more than 200 ft are common, and draughts (depths) are as great as the height of a 6-story building. Numerous accidents each year—most frequently groundings, explosions, structural failures, and collisions—have resulted in oil spills that can have severe consequences for birds and marine life, as well as for the livelihood of local fishermen and resort owners. Among the most dramatic accidents, aside from the wreck of the *Torrey Canyon*, were those involving the *Metula* in the Straits of Magellan in 1974, the *Argo Merchant* near the Georges Bank fisheries off New England in 1976, and the *Amoco Cadiz* off Brittany in 1978, the latter being the largest spill from a tanker in history. Great quantities of oily substances are discharged intentionally from the tankers during tank-cleaning operations or when ballast water is drained. As much as half of the oil pollution in the oceans originates not from vessels but from land sources, such as coastal refineries and industries as well as river runoff (M'Gonigle and Zacher, 1979, pp. 16–17). Blowouts of offshore drilling wells, such as the spectacular one at Pemex's Ixtoc 1 in 1979 which dumped 3.1 million barrels of oil into the waters of the Mexican Gulf Coast, account for only a small fraction of the overall problem of oil pollution, but can have serious localized impacts.

Pollution is inherently an international issue for several other reasons. For one thing, there has been a thriving international trade in chemicals, such as pesticides, with one-half of the world's production crossing political frontiers. Some of these chemicals are so toxic that they are banned or heavily restricted for use in the exporting country because of their serious environmental consequences, which are often unbeknown to officials in the importing country. As much as 25 percent of United States pesticide exports are products that cannot be used domestically (Weir and Schapiro, 1981, p. 4). A significant proportion of these pesticides are applied to crops that are in turn exported to Europe, Japan, and the United States where they then pose a health hazard for consumers (Weir and Shapiro, 1979, p. 4). In Europe there is the phenomenon known as "hazardous waste tourism" in which approximately one-quarter of dangerous industrial wastes produced in the ten Common Market countries gets transported across international boundaries for treatment or disposal (Lewis, 1983, p. 6e). Several United States firms have contacted less developed countries in Africa and Latin America about using their territory for burying hazardous wastes that are difficult or expensive to dispose of locally (Smith, 1980, pp. 962–63).

Finally, some pollution problems, such as photochemical smog in urban areas or threats to health associated with toxic waste dumps, are of widespread concern, not because they spread worldwide, but because they recur in many places. Lacking the scientific expertise required to monitor pollution and to assess its consequences for the environment and the sometimes highly sophisticated technologies that are needed to reduce emissions, many countries must look internationally for advice and assistance on how to cope with these environmental problems that are localized within their borders. What can be intense competition among countries for industrial investment points up another reason why an international approach to the pollution problem is needed: without agreement on minimal standards, polluting industries may play one country off against another in bargaining for lax environmental requirements.

POLLUTION AS AN ISSUE IN SPECIALIZED AND REGIONAL ARENAS

The early international response to pollution as a policy issue was fragmented, which is not unexpected in view of the diversity of pollution problems. Thus, rather than being addressed in a centralized manner by a single international body, pollution issues were taken up by many institutions with functional specialties as diverse as health, agriculture, transport, industrial development, energy, meteorology, and development assistance. Moreover, because of the varying geographical scope of specific problems, pollution has been the subject of bilateral diplomacy, as well as being placed on the agendas of IGOs, both regional and global scope. Environmental matters have been only one of several functional responsibilities of most of these IGOs.

Some of the most noteworthy contributions to international public policy on the environment have been made by the specialized agencies of the United Nations family. WHO, for example, has sought to identify the harmful consequences that many pollutants may be having on human health. WHO has assisted the ILO to study the impact of pollution on workers, such as cotton dust on textile workers or chemical pesticides on agricultural laborers. WMO, through its World Weather Watch, monitors the effects of air pollutants on the weather, such as the degree to which buildups of CO_2 and CFCs are affecting climate. These were among the topics taken up at the World Climate Conference sponsored by WMO in 1979 (see Cain, 1983). The activities of WMO are of interest to the FAO because of the impact of climate on crops. The FAO has also been concerned about the environmental consequences of pesticides for the environment as well as the impact of a variety of pollutants on crops and on ocean fisheries. These findings are of interest to the FAO because of the dependence of agriculture on climatic conditions. As is apparent from these examples, the pollution-related programs of individual specialized agencies can be of considerable value to other agencies that have quite different functions (MacDonald, 1972, pp. 372–81).

Several other specialized agencies are involved in the international struggle to limit the harmful consequences of pollution. Pollution deposited in the oceans from ships has received much of the attention of the renamed International Maritime Organization (IMO), which until 1982 was named the Intergovernmental Maritime Consultative Organization, or IMCO. The organization belatedly came into being in 1958 (ten years after the adoption of its charter) to oversee international shipping. IMO's efforts to protect the marine environment were intensified after the *Torrey Canyon* disaster in 1967, and in 1973 a special Marine Environment Protection Committee was established. Also in the field of transportation, the possibility that pollutants from the operation of supersonic aircraft are depleting the ozone layer has been explored by the ICAO.

Preventing the release of potentially harmful radiation from nuclear power plants (both in normal operation and as a result of accidents) and the disposal of radioactive wastes have been important aspects of the mission of the IAEA. UNESCO has worked to expand the base of knowledge on environmental matters by stimulating and facilitating scientific inquiry on the consequences of pollution and by offering training and education programs on environmental subjects. In 1968 it convened a meeting that became known as the Biosphere Conference, attended by numerous scientists, which led to the continuing research effort called the

Man and the Biosphere Program (see Johnson, 1972, pp. 289–92). Also noteworthy is the role played by the World Bank, sometimes reluctantly, in taking potential adverse impacts into account when making decisions about other proposed projects (see Caldwell, 1984, pp. 91–96).

Regional and bilateral arrangements are the most suitable for addressing pollution problems that are concentrated in a relatively small geographical area. Such is the case in the European region where transboundary pollution has become a major international problem because of the proximity of several highly industrialized countries. Among the regional IGOs that address European environmental problems are the Council of Europe and the European Community whose members are drawn from Western Europe, the United Nations Economic Commission for Europe (ECE) that includes both Eastern and Western European states, the CMEA which is comprised of the Soviet bloc, and the OECD that encompasses the developed countries of the West (see Hetzel, 1980). Pollution has been on the agendas of international river commissions, including those established by the users of the Rhine and Danube rivers, which are among the oldest of the IGOs. In some cases, pollution problems can be effectively dealt with at the bilateral level, perhaps the most successful example being the International Joint Commission, which was established by the Boundary Waters Treaty of 1909 between the United States and Canada.

The activity of NGOs has been more intense on international environmental matters than in most other policy areas. Upwards of 550 NGOs attended the Stockholm conference, 237 of which are international in membership. By 1981, 5,200 NGOS were registered with the Environmental Liaison Centre of UNEP (UNEP, 1982, p. 9). The International Council of Scientific Unions (ICSU), its constituent unions, and special committees, such as the Scientific Committee on Space Research (SCSR), have been a continuing source of scientific expertise and information needed by international bodies in carrying out their environmental responsibilities. The International Union for the Conservation of Nature and Natural Resources (IUCN) was called upon to draft proposals which were considered and adopted at the Stockhom conference. The Friends of the Earth and the Sierra Club are among the better known of numerous NGOs that have been strong advocates of tighter international standards on pollution. On the other side of the issue are NGOs that represent the interests of industries responsible for much of the pollution. The IMO was once looked upon as a "shipowners' club" dominated by NGOs such as the International Chamber of Shipping and the Comité Maritime International (CMI). The CMI, which dates back to 1897, has formulated a number of "private law conventions" that contain regulations through which the shipping industry attempts to regulate itself (Gold, 1981, pp. 152–56). The more recently formed Oil Companies International Marine Forum includes companies that account for about 80 percent of the oil shipped at sea (M'Gonigle and Zacher, 1979, pp. 65–66).

STOCKHOLM, UNEP AND THE COORDINATION OF ENVIRONMENTAL POLICY

A holistic view of the natural environment began to emerge during the 1960s, inspired in part by the satellite photographs of the Earth drifting through the blackness of outer space. From this perspective, pollution in its varied forms is seen as but one of many ways in which human activities are degrading the fragile layer of the ecosphere that sustains human life. The widespread adoption of this "only one earth" way of thinking stimulated efforts to establish a unified response to environmental problems in the international community, such as UNESCO's Biosphere Conference of 1968. Later that year, the General Assembly adopted a Swedish resolution which called for the convening of the United Nations Conference on the Human Environment that took place in Stockholm in 1972.

Held after an extensive series of preparatory meetings, the Stockholm conference symbolically marked the coming of age of the environment as a major global issue. The documents adopted at these meetings included a Declaration of Principles that has given a sense of direction to environmental policy in general, and to pollution policy in particular. But more important was the Action Plan calling for a new international body to coordinate the international response to the new environmental agenda. The General Assembly followed up on the proposal at its 1972 session by establishing the United Nations Environment Programme

(UNEP). Over the past decade, UNEP's 58 member Governing Council has become the focal point of environmental policy making in the international community, this in spite of its headquarters being in Nairobi, Kenya, the first such global organization to be based in the Third World. Locating the headquarters of UNEP in Nairobi was a concession to the less developed members in view of their initial misgivings about the environmental issue, which will be taken up in a later section.

UNEP was not designed to be another operating agency. Nor was the making of global environmental policy and its implementation to be centralized in UNEP, thereby coopting the previously established regulations and programs of specialized agencies or the regional IGOs. Rather, it was to be a small organization with modest resources that would pursue its mission, not by carrying out major projects on its own, but by inspiring, motivating, and persuading national governments and other international institutions to undertake new environmental programs or to strengthen existing ones (UNEP, 1979, pp. 11–12). UNEP is sometimes in a position to provide support to other agencies, such as information or financing. Its role also includes convening numerous ad hoc conferences on specific environmental problems, a typical example being a 1977 scientific meeting on threats to the ozone layer. UNEP occasionally becomes a party in joint projects along with one or more IGOs and NGOs, a notable example being the World Conservation Strategy, which it cosponsors with two INGOs. Thus, with the exception of a few projects of its own that do not fall within the purview of other organizations, UNEP's role is to make other agencies more effective in responding to the environmental problems that are related to their other responsibilities.

GOALS AND PRINCIPLES THAT GUIDE INTERNATIONAL POLLUTION POLICY

The Declaration on the Human Environment adopted at the Stockholm Conference, which was worked out after intense and drawn-out debate, expresses a meeting of the minds on goals and principles that should guide international public policy on the environment. The document did not receive universal acceptance in view of the absence of the Soviet bloc, which boycotted the conference to protest the exclusion of East Germany. Nevertheless, the Declaration has gained stature over the years and, because of the repeated reference to several of its key articles, is considered by some to be a leading example of "new international law" which expresses widely accepted principles of common law (see Gormley, 1976).

Pollution policy can be directed toward either of two basic objectives. One is simply to control the amount of contaminants in the environment. Controlling pollution may mean preventing or limiting any further increases. A more ambitious goal would be to clean up the environment by reducing or even eliminating pollution. The other and perhaps more practical objective would concentrate on minimizing the harmful consequences of pollution. This approach would seek to keep specific contaminants from building up to levels in the environment that are known to be threats to human health or to have other undesirable environmental impacts. Lesser amounts of these pollutants would be tolerated as would those for which no adverse consequences have been detected. Article 6 of the Stockholm Declaration suggests such an emphasis on minimizing harms: "The discharge of toxic substances or of other substances and the release of heat, in such quantities or concentrations as to exceed the capacity of the environment to render them harmless, much be halted in order to insure that serious or irreversible damage is not inflicted upon ecosystems" (UN, 1972).

Rarely can environmental goals be isolated from other social and economic priorities. Pollution is usually a by-product of human activities in which other interests are at stake. It is often impossible or impractical to discontinue these polluting activities, as in the case of life processes that generate sewage, the use of gasoline-powered automobiles for transportation, or the production of electricity from plants burning fossil fuels. The expense of reducing pollution, such as by the use of emission control devices, can heavily tax scarce resources. Thus, policy makers must decide whether the damages caused by pollution warrant the expenditures that would be necessary to clean up the environment. They may also find that the price for eliminating the last 5 or 10 percent of a pollution problem is much greater than what it costs to alleviate a major part of the problem. Thus, a partial cleanup that prevents the worst of the harmful environmental consequences may be the most pragmatic policy objective. Governments of less developed countries have been especially reluctant to expend limited funds on environmental programs that seem a luxury as they are hard pressed to provide for the most basic economic needs of their impoverished populations. These competing priorities are acknowledged in Article 11 of the Stockholm Declaration: "The environmental policies of all states should enhance and not adversely affect the present or future development potential of developing countries, nor should they hamper the attainment of better living conditions for all . . ." (UN, 1972).

The principle of sovereignty raises some interesting questions for international policy on pollution. For example, should polluting activities within the boundaries of a state be the exclusive jurisdiction of its government, even though pollution drifts across international frontiers? Alternatively, is the sovereignty of a state compromised when its environment is degraded by pollutants emanating from neighboring countries with lax environmental standards? Does the pollution constitute foreign interference with the right of the people of a victimized state to fully use its territory and resources, as in the case of transboundary acid rain damaging forests and killing aquatic life in lakes?

The sovereign rights of the countries on the receiving end of transboundary pollution would appear to take precedence. The principle that all nations have a responsibility to prevent pollution that would have harmful environmental effects beyond their boundaries was first recognized in international case law, most notably the Trail Smelter Case. The United States called attention to damage to the environment in the State of Washington from 1925 to 1937 caused by sulfur dioxide emitted from a large, privately owned smelter located at Trail, British Columbia. A specially assembled international tribunal decided in 1941 that "no state has the right to use its territory in such a manner as to cause injury . . . to the territory of another or the properties or persons therein, when the case is of serious consequence and the injury is established by clear and convincing evidence. The tribunal held that Canada was liable for the environmental damage and should pay compensation to the United States and prevent harmful transboundary pollution from the site in the future (see Barros and Johnston, 1974, pp. 177–95). A similar judgment was sought from the International Court of Justice in the Nuclear Test Cases of

1974 in which New Zealand and Australia called for an end to the atmospheric testing of nuclear devices by France in its Polynesian territories that were alleged to have deposited dangerous amounts of nuclear fall-out and radiation over a large area. The issue was declared to be moot when France publicly announced completion of its testing program (see Gormley, 1976, pp. 148–56).

The issue of transboundary pollution is also addressed in the Stockholm Declaration. Article 21 affirms the "sovereign right of states to exploit their resources in accordance with their environmental policies," but places upon them the responsibility to "insure that activities within their own jurisdiction or control do not cause damage to the environment of other states or areas beyond the limits of national jurisdiction." The next article calls upon the states to cooperate in further development of international law regarding liability and compensation for the victims of transboundary pollution (UN, 1972)

Questions also arise when the fundamental tenets of international ocean law are applied to polluting activities. Do states have the right to use the oceans as a sink for disposing of wastes under the same "freedom of the seas" doctrine that permits them to help themselves to the living resources of the oceans and to use the seas for navigation? Alternatively, could it be argued that introducing pollutants into the oceans is a preemptive use of the oceans that interferes with the rights of others to make use of marine resources and is therefore illegal? Discharging pollutants that contaminate fisheries to the point that they are unfit for human consumption would be an example of a preemptive use of the oceans. And finally, under the "common heritage of mankind" principle, would it not be the right of the international community to determine what pollutants may be introduced into the oceans or any other non-national area that is owned by all, such as outer space? Again, international policy fails to recognize a right of a country to pollute areas beyond its boundaries (Gold, 1981, p. 288). The Geneva Convention on the High Seas of 1958 calls upon states to prevent pollution of the oceans, in particular the discharge of oil from ships or pipelines and the dumping of radioactive wastes or other harmful agents. This principle has been reinforced strengthened in later documents, most notably the Stockholm Declaration and the new Law of the Sea Treaty which set forth an obligation to prevent, reduce, and control marine pollution (Schneider, 1982, p. 14).

EXPANDING THE INFORMATION BASE FOR
ENVIRONMENTAL POLICY

An extensive body of scientific information on the global environment is a prerequisite for making appropriate international policies. In the case of pollution, the need is especially critical. Not only is it important to monitor the volume of pollutants being released into the environment, but it is also necessary to have reliable knowledge of the undesirable consequences that occur when the pollutants accumulate to certain levels. The task is an immense one in view of the great number of pollutants and the almost limitless impacts they can have on a complex ecosystem, many of which are unforeseen or become evident only when a critical threshold has been reached. The challenge is compounded by difficulties in isolating the causes and effects of environmental damage.

The development of such a body of knowledge on the global environment has been one of UNEP's primary tasks. Its monitoring activities, which were originally called Earthwatch, is evolving into the Global Environmental Monitoring System (GEMS), one of several of UNEP's program activity centers (PACs). The purpose of GEMS is to coordinate the various international environmental monitoring efforts, including those of several of the specialized agencies of the United Nations that focus on pollution. Data on pollution levels and their impacts on human health are contributed to GEMS by WHO, which has established a network of stations in cities around the world. Other stations have been set up to detect food contamination and to keep track of the quality of water. WMO's Weather Watch Program uses a far-flung network of stations on land and sea to monitor weather conditions, which provides information vital to research on the effects of pollution on climates. Research on the consequences of pollution for the marine environment is being carried out in conjunction with the International Oceanographic Commission, a subsidiary of UNESCO, which has established a pollution monitoring system called the Integrated Global Oceans System. Another part of the GEMS network examines the effects of ionizing radiation on human populations. Monitoring coordinated by GEMS that is not directly related to pollution keeps track of renewable natural resources, wild living resources, desertification, range land, and tropical forests (see UNEP, 1979, pp. 26–27).

A second objective of the Earthwatch program is to facilitate the exchange of information between nations, thus making more efficient use of the resources available worldwide for scientific research on environmental matters. One such network is the International Referral System (INFOTERRA), another of UNEP's PACs, which serves as a clearinghouse that can direct those who need answers to environmental questions to inter-governmental or scientific organizations which may be able to supply helpful information. Sources of environmental information are identified and registered by 107 national "focal points" designated by governments. Yet another PAC, the International Registry of Potentially Toxic Chemicals, collects information on the known environmental hazards of thousands of chemical compounds that have been generated by human activities and issues warnings on those that are especially dangerous. Both of these PACs have been designed to make information that is critical to sound environmental management available to countries which lack the means to carry on extensive research on their own. For those which have such a capability, UNEP's PACs will make it possible to avoid expensive, wasteful duplication of research that had been done in other countries (see UNEP, 1979, pp. 28–29; Ruggie, 1980).

The task of environmental assessment that confronts UNEP and its three PACs is an enormous one. Putting the networks completely into place would be a major accomplishment, but then it will be up to scientists throughout the world to bridge some of the large gaps that remain in man's knowledge of the natural environment and the impact of humanity on it. Beyond that, the challenge is to adopt policies that will limit the flow of harmful pollutants into the environment.

INTERNATIONAL POLICIES TO LIMIT AND REDUCE POLLUTION

Some types of pollution have received much more scrutiny from international policy makers than others. Contamination of marine environments has been the primary subject of an extensive series of agreements negotiated over the past three decades, and a secondary issue in others, such as in the recently adopted Law of the Sea Treaty. By contrast, few international restraints on trans-boundary air pollution have been adopted despite the potentially greater environmental consequences of acid precipitation and the buildup of carbon dioxide.

In the case of marine areas, much more has been accomplished in formulating international public policy designed to restrict or prevent pollution originating from vessels than that which comes from land. The landmark treaty on the subject is the International Convention for the Prevention of Pollution of the Sea by Oil, that was adopted in 1954. Responsibility for implementing the treaty was vested in the newly created IMO, which became the arena for continuing international policy making on vessel-source pollution, including amendments to the 1954 Convention that were adopted in 1962, 1969, and 1971. In 1973 the IMO convened a special conference that adopted the International Convention for the Prevention of Pollution from Ships, or MARPOL '73 for short, which addresses a broader range of pollutants by means of a more complicated set of rules and standards with the objective of the "complete elimination of international pollution of the marine environment by oil and other harmful substances and minimization of accidental discharge of such substances." At the exhortation of the United States, which had had to cope with oil spills from an unusual number of tanker accidents off its coasts during the winter of 1976–77, the IMO called an International Conference on Tanker Safety and Pollution in 1978 which adopted a supplemental Protocol to the MARPOL '73 agreement, or what has become known as MARPOL '78. The MARPOL conventions came into force in 1983.

These treaties were designed primarily to discourage the intentional discharge of polluting substances into the oceans as part of the normal operations of oil tankers and other vessels. This objective was to be accomplished in part by regulations on where oily substances could be discharged from ships. The 1954 Convention prohibited discharges of crude and heavy fuel oils in areas within fifty miles of the coast of states. MARPOL '73 extended this prohibition to "special areas" beyond 50 miles deemed to be particularly vulnerable to oil pollution, including the Mediterranean Sea, Baltic Sea, Black Sea, and Persian Gulf, but only after adjacent coastal states fulfill their responsibility of providing facilities for disposing of oily wastes and ballasts. Limits have also been placed on the quantities of oily substances that may be disposed of in the other regions of the oceans. Another approach to reducing intentional discharges has been to establish specifications for the structure and equipment of tankers. MARPOL '73 requires that new ships of 70,000 dwt. or more be built with segregated ballast tanks (SBT). Operators of ships lacking SBT had been making a practice of pumping water for ballast into empty oil tanks, where it would mix with oily residues before being discharged into the seas. MARPOL '78 made the SBT a requirement of all new ships of 20,000 dwt. or more in addition to having the capacity for crude oil washing as a method of cleaning tanks. Similar requirements were imposed on previously existing tankers of at least 40,000 dwt. (see M'Gonigle and Zacher, 1979; Sielen and McManus, 1983).

Other regulations have been adopted to address the problem of oil spills caused by an epidemic of accidents that occurred as the world's fleet of oil tankers mushroomed during the 1960s and 1970s. Prevention of collisions was the objective of treaties initialed in 1960 and 1972 which, because they regulate the movement of vessels at sea, have become known as "rules of the road." The International Convention for the Safety of Life at Sea, known as SOLAS '74, specified the design and type of equipment that new ships should have for safe operations, in particular to avoid groundings, fires and explosions. A supplementary protocol adopted in 1978 applies many of these rules to vessels of a smaller size and retroactively to previously existing ships. Proposals for double bottoms on tankers that would be more resistant to rupturing during groundings were extensively debated but not adopted. To reduce the incidence of accidents due to human error, the IMO adopted a convention in 1978 on training that specified minimum requirements for crews that are substantially tighter than the very low standards maintained by some countries (see Gold, 1981, p. 342). The *Torrey Canyon* disaster prompted the IMO to convene a conference on marine pollution damage in 1969 which adopted two treaties. The first, the so-called "Public Law" or "Intervention" convention authorizes states to act to prevent or mitigate damage to their environment or other interests that might be caused by a disabled tanker. The other, known as the "Private Law" of "Civil Liability" convention, places strict liability for pollution damage on the owners of ships that transport oil and requires that shipowners carry insurance or other acceptable guarantees that damage claims will be covered. Two years later a special fund was established to compensate victims of pollution beyond the limits of liability that were specified in the 1969 treaty on liability.

The dumping of other types of wastes from vessels is regulated by a separate series of conventions. One that applies globally is the Convention on the Prevention of Marine Pollution by Dumping of Wastes and Other Matter, which was negotiated in London in 1972 upon the recommendation of the Stockholm Conference. Known as the London Convention, it provides for the development of two lists of toxic substances to be added as annexes to the Treaty. A "blacklist" identifies highly toxic substances which may normally not be dumped into the oceans. Among these are mercury, cadmium, persistent plastics, high-level radioactive wastes, agents of chemical and biological warfare, DDT, and PCBs. A "graylist" of wastes, which have less harmful effects on the environment, can be disposed of in the oceans only upon the issuing of "special permit" by one of the ratifying states. Substances on the graylist include arsenic, lead, copper, zinc, flourides, nickel, and their compounds in addition to certain pesticides and low-level radioactive wastes. Regional antidumping agreements containing similar and, in some cases, stricter regulations were established for the North Sea and North Atlantic in 1971 and the Baltic in 1974. These agreements were adopted with relatively little resistance from the states that have engaged in this practice in contrast to the much more politicized negotiations that have taken place on vessel-source oil pollution (McManus, 1983, p. 119).

Less has been accomplished internationally in addressing the much more serious problem of land-based sources of marine pollution, such as industrial wastes, sewage, untreated sewage from municipal systems, and chemical fertilizers and pesticides from agricultural runoffs. The only significant global action on the subject is the new Law of the Sea Treaty which obliges states to take action to prevent, reduce, and control pollution of the oceans from land-based sources. Given the localized nature of the worst part of the environmental consequences of landbased pollution, it is not surprising that much more has been done to address the problem at the regional level. In 1974 a treaty was adopted in Paris that applies to pollution entering into the North Atlantic and

Arctic Oceans. The same year in Helsinki a document was adopted which was directed at the special problems of the shallow, enclosed Baltic Sea. At the prodding of UNEP, which had launched a Regional Seas Program, several groups of states have been developing action plans designed to preserve the environment of bodies of water they share. The most notable of these are the documents adopted by the Mediterranean states beginning 1975, which include a treaty on land-based source of pollution that was adopted in 1980. Kuwait led an effort to develop a similar strategy for the Persian Gulf, through which much of the world's oil trade passes. The Caribbean states have also recently drawn up an action plan for the waters of their region. Other regions that are part of the UNEP program include the Red Sea as well as portions of the Atlantic, Pacific, and Indian oceans (UNEP, 1979, p. 36).

Relatively little has been done internationally to curb transboundary air pollution. A number of national governments have instituted aggressive antipollution policies that have improved air quality, yet only two treaties make noteworthy contributions toward resolving the international aspects of the problem. The earlier one is the Limited Test Ban Treaty of 1963, which prohibits the setting off of nuclear explosions for any purpose in the atmosphere, as well as in outer space and under the waters of the ocean. Usually categorized as an arms control agreement, the treaty was negotiated in response to concerns of scientists that radioactive fallout from the extensive testing of thermonuclear devices by the United States and the Soviet Union in the atmosphere was spreading radioactive debris that would cause genetic damage as it accumulated in the environment. Tests of nuclear devices were permitted underground, but only if they did not cause radioactive materials to be deposited outside the territorial limits of the state conducting the explosions (see U.S. Arms Control and Disarmament Agency, 1982, pp. 41–42).

The only other major international agreement on atmospheric pollution is the Treaty on Long-Range Transboundary Air Pollution, which was negotiated in the ECE. It was accepted in 1979 by 31 of 34 members of the organization, among which are the United States, the Soviet Union, and Canada, in addition to most of the countries of Eastern and Western Europe. The ECE treaty obligates the signatories to limit and, insofar as possible, to reduce gradually and prevent air pollution, especially sulfur dioxide emissions. Prior notice and consultations with neighboring states are required of nations adopting policies that would have a significant impact on levels of transboundary sulphur pollution. Each country promises to use the "best available technology that is economically feasible" to combat air pollution, to cooperate on scientific research on the problem, and to exchange information on policies or undertakings that could cause significant long-term changes in transboundary pollution. Criticized for being vague and lacking provisions for enforcement, the treaty has gained stature as concern over acid precipitation has swelled, especially in Germany, and has provided a legal basis for putting pressure on foreign countries to reduce atmospheric emissions (see Wetstone and Rosencranz, 1983, pp. 133–49). In an effort to implement the ECE treaty, 30 of the original signatories met in Helsinki in 1985 to adopt an agreement that would require them to reduce sulfer dioxide emissions by 30 percent. The potential impact of this latest agreement is diminished, however, by the failure of the United States and the United Kingdom to sign it. Earlier in the year, the EEC countries took a significant step to curb pollution by declaring that within a decade all new automobiles would have to be equipped with emission control devices.

ENFORCEMENT OF ENVIRONMENTAL STANDARDS

Traditionally, responsibility for enforcing international public policies regulating polluting activities has been vested almost exclusively in the governments of the polluters, with the only recourse of the victims being to register complaints with those governments. Thus, violations of the 1954 treaty on vessel-source oil pollution could normally be punished only in accordance with the laws of states in which the ship is registered, or what is known as the "flag state." Under the new Law of the Sea Convention, the flag state is not to permit ships under its registry to sail until they have been certified to have complied with international standards on design, construction, equipment, and crew. The flag state is also obliged to investigate violations that are reported by other states and to apply penalties that are sufficiently severe to discourage further violations. Each party to the London Ocean Dumping Convention is obliged to establish procedures which will ensure that wastes loaded up in its harbors are not dumped illegally into the oceans. The responsibility of the ratifying states also extends to the ships flying their flags that load wastes in the harbors of countries that are not a party to the treaty. Enforcement of the 1979 Treaty on Long-Range Transboundary Air Pollution is also left to the good faith efforts of ratifying states. There is, however, a procedure by which a country can call for consultations with other countries that it believes are contributing to its air pollution problems. Beyond that there is little that a complaining state can do under the terms of the treaty to compel the violator to reduce emissions of the offending pollutants.

Leaving the enforcement of environmental standards to the national governments of the polluters has not proved to be a satisfactory arrangement. Even the states committed to making good faith efforts to support international environmental regulations find it difficult if not impossible to fulfill their obligations. For example, parties to treaties prohibiting or limiting vessel-source pollution are confronted with the almost impossible task of monitoring flagships scattered over the vast expanses of the oceans, whose operators are skilled at concealing their violations, if by no other means than taking advantage of cover of night's darkness. There is also the problem posed by the numerous states that refrain from becoming parties to the treaties designed to limit or reduce pollution and, therefore, are not legally obliged to uphold them. The pace of ratifications of the major treaties on vessel-source ocean pollution has been painfully slow in part because governments are reluctant to put their nation's merchant fleets at a competitive disadvantage by requiring substantially higher standards than are imposed on ships registered with non-treaty states. Several countries have established themselves as "flags of convenience" to attract registration of foreign-owned vessels by offering national havens from international regulations. Two such flags of convenience, Liberia and Panama, have ranked as high as first and fourth, respectively, in tonnage of registered ships and in doing so combining for 25 percent of the total tonnage of the world's merchant fleet (Cuyvers, 1984, p. 110).

One strategy for increasing compliance with international rules on pollution would vest stronger enforcement powers with other states, including those that might be adversely affected by the violations. This possibility has been taken up by IMO as well as in

UNCLOS III with agreements being reached that would authorize states to inspect foreign vessels entering their ports to determine whether they are complying with international standards. Charges could be brought against their operators for discharge violations committed *anywhere* in the world. Port states may also make compliance with certain international standards a condition for entering their harbors. Furthermore, a state may prevent vessels from leaving its ports if they do not meet international safety standards and, in failing to do so, pose a threat to the marine environment. More limited powers are given to coastal states to take action when there are suspected violations taking place within their 12-mile territorial waters and 200-mile EEZs. Normally, the procedure for coastal states will be to call infractions by foreign flag ships to the attention of the state of the next port of call, which is bound to take action against the operators of the violating vessel (see Richardson, 1980, p. 60). Certain limits on the exercise of these enforcement procedures adopted in deference to the principle of "freedom of navigation," as in the case of exemptions for military vessels. Nevertheless, ships flying "flags of convenience" are likely to find it increasingly more difficult to evade international rules.

Enforcement of the Limited Test Ban Treaty is a significant issue not only because of the dangers of radioactive fallout, but also because of its implications for national security. The treaty has been formally ratified by three of the five acknowledged nuclear-weapons states—the United States, Soviet Union, and United Kingdom—and by 93 other countries, most of which currently lack the capacity to explode such a device, India being a notable exception. France and China have refused to sign the treaty, but the former has announced that it does not plan any further atmospheric tests. Verification was an important issue in the earlier stages of the negotiations when a comprehensive ban was under consideration that would also prohibit underground tests, which are less easily detected because it is difficult to distinguish them from natural seismic activity. The United States and United Kingdom insisted on on-sight inspections and international control posts so that outside observers would be in a position to detect violations of the treaty (see U.S. Arms Control and Disarmament Agency, 1982, pp. 35–40). Failing to reach agreement with the Soviet Union on such an arrangement, detection of violations devolves to "national means of verification," which implies that each state is left to its own devices, such as space satellites, to monitor compliance by other states. A party considering an atmospheric explosion in violation of the treaty must contemplate the probability of discovery and the consequences it would have. Not only would the dependability of a violating state's other international commitments be called into question, but other countries might reciprocate by resuming atmospheric testing.

THE POLITICS OF POLLUTION POLICY

The pollution issue is not among the more highly politicized policy problems on international agendas. Preventing the harmful accumulation of pollutants is an international objective that is difficult to argue against, except relative to other priorities. For the most part, pollution continues to be a technical subject on which policy makers look to scientists for guidance as to what needs to be done to prevent significant harms. Furthermore, with the exception of the atmospheric tests of nuclear devices, pollution does not directly affect the military security of countries. The economic stakes can be quite high, however, to the extent that pollution standards can have a bearing on industrial operations, energy generation, and transportation, including international shipping. Nevertheless, these stakes have generally not been high enough to elevate the issue to realm of high politics, a possible exception being the repeated protests of Canadian leaders over the contributions of the United States to their serious problem of acid rain.

This is not to say that conflicts do not arise over international pollution policy. Clearly, the interests of polluters are quite different from those who are unfortunate enough to bear the consequences. Polluters benefit from lax regulations that allow them to dispose of wastes at low cost to themselves, whereas victims are better served by strict standards. Nations with large, complex societies can be difficult to categorize in a general way as being primarily polluters or victims. Most contribute in at least some ways to pollution problems beyond their borders and in turn suffer some of the harmful consequences of the pollution of others. In some instances, such as the contamination of the Mediterranean and other regional seas, the situation is similar to Hardin's "tragedy of the commons" in which all states contribute to the problem and share in its consequences. Agreement on mutual restraints on the discharge of pollution is possible when there is widespread concern about the severity of shared environmental harms.

In some cases, divergent interests are quite clearly defined and, as a result, more difficult to resolve. Because of prevailing wind patterns, Norway and Sweden find themselves on the receiving end of a largely one-way flow of air pollutants originating in the industrial complexes of the British Isles and continental Europe to the south and west (see Wetstone and Rosencranz, 1983, pp. 20–21). Not surprisingly, the United Kingdom and the other net exporters of pollution have resisted efforts to strengthen international agreements that restrict transboundary air pollution. West Germany, a major exporter and importer of pollution, has recently switched from being an opponent of international controls to being one of the most vocal advocates of them. Likewise, international river systems carry pollutants in the direction of the downstream states (Westone and Rosencranz, 1983, pp. 88). In the case of the Rhine, for example, the Netherlands has a far greater stake in maintaining the quality of the water in the river than do Switzerland, France, and West Germany for whose industries it has been a convenient and inexpensive medium for disposing of wastes (Yerkey, 1979). Similarly, coastal states adjacent to heavily traveled shipping routes, such as the Straits of Malacca, the English Channel, and the waters off the southern tip of Africa have borne heavy environmental costs resulting from collisions, groundings, and other types of tanker accidents. As a result, they have a greater stake in international safety standards and international agreements on liability for damages than do the major maritime states whose shipping industries would bear the costs of complying with them and, therefore, resist encroachments on the freedom of navigation (Gold, 1981, p. 320).

Conflicting perspectives on international pollution policy have also surfaced between the developed and less developed countries. In 1972 at Stockholm, numerous Third World states took the stance that the industrialized countries are primarily responsible for the world's pollution problems and, moreover, that it is now only fair that less developed countries not be prevented from polluting the environment as they attempt to undergo rapid industrial growth themselves. Some have gone so far as to embrace pollution as a healthy sign of industrial progress. Concern has also been expressed that being obliged to uphold international standards on pollution could also remove one of the advantages the less developed countries have for attracting industries, that being relatively unpolluted air and more permissive environmental standards.

Growing awareness of how costly the future consequences of pollution can be has led to a moderation of these views and a growing conviction that the Third World should not repeat the mistakes the industrialized countries made in degrading their environments. Nevertheless, the Third World continues to resist efforts to impose strict international pollution standards that would be expensive for them to implement and are considered a luxury in view of the more pressing economic and social needs of their societies. In the case of shipping, it is feared that the expense of complying with standards designed to prevent accident-causing oil spills, such as by equipping vessels with costly navigation equipment, could be a decisive obstacle to the development of merchant fleets that a number of developing countries aspire to develop, in some cases with old, second-hand tonnage that is available at bargain prices (Gold, 1981, p. 336). It has been proposed in some circles that the developed countries, if they have a strong interest in the Third World complying with the strict pollution standards they advocate, should be willing to supplement their economic aid to compensate for these additional costs. This notion, sometimes referred to as the principle of "additionality," was incorporated into Article 11 of the Stockholm Declaration (Juda, 1979, pp. 93, 98).

ASSESSMENT AND PROSPECTS

Rather intensive international activity has been directed at environmental problems, especially since the Stockholm conference. The most notable accomplishment was the establishment of UNEP as a coordinator of environmental programs of various international agencies, both within and outside the United Nations system. In its role of catalyst, UNEP can claim part of the credit for the increase in the number of national governments having environmental agencies from only 10 in 1970 to more than 100 a decade later (UNEP, 1982, p. 9). In regard to pollution specifically, most of UNEP's efforts thus far have gone to establishing an information base that includes monitoring and research on the effects of pollutants. The GEMS network could prove to be a very helpful source of information for policy making on pollution, if and when the problems that have delayed its full implementation can be resolved.

A weightier challenge for international pollution policy, however, will be to induce states to curb activities that spread harmful contaminants beyond their borders. Thus far, much more has been done to restrict pollution of the oceans, especially oil and highly toxic substances that are discharged or dumped from ships, than to contain the transboundary flow of atmospheric pollutants, even though the latter would appear to have more serious consequences for the global environment. But even in the case of vessel-source pollution, the pace of ratifications has been slow and ships flying "flags of convenience" continue to flaut international rules. The recently adopted Treaty on the Law of the Sea may improve the situation by strengthening the enforcement role of coastal and port states.

Ultimately, the success of these international efforts must be judged on the degree to which they ameliorate pollution problems, especially those that are transboundary in nature or involve the oceans or other nonnational areas. It would be premature to expect a substantial across-the-board reduction in the volume of pollutants entering the environment. The more immediate task is to slow down the continuing buildups of several major types of pollutants, such as those of sulfur and nitrogen oxides that cause acid rain and of CO_2 which may have a significant effect on climate (UNEP, 1982, pp. 11–12). Not all of the trends are as discouraging, however. A UNEP sponsored study has detected measurable declines over the past decade in the levels of highly toxic substances such as DCBs, chlorinated hydrocarbons, and harmful metals in the marine environment, particularly in the northern hemisphere.

These more favorable trends can be attributed in large part to ambitious national efforts of some states to control pollution, especially among the developed countries, which have experienced the environmental consequences of high levels of industrial pollution. For example, the United States, acting on its own, has reduced production of aerosol fluorocarbons by 90 percent since 1974, thereby allaying concerns of a rapid depletion of the ozone layer (Stoel, 1983, p. 49). Many Third World countries are only beginning to embark on a process of industrialization which could significantly add to international pollution problems. These countries cannot be expected to forgo industrialization in the interests of the global environment. Recognizing this, it would appear that the interests of the developed world would lie in assisting the Third World in developing strategies of economic growth that minimize the environmental damages yet allow their citizens substantial improvements in their quality of life. If this is done, it is quite possible that some significant improvements in pollution levels will be observed by the end of the century.

REFERENCES

Barros, James and Douglas M. Johnston (1974). *The International Law of Pollution*. New York: Free Press.

Biswas, Asit K. (1982). "Shared Natural Resources." *Development Forum,* Vol. 10, No. 7 (September/October), p. 13.

Cain, Melinda L. (1983). "Carbon Dioxide and the Climate: Monitoring and a Search for Understanding," pp. 45–74 in David A. Kay and Harold K. Jacobson (eds.), *Environmental Protection: The International Dimension*. Totowa, N.J.: Allanheld, Oxmun & Co.

Caldwell, Lynton K. (1984). *International Environmental Policy: Emergence and Dimensions*. Durham, N.C.: Duke University Press.

Cuyvers, Luc (1984). *Ocean Uses and Their Regulation*. New York: John Wiley and Sons.

Gold, Edgar (1981). *Maritime Transport: the Evolution of International Marine Policy and Shipping Law*. Lexington, Mass.: Lexington Books.

Gormley, W. Paul (1976). *Human Rights and Environment: the Need for International Cooperation*. Leyden: A. W. Sijhoff.

Hetzel, Nancy K. (1980). *Environmental Cooperation Among Industrialized Countries: The Role of the Regional Organizations*. Washington, D.C.: University Press of America.

Holdgate, Martin W., Mohammed Kassas, and Gilbert F. White, eds. (1982). *The World Environment: 1972–1982*. Dublin: Tycooly.

Johnson, Brian (1972). "The United Nations' Institutional Response to

Stockholm: A Case Study in the International Politics of Institutional Change," *International Organization,* Vol. 26, No. 2 (Spring), pp. 255–301.

Juda, Lawrence (1979). "International Environmental Concern: Perspectives and Implications for the Developing States," in David W. Orr and Marvin S. Soroos, eds., *The Global Predicament: Ecological Perspectives on World Order.* Chapel Hill: University of North Carolina Press.

Lewis, Paul (1983). "Following U.S., Europe Awakens to Dangers of Toxic Wastes," *New York Times* (February 20), p. 6e.

Likens, George, et al., "Acid Rain," *Scientific American,* Vol. 241, No. 4 (October) pp. 39–47.

MacDonald, Gordon J. (1972). "International Institutions for Environmental Management," *International Organization,* Vol. 26, No. 2 (Spring).

McManus, Robert J. (1983). "Ocean Dumping: Standards in Action," pp. 119–39 in David A. Kay and Harold K. Jacobson (eds.), *Environmental Protection: the International Dimension.* Totowa, N.J.: Allanheld, Osmun & Co.

M'Gonigle, R. Michael and Mark W. Zacher (1979). *Pollution, Politics, and International Law: Tankers at Sea.* Berkeley: University of California Press.

Richardson, Elliot (1980). "Prevention of Vessel-Source Pollution: Part II, Compensation, Monitoring, and Enforcement," *Oceans,* Vol. 13, No. 4 (May), pp. 58–61.

Rosencranz, Armin (1980). "The Problem of Transboundary Pollution," *Environment,* Vol. 22, No. 5 (June).

Ruggie, John Gerard (1980). "On the Problem of 'The Global Problematique': What Roles for International Organizations?" *Alternatives,* Vol. 5, No. 4 (January), pp. 517–60.

Schneider, Jan (1982). "Prevention of Pollution from Vessels or Don't Give Up the Ship," pp. 7–28 in Jonathan I. Charney (ed.) *The New Nationalism and the Use of Common Spaces: Issues in Marine Pollution and the Exploitation of Antarctica.* Totowa, N.J.: Allanheld, Osmund & Co.

Sielen, Alan B. and Robert J. McManus (1983). "IMCO and the Politics of Ship Pollution," pp 140–83 in David A. Kay and Harold K. Jacobson (eds.), *Environmental Protection: The International Dimension,* Totowa, N.J.: Allanheld, Osmun & Co.

Smith, R. Jeffrey (1980). "Hazardous Wastes Cause International Stink," *Science,* Vol. 207, No. 4431 (February 29), pp. 962–63.

Stoel, Thomas B. Jr. (1983). "Flurocarbons: Mobilizing Concern and Action," pp. 45–74 in David A. Kay and Harold K. Jacobson (eds.),

Environmental Protection: The International Dimension. Totowa, N.J.: Allanheld, Osmun & Co.

Stoel, Thomas B., Jr., Alan S. Miller, and Breck Milroy (1980). *Fluorocarbon Regulation.* Lexington, Mass.: Lexington Books.

United Nations Conference on the Human Environment (1972). *Report of the United Nations Conference on the Human Environment.* UN Doc. A/Conf. 48/14.

United Nations Environment Programme (1979). *The State of the World Environment.* New York: UNEP.

United Nations Environment Programme (1980). *The State of the World Environment.* New York: UNEP.

United Nations Environment Programme (1982). *The State of the Environment, 1972–1982.* New York: UNEP.

United Nations Environment Programme (1985). "Ozone Convention to Be Signed," *UNEP News* (March), p. 5.

United States Arms Control and Disarmament Agency (1982). *Arms Control and Disarmament Agreements: Texts and Histories of Negotiations.* Washington, D.C.: U.S. Government Printing Office.

Weir, David and Mark Schapiro (1981). *Circle of Poison: Pesticides and People in a Hungry World.* San Francisco: Institute for Food and Development Policy.

Wetstone, Gregory S. and Armin Rosencranz (1983). *Acid Rain in Europe and North America: National Responses to an International Problem.* Washington, D.C.: Environmental Law Institute.

Yerkey, Gary (1979). "Dutch Upset by Pollutants Floating Down the Rhine River," *International Herald Tribune* (October 11).

10 TELE-COMMUNICATIONS

Managing a Technological Revolution

The invention of the telegraph in the mid-nineteenth century ushered in the era of modern telecommunications. In the decades that followed, a remarkable series of breakthroughs in electronics—the telephone, radio, and television—revolutionized telecommunications by making it possible to transmit voice and video through cables and over the airwaves. But perhaps the most dramatic developments have been taking place in the last two or three decades. Satellites circling the earth in geosynchronous orbit have virtually eliminated time and distance as factors in communications while greatly reducing unit costs. New technologies in the field of fiber optics convert sound waves to laser light waves that are sent through clear glass threads in cables that can carry a much greater volume of information at far faster speeds than was possible using copper wire. Digitalization, a process through which a wide variety of signals can be converted to "off-on" impulses, makes it possible to transmit not only telephone calls, telegrams, and telex messages, but also pictures, music, and data, over communication networks using microwaves, satellites, or optical fiber. The linking of computers, which have the capacity to store and process vast amounts of data, to modern communication systems that can beam it anywhere in the world is bringing on what has been described as an "information society" of global proportions.

Few of the potential applications of these spectacular new technologies have been explored and exploited thus far. Nor is very much understood about the economic, political, and social impact that these applications would be likely to have. Long-haul telephone traffic continues to be the principal use of communications satellites, with television and data transmission continuing to lag far behind. Nevertheless, substantial increases in activities such as teleconferencing and direct satellite broadcasting are foreseen in the not too distant future. The many actors who either use or provide telecommunication services have much at stake. Among these are the superpowers, who have an interest in the many military applications of telecommunications technologies, in particular for communications, navigation, and surveillance. Third World leaders have been intrigued by the possibilities of using the new technologies as instruments for economic development, while expressing concern that they may perpetuate, if not increase, the inequalities between the rich and poor states. Private and public corporations are investing heavily in research and development in the field of telecommunications in hopes of capturing a significant share of what promises to be one of the most lucrative growth industries of the coming decades.

Technologies that can transmit information over great distances have significant implications for the flow of communications across national boundaries. Taking advantage of the tremendous potential in the field of telecommunications requires a high level of international cooperation. For example, steps must be taken to ensure that the equipment which sends signals from one country is compatible with the receivers located in other countries. Thus, one of the earliest as well as one of the continuing challenges for global policy makers in the field of communication has been to establish technical specifications for equipment; for example, on the number of lines per picture and the number of pictures per second in television transmissions. Coordination has also been necessary in establishing international networks, such as in the laying of cables over land and across the oceans, which link national communication networks. Cooperation is also imperative in the handling of payments for transnational communications as well as in formulating operating and administrative procedures.

While the importance of standardization and coordination should not be underestimated, the emphasis of this chapter will be on several other policy problems that have emerged in the field of telecommunications. First, there is the need to manage two types of commonly owned, international resources that are essential to modern forms of communications. One is the spectrum of radio frequencies that can be used to transmit information electronically over great distances. The other is the geosynchronous orbital space, which is the preferred location for communication satellites. A second group of policy issues pertains to the regulation of the flows of transmitted information across national boundaries, in particular those that have been made possible by the new communication technologies. As we shall see, unsolicited information flowing *into* countries poses quite different international policy problems from that which is transmitted *out* of a state against the wishes of its government.

RADIO WAVES AND THE GEOSYNCHRONOUS ARC AS GLOBAL POLICY PROBLEMS

Radio waves and geosynchronous orbital space do not have physical mass as do most familiar natural resources. Moreover, unlike most other natural resources, it is impossible to deplete or damage either radio waves or orbital space permanently. Once use of these resources is discontinued, they resume their original condition and are of undiminished value to future users. There are, however, limits to the numbers of various types of users that the radio spectrum and the orbital arc can accommodate at any one time. Overuse of these resources can result in users interfering with one another in ways that can greatly reduce their value. Thus, to exploit their full potential for transmitting information, it is necessary to regulate the number and types of users.

Radio waves, otherwise known as airwaves, are a portion of the larger spectrum of electromagnetic waves that can be used to transmit information. The spectrum comprises frequencies ranging from 3 Hz in the "extremely low" band to 300 GHz in the "extremely high" band. The abbreviation Hz stands for the number of cycles that pass a fixed point in one second. GHz is the abbreviation for a gigaHertz, or 1,000,000 Hz. By international agreement, sections of the frequency spectrum have been designated "bands." Each band has unique qualities that makes it adaptable to some but not all types of telecommunication, such as telephone, AM and FM radio, UHF and VHF television, air and marine navigation, radar, radio astronomy, meteorology, data transmission, and electronic mail. In order to transmit information at any given time without encountering interference, a user must have exclusive access to a frequency over a geographical area that is determined by the distance the signals travel to targeted receivers. For this reason, there are limits to the number of users that can be simultaneously accommodated by the spectrum (see Leinwoll, 1979, pp. 123–24).

The higher the frequency of the waves, the greater the amount of information that can be transmitted. However, the higher frequency waves have one important limitation. Because they penetrate the atmosphere and continue on a straight line into outer space, they have relatively little range over the curved surface of the earth unless reflected back to the planet by a satellite or relayed by earth stations. Either solution adds considerably to the cost of communication. Signals transmitted at lower frequencies are bent back at an angle toward the earth's surface by the ionosphere, which causes them to follow the curvature of the planet for greater distances. Thus, frequencies below 30 MHz in what is known as the HF sector have been especially popular for long-distance communications. However, with the greater geographical range of the lower frequencies, there is also much more potential for broadcasters to interfere with one other. As a result, the demand for these frequencies often exceeds the supply in certain geographical regions and interference would be a perennial problem without effective international management of the resource.

Satellite communication places heavy demands on the spectrum because different frequencies are normally used when signals are received and transmitted simultaneously. Frequencies toward the upper end of the spectrum are especially useful for communications sent via satellites. The most popular has been the 4 GHz band. However, because this band is shared with terrestrial services, users have experienced substantial interference. New technologies have made it possible to shift some of the rapidly growing demand for frequencies to the 12 GHz band. Here there has been the need to accommodate the requirements of both fixed and broadcast satellite services which, because of the nature of their operations, have a significant potential for interfering with one another. Economic and technical considerations have made it impractical to utilize the even higher frequency 18 GHz band for satellite communication. In the more distant future, satellites may be equipped with transpoders that can relay signals using bands as high as 50 GHz (Whittaker, 1979, p. 161; Dordick, 1983, p. 71).

It is paradoxical that empty space can be considered a "resource" and that any part of the vastness of outer space could be a scarce resource. The explanation lies in the fact that the uses to which a satellite can be put depend on its route. For many types of communication it is advantageous, if not essential, to make use of a satellite that moves in an arc which keeps it above the same location on the rotating earth, or what is known as a geosynchronous orbit. Signals beamed from such a satellite can reach approximately 40 percent of the earth's surface, and three strategically placed ones can provide global coverage. Other orbits require more satellites for similar coverage and, even then, may not be continuously available from any given location on the earth's surface. Furthermore, tracking satellites in other orbits requires special equipment on both the satellite and the ground stations, which adds substantially to the cost. For these reasons, nearly all communications satellites have been launched into a geosynchronous orbit. The arc is also populated with satellites having other functions, among which are those used by the United States military for early warning of nuclear attack, electronic surveillance, and intercepting radio transmissions.

A geosynchronous orbit is possible only in a circular arc at an altitude of approximately 22,300 miles over the equator. Why is this height critical? To maintain any orbit, a satellite must move at a speed that compensates both for the gravitational pull that would draw it closer to the surface of the earth and the inertia that would project it away from the earth in a straight line. Satellites maintaining an orbit at an altitude of 22,300 miles are the only ones whose velocity takes them around the earth at 24-hour intervals. If such a satellite follows an equatorial path in the direction of the earth's rotation, it will remain above the same location on the surface of the planet and from there appear to be stationary (Gorove, 1979, p. 445).

Over the past decade there has been growing anxiety about congestion in the geosynchronous arc, especially in the segments that are most in demand. Exactly how many satellites currently occupy the arc is not known. By one estimate, there are 200 satellites, 120 of which are still operational (Marsh, 1984, p. 9).

While the prospects for collisions between these satellites is remote, there is the more immediate problem that the signals transmitted to and from closely spaced satellites will interfere with one another. The problem of congestion is most immediate in the sections of the arc that can be used to transmit signals within the European and American regions. Originally it was thought that satellites making use of the same frequency bands should be separated by at least four orbital degrees (out of the 360 degrees in the entire arc), which would permit only 15 satellites being in a position to serve audiences in the United States. Taking into account new technologies that reduce the potential for interference, the U.S. Federal Communications Commission in 1983 reduced the minimum permissible separation between the satellites it licenses to two degrees, which would double the capacity of the orbital space. Even tighter packing of satellites may be possible with improved antennas, space platforms, and the use of higher frequency bands. Nevertheless, there is still widespread concern that the arc will not be able to accommodate the explosive increase in governmental and commercial demand for satellite communication circuits that is anticipated in the coming decades.

TRANSBOUNDARY TELECOMMUNICATIONS AS GLOBAL POLICY PROBLEMS

Most governments look upon the flow of information across their boundaries as a mixed blessing. Some regard radio and television broadcasts transmitted from abroad as an intrusion on their sovereignty, regardless of whether they are part of a conscious effort to manipulate the perceptions of their citizens or are simply an inadvertent spillover of signals aimed at an adjacent audience. Governments that try to maintain a tight reign on the information received by their citizens fear that their authority could be undermined by foreign propaganda that is designed to foment political unrest. The Soviet Union has for many years complained about the efforts of the United States to influence its citizens through the Voice of America and Radio Free Europe. Third World countries are bombarded by political broadcasts emanating from both East and West, which can have considerable impact because of limited programming of their own sparse networks of stations. Middle Eastern governments have anxieties about broadcasts from Iran that are aimed at arousing political passions of fundamentalist Shi'ites in the region.

The challenge of controlling the information coming into a country from abroad is being complicated further by the advent of the direct broadcast satellite (DBS). What distinguishes a DBS from other communication satellites is the capacity of its transponder to amplify radio and television signals to the degree necessary to be picked up directly by home receivers in the form of relatively small, inexpensive dishes. Using a DBS, broadcasters can bypass ground receiving stations over which governments commonly exercise control as well as reach remote areas where there are no such stations. Japan and Canada were the first countries to have DBS systems in operation. Not far behind is the United States, which has licensed several firms to offer DBS services beginning in 1986. The possibility of direct television access to foreign populations raises international legal and political issues, and economic ones as well, that are of greater consequence than those pertaining to radio broadcasts, which tend to have less impact on their audience (Webster 1984, p. 1162). Governments that have maintained a monopoly over television broadcasting in their countries may suddenly be confronted with competition from numerous foreign stations, including some of a commercial variety offering popular programming. Recently, 30 countries raised objections to a plan announced by Luxembourg that would beam 16 commercial television channels into households throughout much of Europe (see Tagliabue, 1984). One of the commonly expressed concerns is the fear of cultural imperialism, especially from the United States, which is by far the largest source of television programming.

Paradoxically, the flow of information out of countries is also rapidly becoming a major global policy issue. One such concern is the use of satellites for remote sensing, or what to some governments is an unwelcome form of space-based snooping. In contrast to the geosynchronous orbit of communication satellites, those used for remote sensing are typically launched into relatively low-level, polar orbits which allow them to take pictures of different regions as they circle the planet. The series of LANDSAT satellites operated by United States has been used to gather information pertaining to natural resources, such the presence of deposits of minerals, types of vegetation and forest cover, and the progress of crops. Other satellites are used to monitor weather or for surveillance of military installations, the deployment of weapons, and the launching of missiles. Some states have objected to remote sensing conducted by other states over their territory on grounds that it infringes on their sovereignty. The information collected about their resources, crops, and military forces, they contend, could be used by foreign actors in ways that are contrary to their interests. Many of the same states are also alert to the potential that remote sensing has for generating data that may be of assistance to them in discovering and planning the development of their resources, if they can get access to it.

The linking of computers to telecommunications systems has resulted in massive transborder data flows, or what are commonly known as TDFs. Using satellites, large data sets can be transferred to computers located in foreign countries almost instantaneously or accessed from terminals positioned anywhere in the world. TDFs have already revolutionized the management of multinational corporations that have been quick to take advantage of the possibilities of modern communication networks for coordinating domestic and foreign operations on functions such as production schedules, financial management, accounting, planning, inventory controls, and marketing. For industries that are information intensive, such as international banking, insurance, and tourism, TDFs become the lifeblood of a competitive operation. Already, hundreds of transnational corporations have developed their own transnational computer communications networks, in many cases using privately operated satellite systems. Governments also account for many TDFs, and have even been known to send data to foreign countries for processing and storage. There has also been a rapid growth in publicly available data bases (Sauvant, 1983, pp. 361–63).

Some governments view TDFs as a potential threat to the welfare of their countries. Initially, the primary concern was that the privacy of individual citizens might be violated. It was feared that personal information, such as credit ratings, travel plans, medical reports, and employment records, might be transferred to foreign countries that have fewer legal safeguards on the confidentiality of such data, from where it could be accessed remotely from the country of origin. Copyright protections might be circumvented if the text of articles is transmitted to foreign countries for printing. Anxieties have also been expressed that the vital interests of a country could be jeopardized if, for whatever reason, there were interruptions in access to critical data that have been sent to a foreign country for processing and storage. More recently, questions have been asked about the effect that TDFs might have on employment and the management of multinational corporations. Control of these firms could become even more centralized at the headquarters, with a resulting loss of highly skilled and paid managerial positions in other countries. Conversely, corporations might also find it economical to transfer large numbers of low-skill jobs, such as those involving key punching and data entry, to countries with low wage rates? To prevent such eventualities, some states have enacted national laws that either prohibit or discourage the export of data in ways that hamper the operations of multinational corporations (see Spero, 1982, p. 143).

THE MAKING OF TELECOMMUNICATIONS POLICY

The center arena of global policy making pertaining to telecommunications continues to be the International Telecommunications Union (ITU). One of the oldest of the IGOs, the ITU was founded as the International Telegraph Union in 1865 at the initiative of Napoleon III. The organization adopted its current name in 1932 and became part of the United Nations family of specialized agencies in 1947. Over its lifetime, the primary task of the ITU has been to facilitate cooperation in all types of telcommunications, such as by network planning, standardization of procedures and equipment, and allocation of radio frequencies (see Leive, 1970).

The ITU is unique among IGOs in that it does not have a permanent charter, but is guided by conventions which may be completely revised at Plenipotentiary Conferences that are to be held at intervals of no more than five years. In actual practice these conferences are convened less frequently. The most recent one took place in Nairobi in 1982, which was the first since 1973. The next is scheduled for 1989. During the intervening periods, responsibility for running the organization resides with a smaller Administrative Council that meets annually in Geneva. Much of the work of the ITU is carried out by three partly autonomous bodies that for most practical purposes are IGOs in their own right. Two are Consultative Committees; one focuses on telephone and telegraph, the other on radio. Both of these panels undertake a wide range of activities related to the planning and coordination of international and global communication networks. The third body is the International Frequencies Regulation Board (IFRB). Throughout the history of the ITU, much of the substantive policy making has taken place in conventions. Policies on the use of radio waves have been made at World Administrative Radio Conferences, called WARCs. The most important of these conferences are known as General WARCs, which are held at 20-year intervals to revise the international rules on use of the radio waves. Other WARCs are called on an ad hoc basis to address narrower topics that need special attention. The schedule for the current decades includes mini-WARCs on space broadcasting in the Western Hemisphere (1983), on the HF portion of the radio spectrum (1984, 1986), and on the use of the geosynchronous orbit (1985, 1988).

In recent decades, issues pertaining to telecommunications have been taken up in several other arenas. Satellite communication also falls within the purview of the 53-member UN Committee on the Peaceful Uses of Outer Space (COPUOS), which was established by the United Nations in 1958, and in its two subcommittees specializing on legal and on scientific and technical matters. COPUOS also sponsored a Working Group on Direct Broadcast Satellites from 1969 to 1974. Among the matters that COPUOS considers are the use of the geosynchronous orbital space, remote sensing, satellite broadcasting, and the legal boundary between national air space and outer space. Several of these issues were discussed, but not resolved, at the Second United Nations Conference on the Exploration and Peaceful Uses of Outer Space (UNISPACE), which was held in Vienna in 1982 at the insistence of Third World countries fearful of being excluded from the benefits of space technologies. On most of these issues, the role of COPUOS has been secondary to that of the ITU. Questions related to the regulation of transboundary data flows have come before the OECD, the Council of Europe, and UNC-

TAD, and in the future could be negotiated in GATT as a trade issue. UNESCO has been the forum in which Third World nations have advanced their demands for a "new world information order," parts of which address the dominance of the technologically advanced countries in the field of telecommunications.

The cast of participants in global policy making on telecommunications is diverse. National governments all have an interest in telecommunications, especially those that maintain public communications networks through what are known as Post, Telephone and Telegraph authorities, or PTTs. In addition, many operate state-owned television and radio stations that make use of the airwaves. The governments of a growing number of countries, including India and Indonesia from the Third World, are leasing or purchasing their own satellites, primarily for domestic communications and remote sensing. Moreover, a few states are developing their own launch capabilities rather than rely on the dominant space powers. The field of communications has traditionally been relegated to the realm of low politics, even though the stakes can be quite important. Delegations to meetings of ITU are for the most part made up of engineers who are better able to comprehend the highly technical issues being discussed. Positions taken by many countries are influenced by numerous governmental departments and agencies with an interest in telecommunication. This is especially true of the United States, with the leading roles being played by the Federal Communications Commission and the Department of Defense.

International public policy on telecommunications is of special interest to a host of IGOs. For example, the ICAO is concerned about having adequate clear frequencies available for communication with aircraft; the IMO with satellite navigation systems and communication links to ships at sea. The World Weather Watch network of the WMO makes use of remote sensing and reports transmitted from stations throughout the world. The FAO is interested in the applications of remote sensing for surveying agriculture land and monitoring the progress of crops, as is UNEP for monitoring pollution, deforestation, and the spread of deserts in conjunction with its Earthwatch projects. UNESCO's programs for the exchange of scientific information, educational development, and cultural enrichment can be enhanced by telecommunications. Research on the impact of TDFs, which is still at a nascent stage, is being undertaken by the UN Commission on Transnational Corporations and the Rome-based Intergovernmental Bureau for Informatics.

Also among the intergovernmental organizations most interested in global policy on telecommunications are the public vendors of international communication services, the dominant one being the International Communications Satellite Organization (INTELSAT). INTELSAT along with the Communications Satellite Corporation (COMSAT), its private American subsidiary, provides international satellite communications to 170 countries and domestic services to two dozen states. One of few profit-seeking IGOs, INTELSAT has enjoyed a monopoly on international satellite communications among its 106 members, including telephone, data, and video transmissions. This policy has recently been questioned by the United States, whose private firms are anxious to cash in on the rapidly expanding market for international telecommunication services. Satellite communication services are also provided by INTERSPUTNIK, the Soviet bloc counterpart of INTELSAT; INMARSAT which provides communication links to more than 1600 ships; and EUTELSAT and ARABSAT, two organizations that operate on a regional basis.

Finally, there are many NGOs that have a special interest in the field of telecommunications, a few examples of which are the International Air Transport Association, the International Institute of Communications, the International Broadcasting and Television Organization, the International Council of Scientific Unions, the World Association for Christian Communication, and various associations of ham radio operators. The positions taken in international bodies by a number of states, in particular the United States, are influenced by corporations. These include firms in businesses that depend on access to telecommunication facilities, such as the television networks and the major wire services, as well as the numerous multinational corporations that have invested in communication networks that link their offices or subsidiaries around the world. Not to be overlooked are the high-tech firms that manufacture communication satellites, the leaders being Hughes Aircraft, RCA, and Ford Aerospace. Then, there are the private vendors of satellite communication services, notably COMSAT, American Satellite, RCA Americom, Western Union, and Satellite Business Systems, several of which are poised to provide direct satellite broadcasting services. Lastly, a few companies, most notably Orbital Sciences Corporation, are entering the business of manufacturing launch vehicles.

GLOBAL POLICY ON THE AIRWAVES AND GEOSYNCHRONOUS ARC

Establishing policies on the use of resources is normally the privilege of whoever is recognized as the owner of them. On the question of ownership, the spectrum of electromagnetic frequencies and the geosynchronous arc have been viewed as the common possession of mankind and therefore subject to international regulation. Because radio signals move through space unimpeded by political boundaries, it would be impractical for individual states to exercise the traditional prerogatives of ownership, in particular controlling use of the airwaves over their territory. Thus, nations are no more able to lay claim to the airwaves than they are to the atmosphere and weather. Moreover, with the potential for interference across national boundaries, it is imperative that there be some form of international refereeing of the airwaves. Likewise, an upward extension of the sovereign domain of states from their surface territory into the distant reaches of outer space would be inherently ambiguous in view of the rotation of the earth (Smith, 1976, p. 90). Thus, it is appropriate that the first article of the Outer Space Treaty of 1967 designates outer space to be "the province of all mankind" and, furthermore, provides that the exploration and use of outer space "shall be carried out for the benefit and in the interests of all countries." The subsequent article reinforces the common heritage principle, declaring that outer space "is not subject to national appropriation by claim of sovereignty, by means or use of occupation, or by any other means."

The question of who owns outer space is complicated by two issues that have been raised by a number of states. The first is the ambiguity of the boundary between national air space, over which states have the right to regulate activities such as the overflight of aircraft, and outer space, which is legally open to use by all states. On this matter, it has become a principle of international customary law that the orbits of artificial satellites are within the domain of outer space (Gorove, 1979, p. 44). Thus, use of the geosynchronous orbit would be subject to the provisions of the Outer Space Treaty. COPUOS has reviewed proposals for drawing a definitive boundary between air space and outer space, including one put forth by the Soviet Union which would place the dividing line at an altitude no more than 110 kms above sea level. The second complication is a challenge to the common ownership doctrine that was initially mounted by a group of equatorial states in a document known as the Bogotá Declaration of 1976. In it they argue that the geosynchronous arc should be considered an extension of the national air space of equatorial states in view of both the ambiguity of the boundaries of outer space and the fact that satellites stationed in it remain above the same country. Under the terms of the declaration, each of the 27 equatorial states—all of which are less developed—would have the authority to decide who could position satellites directly above its territory. In taking this position, which few other states accept, the signatories pledged to manage their sections of the arc in a way that would be sensitive to the interests of less developed countries (see Gorove, 1979, pp. 450–55).

It is generally assumed that the radio spectrum and the geosynchronous arc must be regulated internationally to minimize interference that would otherwise reduce significantly the value of these resources to all potential users. In the case of the airwaves, the management scheme of the ITU begins with an allocation of frequency bands to one or more of twenty categories of users known as "services," such as UHF and VHF television, direct satellite broadcasting, AM and FM radio, HF (shortwave) radio, and radio astronomy. The first such allocations were drawn up in 1927 for a relatively narrow range of frequencies. In ensuing years, larger portions of the electromagnetic spectrum were included in the process. The allocations currently in effect were decided upon at the 1979 General WARC and will not come up for general revision until the end of the century. As requests are received for frequencies for new services or an expanded range of frequencies for past ones, consideration is normally given to the impact such an allocation would have on established users, recognizing that requiring them to shift to other frequencies may necessitate expensive adaptations (see Wallenstein, 1973, p. 31).

The ITU does not allocate frequencies directly to states or specific users. Rather it is up to member states to take the initiative by notifying the IFRB of intended uses of particular frequencies by public or private parties within their countries that may transmit signals beyond their boundaries. The Board is empowered to bestow formal international protection to these uses if it determines that they are consistent with the allocation tables in the radio regulations and will not interfere with previously registered uses. This practice of sanctioning the plans of prospective users of the spectrum on what is in effect a first-come, first-served basis has been referred to as a system of institutionalized "squatter rights" (White, 1979, pp. 148–53). Where there is a problem of congestion, as has been the case with the high frequency (HF) sector, the IFRB may recommend ways of accommodating more of the would-be users.

International public policy on the geosynchronous orbital space is less well developed, which is not surprising given that its management is a much newer problem. In the early years of space exploration, countries launching satellites did not seek any international sanction for occupying an orbital space, nor did any encounter protests from other countries for their activities in space. It was an accepted practice that all states had a right to place objects into orbit so long as they did not interfere with satellites of others that were already in place (Gorove, 1979, p. 449). This doctrine of open access on a first-come, first-served basis was reinforced by the first article of the Outer Space Treaty of 1967 which provides that "outer space shall be free for exploration and use by all states." While the treaty goes on to prohibit national appropriations of any part of outer space, satellites are viewed as being a temporary use of orbital space and, thus, not a permanent claim that would violate the treaty. A strict interpretation of the nonappropriation clause to include satellites would effectively rule out the exploration and use of outer space, which was clearly not the intention of the drafters of the treaty.

Rapidly increasing demand for slots in the geosynchronous orbit has prompted the ITU to begin developing plans for managing its use. The 1973 Plenipotentiary Conference recognized the geosynchronous orbit as a scarce resource and authorized the IFRB to record the orbital positions assigned by countries to their satellites and to advise members of the ITU with a view to the "equitable, effective, and economical" use of the orbit (Gorove, 1979, p. 457). The subject was taken up at a special WARC held in 1977 at which the European, African, and Asian states adopted a plan that designated frequency bands and positions in the geo-synchronous orbit for satellite broadcast services in their regions. Each country was allocated five television channels along with a slot in the geostationary orbit. The United States argued that it was premature at that time to adopt such a plan for the remaining region of the Americas in view of new technologies that would be available by the time direct satellite broadcasting would commence in a significant way. Thus, it was not until 1983 that the Western Hemisphere drew up a comparable plan. By then, the availability of interference-reducing technologies, such as multibeam antenna, along with computerized planning of uses made it possible to make significantly more allocations for a given portion of the arc. The United States sought and received 8 orbital slots each with a capacity for 32 channels. On a different, but related matter it was decided at the 1979 General WARC that further negotiations aimed at a more equitable use of the orbit and frequencies for satellite communications would take place at mini-WARCs scheduled for 1984 and 1986.

States have generally made a practice of complying with the rules of the ITU (Jacobson, 1973 p. 74). Those that do not conform to international standards run the risk of being bypassed by the contemporary communications revolution. Moreover, the incentive for violating assignments of radio waves and the geo-synchonous orbit is diminished by the prospect of interference from authorized users of these resources. There was an era during the 1950s and early 1960s when commercial pirate radio stations operating from ships and offshore platforms broadcast popular programming into Europe in violation of ITU rules. Enforcement actions taken by flag states of the ships from which they operated was successful in shutting them down. The new ocean law will allow any state to take action on the high seas against pirate broadcasters whose signals reach their territories (see Robertson, 1982).

GLOBAL POLICY ON TRANSBORDER INFORMATION FLOWS

What rights should governments have to regulate the information that flows across the borders of their state? Two fundamental principles of international law suggest quite different responses to this question. First, there is the doctrine of the freedom of information, which has deep roots in Western democratic theory. It presumes that individuals should be the judges of what information and entertainment they wish to receive. This principle is unequivocally applied to the movement of information across national boundaries in Article 19 of the Universal Declaration of Human Rights, which states that "everyone has the right to freely seek, receive, and impart information and ideas through any media regardless of frontiers." Likewise, the Helsinki Accord of 1975, which was signed by 35 states of Eastern and Western Europe, provides for the free flow of people, ideas, and information as a way of reducing tension in the region. On the other hand, many governments contend that the principle of sovereignty gives them the right to regulate the movement of at least some types information into and out of their countries. Among these are the broadcasting of blatant propaganda beamed from foreign countries that is designed to trigger political unrest and television programming that could undermine cultural values. Also, as it was mentioned above, many governments are sensitive about the information that leaves their countries especially that which could jeopardize national security, have adverse economic consequences, or undermine the cultural integrity of their societies (see Littunen, 1980).

International regulation of transborder flows of information is at a rather primitive state of development. In regard to incoming information, the policies that have been adopted thus far appear to be inconsistent. Over the years, the ITU has allocated generous amounts of the HF band for shortwave broadcasting, much of which is exploited by the United States and the Soviet Union for beaming propaganda throughout the world. One such use has been the Voice of America broadcasts aimed at penetrating the closed information societies of the Soviet bloc. The use of these frequencies for transnational radio broadcasts was further reinforced by a resolution adopted at the 1984 WARC on the HF sector which allows countries to overcome jamming of their transmissions either by increasing their power or by switching frequencies.

Television has been treated in different way, especially with the prospect of direct satellite broadcasting. Several resolutions have been adopted in various forums that affirm the right of states to restrict television broadcasts beamed by satellites into their countries. A 1972 UNESCO resolution endorses satellite broadcasting as a way of spreading education, but only in the spirit of respect for the "sovereignty and equality of countries and the people's right to preserve their culture." In 1982 the General Assembly by an overwhelming vote barred DBS transmissions across national boundaries without the "prior consent" of the receiving country. Under the terms of the resolution, satellite broadcasters are expected to contain the "footprint" of their signals in a way that minimizes spillover into the territory of countries whose governments do not want them. This more restrictive approach to television broadcasts, which the United States strenuously opposed, is motivated by several considerations, not the least of which is the much greater economic stake that countries have in television than in radio. Direct satellite broadcasting could come into direct competition with lucrative cable networks that are being established in a growing number of countries. Moreover, the political and especially the cultural impact of television is generally assumed to be much greater than radio, which in part accounts for the public monopolies over television broadcasting that have been maintained in numerous countries.

International public policy on what states can do to limit the transfer of information to foreign countries is also in a state of relative infancy. Remote sensing activities has generally been recognized as a legitimate use of outer space under the terms of the Outer Space Treaty of 1967, given that the satellites are beyond the territorial jurisdiction of states. Thus, the position taken by some governments that picture taking from satellites is an infringement on their sovereignty, and thus should be subject to their prior approval, has not gained widespread acceptance. However, issues pertaining to the dissemination of the photographs and the data that are generated from them have been continuing topics of discussion in COPUOS. There is substantial support for the principle that states should have timely access to the pictures of their territory at affordable prices and with the assistance needed to interpret them. There is less agreement on whether this right of access extends to the information that is processed from the photographs, which brings up the issue of the proprietary rights of the operators of the satellites, some of whom in the future may be private firms. Another question being discussed is whether the observed state should have the option of vetoing the transfer of remotely gathered information to third parties who might use it to their disadvantage (see Joyner and Miller, 1985).

Transborder data flows (TDFs) are another subject that is just beginning to be addressed internationally. Several governments have taken the initiative on this issue by unilaterally establishing legal restraints on the movement of data beyond their borders. Sweden, Japan, France, Canada, and Brazil are among a growing number of countries that have adopted regulations and tax laws on TDFs that could seriously interfere with the operations of transnational corporations. What progress that has been made in deciding upon international policies is limited primarily to the confidentiality of personal data. Even then, the only noteworthy agreements have been of regional scope, specifically a set of guidelines set forth by the OECD in 1980 and a convention adopted by the Council of Europe in 1981. Both of these documents affirm the right of states to refuse to allow the export of information to countries that do not provide comparable safeguards on its dissemination. More research on the economic impact of TDFs will be necessary before meaningful international policies can be adopted on the movement of nonpersonal types of data (see Bendahmane and McClintock, 1984, pp. 47–66).

THE POLITICS OF TELECOMMUNICATIONS

Throughout most of its history, the ITU has had a reputation for making decisions on scientific and technical grounds. Relatively few extraneous political disputes have arisen of the type that have hampered efforts to reach agreement on international responses to most other policy problems (see Wallenstein, 1973, pp. 101–2). This is at least in part attributable to the practice most governments make of appointing delegates to meetings of the ITU on the basis of expertise rather than political credentials. Another key element in the nonpolitical image of the ITU is the five-member IFRB that is empowered to pass judgment on disputes that arise in applying the organization's rules. The members of the Board, who by tradition are engineers elected for their technical competence, are expected to act as "custodians of an international trust" rather than as representatives of countries or regions. They are neither to request nor to receive instructions from their governments, nor is any government to seek to influence them (Luard, 1977, pp. 27–44).

The policy-making environment in the ITU began to change during the 1970s as issues pertaining to international communications were drawn into the larger dialogue between the North and South over the latter's demands for a NIEO. Of more direct relevance for global telecommunications policy was the contentious debate that began taking place in UNESCO during the 1970s over what became known as the "new world information order" (NWIO). In proposing the NWIO, Third World countries hoped to lessen the dominance of the developed Western countries in the fields of information and communications. Their delegates to the ITU began taking a more serious interest in a variety of issues, such as how the radio waves and geosynchronous orbital space were being managed internationally and how the flow of information across their borders was affecting the security and economic interests of their countries. Moreover, they were looking for ways in which they could share in the fruits of the new technologies in the field of telecommunications and information processing, rather than falling further behind the advanced states.

The growing politicization of the ITU along North-South lines reflects the changing composition of the membership of the organization. The General WARC held in 1959 was dominated by what has been described as an "old boys' club" led by the United States, the United Kingdom, and the Soviet Union (Fore, 1979, p. 498). The General WARC of 1979 was attended by delegations from 65 nations that were not represented at the previous WARC. Almost all of the new members were from the Third World, many of which became independent states during the intervening years. In 1959 the less developed countries lacked the technical expertise needed to understand and represent their interests effectively. Furthermore, because of their lack of unity, many were all to willing to give into pressures to vote as instructed by the United States and the other advanced countries. At the time of the 1979 WARC, the Third World countries were still at a disadvantage in negotiating highly technical issues. However, by pooling their resources and caucusing as a group in preparatory meetings, they were becoming better able to pursue their common interests.

One of the issues Third World representatives have repeatedly raised is what they see as a tendency for the radio spectrum and the geosynchronous arc to be monopolized by the developed countries. At the time of the 1979 WARC it was reported that 90 percent of the radio spectrum was taken up by countries accounting for only 10 percent of the world's population (Hudson, 1979, p. 181). In addition, the technologically advanced countries, with their capacity to manufacture and launch satellites, have been rapidly occupying the choice locations in the geosynchronous orbit. Thus, one of the concerns expressed by Third World delegates is that these limited, common resources will be almost entirely spoken for by the time they develop their capabilities in telecommunications and will desire to make heavier use of them.

These anxieties prompted less developed states to question the first-come, first-served criterion for establishing the right to use the parts of the radio spectrum and the geosynchronous orbit, which they argue discriminates against them as late comers in the telecommunications field. In its place they have pushed for what is called an "a priori" system of allocations, which would allot frequencies and orbital locations to specific countries regardless of whether they had an immediate use for them. Moreover, special consideration would be given to reducing the inequities in the existing distributions. Such a scheme would guarantee that less developed countries would have access to radio spectrum and geosynchronous arc when they had future needs for them. For the most part, the technologically advanced countries have resisted a priori allocations on grounds that highly valued resources would go unused and, in effect, be wasted until the less developed countries are ready to exploit them sometime in the future. The United States has argued for a continuation of the past policy that is in effect based on "demonstrated need and ability to use" (Robinson, 1979, p. 157). The response of advocates of a priori allocations is that efficiency could be realized if less developed states leased their assigned frequencies and orbital slots to the highest bidder until they are ready to make use of them.

Developed and less developed countries have also been at odds over technological matters, in particular the specifications or standards for the equipment that is used. Most of these differences again boil down to the question of whether the primary goal of international policy should be to achieve the most efficient, or "highest," use of the spectrum or orbital arc. Some of the advanced countries, whose demand for telecommunication services is already high and is projected to grow rapidly, advocate requiring equipment that would expand the capacity of the spectrum and orbital arc. This type of proposal is frequently resisted by Third World countries on grounds that purchasing the more sophisticated equipment would impose heavy burdens on their limited economic resources. They prefer, instead, policies that would hold down the cost of their modest requirements for telecommunications.

One such issue has arisen over use of the popular and congested HF region of the radio spectrum, which is used internationally in shortwave radio communication. Over the last 30 years there has been a five-fold increase in the number of shortwave transmitters which, combined with a significant augmenting of the transmitting power of many of them, has left only one-third of the frequencies free of interference (Ronalds, 1979, p. 157). At the 1979 WARC, the United States and several other developed countries argued that additional HF frequencies should be set aside for international shortwave broadcasting of the type done by Voice of America, the BBC, and Radio Moscow. This proposal was opposed by Third World states who use these frequencies for telephone services and other domestic, "point-to-point" communications. The developed countries have tried to persuade other countries to follow their lead in shifting domestic point-to-point services to microwaves and cables, thereby freeing more of the HF region for uses that depend upon its special attributes for long-distance broadcasting. Third World representatives have resisted such a change arguing that it would be very costly and would subject them to more undesired foreign propaganda broadcasts. They in turn argued for assigning shortwave frequencies to specific countries (Mcleod, 1979, p. 878), which as with other a priori allocation schemes, was opposed by the heavy shortwave users on grounds that a valuable and limited resource would be used inefficiently.

Congestion of the HF region can also be alleviated by a switch from double to single side-band transmissions, which would significantly reduce interference and thereby increase substantially the capacity of the region. However, such a change would make it necessary to modify all shortwave transmitters and to replace all shortwave receivers at a cost of billions. Representatives of less developed countries have contended that this would be an unnecessary and excessive expense. Nevertheless, it was agreed at the 1984 mini-WARC on the HF region that all countries would be expected to make the transition to single side-band transmissions over a 20-year period. When asked to comply with more expensive technical specifications such as this, which are primarily for the benefit of the highly developed countries, numerous Third World states have made a practice of insisting upon additional assistance to compensate for the increased costs they would incur.

There is also the broader issue of what should be done to enable less developed countries to take advantage of the opportunities that are unfolding in telecommunications. Third World states point to the "common heritage" principle and more specifically to the first article of the Outer Space Treaty of 1967, which provides that the use of outer space should be for the benefit and interests of all countries, "irrespective of their degree of economic or social development." This clause, it is contended, obliges the highly developed countries to share their advanced technologies with countries that would otherwise be unable to reap the payoffs from the use of outer space to which they are entitled. This may, for example, include sharing communication satellites at affordable prices or even launching them for the countries that lack the requisite space technologies. Third World representatives have also taken the position that the developed countries should commit some of their research and development capacities to adapting technologies to the special needs of less developed societies, such as for low-cost systems for communicating with rural villages. As interpreted by the United States, however, the implies limited responsibilities, in particular the duty not to misuse outer space in a way that would diminish its value for the space activities of other countries.

Deep conflicts have arisen over several other issues related to telecommunications. Soviet bloc governments, which attempt to manage the information their populations receive, have been at odds with the United States and other democratic countries that champion a free flow of communications across international boundaries. Many governments of the Third World countries side with the Soviet bloc on this issue out of frustration with a situation in which their societies are persistently bombarded by uninvited programming originating in the technologically advanced nations, especially when they lack the capacity to reciprocate by transmitting signals to audiences in the developed world. Recently, differences have also cropped up among the highly developed countries on a number of matters, including restrictions on transnational data flows and direct satellite broadcasting. Agreement is sometimes difficult to reach on uniform technical specifications because of the impact they may have on competitive positions of the manufacturers of telecommunications equipment. An inability to agree on the specifications for color television has been an obstacle to interchangeable programming between the countries that have adopted two incompatible systems.

ASSESSMENT AND PROSPECTS

Traditionally, telecommunications policy was looked upon as one of the success stories in international cooperation and a model for efforts to address many of the other problems on global agendas. The tasks of drawing up specifications so that equipment in different countries will be compatible, coordinating international networks, and managing the radio spectrum to reduce interference were effectively handled in the ITU with a minimum of overt political conflict. It appeared that most decisions were made in a rational manner by experts primarily on the basis of technical considerations. And even though the standards and the rules of the ITU are not binding, most states comply with them as a matter of habit without the threat of sanctions (Jacobson, 1973, p. 74). Those that do not conform to international standards run the risk of being bypassed by the contemporary communications revolution. The incentive for violating the radio rules is lessened by the interference from legitimate broadcasters which is likely to be encountered.

The policy problems faced by the ITU and more recently by COPUOS and several regional IGOs became significantly more complicated during the past decade. This is in large part attributable to the new technologies that have revolutionized international communications in ways that could have significant political, economic, and social ramifications. Some of the older problems became more serious and complicated, such as in the congestion of the radio waves. But perhaps more significant are the additional policy problems that have emerged with the development of new technologies. For example, the filling up of the geosynchronous arc was not an international issue until the launching of communication satellites became a frequent and routine phenomenon. Even more recent are the controversies over how DBSs will be used, which became an issue with the development of much more powerful transpoders for communications satellites, and the massive TDFs, which were a product of breakthroughs in digital technologies.

The environment in which international telecommunications policy is made has also become more politically charged as an enlarged and more unified group of Third World countries became a major force in world politics. The proposals for a "new world information order" can be viewed as an offshoot of the demands for a "new international economic order," which were pushed by the Non-Aligned Movement during the 1970s. In the ITU, Third World members became increasingly aware of how unfamiliar technical language masked the interests that they had a stake in the equipment specifications and radio rules that were adopted with little if any overt political conflict. Another major development was the proposal and relatively rapid acceptance of the "common heritage" principle, which added legitimacy to the demands of the less developed countries for a share in the benefits derived from using the radio spectrum and outer space and a greater role in making international policies that pertain to them.

Will telecommunications became as highly politicized as other domains of global policy? Thus far, the conflicts that have emerged over the radio waves, the geosynchronous orbit, and DBSs have not gotten the ITU off the track of making international policy on rational, technical grounds. Forecasts that this would happen at the WARC in 1979 were by and large not borne out. It should be noted, however, that decisions on some of the more sticky issues were postponed to specialized WARCs, which have been fairly successful in addressing them. Some issues, such as the congestion of common resources, are being resolved with the introduction of new technologies that will accommodate many more users. The DBS issue may be defused, at least temporarily, by doubts that have arisen over the profitability of commercial services. The issue that will perhaps be the most difficult to resolve is the regulation of TDFs, which could have major economic implications for both developed and less developed countries. The trend toward the intervention of the state in this form of international commerce is perhaps part of broader tendency toward economic protectionism as countries attempt to cope with trade deficits caused in large part by the oil price rises of the 1970s.

REFERENCES

Bendahmane, Diane B. and David W. McClintock (1984). *Science, Technology, and Foreign Affairs: Vol. I, Global Environment, Communications, and Agriculture.* Washington, D.C.: Department of State.

Dordick, Herbert S. (1983). "The Emerging Information Business," *Columbia Journal of World Business,* Vol. 18, No. 1 (Spring), pp. 69–76.

Fore, William F. (1979). "Communication as Power: WARC 79," *Christian Century,* Vol. 96, No. 16 (May 2), pp. 498–500.

Gorove, Stephen (1979). "The Geostationary Orbit: Issues of Law and Policy," *American Journal of International Law,* Vol. 73, No. 3 (July), pp. 444–61.

Hudson, Heather E. (1979). "Implications for Development Communication," *Journal of Communication,* Vol. 29, No. 1 (Winter), pp. 179–86.

Jacobson, Harold K. (1973). "ITU: A Potpourri of Bureaucrats and Industrialists," pp. 59–101 in Robert W. Cox and Harold K. Jacobson (eds.), *The Anatomy of Influence: Decision-Making in International Organization.* New Haven: Yale University Press.

Joyner, Christopher C. and Douglas Miller (1985). "Selling Satellites: the Commercialization of LANDSAT," *Harvard International Law Journal,* Vol. 26, No. 1 (Winter), pp. 63–102.

Leinwoll, Stanley (1979). *From Spark to Satellite.* New York: Charles Scribner's Sons.

Leive, David M. (1970). *International Telecommunications and International Law: The Regulation of the Radio Spectrum.* Dobbs Ferry, N.Y.: Oceana.

Littunen, Yrjö (1980). "Cultural Problems of Direct Satellite Broadcasting," *International Social Science Journal,* Vol. 32, No. 2, pp. 283–303.

Luard, Evan (1977). *International Agencies: The Emerging Framework of Interdependence.* Dobbs Ferry, N.Y.: Oceana.

Marsh, Peter (1984). "UN Agency Tries to Unscramble Traffic Jam for Satellites in Geostationary Orbit," *Christian Science Monitor* (August 7), p. 9.

Mcleod, Norman (1979). "The World Takes on the Law of the Air," *New Scientist,* Vol. 83, No. 1173, (September 20), pp. 878–80.

Queeny, Kathryn M. (1978). *Direct Broadcast Satellites and the United Nations.* Alphen aan den Rijn, Netherlands: Sijthoff and Noordhoff.

Robertson, Horace B. (1982). "The Suppression of Pirate Radio Broadcasting," *Law and Contemporary Problems,* Vol. 45, No. 1 (Winter), pp. 71–101.

Robinson, Glen O. (1979). "The U.S. Position," *Journal of Communication,* Vol. 29, No. 1 (Winter), pp. 150–57.

Ronalds, Francis S. (1979). "Voices of America," *Foreign Policy,* No. 34, pp. 154–60.

Sauvant, Karl P. (1983). "Transborder Data Flows," *International Organization,* Vol. 37, No. 2, pp. 359–71.

Smith, Delbert D. (1976). *Communication via Satellite: A Vision in Retrospect.* Boston: A. W. Sitjhoff.

Spero, Joan E. (1982). "Information: The Policy Void," *Foreign Affairs,* No. 48, pp. 139–56.

Tagliabue, John (1984). "Luxembourg Draws Ire Over TV Plans," *New York Times* (July 4), p. D1.

Wallenstein, Gerd D. (1973). "Make Room in Space: Harmony and Dissonance in International Telecommunications" (Part 2), *Telecommunication Journal,* Vol. 40, No. 2 (February), pp. 95–102.

Walsh, John (1984). "Will There Be Room on the Arc?" *Science,* Vol. 223 (March 9), pp. 1043–45.

Webster, David (1984). "Direct Broadcast Satellites," *Foreign Affairs,* Vol. 62, No. 5 (Summer), pp. 1161–74.

White, Curtis T. (1979). "Uprooting the Squatters," *Foreign Policy,* No. 34 (Spring), pp. 148–53.

Whittaker, Philip N. (1979). "To Beat the Band," *Foreign Policy,* No. 34 (Spring), pp. 160–64.

11 CONCLUSIONS

Emerging Patterns of Global Policy

In the introductory chapter it was observed that world politics is a rich and perplexing mix of trends and countertrends. States continue to engage in power politics as they assemble large arsenals of increasingly sophisticated conventional and nuclear weapons, threaten to make use of them in attempts to exert influence, and occasionally, become involved in armed conflicts. But not to be ignored are the numerous efforts being made internationally to address an agenda of global problems that cannot be effectively tackled by states acting individually. The objective of this book has been to illuminate this latter, more constructive dimension of world politics. Concepts and theories derived from the field of policy studies, which previously have been applied primarily to national and subnational levels of political organization, were adopted to describe and analyze efforts at global problem solving. In this concluding chapter we shall review and assess the experience of the international community in developing and implementing global public policies. The six case studies that comprise the latter half of the book will be reviewed and compared in terms of the theoretical framework that was sketched in the first part.

THE NATURE OF THE PROBLEMS

The array of problems appearing on the contemporary global agenda is indeed both extensive and varied. In view of the serious and interrelated nature of many of them, it has been said that humanity faces a "problematique" that is of historically unprecedented proportions. The set of policy problems that defined the six case studies are a diverse lot in several respects other than representing different substantive domains—political, economic, social, resources, environment, and communication and transportation. Most of the policy problems that were examined are of a negative nature, implying actual or potential conditions that are generally considered undesirable. For example, there is the absolute poverty that is symptomatic of underdevelopment, as well as the widespread use of torture and executions by governments to deal with political opponents. Water and air pollution and the depletion of ocean fisheries are unfortunate developments that seem to be getting progressively worse. Proliferation of nuclear weapons is directed not so much at the present group of acknowledged nuclear states, which is still quite small, but at the prospect of a flurry of new entries into the nuclear weapons club, which could have a serious destabilizing effect on world politics. By contrast, policy problems related to telecommunications and the use of the seabed are of a more positive nature in that one of the primary objectives is to take advantage of opportunities presented by new technologies.

Policy problems appear on global agendas for a variety of reasons, usually a combination of several of them. Some problems are transnational in character because they involve relationships between states. Thus, telecommunications initially became a subject of global policy when technological breakthroughs opened up new possibilities for interactions across national boundaries. Trade essential to the development of Third World countries is a form of international transaction. Likewise, exports of nuclear technologies and materials are an integral part of the proliferation problem. Pollution introduced into the of the atmosphere or terrestrial river systems is a classic example of a "spillover" problem, as is interference from radio signals originating in other countries. Possibilities for proliferation also illustrate how the policies of one state can potentially cause problems for others; specifically, the acquisition of nuclear weapons by additional states diminishes the security of their neighbors. Concessions on taxes and environmental standards by Third World countries attempting to attract foreign investment illustrate a situation in which mutually disadvantageous competition dictates an international policy response.

Not all problems appearing on global agendas cut across national boundaries. Some involve areas that are beyond the territorial jurisdiction of states, as is the case with conflicts over rights to harvest the living resources of the oceans, to mine the mineral-rich nodules found on the deep seabed, and to position satellites in geosynchronous orbit. What appears to be an internal problem may also become the subject of global policy, especially if it is common to many countries or is of special interest to the broader community. A majority of countries are mired in an underdeveloped condition, which is attributable in large part to internal causes that cannot be corrected without economic and technical assistance from abroad. This is not, however, to deny that the task of development faced by the Third World is greatly complicated by external factors. The protection of human rights is another global policy problem that is primarily internal in character. The prominence of human rights issues on international agendas is best explained by the strong concern about how people of foreign countries are treated by their governments, which was initially aroused by revelations about the atrocities committed during World War II.

ACTORS

Governments of states are the key actors in efforts to address any global problem. Collectively, they make the decisions on global public policies; individually, they decide whether to be bound by each policy. Moreover, it is up to governments to enforce the regulations contained in the policies, both upon themselves and their nationals, and to provide the financial support for international programs. While none of the six case studies was an exception to this general rule, there were differences in the extent to which policy problems attracted the interest and involvement of top-level governmental officials. Human rights are clearly in the realm of "high" politics for most countries because of the domestic political implications that a faithful observance of them might have. Development has a similar status, especially for the Third World countries, as can be seen in the impressive number of heads of states and high level ministers that attend the meetings of the Non-Aligned Movement every four years, at which economic issues are the predominant subject of discussion. At the other extreme of "low politics," global policies on telecommunications, and to a lesser extent on pollution and ocean fisheries, are worked out by delegates chosen for their knowledge or expertise rather than political status.

IGOs frequently play important roles in global problem solving, albeit ones that are not only secondary to those of the governments of states, but also quite different in terms of the contributions that are made. IGOs are frequently looked to for information and recommendations. It is also not uncommon for IGOs to play a critical part in implementing policies, particularly in monitoring compliance with regulations and administering programs. Of the six case studies, IGOs are perhaps the most active in addressing the problem of economic development, in view of the roles played by the World Bank group, the IMF, the UNDP, and the regional development banks in dispensing economic and technical assistance. Most of the other specialized agencies also contribute in some way to international development programs, two notable examples being the FAO in the field of agriculture and UNESCO in combatting illiteracy and improving education generally. Numerous IGOs are actors in the creation and implementation of pollution policy, among which are WHO, WMO, IMO, IAEA, ILO, and UNESCO, whose efforts are now being coordinated and stimulated by UNEP. By contrast, only one global IGO is actively involved in nonproliferation policy, namely the IAEA, which monitors nuclear power facilities to detect significant diversions of fissionable material to weapons production.

Far more numerous than IGOs, INGOs have become an ever-present feature of the global policy process. The participation of a selected group of INGOs in global policy making has been institutionalized through the granting of "consultative status" with certain IGOs. Many INGOs act as pressure groups in seeking to influence the direction of global policy. Some advance a public cause, as is the case with environmentally oriented associations that have promoted restrictions that would limit pollution or conserve marine mammals and with the many groups that have pushed for higher standards on human rights. International trade associations have been prominent advocates of the interests of industries that would be affected by global policies on the proliferation of nuclear weapons, extracting the mineral wealth of the seabed, the curbing of pollution, and the use of airwaves and the geosynchronous orbit. International scientific and professional associations—perhaps the most prominent being the International Council of Scientific Unions—are looked to as reliable sources of information and draft resolutions on technical subjects, as was observed in the case studies on pollution and ocean fisheries. INGOs may also be the most vigorous monitors of compliance with international regulations, the best example from among the case studies being the efforts of Amnesty International and the other INGOs comprising the "human rights industry" to investigate and issue reports of human rights violations.

THE POLICY PROCESS

A policy process is a multi-staged effort by a group of actors who contribute to the making and implementing of strategies that address problems. Ideally, the process proceeds through a series of steps similar to those typically incorporated into models of rational decision making. The policy process begins with the recognition of a problem, then moves on to an agreement on procedures and a specification of values and principles. Next, policy alternatives are formulated and considered before one is settled upon. Finally, the policy is implemented and, following the passage of a reasonable amount of time, is reviewed before a decision is made on whether to terminate, continue, modify, or replace it.

Many of these steps can be observed in the case studies, although they are quite often not as distinctive, nor in as orderly a progression, as the model would suggest. It is not uncommon for steps to be bypassed or merged with others. The allocation of electromagnetic frequencies is an example of the policy process running the full cycle. Decisions on whether to continue certain policies dating back to 1959 were made at the General WARC convened in 1979, which in turn marked the beginning of a new policy cycle that is to run for the next twenty years. All stages are also identifiable in the making and implementing of global policies on the proliferation of nuclear weapons. Review conferences that consider the future of the Non-Proliferation Treaty (NPT) have been held at 5-year intervals beginning in 1975. Likewise, global policy on economic development has reached the stage of review and revision several times. Major evaluations have been taking place at 10-year intervals, coinciding with the drafting of plans for each Development Decade. The proposals for a new international economic order (NIEO) are a more complicated case. The Charter of Economic Rights and Duties and States, which was adopted in 1974, could be viewed as a revised statement of goals, principles, and policy alternatives. Further efforts to decide on specific policies and how they will be implemented have become bogged down in procedural disputes over the conduct of the postponed Global Negotiations. The policy process on several of the other problems has not proceeded nearly as far. Policies on human rights, the use of the seabed, and marine pollution have been spelled out in considerable detail, but much still remains to be done to implement and review them. Regulations on the control of transboundary air pollution have not as yet been defined in very specific terms.

What observations can be made about the arenas in which the policy making activities took place? In all of the case studies, activity occurred in a combination of permanent and ad hoc arenas. The largest number of permanent forums has been used in discussions of development policy, among which are the General Assembly and ECOSOC, as well as the deliberative bodies of many lending institutions and other specialized agencies. Human rights issues also appear regularly on the agenda of the General Assembly in addition to being an exclusive concern of several commissions that answer to ECOSOC and a secondary matter for several of the specialized agencies. Past efforts to prevent an enactment of Hardin's "tragedy of the commons" in the harvesting of the living resources of the oceans have been decentralized among a score of fishery commissions loosely coordinated by the FAO. When the 200-mile EEZs come into effect, as provided for in the new law of the sea, fishery conservation will fall almost exclusively within the jurisdiction of coastal states.

By contrast, policy making directed at some problems is centralized in a few specialized arenas. Telecommunications have been dealt with almost exclusively by the ITU, although several policies that apply to satellite communication were adopted in the Committee on the Peaceful Uses of Outer Space. The formulation of policies aimed at stemming the proliferation of nuclear weapons took place in the Eighteen Nation Disarmament Committee and its successors. Most decisions on the procedures for safe-guards and inspections of nuclear facilities have been made in the IAEA, although the nuclear supplier states have occasionally met, sometimes secretly, in efforts to agree on a common export policy for "sensitive" equipment. Almost all of the recent policy making on the exploitation of the resources of the seabed has taken place in UNCLOS III and the special committees established by the General Assembly to do the preliminary work on a new ocean law.

Ad hoc arenas have become an important setting for global policy making, a trend that was borne out in the cases that were examined. The 1972 Conference on the Human Environment, at which the issue of pollution was a leading agenda item, and the 1979 Conference on Science and Technology for Development are prototypes of single-issue world conferences. These "global town meetings" last a few weeks following an extended series of a preparatory meetings sometimes strung out over several years. On the subject of human rights, the conferences held in 1975, 1980, and 1985 in conjunction with the United Nations Decade for Women are in much the same mold of ad hoc meetings, as was the International Labor Conference of 1976 and the World Conference to Combat Racism and Racial Discrimination of 1978. Special sessions of the General Assembly called in 1974, 1975, and 1980 were the site for some of the most intensive discussions of the NIEO. UNCLOS III could also be classified as an ad hoc arena, but one that differs from other world conferences in several re-spects. Rather than being a single-shot conference, it was a series of eleven sessions, each lasting several weeks that were held at irregular intervals over a 9-year period in three different cities. Moreover, the objective of the conference was a treaty that states would be invited to ratify, rather than a spate of resolutions to be acted upon by the General Assembly or some other sponsoring international body.

The policy process usually proceeds through a series of perma-nent and temporary arenas. As diagrammed in figure 3.1, a model path begins with some form of exploratory meetings. If the prob-lem is deemed to be serious and of general interest, it is next taken up in the General Assembly. Because of its limited time, the General Assembly may elect to convene a supplementary, ad hoc arena, either a special session or a world conference, to explore the matter in more detail and draw up a set of guiding principles and a plan of action. In the implementation stage, the assemblies and councils of specialized IGOs typically become the center of policy-related activity. The model is a fairly good representation of how environmental problems were considered in UNESCO's Biosphere Conference of 1968, the General Assembly, the Stockholm Conference of 1972, and over the past decade by UNEP. Likewise, on the subject of ocean law, the General Assembly convened three conferences for intensive negotiations and the adoption of treaties. Implementation of parts of the recently adopted Law of the Sea Treaty will be carried out by a newly established body to be known as the International Seabed Authority. Policy problems related to economic development are discussed in so many arenas simultaneously that it is difficult to chart a sequence among them. Part of the model can be observed in the discussions of the NIEO beginning in the mid-1970s, which shifted back and forth between the General Assembly and special sessions held in 1974, 1975, and 1980.

In some cases, the route of an international policy process diverges significantly from the model sequence of arenas. Permanent bodies, rather than ad hoc conferences, were established to draft global policies on human rights and arms control. Writing an "international bill of rights" was the original charge given the Commission on Human Rights, which was created by ECOSOC in 1946. The NPT was the first major arms control effort of ENDC, now the Committee on Disarmament, which was reconstituted by the General Assembly in 1961. There were also instances in which policy problems were addressed first in specialized agencies. Various aspects of pollution problems were initially taken up, not in the General Assembly or at the Stockholm Conference, but in several of the specialized agencies and regional organizations. For example, as far back as the early 1950s, IMO has been the principal forum for negotiating treaties designed to limit vessel-source pollution. Likewise, the ITU has been the primary if not the exclusive arena for policies on telecommunications for more than a century. The policy process of the ITU is notable in one other respect. In contrast to the other specialized agencies, which have permanent deliberative bodies, decisions of the ITU are made at WARCs, which have many of the trappings of ad hoc conferences.

GOALS AND PRINCIPLES

Values in the form of goals and principles not only lend a sense of direction to the policy process, but also, influence what is identified as a problem. In this study, goals have been defined as the objectives of public policies; principles as the ground rules that should not be violated in the pursuit of goals. The goals and principles that ostensibly guide global policies can be readily found in the preambles of most charters of international organizations, resolutions, and treaties.

Goals can usually be arranged in a hierarchy. Lower-level objectives are instrumental to progress toward other higher-level values leading eventually to ultimate goals, which are desirable in their own right, rather than as the means to some other end. Several of the goals highlighted in the case studies contribute quite directly to an ultimate objective of making it possible for individuals to achieve their full potential as human beings. This is particularly true of the fundamental rights and freedoms for individuals, including entitlements to basic needs, that are enshrined in the Universal Declaration of Human Rights of 1948 and in the many other documents that spell out specific types of rights in more detail. The NPT is a clear-cut example of a policy aimed at somewhat lower-level, instrumental values. The relevant higher-order goal is ostensibly to avoid nuclear war, an objective that is to be achieved by policies that would prevent additional countries from acquiring nuclear weaons. This intermediate objective in turn is to be achieved by denying aspiring states the opportunity to acquire or produce the fissionable materials needed to construct a nuclear bomb. Likewise, policies in the fields of telecommunications and the exploitation of the deep seas contribute less directly to the achievement of an ultimate objective.

Conflict over the goals of global policies can be observed in all of the case studies. For example, should global policies on economic development be oriented primarily toward industrialization? Or, should they also be directed toward the prompt satisfaction of the "basic needs" of the hundreds of millions of desperately poor in the world? In a related vein, should greater emphasis be placed on political and civil rights, such as freedom of speech and other democratic values, or be focused on economic and social entitlements to food, shelter, education, and medical care. In deciding on international policies for ocean fisheries, there has been tension over whether the primary goal should be maximizing the short-term profitability of the world's fishing industry as opposed to conserving the resource for the future. Competing goals can usually be smoothed over, at least temporarily, through the use of bland, abstract concepts that lend themselves to widely varying interpretations. An example of such a concept is "maximum sustainable yield," which is a compromise between economic and environmental values in the management of ocean fisheries. Differing views often surface again later and become a bone of contention throughout the policy process.

As with other ground rules, principles limit the range of action that is considered appropriate given the values of a community. The principle supporting soverignty of national governments over internal matters has been a continuing obstacle to the development of strong international policies. Several of the case studies, however, revealed a willingness of states to compromise on what was once regarded as an absolute principle. Shock over the magnitude of the atrocities committed in Nazi Germany gave rise to the establishment of international standards on human rights, which are a direct challenge to the doctrine of sovereignty. Nevertheless, a number of governments, including some of the most flagrant violators of human rights, contend that international efforts to monitor their performance and to investigate alleged violations are an unwarranted infringement on their sovereignty. The NPT impinges on another aspect of sovereignty, namely the prerogative of states to acquire or produce weapons that might be needed for their self-defense. Provisions of the treaty for "full-scope" safeguards of nuclear facilities by the IAEA is another example of sovereignty being compromised in the interests of global policy. The doctrine of sovereignty cuts in two ways when applied to the issue of transboundary pollution. States commonly claim the exclusive right to regulate pollution causing activities within their boundaries. It could also be argued that the sovereignty of a state is compromised when the value of its resources and the quality of its environment is diminished by pollution that flows or drifts into its territory from other states.

Other principles have a bearing on global policies that apply to areas beyond the territorial jurisdiction of states. For centuries, the doctrine of the "freedom of the seas" has governed use of the oceans and seabed beyond the territorial waters of the coastal states. This tenet of customary law permitted all countries to make use of the ocean areas for their own gain so long as they did not unduly interfere with the legitimate activities of others or establish permanent claims. In the case of the seabed, the freedom of the seas has been superseded by the concept of the "common heritage of mankind" which treats the area and its resources as the joint property of all states. As usually interpreted, the common heritage doctrine implies that all states have a right to participate in policy decisions on who may exploit the resources of the seabed and under what conditions, as well as a right to expect a share of the proceeds. Likewise, outer space, which includes the geosynchronous orbital arc that is critical to satellite communications, was declared to be the "province of all mankind" to be explored and used for the benefit of all countries. The spectrum of electromagnetic frequencies, or airwaves, has also been treated as a common resource, presumably because of the impracticality of dividing it up geographically for the exclusive use of individual states. The sovereignty principle has not been entirely divorced from non-national areas. Ships plying the high seas are regarded as tiny areas of "floating sovereignty," that are subject to the jurisdiction of states whose flags they fly. Some states contend that foreign-operated satellites that collect information on their weapons, crops, or natural resources are an infringement on their sovereignty. A similar argument has been made with regard to the use of the airwaves to beam propaganda to the residents of a country against the wishes of its government.

The issue of equity inevitably arises because of the unequal benefits and costs that global policies have for states. For example, the inherent fairness of the NPT has been challenged on grounds that it permits a few military "have" states to build up large nuclear arsenals, while denying this ultimate weapon to all others, who are thereby relegated to a permanent condition of military inferiority. Fishery commissions have weighed a variety of factors in efforts to equitably allocate quotas to countries, including population, investments in fishing fleets, historical share of the catch, and proximity to the fishing grounds. Equity was hardly the governing consideration in incorporating the 200-mile exclusive economic zone (EEZ) into the new Law of the Sea Treaty, inasmuch as a small number of states will derive enormous benefits from being permitted to claim first rights to harvest high productive fisheries located off their coasts. Fairness has been a more important issue in establishing the conditions under which the highly developed countries may use their advanced technologies to exploit common property resources, in particular the mineral-rich nodules found on the seabed. Third World governments have argued that the common heritage principle entitles them to a share of the profits from such ventures, and even to participate in them. Similarly, the first-come, first-served procedure for registering users of the airwaves and orbital spaces has been challenged on grounds that it permits the advanced countries unfairly to monopolize these limited resources. Equity can also be an objective as opposed to a ground rule for global policy, which has been the case with the sometimes stridently stated demands of Third World leaders for an NIEO that would allow their countries to enjoy a greater proportion of the world's wealth.

POLICY RESPONSES

International public policies take the form of either regulations or programs, or a combination of the two. Regulations are the staple of strategies for addressing problems that are transboundary in character or involve the use of areas beyond the territorial jurisdiction of states. Solutions to these types of problems usually entail constraints on actions of states that are harmful to others while encouraging behaviors that are beneficial to the larger community. Programs providing international assistance or a service are the principal ingredient of policies directed at problems that are basically internal, but are experienced by many countries that can benefit from outside assistance in addressing them.

Most international regulations fall into one of four categories: restrictions, obligations, standards, or rights. Ample examples of each can be noted from among the case studies. Restrictions are perhaps the most common type of regulation. Under the terms of the NPT, states having nuclear weapons or advanced nuclear technologies are prohibited from assisting other countries to share in the forbidden fruit of nuclear weapons. Human rights conventions prohibit many practices, such as slavery and forced labor, genocide, racial discrimination, and torture, as well as arbitrary arrest, detention, and exile. The Oslo and London Conventions completely ban the ocean dumping of highly toxic substances appearing on "black" lists and limit the disposal of less toxic wastes that have been placed on "gray" lists. Restrictions have also been the key element in strategies designed to conserve fisheries. The International Whaling Commission has recently extended a moratorium on the harvesting of endangered species of whales to almost all commercial whaling activities. Other fishery commissions have imposed a variety of limitations, such as closed seasons and national and global quotas.

Examples of obligations and standards can also be cited. In conjunction with the United Nations Development Decades, the industrialized countries have been asked to provide development assistance in an amount that is at least equal to 0.7 percent of their GNPs. This is not a binding obligation, however, which in part explains why the assistance programs of all but a few of the donor countries have fallen far short of the targeted figure. Human rights policies outline many responsibilities that governments have to their citizens, such as in satisfying the requirements of due process for individuals taken into custody. The NPT not only calls upon the nuclear-weapons states to assist the nonweapons states in the peaceful applications of nuclear technologies, but also obligates them to make serious efforts to negotiate a reduction of their nuclear arsenals. Corporations that engage in deep-sea mining under the terms of the new law of the sea are required to make their technologies available at a fair price to the mining enterprise that will be created as an arm of the new International Seabed Authority. The best examples of standards can be found in the series of conventions of the IMO, the most prominent ones being MARPOL 73 and SOLAS 74. These documents set forth specifications on matters such as the structure and navigation equipment of tankers and the training of crews, which were designed not only to reduce discharges of oil and oily substances during routine operations, but also to reverse an alarming increase in accidents. In the field of telecommunications, specifications for equipment have been set in the interests of reducing interference in the use of airwaves and of ensuring the compatibility of transmitters and receivers located in different countries.

Often overlooked are the rights which are the reciprocal of restrictions on the behavior of other countries. The radio rules of the ITU make it possible for countries to have exclusive use of certain frequencies that they have registered with the International Frequency Registration Board. States swearing off nuclear weapons by ratifying the NPT have the explicit right to adapt nuclear technologies to peaceful purposes. Under the long-standing doctrine of the freedom of seas, states have the right of open access to the oceans. The Outer Space Treaty of 1967 affirms the right of states to make use of outer space, which includes the option of putting satellites into unoccupied orbital spaces. The new Law of the Sea Treaty bestows on coastal states major new rights to manage the resources within EEZs that extend 200 nautical miles from their shorelines. Human rights documents are replete with the rights of individuals to satisfy their basic needs, to be free to form trade unions, to be granted a fair and speedy trial if arrested, and to enjoy other specified perogatives. Finally, societies are to have the right to choose their own type of government, or what is known as "self-determination."

The role of programs in international policy responses varies greatly depending on the problem being addressed. It is only natural that economic and technical assistance would be the key elements in development policy aimed at industrializing Third World countries and improving the living standards of their populations. The primary multilateral sources of funds have been the UNDP, which finances many of the programs of the specialized agencies, and the World Bank Group, which through its three windows has lent out nearly $100 billion dollars. The IDA was set up as an affiliate of the World Bank to provide loans to the poorer countries on "soft" terms. Another affiliate, the IFC provides loans to private companies investing in the Third World. Technical assistance, which is sometimes geared to making it possible for countries to comply with international standards, is a secondary part of several of the global policies that were reviewed. Accordingly, the ITU aids poorer countries in conforming with international specifications on radio equipment and the IMO on the development of harbor facilities that meet international standards.

Various information services are key ingredients of several of the global policies that were considered. Such is the case with data on fish stocks and catches that are assembled by several of the fishery commissions and by the independent International Council for the Exploration of the Sea. This information, when combined with knowledge of regeneration rates of species, becomes critical for setting "maximum sustainable yields" for fisheries under international supervision. Various types of scientific information are an important part of UNEP's attack on pollution problems through its Program Activity Centers. Among these are the Global Environmental Monitoring System (GEMS) being created to record pollution levels and investigate the impact of them on the environment; INFOTERRA, which serves as a clearing house for information on research pertaining to specific environmental problems that is being conducted in various countries; and the International Registry of Potentially Toxic Chemicals, a repository of research findings on the dangers associated with particular chemicals.

IMPLEMENTATION

Carrying out policies in the horizontally ordered community of states is a different proposition from what it is in nations that have a strong vertical structure of authority. It is normally up to the governments of states to decide whether to be bound by international regulations or to help finance programs. Not surprisingly, governments have been reluctant to ratify the treaties that are the foundation of several of the policies noted in the case studies. Conspicuously absent from the list of 127 states that have become parties to the NPT are some of the very states that are the greatest threats to join the nuclear weapons club, if they have not done so clandestinely already. It is also notable that 10 years passed before the 2 major convenants on human rights adopted by the General Assembly in 1966 came into effect upon the ratification of the thirty-fifth state. Even slower has been the trickle of acceptance of the optional protocol appended to the Covenant on Civil and Political Rights, which authorizes the Human Rights Committee to receive complaints from a ratifying state's own citizens. States have also been notoriously dilatory in ratifying the treaties of the IMO that address, among other things, the problem of vessel-source oil pollution. The four treaties adopted at UNCLOS I in 1958 fell into disrepute because none attracted the ratifications of as many as one-third of the eligible states.

Formalities aside, the rate of compliance varies considerably from one treatment to the next. Most states make a practice of obeying the rules of the ITU on the use of airwaves, presumably in part because nonconforming uses would encounter interference from the signals of legitimate users. It also appears that the parties to the NPT conform to most if not all of its provisions. A glaring exception is the obligation of the nuclear weapons states to first limit and then reduce their nuclear arsenals. Aside from a series of atmospheric explosions conducted by China and France, which are banned by the Limited Test Ban Treaty of 1963, testing of nuclear weapons has taken place underground, as permitted by the treaty. Most states comply with limits imposed by the International Whaling Commission in the interests of conserving endangered species of whales. Unfortunately, their restraint has been taken advantage of by a few "pirate whalers." Other treaties mentioned in the case studies have been observed less consistently. A disturbing number of governments, including ratifiers of conventions on human rights, blatantly engage in internationally forbidden practices, such as torture, arbitrary imprisonment, and press censorship—rationalizing their behavior on the grounds that political order is a prerequisite to economic development. Few of the parties to the 1979 Treaty on Long-Range Transbourday Air Pollution have made serious efforts to fulfill their obligation to reduce emissions of the airborne pollutants that cause such problems as acid rain.

The first step in a more aggressive enforcement of international rules is the detection of violations by systematic monitoring performed by outside groups. In this regard, two of the case studies are noteworthy. The IAEA has developed an elaborate set of procedures for inspecting nuclear facilities to discover whether enough fissionable materials are unaccounted for to warrant concern that a nuclear bomb is being produced clandestinely. The performance of governments in observing human rights is scrutinized by several United Nations bodies, most notably the Commission on Human Rights and the more recently formed Human Rights Committee. Even more penetrating investigations of human rights records are conducted by Amnesty International and several other respected INGOs, which not only feed information to the appropriate IGOs, but also issue their own public reports. Fishery commissions have assigned inspectors to fishing vessels on either a routine or spot basis to verify that quotas or other rules are not being breached. With other policies, such as those that apply to pollution, it is up to each state to monitor its own behavior and that of its nationals, although other states may issue complaints when they observe violations.

Stronger pressure can be exerted on offending states in a number of ways. The tactic of publicizing and condemning violations, or what is popularly known as "mobilizing shame," has been used extensively by both IGOs and INGOs to induce reforms from governments guilty of serious human rights violations. The highly organized "prisoner of conscience" campaigns by Amnesty International have had some apparent success, especially in gaining the release of more celebrated political prisoners, whose fate was known to the outside world. A similar tactic has been employed by other INGOs against nations that persist in harvesting whales in disregard of the regulations of the International Whaling Commission. Internationally decreed economic sanctions are imposed infrequently to encourage compliance with international policies. Among the case studies, the most notable examples were again directed against human rights violators, specifically the mandatory embargoes declared by the Security Council on all trade with Rhodesia from 1968 to 1980 and on arms shipments to South Africa since 1977. Even without being a party to the NPT, India was soundly condemned for detonating a nuclear device in 1974, the first major transgression of the treaty's ban on such tests. In this case, however, the sanctions in the form of a curtailing of the sale of nuclear materials and technology to India were imposed by supplier states acting unilaterally. When the new law of the sea comes into effect, coastal states will have expanded powers to punish operators of ships entering their ports that have been observed to be violating international regulations. Thus far, military force has not been used to compel compliance with any of the policies discussed in the case studies, with the questionable exceptions of a few instances of armed forces crossing international boundaries under the guise of a "humanitarian intervention" that would bring an end to atrocities being committed by a government against its people.

Securing adequate funding is a major challenge in implementing global policies that involve programs, which has especially been the case with international development assistance. Aside from the investments of private parties that are loaned out by the World

Bank, most of the money for development programs comes from the contributions of members of the OECD. The assistance provided by most OECD states falls far short of the international standard of 0.7 percent of their GNPs. During the past decade, OPEC countries shared some of their oil wealth, but became less generous as their oil sales dropped off. Because of the political motivations for assistance programs of the major donor states, the lion's share of the funds from these sources is distributed bilaterally to a small group of favored recipients. Only a modest amount has been made available for financing the assistance programs of international institutions. Pledges to the IDA, upon which the poorest countries depend for development assistance on "soft" terms, have fallen well below the goals set for the program, especially in recent years after deep cutbacks by the United States. A chronic shortfall in contributions has made it difficult for UNEP to launch many of its ambitious plans, including the GEMS and the Regional Seas Program.

CONFLICT

Efforts to address problems collectively inevitably lead to conflict as the participants push for the adoption of those policies that will best serve their interests. The intensity of the disputes, or degree of politicization of the policy process, varies considerably from one issue area to the next. Historically, the field of telecommunication has been characterized by a low level of politicization. In the conferences of the ITU, policy decisions have customarily been made on technical grounds by delegates who were appointed for their expertise. More conflict has arisen in recent years, however, as representatives from the Third World recognized the interests they had at stake. Likewise, international policy on pollution has generally not been very highly politicized, with the exception of a few regional contexts, most notably the discord between the United States and Canada over acid precipitation. Issues pertaining to the mining of the deep seabed evoked the greatest controversy at UNCLOS III, which overall was a moderately politicized forum. Fairly intense conflict has arisen over issues involving human rights—in particular on the subject of international enforcement of political freedoms. The 5-year review conferences of the NPT have been contentious affairs, as states that had sworn off nuclear weapons strongly criticized not only the superpowers for their failure to limit, much less reduce, their arsenals, but also the supplier states for restrictions imposed on exports of "sensitive" nuclear technologies. Finally, global development policy has been quite highly politicized since the early 1970s when Third World leaders came forward with proposals for a NIEO.

Conflict may surface at any stage of the policy process. Disagreements over global development policy have arisen at several points in a very complex international effort. During the 1950s, the issue was whether any type of global commitment should be made to the economic development of the Third World. The 1970s saw the debate over the alternative goals of economic growth or satisfying basic needs. Deep divisions could also be observed over policy alternatives as the United States and several of its OECD allies took sharp issue with numerous Third World proposals for a NIEO. Recently, the "North-South dialogue" has come to a standstill over the procedural issue of which forums should be used for the Global Negotiations on implementing the NIEO. The principal issues that have arisen over international law on the oceans and the seabed have been policy questions, namely who has the right to exploit the vast quantities of living and nonliving resources, and under what conditions. Likewise, disagreements over the use of the airwaves and geosynchronous orbital spaces are disputes over policies. The policy debates over all of these types of nonnational resources reflect deeper disagreement over values. Should they be managed for economic efficiency to the benefit of the industrially advanced states or, alternatively, for equity in a way that would ensure the less developed countries a share of the proceeds? In addressing the problems of human rights and proliferation of nuclear weapons, the most visible conflicts have arisen over the implementation of policies that have been widely accepted, namely the "international bill of rights" and the NPT.

The most salient line of conflict pertinent to global policy has not been the one between the Cold War blocs led by the two superpowers. The East-West division was only an occasional factor in the six case studies; human rights being the primary example. Ironically, the United States and Soviet Union collaborated on joint drafts of the NPT during the 1960s. Much more in evidence has been the "North-South dialogue" between the developed countries, known as either the "West" or "North," and the less developed countries of the Third World, or "South." The North includes the members of the OECD, while the South has achieved a degree of unity through the meetings of the Non-Aligned Movement and the Group of 77. The conflict heated up during the 1970s as the activism of the South that accompanied demands for a NIEO spilled over into a wide range of other global issues, including the mining of seabed resources and rights to use the airwaves and geosynchronous orbital space. Initially, North and South were also at odds over the priority that should be given to pollution problems and the quality of the natural environment generally. This latter conflict has receded as Third World governments were reassured that international environmental action would not be at the expense of a continued commitment to economic development.

Other lines of conflict are specific to single issues. On the subject of nuclear proliferation, the primary division has been between the nuclear-weapon "haves" and "have nots," with China, a Third World country, being a member of the former group. Serious disputes have arisen between the United States and its allies possessing advanced nuclear industries over the question of exports of technologies that may make it possible for states to produce their first bombs. Among the vast majority of states without nuclear weapons, there is a divergence of interests between the relatively small number of countries that aspire to have the bomb and the much larger group that supports the objectives of the NPT and would feel threatened by the introduction of nuclear weapons into their regions. Overlapping lines of conflict were evident at UNCLOS III. Coastal states whose shore-based fishermen work nearby waters using traditional methods were pitted against a group of countries that have invested heavily in highly mechanized, fishing fleets designed to work productive fisheries off the shores of distant states. States with long coastlines or islands were in conflict with landlocked and "geographically disadvantaged" states on issues such as the breadth of coastal zones and the rights of the later to share in the resources that lie within EEZs. The interests of states that border narrow straits were at odds with those that have large merchant marines and naval forces which frequently use them as shipping channels. These other lines of conflict blunt tendencies toward polarization of the community of states along the major cleavages that were noted earlier.

ASSESSING THE GLOBAL EXPERIENCE

How successful has the enterprise of international policy making been in addressing the global agenda? In a word, it has been varied. Much more progress has clearly been made in addressing some policy problems than others. The evaluation of the response to any specific problem depends on the criteria upon which it is based. Thus, an assessment that focuses on what has been accomplished thus far may be quite at odds with one that concentrates on what remains to be done to complete the task?

Which problems rank highly in terms of what has already been done to address them? Among the case studies, economic development stands out in view of the strategies set forth for the United Nations Development Decades and the many assistance programs that have been established for less developed countries. The relative size of the effort directed at development problems is also apparent from the fact that about 80 percent of the budget of the United Nations is directed at the many dimensions of this problem. Much has also been accomplished in efforts to promote the observance of human rights, especially in defining a wide range of rights, freedoms, and entitlements of individuals and groups. Substantial progress has also been made on procedures for monitoring the performance of governments in protecting human rights. Numerous conventions have been adopted on pollution of the oceans, especially under the auspices of the IMO in regard to oil pollution from the world's enormous fleet of tankers. In all three cases, much remains to be done. The number of people that experience the poverty and misery of underdevelopment has not declined significantly, and in fact, may have increased. Human rights are flagrantly violated in many countries. Finally, little has been done to control land-based sources of ocean pollution or air pollution that contributes to acid rain and the "green house" effect, or to regulate direct satellite broadcasts, remote-sensing activities, and transborder data flows.

Efforts to address other global problems could be rated higher on the criterion on how close the task is to being completed. International policies on the use of radio waves are not only reasonably comprehensive, but have also been implemented rather thoroughly. Much the same assessment could be made of global policy on the proliferation of nuclear weapons, taking into account the elaborate inspection and accounting procedures of the IAEA. Relatively little remains to be done internationally in managing the living resources of the oceans inasmuch as most of the world's fisheries fall within the EEZs of coastal states under the new Law of the Sea Treaty. However, species that migrate across the high seas will continue to be an international policy problem. In the case of whales, international policies are well established, but stronger measures are needed for dealing with pirate whalers. In general, relatively little remains to be done only in those cases in which the problem is fairly well contained, and as a result more manageable, in contrast to the much more formidable challenges presented by the highly complex problems of economic development and human rights.

The ultimate test of a policy is the impact that it has had on the problems that it is designed to address. This is often difficult if not impossible to assess for lack of knowledge of how history would have been different if the policy had not been implemented. It is usually possible to compare the conditions present when a policy was initiated with those that prevail after it has been in effect for some time. However, such comparisons can be misleading. Apparent achievements may have occurred not because of the policies, but in spite of them. For example, the failure of the nuclear weapons club to grow rapidly as feared 20 years ago may be less the result of the NPT than an unrelated calculation by states that their security would not be enhanced by the acquisition of nuclear weapons. Naturally, it is also possible that the impact of policies has been greater than it appears to have been. Much of the success of international development and nutrition programs has been obscured by worsening conditions that further complicate the problems being tackled, such as mushrooming population, adverse trends in the world economy, or persistent drought. In such cases, the success of a policy may be in reducing the rate at which a situation deteriorates rather than in improving it substantially.

Global policy makers face a never-ending series of challenges.

Considerable effort may be needed simply to preserve the modest accomplishments made thus far. Changing circumstances sometimes alter the nature of policy problems necessitating modified policy responses. Then there are completely new problems that must be addressed or heightened concerns over conditions that have been ignored or neglected. The customary law of the sea dating back to the early seventeenth century became obsolete rather quickly as technological advances led to an acceleration in the harvesting of fish and raised the possibility of mining the deep seabed. Existing policy designed to prevent proliferation of nuclear weapons may prove to be inadequate with the development of simpler and less costly processes for enriching and reprocessing fissionable materials. The making of policy on telecommunications has become more contentious with the realization in the Third World of what was at stake in decisions that had previously been left to the technical experts of the advanced countries. Pollution problems take on greater urgency as industrial development becomes a worldwide phenomenon and scientific research reveals more about the dangers posed for human health and the environment.

What accounts for the successes and failures in the international response to global problems? Perhaps the answer can be found in the nature of the policy problems. Some problems are more complex than others and therefore present a far greater challenge for policy makers. Alternatively, it may be that the procedures used to make decisions in some international policy-making arenas are less cumbersome than in others. The answer may lie in the characteristics of the national delegates. Are their credentials political or scientific? Do they receive detailed instructions from their home governments? Agreement on goals and principles can be an important factor. The politicization of policy issues may significantly reduce the prospects for a successful response to the problem. Some policies may simply be a more rational strategy for tackling the problem at hand. Then, there is the thoroughness of the monitoring procedures used to detect violations or the strength and regularity of the sanctions that are imposed on violators of international rules. Success may depend on the commitment of wealthy countries to finance programs. Finally, a key factor over the long run may be the depth of policy evaluations and the willingness of decision makers to enact needed changes. These are but a few of many explanations which space does not permit us to explore here.

One factor that stands out as being related to the success of international policy responses is whether or not a balance exists in the interests that are served by global policies. Little progress should be expected when some states, especially the key ones, endure most of the costs, while others enjoy most of the benefits. The highly developed countries perceive that there is little to gain and potentially much to lose from implementing the NIEO. States whose geographical position is upwind or upstream from others see little reason to be enthusiastic about international regulations on transboundary pollution. More can be accomplished when tradeoffs can be made so that all major actors gain something of importance. The willingness of so many of the nonweapons states to abide by the NPT would seem to depend on the technical assistance they receive in developing peaceful applications of nuclear technology. Most states are willing to abide by ITU rules, presumably because all would be disadvantaged by a condition of anarchy in the use of the airwaves. The new ocean law was acceptable to so many states as a package, not because their interests were served by all of its provisions, but because they got at least some of what was important to them. The concerns of the United States and several other advanced states that they had much more to lose than to gain from the section on deep sea mining may prove to be the treaty's undoing.

Numerous proposals have been advanced for improving the way the international community sets about the task of global problem solving. Considerable attention has been given to voting procedures in international deliberative bodies, which in most cases assign a single vote to each member state. It is argued that international resolutions would carry greater weight if voting strength was made proportionate to the population and size of the economies of states. Others contend that stronger and more predictable sanctions are needed in order to deter states from violating international regulations. To provide adequate and stable financing of international programs, IGOs should have funding sources that are independent of the whims of states. One possibility is a tax on certain uses of global commons, such as the exploitation of ocean resources. Significant changes of this nature would obviously be difficult to enact. The numerous smaller states that benefit from the one-nation, one-vote rule can use their votes to defeat proposals for weighted voting. Most governments are reluctant to approve stronger international sanctions for fear of being embarrassed by becoming the target of them at some future time. New revenue sources would be probably be resisted by a number of key states for fear of jeopardizing the profitability of industries that make use of international commons. Perhaps the most important concern is that independent funding would diminish the accountability of IGOs to the member states.

Even if such changes as these were implemented, the larger question turns on whether the international policy making apparatus can cope with the evolving global agenda. The pessimistic point of view is that the problems will continue to surface and intensify at a rate that outstrips the capacity of international problem solvers to address them satisfactorily. Such a forecast usually presumes that states will not be willing to compromise their sovereignty to the degree necessary for creating a less cumbersome international policy process. In recent years, this gloomy outlook has been reinforced by an apparent resurgence in the practice of power politics, especially among the superpowers. The more optimistic view is that remarkable progress can be observed in addressing numerous global problems, especially if one steps back and assesses what has transpired over the longer sweep of modern history. Moreover, this trend is likely to continue and perhaps even accelerate because governments of states are becoming less insistent on viewing sovereignty as an absolute principle, having recognized that their national interests in an interdependent world are tied to the success of international cooperation on a global scale. Only time will tell which of these two visions is more realistic.

In any event, this volume has demonstrated the applicability of the policy approach to the study of world politics. An agenda of global problems can be identified. Elements of an international policy process have been in place for at least several decades. Policies containing regulations and programs have been incorporated into treaties and resolutions. Finally, steps have been taken to implement and review the policies that have been adopted. The nature of contemporary world politics cannot be adequately understood without knowledge of these cooperative efforts at global problem solving.

INDEX